BARRON'S

W9-BNT-769

AP*
COMPUTER
SCIENCE A

6TH EDITION

Roselyn Teukolsky, M.S.
Formerly, Computer Science Teacher
Ithaca High School
Ithaca, New York

BARRON'S

About the Author:

Roselyn Teukolsky has an M.S. degree from Cornell University, and has been teaching programming and computer science since 1980. She has published articles in *The Mathematics Teacher* and in the National Council of Teachers of Mathematics Yearbook. She is the author of Barron's *ACT Math and Science Workbook* and co-author of Barron's *SAT 2400: Aiming for the Perfect Score.* She has received the Edyth May Sliffe Award for Distinguished Mathematics Teaching and the Alfred Kalfus Distinguished Coach Award from the New York State Math League (NYSML).

© Copyright 2013, 2010 by Barron's Educational Series, Inc.
Previous editions © copyright 2007 under the title
AP Computer Science Levels A and AB, 2003 under the title
*How to Prepare for the AP Computer Science Advanced
Placement Examination, JAVA Version*, and 2001
under the title *How to Prepare for the AP Computer
Science Advanced Placement Examination*
by Barron's Educational Series, Inc.

All inquiries should be addressed to:
Barron's Educational Series, Inc.
250 Wireless Boulevard
Hauppauge, New York 11788
www.barronseduc.com

ISBN: 978-1-4380-0152-4
ISBN (with CD-ROM): 978-1-4380-7277-7

ISSN (Print): 2169-5571
ISSN (Print with CD-ROM): 2169-558X

PRINTED IN THE UNITED STATES OF AMERICA
9 8 7 6 5 4 3 2

**10%
POST-CONSUMER
WASTE**
Paper contains a minimum
of 10% post-consumer
waste (PCW). Paper used
in this book was derived
from certified, sustainable
forestlands.

Contents

Barron's Essential 5

As you review the content in this book to work toward earning that **5** on your AP Computer Science A exam, here are five things that you **MUST** know above everything else:

1

The Basics. Every AP exam question uses at least one of these:
- Types and Identifiers (p. 58)
- Operators (p. 62)
- Control structures (p. 67)

2

Objects, Classes, and Inheritance. You may have to write your own class. You'll definitely need to interpret at least one class that's given.
- Methods (p. 92)
- Subclasses (p. 128)
- Abstract classes (p. 138)
- Interfaces (p. 140)

3

Lists and Arrays. Learn to manipulate a list. Search, delete an item, insert an item. It seems as if every second question on the AP exam uses a list!
- One-dimensional arrays (p. 230)
- ArrayLists (p. 241)
- Two-dimensional arrays (p. 246)

4

Sorting and Searching. Know these algorithms!
- Selection Sort (p. 319)
- Insertion Sort (p. 320)
- Merge Sort (p. 320)
- Binary Search (p. 324)

5

The GridWorld Case Study. Those critters make up 25% of the exam!
- The Bug Class (p. 352)
- The BoxBug Class (p. 354)
- The Critter Class (p. 355)
- The ChameleonCritter Class (p. 357)

Preface

This book is aimed at students reviewing for the AP Computer Science A exam. It would normally be used at the completion of an AP course. However, it contains a complete summary of all topics for the exam, and it can be used for self-study if accompanied by a suitable textbook.

The book provides a review of object-oriented programming, algorithm analysis, and data structures. It can therefore be used as a supplement to first-year college courses where Java is the programming language, and as a resource for teachers of high school and introductory college courses.

This sixth edition includes some features of Java 5.0 and later: generic lists and the enhanced `for` loop. Static imports and auto-boxing and -unboxing are also discussed in the book, but these topics will not be tested on the AP exam.

All of the changes introduced by the AP Computer Science Development Committee for the May 2011 exam have been incorporated into the book. Specifically, new sections on each of the following have been added:

- the `java.util.List` interface
- the Java constants `Integer.MIN_VALUE` and `Integer.MAX_VALUE`
- static variables.

Additionally, the material on two-dimensional arrays that was formerly for Level AB students only is now presented in the main text. All students should be able to create, initialize, modify, and traverse two-dimensional arrays. More questions on two-dimensional arrays have been added for this edition.

Each review chapter is followed by AP exam-style multiple-choice questions with detailed explanations of the answers.

There is a similarly thorough review of the GridWorld Case Study.

There are three complete practice exams. These exams have been revised to be more in keeping with the evolution of the actual exams. The exams follow the format of the AP exam, with multiple-choice and free-response sections. One exam is presented after the introduction to the book for possible use as a diagnostic test. A diagnostic chart accompanies this test. Detailed solutions with explanations are provided for all exams. Two additional exams are provided on the optional CD-ROM. This edition contains several new questions. There is no overlap of questions between the exams.

Note that the scoring worksheets that accompany each exam, in both the book and CD-ROM, have been updated in this edition. They reflect the new College Board policy of not penalizing students for wrong answers on the multiple-choice section.

ACKNOWLEDGMENTS

I owe thanks to many people who helped in the creation of this book.

I am most grateful to my excellent editor, Linda Turner, of Barron's, for her friendly guidance and moral support throughout this project, over many years. I also thank all the other members of the Barron's staff who worked on the production of the book.

I am grateful to Steven Andrianoff and David Levine of St. Bonaventure University, New York, for their outstanding workshops that gave me a leg up in computer science. Many ideas from their Java workshops found their way into this book. Thanks also to Chris Nevison, Richard Kick, and Mark Stehlik for invaluable advice and suggestions.

A big thank-you goes to my AP computer science students who helped in the debugging of problems. Special thanks to Ben Zax and Ian Lenz for contributing their hours and expertise, and to Johnathon Schultz and Daniel Birman for sharing a couple of clever algorithms.

Many thanks to Rachel Zax and April Shen, who did an amazing job of checking the practice exams.

Thank you to all of the computer science teachers throughout the country who took time to write to me with suggestions for the new edition.

My husband, Saul, continues to be my partner in this project—typesetting the manuscript, producing the figures, and giving advice and moral support every step of the way. This book is dedicated to him.

Roselyn Teukolsky
Ithaca, NY
July 2012

Introduction

*Computer Science: The boring art
of coping with a large number of trivialities.*
—Stan Kelly-Bootle, The Devil's DP Dictionary *(1981)*

GENERAL INFORMATION ABOUT THE EXAM

The AP Computer Science exam is a three-hour written exam. No books, calculators, or computers are allowed! The exam consists of two parts that have equal weight:

- Section I: 40 multiple-choice questions in 1 hour and 15 minutes.
- Section II: 4 free-response questions in 1 hour and 45 minutes.

Section I is scored by machine—you will bubble your answers with a pencil on a mark-sense sheet. Each question correctly answered is worth 1 point. There are no deductions for incorrect answers, and a question left blank is ignored.

Section II is scored by human readers—you will write your answers in a booklet provided. Free-response questions typically involve writing methods in Java to solve a given problem. Sometimes there are questions analyzing algorithms or designing and modifying data structures. You may be asked to write or design an entire class. To ensure consistency in the grading, each grader follows the same rubric, and each of your four answers may be examined by more than one reader. Each question is worth 9 points, with partial credit awarded where applicable. Your name and school are hidden from the readers.

> **SCORING CHANGE**
>
> The College Board has announced a change to how the AP Computer Science A exam is scored. There will no longer be any penalty for wrong answers on the multiple-choice section.

Your raw score for both sections is converted to an integer score from 1 to 5, where 1 represents "Not at all qualified" and 5 represents "Extremely well qualified." Be aware that the awarding of AP credit varies enormously from college to college. The exam covers roughly a one-semester introductory college course.

The language of the AP exam is Java. Only a subset of the Java language will be tested on the exam. In writing your solutions to the free-response questions, however, you may use any Java features, including those that are not in the AP subset. For a complete description of this subset, see the College Board website at *http://www.collegeboard.com/student/testing/ap/subjects.html.* **Every language topic in this review book is part of the AP Java subset unless explicitly stated otherwise. Note that the entire subset is covered in the book.**

At least one free-response and five multiple-choice questions will be based on the GridWorld Case Study. The full text of the case study can be found at the College Board website *http://www.collegeboard.com/student/testing/ap/compsci_a/case.html?compscia.*

For both the multiple-choice and free-response sections of the exam, there will be a quick reference in the appendix. You can look at this ahead of time at *http://apcentral. collegeboard.com/apc/public/repository/ap_comp_sci_a_quick_reference.pdf*

The quick reference contains

- A copy of the testable case study code.
- The "black box" classes of the case study, with lists of their required methods.
- The standard Java interfaces and classes with lists of their required methods.

HINTS FOR TAKING THE EXAM

The Multiple-Choice Section

- Since there are no deductions for wrong answers, you should guess when you've eliminated what you can.

- You have a little less than two minutes per question, so don't waste time on any given question. You can always come back to it if you have time at the end.

- Seemingly complicated array questions can often be solved by hand tracing the code with a small array of two or three elements. The same is true for matrices.

- Many questions ask you to compare two pieces of code that supposedly implement the same algorithm. Often one program segment will fail because it doesn't handle endpoint conditions properly (e.g., num == 0). *Be aware of endpoint conditions throughout the exam.*

- Since the mark-sense sheet is scanned by machine, make sure that you erase completely if you change an answer.

The Free-Response Section

- Each free-response question is worth 9 points. Take a minute to read through the whole exam so that you can start with a question that you feel confident about. It gives you a psychological leg up to have a solid question in the bag.

- Don't omit a question just because you can't come up with a complete solution. Remember, partial credit is awarded. Also, if you can't do part (a) of a question, don't omit part (b)—they are graded independently.

- In writing solutions to a question, you must use the public methods of classes provided in that question wherever possible. If you write a significant chunk of code that can be replaced by a call to one of these methods, you will probably not receive full credit for the question.

- If an algorithm is suggested to solve a problem, just follow it. Don't reinvent the wheel.

- Don't waste time writing comments: the graders generally ignore them. The occasional brief comment that clarifies a segment of code is OK.

- Points are not deducted for inefficient code unless efficiency is an issue in the question.

- Most of the standard Java library methods are not included in the AP subset. They are accepted on the exam if you use them correctly. However, there is always an alternative solution that uses the AP subset and you should try to find it.

- Don't cross out an answer until you have written a replacement. Graders are instructed not to read anything crossed out, even if it would have gotten credit.

- Have some awareness that this section is graded by humans. It is in your interest to have the graders understand your solutions. With this in mind,

  - Use a sharp pencil, write legibly, space your answers, and indent correctly.
  - Use self-documenting names for variables, methods, and so on.
  - Use the identifiers that are given in a question. You will lose usage points if you persist in using the wrong names.
  - Write clear readable code. This is your goal. Don't write one obscure convoluted statement when you can write two short clear statements. The APCS exam is not the place to demonstrate that you're a genius.

HOW TO USE THIS BOOK

Each chapter in the book contains a comprehensive review of a topic, multiple-choice questions that focus on the topic, and detailed explanations of answers. These focus questions help you to review parts of the Java subset that you should know. A few questions are not typical AP exam questions—for example, questions that test low-level details of syntax. Most of the focus questions, however, and all the multiple-choice questions in the practice exams are representative of actual exam questions.

You should also note that several groups of focus questions are preceded by a single piece of code to which the questions refer. Be aware that the AP exam will usually restrict the number of questions per code example to two.

In both the text and questions/explanations, a special code font is used for parts of the text that are Java code.

```
//This is an example of code font
```

A different font is used for pseudo-code.

< Here is pseudo-code font. >

A small number of optional topics that are not part of the AP Java subset are included in the book because they are useful in the free-response questions. Sections in the text and multiple-choice questions that are optional topics are clearly marked as such.

Three complete practice exams are provided in the book. One exam is at the start of the book and may be used as a diagnostic test. It is accompanied by a diagnostic chart that refers you to related topics in the review book. The other two exams are at the end of the book. There are two additional exams on the optional CD-ROM provided with the book.

Each of the five exams has an answer key, complete solutions and explanations for the free-response questions, and detailed explanations for the multiple-choice questions. There is no overlap in the questions.

Each practice exam contains at least five multiple-choice questions and one free-response question on the GridWorld Case Study.

An answer sheet is provided for the Section I questions of each exam. When you have completed an entire exam, and have checked your answers, you may wish to calculate your approximate AP score. Use the scoring worksheet provided on the back of the answer sheet.

An appendix at the end of the book provides a glossary of computer terms that occasionally crop up on the exam.

A final hint about the book: Try the questions before you peek at the answers. Good luck!

PRACTICE EXAM ONE / DIAGNOSTIC TEST

The exam that follows has the same format as that used on the actual AP exam. There are two ways you may use it:

1. As a diagnostic test before you start reviewing. Following the answer key is a diagnostic chart that relates each question to sections that you should review. In addition, complete explanations are provided for each solution.
2. As a practice exam when you have completed your review.

    Complete solutions with explanations are provided for the free-response questions.

Answer Sheet: Practice Exam One

1. Ⓐ Ⓑ Ⓒ Ⓓ Ⓔ
2. Ⓐ Ⓑ Ⓒ Ⓓ Ⓔ
3. Ⓐ Ⓑ Ⓒ Ⓓ Ⓔ
4. Ⓐ Ⓑ Ⓒ Ⓓ Ⓔ
5. Ⓐ Ⓑ Ⓒ Ⓓ Ⓔ
6. Ⓐ Ⓑ Ⓒ Ⓓ Ⓔ
7. Ⓐ Ⓑ Ⓒ Ⓓ Ⓔ
8. Ⓐ Ⓑ Ⓒ Ⓓ Ⓔ
9. Ⓐ Ⓑ Ⓒ Ⓓ Ⓔ
10. Ⓐ Ⓑ Ⓒ Ⓓ Ⓔ
11. Ⓐ Ⓑ Ⓒ Ⓓ Ⓔ
12. Ⓐ Ⓑ Ⓒ Ⓓ Ⓔ
13. Ⓐ Ⓑ Ⓒ Ⓓ Ⓔ
14. Ⓐ Ⓑ Ⓒ Ⓓ Ⓔ

15. Ⓐ Ⓑ Ⓒ Ⓓ Ⓔ
16. Ⓐ Ⓑ Ⓒ Ⓓ Ⓔ
17. Ⓐ Ⓑ Ⓒ Ⓓ Ⓔ
18. Ⓐ Ⓑ Ⓒ Ⓓ Ⓔ
19. Ⓐ Ⓑ Ⓒ Ⓓ Ⓔ
20. Ⓐ Ⓑ Ⓒ Ⓓ Ⓔ
21. Ⓐ Ⓑ Ⓒ Ⓓ Ⓔ
22. Ⓐ Ⓑ Ⓒ Ⓓ Ⓔ
23. Ⓐ Ⓑ Ⓒ Ⓓ Ⓔ
24. Ⓐ Ⓑ Ⓒ Ⓓ Ⓔ
25. Ⓐ Ⓑ Ⓒ Ⓓ Ⓔ
26. Ⓐ Ⓑ Ⓒ Ⓓ Ⓔ
27. Ⓐ Ⓑ Ⓒ Ⓓ Ⓔ
28. Ⓐ Ⓑ Ⓒ Ⓓ Ⓔ

29. Ⓐ Ⓑ Ⓒ Ⓓ Ⓔ
30. Ⓐ Ⓑ Ⓒ Ⓓ Ⓔ
31. Ⓐ Ⓑ Ⓒ Ⓓ Ⓔ
32. Ⓐ Ⓑ Ⓒ Ⓓ Ⓔ
33. Ⓐ Ⓑ Ⓒ Ⓓ Ⓔ
34. Ⓐ Ⓑ Ⓒ Ⓓ Ⓔ
35. Ⓐ Ⓑ Ⓒ Ⓓ Ⓔ
36. Ⓐ Ⓑ Ⓒ Ⓓ Ⓔ
37. Ⓐ Ⓑ Ⓒ Ⓓ Ⓔ
38. Ⓐ Ⓑ Ⓒ Ⓓ Ⓔ
39. Ⓐ Ⓑ Ⓒ Ⓓ Ⓔ
40. Ⓐ Ⓑ Ⓒ Ⓓ Ⓔ

How to Calculate Your (Approximate) AP Computer Science Score

Multiple Choice

Number correct (out of 40) = _____ ⟸ Multiple-Choice Score

Free Response

Question 1 _____
(out of 9)

Question 2 _____
(out of 9)

Question 3 _____
(out of 9)

Question 4 _____
(out of 9)

Total _____ × 1.11 = _____ ⟸ Free-Response Score
(Do not round.)

Final Score

_____ + _____ = _____
Multiple-   Free-   Final Score
Choice   Response   (Round to nearest
Score   Score   whole number.)

Chart to Convert to AP Grade
Computer Science

Final Score Range	AP Grade[a]
60–80	5
45–59	4
33–44	3
25–32	2
0–24	1

[a]The score range corresponding to each grade varies from exam to exam and is approximate.

Practice Exam One
COMPUTER SCIENCE
SECTION I

Time—1 hour and 15 minutes
Number of questions—40
Percent of total grade—50

Directions: Determine the answer to each of the following questions or incomplete statements, using the available space for any necessary scratchwork. Then decide which is the best of the choices given and fill in the corresponding oval on the answer sheet. Do not spend too much time on any one problem.

Notes:
- Assume that the classes in the Quick Reference have been imported where needed.
- Assume that variables and methods are declared within the context of an enclosing class.
- Assume that method calls that have no object or class name prefixed, and that are not shown within a complete class definition, appear within the context of an enclosing class.
- Assume that parameters in method calls are not null unless otherwise stated.

1. Consider this inheritance hierarchy, in which Novel and Textbook are subclasses of Book.

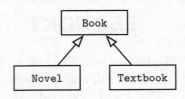

   Which of the following is a *false* statement about the classes shown?
   (A) The Textbook class can have private instance variables that are in neither Book nor Novel.
   (B) Each of the classes—Book, Novel, and Textbook—can have a method computeShelfLife, whose code in Book and Novel is identical, but different from the code in Textbook.
   (C) If the Book class has private instance variables myTitle and myAuthor, then Novel and Textbook inherit them but cannot directly access them.
   (D) Both Novel and Textbook inherit the constructors in Book.
   (E) If the Book class has a private method called readFile, this method may not be accessed in either the Novel or Textbook classes.

GO ON TO THE NEXT PAGE.

2. A programmer is designing a program to catalog all books in a library. He plans to have a Book class that stores features of each book: author, title, isOnShelf, and so on, with operations like getAuthor, getTitle, getShelfInfo, and setShelfInfo. Another class, LibraryList, will store an array of Book objects. The LibraryList class will include operations such as listAllBooks, addBook, removeBook, and searchForBook. The programmer plans to implement and test the Book class first, before implementing the LibraryList class. The programmer's plan to write the Book class first is an example of
    (A) top-down development.
    (B) bottom-up development.
    (C) procedural abstraction.
    (D) information hiding.
    (E) a driver program.

Questions 3–4 refer to the `Card` and `Deck` classes shown below.

```
public class Card
{
    private String mySuit;
    private int myValue;        //0 to 12

    public Card(String suit, int value)
    { /* implementation */ }

    public String getSuit()
    { return mySuit; }

    public int getValue()
    { return myValue; }

    public String toString()
    {
        String faceValue = "";
        if (myValue == 11)
            faceValue = "J";
        else if (myValue == 12)
            faceValue = "Q";
        else if (myValue == 0)
            faceValue = "K";
        else if (myValue == 1)
            faceValue = "A";
        if (myValue >= 2 && myValue <= 10)
            return myValue + " of " + mySuit;
        else
            return faceValue + " of " + mySuit;
    }
}

public class Deck
{
    private Card[] myDeck;
    public final static int NUMCARDS = 52;

    public Deck()
    { ...

    //Simulate shuffling the deck.
    public void shuffle()
    { ...

    //other methods not shown ...
}
```

GO ON TO THE NEXT PAGE.

3. Which of the following represents correct /* *implementation* */ code for the constructor in the Card class?

    (A) ```
mySuit = suit;
myValue = value;
```

    (B) ```
suit = mySuit;
value = myValue;
```

    (C) ```
Card = new Card(mySuit, myValue);
```

    (D) ```
Card = new Card(suit, value);
```

    (E) ```
mySuit = getSuit();
myValue = getValue();
```

4. Consider the implementation of a writeDeck method that is added to the Deck class.

```
//Write the cards in myDeck, one per line.
public void writeDeck()
{
    /* implementation code */
}
```

Which of the following is correct /* *implementation code* */?

   I ```
System.out.println(myDeck);
```

   II ```
for (Card card : myDeck)
    System.out.println(card);
```

  III ```
for (Card card : myDeck)
    System.out.println((String) card);
```

    (A) I only
    (B) II only
    (C) III only
    (D) I and III only
    (E) II and III only

GO ON TO THE NEXT PAGE.

5. Refer to the following method that finds the smallest value in an array.

```
//Precondition:  arr is initialized with int values.
//Postcondition: Returns the smallest value in arr.
public static int findMin(int[] arr)
{
    int min = /* some value */;
    int index = 0;
    while (index < arr.length)
    {
        if (arr[index] < min)
            min = arr[index];
        index++;
    }
    return min;
}
```

Which replacement(s) for /* *some value* */ will always result in correct execution of the findMin method?

   I Integer.MIN_VALUE

  II Integer.MAX_VALUE

 III arr[0]

(A) I only
(B) II only
(C) III only
(D) I and III only
(E) II and III only

Refer to the following class for Questions 6 and 7.

```
public class Tester
{
    private int[] testArray = {3, 4, 5};

    //Add 1 to n.
    public void increment (int n)
    { n++; }

    public void firstTestMethod()
    {
        for (int i = 0; i < testArray.length; i++)
        {
            increment(testArray[i]);
            System.out.print(testArray[i] + " ");
        }
    }

    public void secondTestMethod()
    {
        for (int element : testArray)
        {
            increment(element);
            System.out.print(element + " ");
        }
    }
}
```

6. What output will be produced by invoking `firstTestMethod` for a `Tester` object?
   (A) 3 4 5
   (B) 4 5 6
   (C) 5 6 7
   (D) 0 0 0
   (E) No output will be produced. An `ArrayIndexOutOfBoundsException` will be thrown.

7. What output will be produced by invoking `secondTestMethod` for a `Tester` object, assuming that `testArray` contains 3,4,5?
   (A) 3 4 5
   (B) 4 5 6
   (C) 5 6 7
   (D) 0 0 0
   (E) No output will be produced. An `ArrayIndexOutOfBoundsException` will be thrown.

8. Consider the following loop, where n is some positive integer.

```
for (int i = 0; i < n; i += 2)
{
    if (/* test */)
        /* perform some action */
}
```

In terms of n, which Java expression represents the maximum number of times that /* *perform some action* */ could be executed?
(A) n / 2
(B) (n + 1) / 2
(C) n
(D) n - 1
(E) (n - 1) / 2

9. A method is to be written to search an array for a value that is larger than a given item and return its index. The problem specification does not indicate what should be returned if there are several such values in the array. Which of the following actions would be best?
(A) The method should be written on the assumption that there is only one value in the array that is larger than the given item.
(B) The method should be written so as to return the index of every occurrence of a larger value.
(C) The specification should be modified to indicate what should be done if there is more than one index of larger values.
(D) The method should be written to output a message if more than one larger value is found.
(E) The method should be written to delete all subsequent larger items after a suitable index is returned.

10. When will method `whatIsIt` cause a stack overflow (i.e., cause computer memory to be exhausted)?

```
public static int whatIsIt(int x, int y)
{
    if (x > y)
        return x * y;
    else
        return whatIsIt(x - 1, y);
}
```

   (A) Only when $x < y$
   (B) Only when $x \leq y$
   (C) Only when $x > y$
   (D) For all values of x and y
   (E) The method will never cause a stack overflow.

11. The boolean expression `a[i] == max || !(max != a[i])` can be simplified to
   (A) `a[i] == max`
   (B) `a[i] != max`
   (C) `a[i] < max || a[i] > max`
   (D) `true`
   (E) `false`

12. Suppose the characters $0, 1, \ldots, 8, 9, A, B, C, D, E, F$ are used to represent a hexadecimal (base-16) number. Here $A = 10, B = 11, \ldots, F = 15$. What is the largest base-10 integer that can be represented with a two-digit hexadecimal number, such as 14 or 3A?
   (A) 32
   (B) 225
   (C) 255
   (D) 256
   (E) 272

13. Consider a `Clown` class that has a default constructor. Suppose a list `ArrayList<Clown> list` is initialized. Which of the following will *not* cause an `IndexOutOfBoundsException` to be thrown?

   (A) `for (int i = 0; i <= list.size(); i++)`
       `    list.set(i, new Clown());`

   (B) `list.add(list.size(), new Clown());`

   (C) `Clown c = list.get(list.size());`

   (D) `Clown c = list.remove(list.size());`

   (E) `list.add(-1, new Clown());`

GO ON TO THE NEXT PAGE.

Questions 14–16 refer to the Point, Quadrilateral, and Rectangle classes below:

```
public class Point
{
    private int xCoord;
    private int yCoord;

    //constructor
    public Point(int x, int y)
    {
        ...
    }

    //accessors

    public int get_x()
    {
        ...
    }

    public int get_y()
    {
        ...
    }

    //other methods not shown ...

}

public abstract class Quadrilateral
{
    private String myLabels;    //e.g., "ABCD"

    //constructor
    public Quadrilateral(String labels)
    { myLabels = labels; }

    public String getLabels()
    { return myLabels; }

    public abstract int perimeter();
    public abstract int area();
}
```

```
public class Rectangle extends Quadrilateral
{
    private Point myTopLeft;    //coords of top left corner
    private Point myBotRight;   //coords of bottom right corner

    //constructor
    public Rectangle(String labels, Point topLeft, Point botRight)
    { /* implementation code */ }

    public int perimeter()
    { /* implementation not shown */ }

    public int area()
    { /* implementation not shown */ }

    //other methods not shown ...
}
```

14. Which statement about the `Quadrilateral` class is *false*?
    (A) The perimeter and area methods are abstract because there's no suitable default code for them.
    (B) The getLabels method is not abstract because any subclasses of Quadrilateral will have the same code for this method.
    (C) If the Quadrilateral class is used in a program, it *must* be used as a super-class for at least one other class.
    (D) No instances of a Quadrilateral object can be created in a program.
    (E) Any subclasses of the Quadrilateral class *must* provide implementation code for the perimeter and area methods.

15. Which represents correct /* *implementation code* */ for the Rectangle constructor?

    I super(labels);

    II super(labels, topLeft, botRight);

    III super(labels);
        myTopLeft = topLeft;
        myBotRight = botRight;

    (A) I only
    (B) II only
    (C) III only
    (D) I and II only
    (E) II and III only

GO ON TO THE NEXT PAGE.

16. Refer to the `Parallelogram` and `Square` classes below.

```
public class Parallelogram extends Quadrilateral
{
    //private instance variables and constructor not shown
        ...

    public int perimeter()
    { /* implementation not shown */ }

    public int area()
    { /* implementation not shown */ }
}

public class Square extends Rectangle
{
    //private instance variables and constructor not shown
        ...

    public int perimeter()
    { /* implementation not shown */ }

    public int area()
    { /* implementation not shown */ }
}
```

Consider an `ArrayList<Quadrilateral>` quadList whose elements are of type
`Rectangle`, `Parallelogram`, or `Square`.
Refer to the following method, `writeAreas`:

```
/* Precondition:  quadList contains Rectangle, Parallelogram, or
 *                Square objects in an unspecified order. */
public static void writeAreas(List<Quadrilateral> quadList)
{
    for (Quadrilateral quad : quadList)
        System.out.println("Area of " + quad.getLabels()
            + " is " + quad.area());
}
```

What is the effect of executing this method?
(A) The area of each `Quadrilateral` in quadList will be printed.
(B) A compile-time error will occur, stating that there is no area method in
abstract class `Quadrilateral`.
(C) A compile-time error will occur, stating that there is no `getLabels` method
in classes `Rectangle`, `Parallelogram`, or `Square`.
(D) A `NullPointerException` will be thrown.
(E) A `ClassCastException` will be thrown.

17. Refer to the doSomething method:

```
// postcondition
public static void doSomething(List<SomeType> list, int i, int j)
{
    SomeType temp = list.get(i);
    list.set(i, list.get(j));
    list.set(j, temp);
}
```

Which best describes the *postcondition* for doSomething?
(A) Removes from list the objects indexed at i and j.
(B) Replaces in list the object indexed at i with the object indexed at j.
(C) Replaces in list the object indexed at j with the object indexed at i.
(D) Replaces in list the objects indexed at i and j with temp.
(E) Interchanges in list the objects indexed at i and j.

18. Consider the NegativeReal class below, which defines a negative real number object.

```
public class NegativeReal
{
    private Double myNegReal;

    //constructor. Creates a NegativeReal object whose value is num.
    //Precondition: num < 0.
    public NegativeReal(double num)
    { /* implementation not shown */ }

    //Postcondition: Returns the value of this NegativeReal.
    public double getValue()
    { /* implementation not shown */ }

    //Postcondition: Returns this NegativeReal rounded to the nearest integer.
    public int getRounded()
    { /* implementation */ }
}
```

Here are some rounding examples:

Negative real number	Rounded to nearest integer
−3.5	−4
−8.97	−9
−5.0	−5
−2.487	−2
−0.2	0

Which /* *implementation* */ of getRounded produces the desired postcondition?
(A) return (int) (getValue() - 0.5);
(B) return (int) (getValue() + 0.5);
(C) return (int) getValue();
(D) return (double) (getValue() - 0.5);
(E) return (double) getValue();

GO ON TO THE NEXT PAGE.

19. Consider the following method.

```
public static void whatsIt(int n)
{
    if (n > 10)
        whatsIt(n / 10);
    System.out.print(n % 10);
}
```

What will be output as a result of the method call `whatsIt(347)`?
(A) 74
(B) 47
(C) 734
(D) 743
(E) 347

20. A large list of numbers is to be sorted into ascending order. Assuming that a "data movement" is a swap or reassignment of an element, which of the following is a *true* statement?
    (A) If the array is initially sorted in descending order, then insertion sort will be more efficient than selection sort.
    (B) The number of comparisons for selection sort is independent of the initial arrangement of elements.
    (C) The number of comparisons for insertion sort is independent of the initial arrangement of elements.
    (D) The number of data movements in selection sort depends on the initial arrangement of elements.
    (E) The number of data movements in insertion sort is independent of the initial arrangement of elements.

GO ON TO THE NEXT PAGE.

21. Refer to the definitions of `ClassOne` and `ClassTwo` below.

```
public class ClassOne
{
    public void methodOne()
    {
        ...
    }

    //other methods not shown
}

public class ClassTwo extends ClassOne
{
    public void methodTwo()
    {
        ...
    }

    //other methods not shown
}
```

Consider the following declarations in a client class. You may assume that `ClassOne` and `ClassTwo` have default constructors.

```
ClassOne c1 = new ClassOne();
ClassOne c2 = new ClassTwo();
```

Which of the following method calls will cause an error?

I `c1.methodTwo();`

II `c2.methodTwo();`

III `c2.methodOne();`

(A) None
(B) I only
(C) II only
(D) III only
(E) I and II only

22. Consider the code segment

```
if (n == 1)
    k++;
else if (n == 4)
    k += 4;
```

Suppose that the given segment is rewritten in the form

```
if (/* condition */)
    /* assignment statement */;
```

Given that n and k are integers and that the rewritten code performs the same task as the original code, which of the following could be used as

  (1) /* *condition* */ and (2) /* *assignment statement* */?

(A) (1) n == 1 && n == 4   (2) k += n

(B) (1) n == 1 && n == 4   (2) k += 4

(C) (1) n == 1 || n == 4   (2) k += 4

(D) (1) n == 1 || n == 4   (2) k += n

(E) (1) n == 1 || n == 4   (2) k = n - k

23. Which of the following will execute *without* throwing an exception?

```
 I  String s = null;
    String t = "";
    if (s.equals(t))
        System.out.println("empty strings?");

II  String s = "holy";
    String t = "moly";
    if (s.equals(t))
        System.out.println("holy moly!");

III String s = "holy";
    String t = s.substring(4);
    System.out.println(s + t);
```

(A) I only
(B) II only
(C) III only
(D) I and II only
(E) II and III only

24. Three numbers *a*, *b*, and *c* are said to be a *Pythagorean Triple* if and only if the sum of the squares of two of the numbers equals the square of the third. A programmer writes a method isPythTriple to test if its three parameters form a Pythagorean Triple:

```
//Returns true if a * a + b * b == c * c; otherwise returns false.
public static boolean isPythTriple(double a, double b, double c)
{
    double d = Math.sqrt(a * a + b * b);
    return d == c;
}
```

When the method was tested with known Pythagorean Triples, isPythTriple sometimes erroneously returned false. What was the most likely cause of the error?
(A) Round-off error was caused by calculations with floating-point numbers.
(B) Type boolean was not recognized by an obsolete version of Java.
(C) An overflow error was caused by entering numbers that were too large.
(D) c and d should have been cast to integers before testing for equality.
(E) Bad test data were selected.

25. Refer to the following class, containing the mystery method.

```
public class SomeClass
{
    private int[] arr;

    //Constructor. Initializes arr to contain nonnegative
    // integers k such that 0 <= k <= 9.
    public SomeClass()
    { /* implementation not shown */ }

    public int mystery()
    {
        int value = arr[0];
        for (int i = 1; i < arr.length; i++)
            value = value * 10 + arr[i];
        return value;
    }
}
```

Which best describes what the mystery method does?
(A) It sums the elements of arr.
(B) It sums the products 10*arr[0]+10*arr[1]+⋯+10*arr[arr.length-1].
(C) It builds an integer of the form $d_1 d_2 d_3 \ldots d_n$, where $d_1 =$ arr[0], $d_2 =$ arr[1], ..., $d_n =$ arr[arr.length-1].
(D) It builds an integer of the form $d_1 d_2 d_3 \ldots d_n$, where $d_1 =$ arr[arr.length-1], $d_2 =$ arr[arr.length-2], ..., $d_n =$ arr[0].
(E) It converts the elements of arr to base-10.

GO ON TO THE NEXT PAGE.

Questions 26 and 27 refer to the search method in the Searcher class below.

```
public class Searcher
{
    private int[] arr;

    //Constructor. Initializes arr with integers.
    public Searcher()
    { /* implementation not shown */ }

    /* Precondition:  arr[first]...arr[last] sorted in ascending order.
     * Postcondition: Returns index of key in arr. If key not in arr,
     *                returns -1. */
    public int search(int first, int last, int key)
    {
        int mid;
        while (first <= last)
        {
            mid = (first + last) / 2;
            if (arr[mid] == key)        //found key, exit search
                return mid;
            else if (arr[mid] < key)  //key to right of arr[mid]
                first = mid + 1;
            else                        //key to left of arr[mid]
                last = mid - 1;
        }
        return -1;                      //key not in list
    }
}
```

26. Which assertion is true just before each execution of the while loop?
    (A) arr[first] < key < arr[last]
    (B) arr[first] ≤ key ≤ arr[last]
    (C) arr[first] < key < arr[last] or key is not in arr
    (D) arr[first] ≤ key ≤ arr[last] or key is not in arr
    (E) key ≤ arr[first] or key ≥ arr[last] or key is not in arr

27. Consider the array a with values as shown:

    4, 7, 19, 25, 36, 37, 50, 100, 101, 205, 220, 271, 306, 321

    where 4 is a[0] and 321 is a[13]. Suppose that the search method is called with
    first = 0 and last = 13 to locate the key 205. How many iterations of the while
    loop must be made in order to locate it?
    (A) 3
    (B) 4
    (C) 5
    (D) 10
    (E) 13

GO ON TO THE NEXT PAGE.

28. Consider the following `RandomList` class.

```
public class RandomList
{
    private int[] myList;

    //constructor
    public RandomList()
    { myList = getList(); }

    /* Read random Integers from 0 to 100 inclusive into array list. */
    public int[] getList()
    {
        System.out.println("How many integers? ");
        int listLength = IO.readInt();      //read user input
        int[] list = int[listLength];
        for (int i = 0; i < listLength; i++)
        {
            /* code to add integer to list */
        }
        return list;
    }

    /* Print all elements of this list. */
    public void printList()
    { ... }
}
```

Which represents correct /* *code to add* integer *to* list */?

(A) `list[i] = (int) (Math.random() * 101);`

(B) `list.add((int) (Math.random() * 101));`

(C) `list[i] = (int) (Math.random() * 100);`

(D) `list.add(new Integer(Math.random() * 100))`

(E) `list[i] = (int) (Math.random() * 100) + 1;`

29. Refer to method `insert` described here. The `insert` method has two string parameters and one integer parameter. The method returns the string obtained by inserting the second string into the first starting at the position indicated by the integer parameter pos. For example, if `str1` contains xy and `str2` contains cat, then

$$
\begin{array}{lll}
\text{insert(str1, str2, 0)} & \text{returns} & \text{catxy} \\
\text{insert(str1, str2, 1)} & \text{returns} & \text{xcaty} \\
\text{insert(str1, str2, 2)} & \text{returns} & \text{xycat}
\end{array}
$$

Method `insert` follows:

```
//Precondition:  0 <= pos <= str1.length().
//Postcondition:   If str1 = a₀a₁...aₙ₋₁ and str2 = b₀b₁...bₘ₋₁,
                   returns a₀a₁...a_{pos-1}b₀b₁...b_{m-1}a_{pos}a_{pos+1}...a_{n-1}
public static String insert(String str1, String str2, int pos)
{
    String first, last;
        /* more code */
    return first + str2 + last;
}
```

Which of the following is a correct replacement for /* *more code* */?

(A) `first = str1.substring(0, pos);`
     `last = str1.substring(pos);`

(B) `first = str1.substring(0, pos - 1);`
     `last = str1.substring(pos);`

(C) `first = str1.substring(0, pos + 1);`
     `last = str1.substring(pos + 1);`

(D) `first = str1.substring(0, pos);`
     `last = str1.substring(pos + 1, str1.length());`

(E) `first = str1.substring(0, pos);`
     `last = str1.substring(pos, str1.length() + 1);`

GO ON TO THE NEXT PAGE.

30. A matrix (two-dimensional array) is declared as

```
int[][] mat = new int[2][3];
```

Consider the following method:

```
public static void changeMatrix(int[][] mat)
{
    for (int r = 0; r < mat.length; r++)
        for (int c = 0; c < mat[r].length; c++)
            if (r == c)
                mat[r][c] = Math.abs(mat[r][c]);
}
```

If mat is initialized to be

```
-1 -2 -6
-2 -4  5
```

which matrix will be the result of a call to changeMatrix(mat)?

(A)   1 -2 -6
     -2 4 5

(B) -1 2 -6
      2 -4 5

(C) -1 -2 -6
     -2 -4 -5

(D)   1 2 -6
      2 4 5

(E)   1 2 6
      2 4 5

Use the following program description for Questions 31–33.

A programmer plans to write a program that simulates a small bingo game (no more than six players). Each player will have a bingo card with 20 numbers from 0 to 90 (no duplicates). Someone will call out numbers one at a time, and each player will cross out a number on his card as it is called. The first player with all the numbers crossed out is the winner. In the simulation, as the game is in progress, each player's card is displayed on the screen.

The programmer envisions a short driver class whose `main` method has just two statements:

```
BingoGame b = new BingoGame();
b.playBingo();
```

The `BingoGame` class will have several objects: a `Display`, a `Caller`, and a `PlayerGroup`. The `PlayerGroup` will have a list of `Players`, and each `Player` will have a `BingoCard`.

31. The relationship between the `PlayerGroup` and `Player` classes is an example of
    (A) an interface.
    (B) encapsulation.
    (C) composition.
    (D) inheritance.
    (E) independent classes.

32. Which is a reasonable data structure for a `BingoCard` object? Recall that there are 20 integers from 0 to 90 on a `BingoCard`, with no duplicates. There should also be mechanisms for crossing off numbers that are called, and for detecting a winning card (i.e., one where all the numbers have been crossed off).

```
 I int[] myBingoCard;   //will contain 20 integers
                 //myBingoCard[k] is crossed off by setting it to -1.
    int numCrossedOff;   //player wins when numCrossedOff reaches 20.

II boolean[] myBingoCard;  //will contain 91 boolean values, of which
                    //20 are true. All the other values are false.
                    //Thus, if myBingoCard[k] is true, then k is
                    //on the card, 0 <= k <= 90. A number k is
                    //crossed off by changing the value of
                    //myBingoCard[k] to false.
    int numCrossedOff; //player wins when numCrossedOff reaches 20.

III ArrayList<Integer> myBingoCard;  //will contain 20 integers.
        //A number is crossed off by removing it from the ArrayList.
        //Player wins when myBingoCard.size() == 0.
```

    (A) I only
    (B) II only
    (C) III only
    (D) I and II only
    (E) I, II, and III

GO ON TO THE NEXT PAGE.

33. The programmer decides to use a List<Integer>, which is implemented as an ArrayList<Integer>, to store the numbers to be called by the Caller:

```
public class Caller
{
    private List<Integer> myNumbers;

    //constructor
    public Caller()
    {
        myNumbers = getList();
        shuffleNumbers();
    }

    //Return the numbers 0...90 in order.
    private List<Integer> getList()
    { /* implementation not shown */ }

    //Shuffle the numbers.
    private void shuffleNumbers()
    { /* implementation not shown */ }
}
```

When the programmer tests the constructor of the Caller class she gets a NullPointerException. Which could be the cause of this error?

(A) The Caller object in the driver class was not created with new.

(B) The programmer forgot the return statement in getList that returns the list of Integers.

(C) The declaration of myNumbers is incorrect. It needed to be

   private List<Integer> myNumbers = null;

(D) In the getList method, an attempt was made to add an Integer to an ArrayList that had not been created with new.

(E) The shuffleNumbers algorithm went out of range, causing a null Integer to be shuffled into the ArrayList.

Questions 34–40 involve reasoning about the code from the GridWorld Case Study. A Quick Reference to the case study is provided as part of this exam. The actors in GridWorld are represented in this book with the pictures shown below. Each actor is shown facing north. These pictures almost certainly will be different from those used on the AP exam!

Actor   Bug   Flower   Rock   Critter   ChameleonCritter

34. Which is a *false* statement about Bug movement?
    (A) A Bug can move on a diagonal line across the grid.
    (B) If a Flower is directly in front of a Bug, the Bug will replace the Flower in the Flower's location.
    (C) If a Rock is directly in front of a Bug, the Bug will not change its location.
    (D) If a Bug is at the edge of the grid, the Bug will change its direction to Location.RIGHT + its current direction.
    (E) It is possible for a Bug to turn through a complete circle without changing its location.

35. Consider an actor whose current direction is Location.NORTHWEST. The following method call is made for this actor:

    ```
    setDirection(getDirection() + Location.HALF_LEFT);
    ```

    What is the int value of the actor's resulting direction?
    (A) 0
    (B) 45
    (C) 90
    (D) 225
    (E) 270

36. Suppose Bug and BoxBug behavior will be modified to allow bugs and box bugs to move onto Rocks in the same way that they move onto Flowers. Which classes will need to be modified to effect this change?

    I Actor

    II Bug

    III BoxBug

    (A) I only
    (B) II only
    (C) III only
    (D) II and III only
    (E) I, II, and III

GO ON TO THE NEXT PAGE.

37. Consider the small bounded grid in the diagram.

It shows a red `Bug` facing north at (0, 2); a black `Rock` at (1, 0); and a blue `ChameleonCritter` facing south at (1, 1). After one step of the simulation, the bug is facing northeast at location (0, 2), and the rock is still at location (1, 0). Which represents a legitimate state for the `ChameleonCritter`?
(A) Color is blue, location is (2, 1), and direction is south.
(B) Color is black, location is (1, 1), and direction is east.
(C) Color is red, location is (1, 2), and direction is northeast.
(D) Color is red, location is (0, 0), and direction is northwest.
(E) Color is black, location is (2, 0), and direction is south.

38. The `moveTo` method of the `Actor` class would *not* be suitable for which of the following operations? You may assume that each scenario below is contained in the context of a two-dimensional grid.
(A) Capturing a piece in Chess (namely, removing that piece from the board and taking its place on the board).
(B) Moving a piece on a Checkers board into an empty location.
(C) Rearranging the furniture in a room that has a rectangular floor plan.
(D) Changing a reserved seat to another location in a theater that has a rectangular arrangement of seats.
(E) Placing two monkeys in the same cage at a zoo, where the zoo has a rectangular arrangement of cages.

GO ON TO THE NEXT PAGE.

39. Consider the bounded grid shown, and the Actor in location (1, 1).

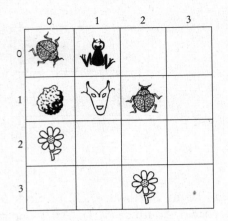

If it is the Actor's turn to act, which are valid possibilities for a new location, if the Actor is a

(1) Critter
(2) ChameleonCritter

(A) (1) (0, 0), (2, 0), (2, 1), (2, 2), (1, 2), (0, 2)
    (2) (2, 1), (2, 2), (0, 2)

(B) (1) (0, 0), (2, 0), (1, 2)
    (2) (3, 0), (3, 1), (2, 1), (2, 2), (3, 3), (2, 3), (1, 3), (0, 2), (0, 3)

(C) (1) (0, 0), (0, 1), (0, 2), (1, 0), (1, 2), (2, 0), (2, 1), (2, 2)
    (2) (2, 1), (2, 2), (0, 2)

(D) (1) (0, 0), (0, 1), (1, 1), (1, 2), (2, 0), (3, 2)
    (2) (3, 0), (3, 1), (2, 1), (2, 2), (3, 3), (2, 3), (1, 3), (0, 2), (0, 3)

(E) (1) (0, 0), (0, 1), (0, 2), (1, 2), (2, 0), (2, 1), (2, 2)
    (2) (0, 2), (2, 0), (2, 1), (2, 2)

40. Suppose the program is changed so that a `Critter` is allowed to age. A `Critter` will start out at age 1, and have its age incremented by 1 each time it acts. To make this change, a private instance variable `age` is added to the `Critter` class, as well as an accessor method, `getAge`. A constructor is provided that initializes age to 1. What other changes must be made?

I The act method of the `Actor` class must be modified.

II The act method of the `Critter` class must be modified.

III The act method of the `ChameleonCritter` class must be overridden.

(A) I only
(B) II only
(C) III only
(D) I and II only
(E) I, II, and III

END OF SECTION I

COMPUTER SCIENCE
SECTION II

Time—1 hour and 45 minutes
Number of questions—4
Percent of total grade—50

Directions: SHOW ALL YOUR WORK. REMEMBER THAT
PROGRAM SEGMENTS ARE TO BE WRITTEN IN Java.

Write your answers in pencil only in the booklet provided.

Notes:

- Assume that the classes in the Quick Reference have been imported where needed.

- Unless otherwise stated, assume that parameters in method calls are not null and that methods are called only when their preconditions are satisfied.

- In writing solutions for each question, you may use any of the accessible methods that are listed in classes defined in that question. Writing significant amounts of code that can be replaced by a call to one of these methods may not receive full credit.

---

1. A chemical solution is said to be *acidic* if it has a pH integer value from 1 to 6, inclusive. The lower the pH, the more acidic the solution.

   An experiment has a large number of chemical solutions arranged in a line and a mechanical arm that moves back and forth along the line, so that the acidity of each solution can be altered by adding various chemicals. A chemical solution is specified by the Solution interface below.

```
public interface Solution
{
    /** @return an integer value that ranges from 1 (very acidic)
     *  to 14 */
    int getPH();

    /** Set PH to newValue.
     *  @param newValue the new PH value */
    void setPH(int newValue);
}
```

The experiment keeps track of the solutions and the mechanical arm. The figure below represents the solutions and mechanical arm in an experiment. The arm, indicated by the arrow, is currently at index 4 and is facing left. The second row of integers represents the pH values of the solutions.

index	0	1	2	3	4	5	6
pH	7	4	10	5	6	7	13

←

In this experiment, the most acidic solution is at index 1, since its pH value is the lowest.

The state of the mechanical arm includes the index of its location and direction it is facing (to the right or to the left). A mechanical arm is specified by the `MechanicalArm` interface below.

```
public interface MechanicalArm
{
    /** @return the index of the current location of the
     *  mechanical arm */
    int getCurrentIndex();

    /** @return true if the mechanical arm is facing right
     *  (toward solutions with larger indexes),
     *  false if the mechanical arm is facing left
     *  (toward solutions with smaller indexes)
     */
    boolean isFacingRight();

    /** Changes the current direction of the mechanical arm */
    void changeDirection();

    /** Moves the mechanical arm forward in its current direction
     *  by the number of locations specified.
     *  @param numLocs the number of locations to move
     *  Precondition: numLocs > 0. */
    void moveForward(int numLocs);
}
```

An experiment is represented by the `Experiment` class shown below.

GO ON TO THE NEXT PAGE.

```
public class Experiment
{
    /** The mechanical arm used to process the solutions */
    private MechanicalArm arm;

    /** The list of solutions */
    private List<Solution> solutions;

    /** Resets the experiment.
     * Postcondition:  The mechanical arm has a current index of 0
     *                 and is facing right.
     */
    public void reset()
    { /* to be implemented in part (a) */ }

    /** Finds and returns the index of the most acidic solution.
     * @return index the location of the most acidic solution
     * or -1 if there are no acidic solutions
     * Postcondition: The mechanical arm is facing right, and its
     *                current index is at the most acidic solution,
     *                or at 0 if there are no acidic solutions.
     */
    public int mostAcidic()
    { /* to be implemented in part (b) */ }
}
```

(a) Write the `Experiment` method reset that places the mechanical arm facing right, at index 0.

For example, suppose the experiment contains the solutions with pH values shown. The arrow represents the mechanical arm.

A call to reset will result in

Information repeated from the beginning of the question

```
public interface Solution

int getPH()
void setPH(int newValue)

public interface MechanicalArm

int getCurrentIndex()
boolean isFacingRight()
void changeDirection()
void moveForward(int numLocs)

public class Experiment

private MechanicalArm arm
private List<Solution> solutions
public void reset()
public int mostAcidic()
```

Complete method reset below.

```
/** Resets the experiment.
 *  Postcondition: The mechanical arm has a current index of 0
 *               and is facing right.
 */
public void reset()
```

(b) Write the Experiment method mostAcidic that returns the index of the most acidic solution and places the mechanical arm facing right at the location of the most acidic solution. A solution is acidic if its pH is less than 7. The lower the pH, the more acidic the solution. If there are no acidic solutions in the experiment, the mostAcidic method should return –1 and place the mechanical arm at index 0, facing right.

For example, suppose the experiment has this state:

A call to mostAcidic should return the value 1 and result in the following state for the experiment:

GO ON TO THE NEXT PAGE.

If the experiment has this state,

a call to mostAcidic should return the value −1 and result in the following state for the experiment:

Information repeated from the beginning of the question

<u>public interface Solution</u>

```
int getPH()
void setPH(int newValue)
```

<u>public interface MechanicalArm</u>

```
int getCurrentIndex()
boolean isFacingRight()
void changeDirection()
void moveForward(int numLocs)
```

<u>public class Experiment</u>

```
private MechanicalArm arm
private List<Solution> solutions
public void reset()
public int mostAcidic()
```

Complete method mostAcidic below.

```
/** Finds and returns the index of the most acidic solution.
 *  @return index the location of the most acidic solution
 *  or -1 if there are no acidic solutions
 *  Postcondition: The mechanical arm is facing right, and its
 *                 current index is at the most acidic solution,
 *                 or at 0 if there are no acidic solutions.
 */
public int mostAcidic()
```

2. A WordSet, shown in the class declaration below, stores a set of String objects in no particular order and contains no duplicates. Each word is a sequence of capital letters only.

```
public class WordSet
{
    /**
     * Constructor initializes set to empty
     */
    public WordSet()
    { /* implementation not shown */ }

    /**
     * @return the number of words in set
     */
    public int size()
    { /* implementation not shown */ }

    /**
     * Adds word to set (no duplicates)
     * @param word the word to be added
     */
    public void insert(String word)
    { /* implementation not shown */ }

    /**
     * Removes word from set if present, else does nothing
     * @param word the word to be removed
     */
    public void remove(String word)
    { /* implementation not shown */ }

    /**
     * Returns kth word in alphabetical order, where 1 <= k <= size().
     * @param k position of word to be returned
     * @return the kth word
     */
    public String findkth(int k)
    { /* implementation not shown */ }

    /**
     * @return true if set contains word, false otherwise
     */
    public boolean contains(String word)
    { /* implementation not shown */ }

    //There may be instance variables, constructors, and methods
    //that are not shown.
}
```

The findkth method returns the *k*th word in alphabetical order in the set, even though the implementation of WordSet may not be sorted. The number *k* ranges from 1 (corresponding to first in alphabetical order) to *N*, where *N* is the number of words in the set. For example, if WordSet s stores the words {"GRAPE", "PEAR", "FIG", "APPLE"}, here are the values when s.findkth(k) is called.

k	values of s.findkth(k)
1	APPLE
2	FIG
3	GRAPE
4	PEAR

(a) Write a client method countA that returns the number of words in WordSet s that begin with the letter "A." In writing countA, you may call any of the methods of the WordSet class. Assume that the methods work as specified.

Complete method countA below.

```
/**
 * @param s the current WordSet
 * @return the number of words in s that begin with "A"
 */
public static int countA(WordSet s)
```

(b) Write a client method removeA that removes all words that begin with "A." If there are no such words in s, then removeA does nothing. In writing removeA, you may call method countA specified in part (a). Assume that countA works as specified, regardless of what you wrote in part (a).

```
Information repeated from the beginning of the question

public class WordSet

public WordSet()
public int size()
public void insert(String word)
public void remove(String word)
public String findkth(int k)
public boolean contains(String word)
```

Complete method removeA below:

```
/**
 * @param s the current WordSet
 * Postcondition: WordSet s contains no words that begin with "A",
 *                but is otherwise unchanged.
 */
public static void removeA(WordSet s)
```

GO ON TO THE NEXT PAGE.

(c) Write a client method `commonElements` that returns the `WordSet` containing just those elements occurring in both of its `WordSet` parameters.

For example, if s1 is {"BE", "NOT", "AFRAID"} and s2 is {"TO", "BE", "OR", "NOT"}, then `commonElements(s1, s2)` should return the `WordSet` {"BE", "NOT"}. (If you are familiar with mathematical set theory, `commonElements` returns the intersection of s1 and s2.)

Complete method `commonElements` below.

```
/**
 * @param s1 the first given set
 * @param s2 the second given set
 * @return the WordSet containing only the elements that occur
 *          in both s1 and s2
 */
public static WordSet commonElements(WordSet s1, WordSet s2)
```

3. In this question you will implement two methods for a class `Tournament` that keeps track of the players who have registered for a tournament. The `Tournament` class uses the `Player` class shown below. A `Player` has a name and player number specified when a player is constructed.

```
public class Player
{
    public Player(String name, int playerNumber)
    { /* implementation not shown */ }

    public int getPlayerNumber()
    { /* implementation not shown */ }

    //private instance variables and other methods not shown
}
```

An incomplete declaration for the `Tournament` class is shown below. There are 100 available slots for players in the tournament, and the players are numbered $0, 1, 2, \ldots, 99$.

```
public class Tournament
{
    /** The list of slots in the tournament.
     * Each element corresponds to a slot in the tournament.
     * If slots[i] is null, the slot is not yet taken;
     * otherwise it contains a reference to a Player.
     * For example, slots[i].getPlayerNumber() returns i. */
    private Player[] slots;

    /** The list of names of players who wish to participate in
     * the tournament, but cannot because all slots are taken. */
    private List<String> waitingList;
```

```
/**
 * If there are any empty slots (slots with no Player)
 * assign the player with the specified playerName to an
 * empty slot. Create and return the new Player.
 * If there are no available slots, add the player's name
 * to the end of the waiting list and return null.
 * @playerName the name of the person requesting a slot
 * @return the new Player
 */
public Player requestSlot(String playerName)
{ /* to be implemented in part (a) */ }

/**
 * Release the slot for player p, thus removing that player
 * from the tournament. If there are any names in waitingList,
 * remove the first name and create a Player in the
 * canceled slot for this person. Return the new Player.
 * If waitingList is empty, mark the slot specified by p as
 * empty and return null.
 * Precondition: p is a valid Player for some slot in this
 *                     tournament.
 * @param p the player who will be removed from the tournament
 * @return the new Player placed in the canceled slot
 */
public Player cancelAndReassignSlot(Player p)
{ /* to be implemented in part (b) */ }

    // constructor and other methods not shown.
}
```

(a) Write the `Tournament` method `requestSlot`. Method `requestSlot` tries to reserve a slot in the tournament for a given player. If there are any available slots in the tournament, one of them is assigned to the named player, and the newly created `Player` is returned. If there are no available slots, the player's name is added to the end of the waiting list and `null` is returned.

Complete method `requestSlot` below.

```
/**
 * If there are any empty slots (slots with no Player)
 * assign the player with the specified playerName to an
 * empty slot. Create and return the new Player.
 * If there are no available slots, add the player's name
 * to the end of the waiting list and return null.
 * @playerName the name of the person requesting a slot
 * @return the new Player
 */
public Player requestSlot(String playerName)
```

(b) Write the `Tournament` method `cancelAndReassignSlot`. This method releases a previous player's slot. If the waiting list for the tournament contains any names, the newly available slot is reassigned to the person at the front of the list. That person's name is removed from the waiting list and the newly created `Player` is returned. If the waiting list is empty, the newly released slot is marked as empty and null is returned.

In writing `cancelAndReassignSlot` you may use any accessible methods in the `Player` and `Tournament` classes. Assume that these methods work as specified.

Information repeated from the beginning of the question

```
public class Player

public Player(String name, int playerNumber)
public int getPlayerNumber()

public class Tournament

private Player[] slots
private List<String> waitingList
public Player requestSlot(String playerName)
public Player cancelAndReassignSlot(Player p)
```

Complete method `cancelAndReassignSlot` below.

```
/**
 * Release the slot for player p, thus removing that player
 * from the tournament. If there are any names in waitingList,
 * remove the first name and create a Player in the
 * canceled slot for this person. Return the new Player.
 * If waitingList is empty, mark the slot specified by p as
 * empty and return null.
 * Precondition: p is a valid Player for some slot in this
 *               tournament.
 * @param p the player who will be removed from the tournament
 * @return the new Player placed in the canceled slot
 */
public Player cancelAndReassignSlot(Player p)
```

4. This question involves reasoning about the code from the GridWorld Case Study. A Quick Reference to the case study is provided as part of this exam.

Consider defining a new kind of ChameleonCritter, a HungryChameleon, that attempts to eat a Bug when it acts. If it succeeds in eating a bug, a HungryChameleon does not change color. If it fails to eat, then it changes color in the same way a ChameleonCritter does. After eating or changing color, a HungryChameleon moves like a ChameleonCritter. Here is a partial definition of the class HungryChameleon.

```
/**
 * A HungryChameleon eats neighboring bugs if there are any;
 * otherwise it takes on the color of neighboring actors as it
 * moves through the grid.
 */
public class HungryChameleon extends ChameleonCritter
{
    /**
     * Gets a list of adjacent bugs.
     * @param actors the list of all adjacent neighbors
     * @return a list of adjacent bugs
     */
    private ArrayList<Bug> getBugs(ArrayList<Actor> actors)
    { /* to be implemented in part (a) */ }

    /**
     * Randomly "eats" one of the bugs in the list of bugs.
     * Precondition: bugs.size() > 0.
     * @param bugs the list of adjacent bugs
     */
    private void eatBug(ArrayList<Bug> bugs)
    { /* to be implemented in part (b) */ }

    /**
     * Gets a list of adjacent neighboring bugs and eats one.
     * If there are no bugs to eat, the HungryChameleon takes
     * on the color of a neighboring actor.
     * @param actors the list of all adjacent neighbors
     */
    public void processActors(ArrayList<Actor> actors)
    { /* to be implemented in part (c) */ }
}
```

(a) Write the private HungryChameleon method getBugs. This method should return a list of adjacent neighboring actors that are bugs.

Complete method getBugs below.

```
/**
 * Gets a list of adjacent bugs.
 * @param actors the list of all adjacent neighbors
 * @return a list of adjacent bugs
 */
private ArrayList<Bug> getBugs(ArrayList<Actor> actors)
```

GO ON TO THE NEXT PAGE.

(b) Write the private `HungryChameleon` method `eatBug`. Method `eatBug` randomly selects a `Bug` from its bugs parameter and "eats" (i.e., removes) it.

Complete method `eatBug` below.

```
/**
 * Randomly "eats" one of the bugs in the list of bugs.
 * Precondition: bugs.size() > 0.
 * @param bugs the list of adjacent bugs
 */
private void eatBug(ArrayList<Bug> bugs)
```

(c) Override the `processActors` method of the `ChameleonCritter` superclass. A `HungryChameleon` processes actors by getting a list of neighboring bugs and randomly selecting one to eat. If there are no bugs to eat, the `HungryChameleon` takes on the color of one of its neighbors, behaving just like a `ChameleonCritter`.

Complete method `processActors` below.

```
/**
 * Gets a list of adjacent neighboring bugs and eats one.
 * If there are no bugs to eat, the HungryChameleon takes
 * on the color of a neighboring actor.
 * @param actors the list of all adjacent neighbors
 */
public void processActors(ArrayList<Actor> actors)
```

END OF EXAMINATION

ANSWER KEY (Section I)

1. D	15. C	29. A
2. B	16. A	30. A
3. A	17. E	31. C
4. B	18. A	32. E
5. E	19. E	33. D
6. A	20. B	34. D
7. A	21. E	35. E
8. B	22. D	36. B
9. C	23. E	37. D
10. B	24. A	38. E
11. A	25. C	39. A
12. C	26. D	40. B
13. B	27. B	
14. E	28. A	

DIAGNOSTIC CHART FOR PRACTICE EXAM

Each multiple-choice question has a complete explanation (p. 46).

The following table relates each question to sections that you should review. For any given question, the topic(s) in the chart represent the concept(s) tested in the question. These topics are explained on the corresponding page(s) in the chart and should provide further insight into answering that question.

ANSWERS EXPLAINED

Section I

1. **(D)** Constructors are never inherited. If a subclass has no constructor, the default constructor for the superclass is generated. If the superclass does not have a default constructor, a compile-time error will occur.

2. **(B)** The programmer is using an object-oriented approach to writing the program and plans to test the simplest classes first. This is bottom-up development. In *top-down* development (choice A), high-level classes are broken down into subsidiary classes. Procedural abstraction (choice C) is the use of helper methods in a class. Information hiding (choice D) is restriction of access to private data and methods in a class. Choice E is wrong because a driver program is one whose sole purpose is to test a given method or class. Implementing the simplest classes first may involve driver programs that test the various methods, but the overall plan is not an example of a driver program.

3. **(A)** In the constructor, the private instance variables `mySuit` and `myValue` must be initialized to the appropriate parameter values. Choice A is the only choice that does this.

4. **(B)** Implementation II invokes the `toString` method of the `Card` class. Implementation I fails because there is no default `toString` method for arrays. Implementation III will cause a `ClassCastException`: You cannot cast a `Card` to a `String`.

5. **(E)** Since the values in `arr` cannot be greater than `Integer.MAX_VALUE`, the test in the `while` loop will be true at least once and will lead to the smallest element being stored in `min`. (If *all* the elements of the array are `Integer.MAX_VALUE`, the code still works.) Similarly, initializing `min` to `arr[0]`, the first element in the array, ensures that all elements in `arr` will be examined and the smallest will be found. Choice I, `Integer.MIN_VALUE`, fails because the test in the loop will always be false! There is no array element that will be less than the smallest possible integer. The method will (incorrectly) return `Integer.MIN_VALUE`.

6. **(A)** The array will not be changed by the `increment` method. Here are the memory slots:

Before the first call, `increment(3)`:

Just after the first call:

Just before exiting `increment(3)`:

Just after exiting `increment(3)`:

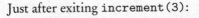

The same analysis applies to the method calls `increment(4)` and `increment(5)`.

7. **(A)** As in the previous question, the array will not be changed by the `increment` method. Nor will the local variable `element`! What *will* be changed by `increment` is the copy of the parameter during each pass through the loop.

8. **(B)** The maximum number will be achieved if /* *test* */ is true in each pass through the loop. So the question boils down to: How many times is the loop executed? Try one odd and one even value of n:

$$\text{If } n = 7, \quad i = 0, 2, 4, 6 \quad \text{Ans} = 4$$
$$\text{If } n = 8, \quad i = 0, 2, 4, 6 \quad \text{Ans} = 4$$

Notice that choice B is the only expression that works for both $n = 7$ and $n = 8$.

9. **(C)** Here is one of the golden rules of programming: Don't start planning the program until every aspect of the specification is crystal clear. A programmer should never make unilateral decisions about ambiguities in a specification.

10. **(B)** When $x \leq y$, a recursive call is made to `whatIsIt(x-1, y)`. If x decreases at every recursive call, there is no way to reach a successful base case. Thus, the method never terminates and eventually exhausts all available memory.

11. **(A)** The expression `!(max != a[i])` is equivalent to `max == a[i]`, so the given expression is equivalent to `a[i] == max || max == a[i]`, which is equivalent to `a[i] == max`.

12. **(C)** A base-`b` number can be represented with `b` characters. Thus, base-2 uses 0,1 for example, and base-10 uses $0, 1, \ldots, 8, 9$. A hexadecimal (base-16) number is represented with 16 characters: $0, 1, \ldots, 8, 9, A, B, C, D, E, F$, where $A = 10, B = 11, \ldots, F = 15$. The largest two-place base-2 integer is

$$11 = 1 \times 2^0 + 1 \times 2^1 = 3$$

The largest two-place base-10 integer is

$$99 = 9 \times 10^0 + 9 \times 10^1$$

The largest two-place base-16 integer is

$$FF = F \times 16^0 + F \times 16^1$$

The character F represents 15, so

$$FF = 15 \times 16^0 + 15 \times 16^1 = 255$$

Here's another way to think about this problem: Each hex digit is 4 binary digits (bits), since $16 = 2^4$. Therefore a two-digit hex number is 8 bits. The largest base-10 number that can be represented with 8 bits is $2^8 - 1 = 255$.

13. **(B)** The index range for `ArrayList` is $0 \leq \text{index} \leq \text{size}()-1$. Thus, for methods `get`, `remove`, and `set`, the last in-bounds index is `size()-1`. The one exception is the `add` method—to add an element to the end of the list takes an index parameter `list.size()`.

14. **(E)** Subclasses of `Quadrilateral` may also be abstract, in which case they will inherit `perimeter` and/or `area` as abstract methods.

15. **(C)** Segment I starts correctly but fails to initialize the additional private variables of the `Rectangle` class. Segment II is wrong because by using `super` with `topLeft` and `botRight`, it implies that these values are used in the `Quadrilateral` superclass. This is false—there isn't even a constructor with three arguments in the superclass.

16. **(A)** During execution the appropriate `area` method for each quad in `quadList` will be determined (polymorphism or dynamic binding).

17. **(E)** The algorithm has three steps:

    1. Store the object at `i` in `temp`.
    2. Place at location `i` the object at `j`.
    3. Place `temp` at location `j`.

    This has the effect of swapping the objects at `i` and `j`. Notice that choices B and C, while incomplete, are not incorrect. The question, however, asks for the *best* description of the postcondition, which is found in choice E.

18. **(A)** Subtracting 0.5 from a negative real number and then truncating it produces the number correctly rounded to the nearest integer. Note that casting to an `int` truncates a real number. The expression in choice B is correct for rounding a *positive* real number. Choice C won't round correctly. For example, −3.7 will be rounded to −3 instead of −4. Choices D and E don't make sense. Why cast to `double` if you're rounding to the nearest integer?

19. **(E)** The method call `whatsIt(347)` puts on the stack `System.out.print(7)`.
    The method call `whatsIt(34)` puts on the stack `System.out.print(4)`.
    The method call `whatsIt(3)` is a base case and writes out 3.
    Now the stack is popped from the top, and the 3 that was printed is followed by 4, then 7. The result is 347.

20. **(B)** Recall that insertion sort takes each element in turn and (a) finds its insertion point and (b) moves elements to insert that element in its correct place. Thus, if the array is in reverse sorted order, the insertion point will always be at the front of the array, leading to the maximum number of comparisons and data moves—very inefficient. Therefore choices A, C, and E are false.

    Selection sort finds the smallest element in the array and swaps it with `a[0]` and then finds the smallest element in the rest of the array and swaps it with `a[1]`, and so on. Thus, the same number of comparisons and moves will occur, irrespective of the original arrangement of elements in the array. So choice B is true, and choice D is false.

21. **(E)** Method call I fails because `ClassOne` does not have access to the methods of its subclass. Method call II fails because `c2` needs to be cast to `ClassTwo` to be able to access `methodTwo`. Thus, the following would be OK:

    ```
    ((ClassTwo) c2).methodTwo();
    ```

    Method call III works because `ClassTwo` inherits `methodOne` from its superclass, `ClassOne`.

22. **(D)** Notice that in the original code, if `n` is 1, `k` is incremented by 1, and if `n` is 4, `k` is incremented by 4. This is equivalent to saying "if `n` is 1 or 4, `k` is incremented by `n`."

23. **(E)** Segment I will throw a `NullPointerException` when `s.equals...` is invoked, because `s` is a null reference. Segment III looks suspect, but when the `startIndex` parameter of the `substring` method equals `s.length()`, the value returned is the empty string. If, however, `startIndex > s.length()`, a `StringIndexOutOfBoundsException` is thrown.

24. **(A)** Since results of calculations with floating-point numbers are not always represented exactly (round-off error), direct tests for equality are not reliable. Instead of the boolean expression `d == c`, a test should be done to check whether the difference of `d` and `c` is within some acceptable tolerance interval (see the Box on comparing floating-point numbers, p. 63).

25. **(C)** If `arr` has elements 2, 3, 5, the values of `value` are

```
2                      //after initialization
2*10 + 3 = 23          //when i = 1
23*10 + 5 = 235    //when i = 2
```

26. **(D)** The point of the binary search algorithm is that the interval containing `key` is repeatedly narrowed down by splitting it in half. For each iteration of the `while` loop, if `key` is in the list, `arr[first]` $\leq$ `key` $\leq$ `arr[last]`. Note that (i) the endpoints of the interval must be included, and (ii) `key` is not necessarily in the list.

27. **(B)**

	first	last	mid	a[mid]
After first iteration	0	13	6	50
After second iteration	7	13	10	220
After third iteration	7	9	8	101
After fourth iteration	9	9	9	205

28. **(A)** The data structure is an array, not an `ArrayList`, so you cannot use the `add` method for inserting elements into the list. This eliminates choices B and D. The expression to return a random integer from 0 to k-1 inclusive is

```
(int) (Math.random() * k)
```

Thus, to get integers from 0 to 100 requires `k` to be 101, which eliminates choice C. Choice E fails because it gets integers from 1 to 100.

29. **(A)** Suppose `str1` is `strawberry` and `str2` is `cat`. Then `insert(str1, str2, 5)` will return the following pieces, concatenated:

```
straw + cat + berry
```

Recall that `s.substring(k, m)` (a method of `String`) returns a substring of `s` starting at position `k` and ending at position `m-1`. String `str1` must be split into two parts, `first` and `last`. Then `str2` will be inserted between them. Since `str2` is inserted starting at position 5 (the "b"), `first` = `straw`, namely `str1.substring(0,pos)`. (Start at 0 and take all the characters up to and including location `pos-1`, namely 4.) Notice that `last`, the second substring of `str1`, must start at the index for "b", which is `pos`, the index at which `str2` was inserted. The expression `str1.substring(pos)` returns the substring of `str1` that starts at `pos` and continues to the end of the string, which was required. Note that you don't need any "special case" tests. In the cases where `str2` is inserted at the front of `str1` (i.e., `pos` is 0) or the back of `str1` (i.e., `pos` is `str1.length()`), the code for the general case works.

30. **(A)** Method `changeMatrix` examines each element and changes it to its absolute value if its row number equals its column number. The only two elements that satisfy the condition `r == c` are `mat[0][0]` and `mat[1][1]`. Thus, –1 is changed to 1 and –4 is changed to 4, resulting in the matrix in choice A.

31. **(C)** Composition is the *has-a* relationship. A `PlayerGroup` *has-a* `Player` (several of them, in fact). Inheritance, (choice D) is the *is-a* relationship, which doesn't apply here. None of the choices A, B, or E apply in this example: An interface is a single class composed of only abstract methods (see p. 140); encapsulation is the bundling together of data fields and operations into a single unit, a class (see p. 91); and `PlayerGroup` and `Player` are clearly dependent on each other since `PlayerGroup` contains several `Player` objects (see p. 211).

32. **(E)** All of these data structures are reasonable. They all represent 20 bingo numbers in a convenient way and provide easy mechanisms for crossing off numbers and recognizing a winning card. Notice that data structure II provides a very quick way of searching for a number on the card. For example, if 48 is called, `myBingoCard[48]` is inspected. If it is `true`, then it was one of the 20 original numbers on the card and gets crossed out. If `false`, 48 was not on that player's card. Data structures I and II require a linear search to find any given number that is called. (Note: There is no assumption that the array is sorted, which would allow a more efficient binary search.)

33. **(D)** A `NullPointerException` is thrown whenever an attempt is made to invoke a method with an object that hasn't been created with `new`. Choice A doesn't make sense: To test the `Caller` constructor requires a statement of the form

    ```
    Caller c = new Caller();
    ```

    Choice B is wrong: A missing `return` statement in a method triggers a compile-time error. Choice C doesn't make sense: In the declaration of `myNumbers`, its default initialization is to `null`. Choice E is bizarre. Hopefully you eliminated it immediately!

34. **(D)** `Location.RIGHT` is 90. A `Bug` that doesn't move, however, turns right through 45°, or `Location.HALF_RIGHT`. Choice A could happen if the `Bug` is facing northeast, for example, at its turn to move. If there are no obstacles in its path, the `Bug` will keep moving in that direction, on a diagonal path. For choice B, refer to the bug's `canMove` method, and notice that the `Bug` can move either into an empty location or onto a `Flower`. It may not, however, move onto a `Rock`, so choice C is true. Choice E will happen whenever a `Bug` is blocked in all adjacent locations, either by an actor other than a `Flower` or an edge of the grid. The `Bug` can't move, so it keeps on turning right.

35. **(E)**   `getDirection() = Location.NORTHWEST`

    $$= 315$$

    `Location.HALF_LEFT = -45`

    Answer: $315 - 45 = 270$

36. **(B)** The `canMove` method in the `Bug` class is the only code that needs to be changed. Here is the change:

```
return (neighbor == null) || (neighbor instanceof Flower)
    || (neighbor instanceof Rock);
```

Note that the `BoxBug` class does not need to be changed. In the `act` method, the inherited `canMove` method will now return `true` if the location in front of the `BoxBug` is empty, or contains a flower, or contains a rock. The `Actor` class too does not need to be changed. The `moveTo` method specifies that if there is another `Actor` at the new location, that actor will be removed.

37. **(D)** The `ChameleonCritter` randomly picks either the rock or the bug, and changes its color to match that of the selected actor. Eliminate choice A—the `ChameleonCritter` cannot remain blue. Next, the `ChameleonCritter` moves to an empty neighboring location, changing its direction to match the direction in which it moved. Eliminate choice B, since (1, 1) is not an empty neighboring location. Choices C and E both change color correctly and move to a valid location. The `ChameleonCritter`, however, ends up facing the wrong direction. The direction from (1, 1) to (1, 2) is east, not northeast. The direction from (1, 1) to (2, 0) is southwest, not south.

38. **(E)** The specification for `moveTo` states that

    - the actor will be moved to a new location.
    - if there's already another actor in this location, it will be removed.

    The key here is that *two* actors may not occupy the same location simultaneously. Therefore, you cannot use `moveTo` to place two `Monkey` objects in the same location at a zoo.

39. **(A)** The `Critter` will eat the bugs in (0, 0) and (1, 2) and the flower in (2, 0), leaving those locations empty and available. Also available are the other empty locations: (2, 1), (2, 2), and (0, 2). The `ChameleonCritter` doesn't eat its neighbors, so the only available locations are the ones that were empty to begin with: (2, 1), (2, 2), and (0, 2).

40. **(B)** The `act` method of the `Critter` class must be changed so that the `age` variable is increased by 1 each time `act` is called. Statement I is wrong because not all actors age. Statement III is wrong because a `ChameleonCritter` inherits the `Critter`'s `act` method.

Section II

1. (a)
```
public void reset()
{
    if(arm.isFacingRight())
        arm.changeDirection();
    arm.moveForward(arm.getCurrentIndex());
    arm.changeDirection();
}
```

(b)
```
public int mostAcidic()
{
    reset();
    int minPH = Integer.MAX_VALUE, minIndex = 0;
    int index = 0;
    while (index < solutions.size())
    {
        Solution s = solutions.get(index);
        if (s.getPH() < minPH)
        {
            minPH = s.getPH();
            minIndex = index;
        }
        index++;
    }
    if (minPH >= 7)
        return -1;
    else
    {
        arm.moveForward(minIndex);
        return minIndex;
    }
}
```

NOTE

- In part (b), a for-each loop won't work, because you need to save an index.
- In part (b), notice that resetting the mechanical arm causes the arm to face right.
- In part (b), you could initialize minPh to any integer greater than or equal to 7 for this algorithm to work. You just must be careful not to set it to an "acidic" number, namely 1 to 6.

2. (a)
```
public static int countA(WordSet s)
{
    int count = 0;
    while (count < s.size() &&
            s.findkth(count + 1).substring(0, 1).equals("A"))
        count++;
    return count;
}
```

Alternatively,

```
public static int countA(WordSet s)
{
    boolean done = false;
    int count = 0;
    while (count < s.size() && !done)
    {
        String nextWord = s.findkth(count + 1);
        if (nextWord.substring(0,1).equals("A"))
            count++;
        else
            done = true;
    }
    return count;
}
```

(b)
```
public static void removeA(WordSet s)
{
    int numA = countA(s);
    for (int i = 1; i <= numA; i++)
        s.remove(s.findkth(1));
}
```

Alternatively,

```
public static void removeA(WordSet s)
{
    while (s.size() != 0 &&
            s.findkth(1).substring(0, 1).equals("A"))
        s.remove(s.findkth(1));
}
```

(c)
```
public static WordSet commonElements(WordSet s1, WordSet s2)
{
    WordSet temp = new WordSet();
    for (int i = 1; i <= s1.size(); i++)
    {
        String nextWord = s1.findkth(i);
        if (s2.contains(nextWord))
            temp.insert(nextWord);
    }
    return temp;
}
```

NOTE

- To test whether a word starts with "A", you must compare the first letter of word, that is, word.substring(0,1), with "A".
- In part (a), you must check that your solution works if s is empty. For the given algorithm, count < s.size() will fail and short circuit the test, which is desirable since s.findkth(1) will violate the precondition of findkth(k), namely that k cannot be greater than size().
- The parameter for s.findkth must be greater than 0. Hence the use of s.findkth(count+1) in part (a).

- For the first solution in part (b), you get a subtle intent error if your last step is `s.remove(s.findkth(i))`. Suppose that s is initially {"FLY", "ASK", "ANT"}. After the method call `s.remove(s.findkth(1))`, s will be {"FLY", "ASK"}. After the statement `s.remove(s.findkth(2))`, s will be {"ASK"}!! The point is that s is adjusted after each call to `s.remove`. The algorithm that works is this: If N is the number of words that start with "A", simply remove the first element in the list N times. Note that the alternative solution avoids the pitfall described by simply repeatedly removing the first element if it starts with 'A." The alternative solution, however, has its own pitfall: The algorithm can fail if a test for s being empty isn't done for each iteration of the `while` loop.
- Part (c) could also be accomplished by going through each element in s2 and checking if it's included in s1.

3. (a)
```java
public Player requestSlot(String playerName)
{
    for (int i = 0; i < slots.length; i++)
    {
        if (slots[i] == null)
        {
            Player p = new Player(playerName, i);
            slots[i] = p;
            return p;
        }
    }
    waitingList.add(playerName);
    return null;
}
```

(b)
```java
public Player cancelAndReassignSlot(Player p)
{
    int i = p.getPlayerNumber();
    if (waitingList.size() != 0)
    {
        slots[i] = new Player(waitingList.get(0), i);
        waitingList.remove(0);
    }
    else
    {
        slots[i] = null;
    }
    return slots[i];
}
```

NOTE

- In part (a), the last two lines of the method will be executed only if you are still in the method, namely no available slot was found.
- In part (b), the final line will return either a new player, or `null` if the waiting list was empty.

4. (a)
```
    private ArrayList<Bug> getBugs(ArrayList<Actor> actors)
    {
        ArrayList<Bug> bugs = new ArrayList<Bug>();
        for (Actor a : actors)
        {
            if (a instanceof Bug)
                bugs.add((Bug)a);
        }
        return bugs;
    }
```

    (b)
```
    private void eatBug(ArrayList<Bug> bugs)
    {
        int n = bugs.size();
        int r = (int) (Math.random() * n);
        Bug b = bugs.get(r);
        b.removeSelfFromGrid();
    }
```

    (c)
```
    public void processActors(ArrayList<Actor> actors)
    {
        ArrayList<Bug> bugList = getBugs(actors);
        if (bugList.size() == 0)
            super.processActors(actors);
        else
            eatBug(bugList);
    }
```

NOTE

- In part (a), the bugs ArrayList contains only Bug objects. Notice that in the for loop, the object a that is being examined is an Actor. Therefore you need the cast to Bug in the add statement in the body of the loop.
- In part (c), if there is at least one bug in bugList, the HungryChameleon will eat; otherwise it will do what its superclass, ChameleonCritter, does:

```
super.processActors(actors);
```

Introductory Java Language Features

Fifty loops shalt thou make ...
—Exodus 26:5

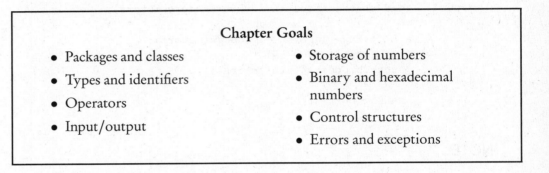

Chapter Goals

- Packages and classes
- Types and identifiers
- Operators
- Input/output

- Storage of numbers
- Binary and hexadecimal numbers
- Control structures
- Errors and exceptions

The AP Computer Science course includes algorithm analysis, data structures, and the techniques and methods of modern programming, specifically, object-oriented programming. A high-level programming language is used to explore these concepts. Java is the language currently in use on the AP exam.

Java was developed by James Gosling and a team at Sun Microsystems in California; it continues to evolve. The AP exam covers a clearly defined subset of Java language features that are presented throughout this book, including some new features of Java 5.0 that were tested for the first time in May 2007. The College Board website, *http://www.collegeboard.com/student/testing/ap/subjects.html*, contains a complete listing of this subset.

Java provides basic control structures such as the `if-else` statement, `for` loop, for-each loop, and `while` loop, as well as fundamental built-in data types. But the power of the language lies in the manipulation of user-defined types called objects, many of which can interact in a single program.

PACKAGES AND CLASSES

A typical Java program has user-defined classes whose objects interact with those from Java class libraries. In Java, related classes are grouped into *packages*, many of which are provided with the compiler. You can put your own classes into a package—this facilitates their use in other programs.

The package `java.lang`, which contains many commonly used classes, is automatically provided to all Java programs. To use any other package in a program, an `import` statement must be used. To import all of the classes in a package called `packagename`, use the form

```
import packagename.*;
```

To import a single class called `ClassName` from the package, use

```
import packagename.ClassName;
```

Java has a hierarchy of packages and subpackages. Subpackages are selected using multiple dots:

```
import packagename.subpackagename.ClassName;
```

The `import` statement allows the programmer to use the objects and methods defined in the designated package. By convention Java package names are lowercase. The AP exam does not require knowledge of packages. You will not be expected to write any `import` statements.

A Java program must have at least one class, the one that contains the *main method*. The java files that comprise your program are called *source files*.

A *compiler* converts source code into machine-readable form called *bytecode*.

Here is a typical source file for a Java program.

```
/* Program FirstProg.java
   Start with a comment, giving the program name and a brief
   description of what the program does. */

import package1.*;
import package2.subpackage.ClassName;

public class FirstProg  //note that the file name is FirstProg.java
{
    public static type1 method1(parameter list)
    {
        < code for method 1 >
    }
    public static type2 method2(parameter list)
    {
        < code for method 2 >
    }
    ...

    public static void main(String[] args)
    {
        < your code >
    }
}
```

NOTE

1. All Java methods must be contained in a class, and all program statements must be placed inside a method.

2. Typically, the class that contains the `main` method does not contain many additional methods.

3. The words `class`, `public`, `static`, `void`, and `main` are *reserved words*, also called *keywords*.

4. The keyword `public` signals that the class or method is usable outside of the class, whereas `private` data members or methods (see Chapter 2) are not.

5. The keyword `static` is used for methods that will not access any objects of a class, such as the methods in the `FirstProg` class in the example on the previous page. This is typically true for all methods in a source file that contains no *instance variables* (see Chapter 2). Most methods in Java do operate on objects and are not static. The `main` method, however, must always be static.

6. The program shown on the previous page is a Java *application*. This is not to be confused with a Java *applet*, a program that runs inside a web browser or applet viewer. Applets are not part of the AP subset.

TYPES AND IDENTIFIERS

Identifiers

An *identifier* is a name for a variable, parameter, constant, user-defined method, or user-defined class. In Java an identifier is any sequence of letters, digits, and the underscore character. Identifiers may not begin with a digit. Identifiers are case-sensitive, which means that `age` and `Age` are different. Wherever possible identifiers should be concise and self-documenting. A variable called `area` is more illuminating than one called `a`.

By convention identifiers for variables and methods are lowercase. Uppercase letters are used to separate these into multiple words, for example `getName`, `findSurfaceArea`, `preTaxTotal`, and so on. Note that a class name starts with a capital letter. Reserved words are entirely lowercase and may not be used as identifiers.

Built-in Types

Every identifier in a Java program has a type associated with it. The *primitive* or *built-in* types that are included in the AP Java subset are

`int`	An integer. For example, 2, -26, 3000
`boolean`	A boolean. Just two values, `true` or `false`
`double`	A double precision floating-point number. For example, 2.718, -367189.41, 1.6e4

(Note that primitive type `char` is not included in the AP Java subset.)

Integer values are stored exactly. Because there's a fixed amount of memory set aside for their storage, however, integers are bounded. If you try to store a value whose magnitude is too big in an `int` variable, you'll get an *overflow error*. (Java gives you no warning. You just get a wrong result!)

An identifier, for example a *variable*, is introduced into a Java program with a *declaration* that specifies its type. A variable is often initialized in its declaration. Some examples follow:

```
int x;
double y,z;
boolean found;
int count = 1;            //count initialized to 1
double p = 2.3, q = 4.1;    //p and q initialized to 2.3 and 4.1
```

One type can be cast to another compatible type if appropriate. For example,

```
int total, n;
double average;
    ...
average = (double) total/n;    //total cast to double to ensure
                               //real division is used
```

Alternatively,

```
average = total/(double) n;
```

Assigning an int to a double automatically casts the int to double. For example,

```
int num = 5;
double realNum = num;    //num is cast to double
```

Assigning a double to an int without a cast, however, causes a compile-time error. For example,

```
double x = 6.79;
int intNum = x;      //Error. Need an explicit cast to int
```

Note that casting a floating-point (real) number to an integer simply truncates the number. For example,

```
double cost = 10.95;
int numDollars = (int) cost;     //sets numDollars to 10
```

If your intent was to round cost to the nearest dollar, you needed to write

```
int numDollars = (int) (cost + 0.5);  //numDollars has value 11
```

To round a negative number to the nearest integer:

```
double negAmount = -4.8;
int roundNeg = (int) (negAmount - 0.5);   //roundNeg has value -5
```

The strategy of adding or subtracting 0.5 before casting correctly rounds in all cases.

Storage of Numbers

INTEGERS

Integer values in Java are stored exactly, as a string of bits (binary digits). One of the bits stores the sign of the integer, 0 for positive, 1 for negative.

The Java built-in integral type, byte, uses one byte (eight bits) of storage.

The picture represents the largest positive integer that can be stored using type byte: $2^7 - 1$.

Type int in Java uses four bytes (32 bits). Taking one bit for a sign, the largest possible integer stored is $2^{31} - 1$. In general, an *n*-bit integer uses $n/8$ bytes of storage, and stores integers from -2^{n-1} to $2^{n-1} - 1$. (Note that the extra value on the negative side comes from not having to store −0.) There are two Java constants that you should know. Integer.MAX_VALUE holds the maximum value an int can hold, $2^{31} - 1$. Integer.MIN_VALUE holds the minimum value an int can hold, -2^{31}.

Built-in types in Java are byte (one byte), short (two bytes), int (four bytes), and long (eight bytes). Of these, only int is in the AP Java subset.

FLOATING-POINT NUMBERS

There are two built-in types in Java that store real numbers: float, which uses four bytes, and double, which uses eight bytes. A *floating-point number* is stored in two parts: a *mantissa*, which specifies the digits of the number, and an exponent. The JVM (Java Virtual Machine) represents the number using scientific notation:

$$\text{sign} * \text{mantissa} * 2^{\text{exponent}}$$

In this expression, 2 is the *base* or *radix* of the number. In type double eleven bits are allocated for the exponent, and (typically) 52 bits for the mantissa. One bit is allocated for the sign. This is a *double-precision* number. Type float, which is *single-precision*, is not in the AP Java subset.

When floating-point numbers are converted to binary, most cannot be represented exactly, leading to *round-off error*. These errors are compounded by arithmetic operations. For example,

$$0.1*26 \neq 0.1+0.1+\cdots+0.1 \quad (26 \text{ terms})$$

In Java, no exceptions are thrown for floating-point operations. There are two situations you should be aware of:

- When an operation is performed that gives an undefined result, Java expresses this result as NaN, "not a number." Examples of operations that produce NaN are: taking the square root of a negative number, and 0.0 divided by 0.0.

- An operation that gives an infinitely large or infinitely small number, like division by zero, produces a result of Infinity or -Infinity in Java.

Hexadecimal and Octal Numbers

A *hexadecimal number* or *hex number* uses base (radix) 16, and is represented with the symbols 0 – 9 and A – F (occasionally a – f), where A represents 10, and F represents 15. To denote a hex number in Java, the prefix "0x" or "0X" is used, for example, 0xC2A. On the AP exam, the representation is likely to be with the subscript hex: $C2A_{hex}$. In expanded form, this number means

$$(C)(16^2) + (2)(16^1) + (A)(16^0)$$
$$= (12)(16^2) + (2)(16) + (10)(1)$$
$$= 3114, \text{ or } 3114_{dec}$$

The advantages of hex numbers are their compactness, and the ease of conversion between hex and binary. Notice that any hex digit expands to four bits. For example,

$$5_{hex} = 0101_{bin} \quad \text{and} \quad F_{hex} = 1111_{bin}$$

Thus, $5F_{hex} = 01011111_{bin}$, which is 1011111_{bin}.

Similarly, to convert a binary number to hex, convert in groups of four from right to left. If necessary, pad with zeroes to complete the last group of four. For example,

$$
\begin{aligned}
1011101_{bin} &= 0101 \quad 1101_{bin} \\
&= 5 \quad\quad D_{hex} \\
&= 5D_{hex}
\end{aligned}
$$

An *octal number* uses base 8, and is represented with the symbols 0 – 7. On the AP exam, the representation is likely to be with the subscript oct: 132_{oct}. In expanded form, 132_{oct} means

$$
\begin{aligned}
&(1)(8^2) + (3)(8^1) + (2)(8^0) \\
&= (1)(64) + (3)(8) + (2)(1) \\
&= 64 + 24 + 2 \\
&= 90, \text{ or } 90_{dec}
\end{aligned}
$$

Final Variables

A *final variable* or *user-defined constant*, identified by the keyword `final`, is used to name a quantity whose value will not change. Here are some examples of `final` declarations:

```
final double TAX_RATE = 0.08;
final int CLASS_SIZE = 35;
```

NOTE

1. Constant identifiers are, by convention, capitalized.
2. A `final` variable can be declared without initializing it immediately. For example,

    ```
    final double TAX_RATE;
    if (< some condition >)
        TAX_RATE = 0.08;
    else
        TAX_RATE = 0.0;
    // TAX_RATE can be given a value just once: its value is final!
    ```

3. A common use for a constant is as an array bound. For example,

    ```
    final int MAXSTUDENTS = 25;
    int[] classList = new int[MAXSTUDENTS];
    ```

4. Using constants makes it easier to revise code. Just a single change in the `final` declaration need be made, rather than having to change every occurrence of a value.

OPERATORS

Arithmetic Operators

Operator	Meaning	Example
+	addition	`3 + x`
−	subtraction	`p - q`
*	multiplication	`6 * i`
/	division	`10 / 4` `//returns 2, not 2.5!`
%	mod (remainder)	`11 % 8` `//returns 3`

NOTE

1. These operators can be applied to types `int` and `double`, even if both types occur in the same expression. For an operation involving a `double` and an `int`, the `int` is promoted to `double`, and the result is a `double`.

2. The mod operator `%`, as in the expression `a % b`, gives the remainder when `a` is divided by `b`. Thus `10 % 3` evaluates to `1`, whereas `4.2 % 2.0` evaluates to `0.2`.

3. Integer division `a/b` where both `a` and `b` are of type `int` returns the integer quotient only (i.e., the answer is truncated). Thus, `22/6` gives `3`, and `3/4` gives `0`. If at least one of the operands is of type `double`, then the operation becomes regular floating-point division, and there is no truncation. You can control the kind of division that is carried out by explicitly casting (one or both of) the operands from `int` to `double` and vice versa. Thus

   ```
   3.0 / 4            →   0.75
   3 / 4.0            →   0.75
   (int) 3.0 / 4      →   0
   (double) 3 / 4     →   0.75
   ```

   You must, however, be careful:

   ```
   (double) (3 / 4)   →   0.0
   ```

   since the integer division `3/4` is computed first, before casting to `double`.

4. The arithmetic operators follow the normal precedence rules (order of operations):

   (1)   parentheses, from the inner ones out (highest precedence)
   (2)   *, /, %
   (3)   +, − (lowest precedence)

   Here operators on the same line have the same precedence, and, in the absence of parentheses, are invoked from left to right. Thus the expression `19 % 5 * 3 + 14 / 5` evaluates to `4 * 3 + 2 = 14`. Note that casting has precedence over all of these operators. Thus, in the expression `(double) 3/4`, `3` will be cast to `double` before the division is done.

Relational Operators

Operator	Meaning	Example
==	equal to	if (x == 100)
!=	not equal to	if (age != 21)
>	greater than	if (salary > 30000)
<	less than	if (grade < 65)
>=	greater than or equal to	if (age >= 16)
<=	less than or equal to	if (height <= 6)

NOTE

1. Relational operators are used in *boolean expressions* that evaluate to `true` or `false`.

```
boolean x = (a != b);      //initializes x to true if a != b,
                           // false otherwise
return p == q;    //returns true if p equals q, false otherwise
```

2. If the operands are an int and a `double`, the int is promoted to a `double` as for arithmetic operators.
3. Relational operators should generally be used only in the comparison of primitive types (i.e., int, `double`, or `boolean`). User-defined types are compared using the `equals` and `compareTo` methods (see pp. 141 and 173).
4. Be careful when comparing floating-point values! Since floating-point numbers cannot always be represented exactly in the computer memory, they should not be compared directly using relational operators.

> Do not routinely use == to test for equality of floating-point numbers.

Comparing Floating-Point Numbers

Because of round-off errors in floating-point numbers, you can't rely on using the == or != operators to compare two `double` values for equality. They may differ in their last significant digit or two because of round-off error. Instead, you should test that the magnitude of the difference between the numbers is less than some number about the size of the machine precision. The machine precision is usually denoted ϵ and is typically about 10^{-16} for double precision (i.e., about 16 decimal digits). So you would like to test something like $|x - y| \leq \epsilon$. But this is no good if x and y are very large. For example, suppose $x = 1234567890.123456$ and $y = 1234567890.123457$. These numbers are essentially equal to machine precision, since they differ only in the 16th significant digit. But $|x - y| = 10^{-6}$, not 10^{-16}. So in general you should check the *relative* difference:

$$\frac{|x - y|}{\max(|x|, |y|)} \leq \epsilon$$

To avoid problems with dividing by zero, code this as

$$|x - y| \leq \epsilon \max(|x|, |y|)$$

An example of code that uses a correct comparison of real numbers can be found in the Shape class on p. 142.

Logical Operators

Operator	Meaning	Example
!	NOT	if (!found)
&&	AND	if (x < 3 && y > 4)
||	OR	if (age < 2 || height < 4)

NOTE

1. Logical operators are applied to boolean expressions to form *compound boolean expressions* that evaluate to true or false.
2. Values of true or false are assigned according to the truth tables for the logical operators.

&&	T	F		||	T	F		!	
T	T	F		T	T	T		T	F
F	F	F		F	T	F		F	T

For example, F && T evaluates to F, while T \|\| F evaluates to T.

3. *Short-circuit evaluation.* The subexpressions in a compound boolean expression are evaluated from left to right, and evaluation automatically stops as soon as the value of the entire expression is known. For example, consider a boolean OR expression of the form A \|\| B, where A and B are some boolean expressions. If A is true, then the expression is true irrespective of the value of B. Similarly, if A is false, then A && B evaluates to false irrespective of the second operand. So in each case the second operand is not evaluated. For example,

```
if (numScores != 0 && scoreTotal/numScores > 90)
```

will not cause a run-time ArithmeticException (division-by-zero error) if the value of numScores is 0. This is because numScores != 0 will evaluate to false, causing the entire boolean expression to evaluate to false without having to evaluate the second expression containing the division.

Assignment Operators

Operator	Example	Meaning
=	x = 2	simple assignment
+=	x += 4	x = x + 4
-=	y -= 6	y = y - 6
*=	p *= 5	p = p * 5
/=	n /= 10	n = n / 10
%=	n %= 10	n = n % 10

NOTE

1. All these operators, with the exception of simple assignment, are called *compound assignment operators.*
2. *Chaining* of assignment statements is allowed, with evaluation from right to left.

```
int next, prev, sum;
next = prev = sum = 0;  //initializes sum to 0, then prev to 0
                        //then next to 0
```

Increment and Decrement Operators

Operator	Example	Meaning
++	i++ or ++i	i is incremented by 1
--	k-- or --k	k is decremented by 1

Note that i++ (postfix) and ++i (prefix) both have the net effect of incrementing i by 1, but they are not equivalent. For example, if i currently has the value 5, then System.out.println(i++) will print 5 and then increment i to 6, whereas System.out.println(++i) will first increment i to 6 and then print 6. It's easy to remember: if the ++ is first, you first increment. A similar distinction occurs between k-- and --k. (Note: You do not need to know these distinctions for the AP exam.)

Operator Precedence

highest precedence → (1) !, ++, --
(2) *, /, %
(3) +, -
(4) <, >, <=, >=
(5) ==, !=
(6) &&
(7) ||
lowest precedence → (8) =, +=, -=, *=, /=, %=

Here operators on the same line have equal precedence. The evaluation of the operators with equal precedence is from left to right, except for rows (1) and (8) where the order is right to left. It is easy to remember: The only "backward" order is for the unary operators (row 1) and for the various assignment operators (row 8).

Example

What will be output by the following statement?

```
System.out.println(5 + 3 < 6 - 1);
```

Since + and - have precedence over <, 5 + 3 and 6 - 1 will be evaluated before evaluating the boolean expression. Since the value of the expression is false, the statement will output false.

INPUT/OUTPUT

Input

Since there are so many ways to provide input to a program, user input is not a part of the AP Java subset. If reading input is a necessary part of a question on the AP exam, it will be indicated something like this:

```
double x = call to a method that reads a floating-point number
```

or

```
double x = IO.readDouble();    //read user input
```

NOTE

The Scanner class, new in Java 5.0, simplifies both console and file input. It will not, however, be tested on the AP exam.

Output

Testing of output will be restricted to System.out.print and System.out.println. Formatted output will not be tested.

System.out is an object in the System class that allows output to be displayed on the screen. The println method outputs an item and then goes to a new line. The print method outputs an item without going to a new line afterward. An item to be printed can be a string, or a number, or the value of a boolean expression (true or false). Here are some examples:

```
System.out.print("Hot");          }  prints  Hotdog
System.out.println("dog");         }

System.out.println("Hot");}  prints   Hot
System.out.println("dog");}           dog

System.out.println(7 + 3);     }  prints  10

System.out.println(7 == 2 + 5); }  prints  true

int x = 27;
System.out.println(x);      }  prints  27
System.out.println("Value of x is " + x);
                           prints   Value of x is 27
```

In the last example, the value of x, 27, is converted to the string "27", which is then concatenated to the string "Value of x is ".

To print the "values" of user-defined objects, the toString() method is invoked (see p. 172).

Escape Sequences

An *escape sequence* is a backslash followed by a single character. It is used to print special characters. The three escape sequences that you should know for the AP exam are

Escape Sequence	Meaning
\n	newline
\"	double quote
\\	backslash

Here are some examples:

```
System.out.println("Welcome to\na new line");
```

prints

```
Welcome to
a new line
```

The statement

```
System.out.println("He is known as \"Hothead Harry\".");
```

prints

```
He is known as "Hothead Harry".
```

The statement

```
System.out.println("The file path is d:\\myFiles\\..");
```

prints

```
The file path is d:\myFiles\..
```

CONTROL STRUCTURES

Control structures are the mechanism by which you make the statements of a program run in a nonsequential order. There are two general types: decision making and iteration.

Decision-Making Control Structures

These include the `if`, `if...else`, and `switch` statements. They are all selection control structures that introduce a decision-making ability into a program. Based on the truth value of a boolean expression, the computer will decide which path to follow. The `switch` statement is not part of the AP Java subset.

THE `if` STATEMENT

```
if (boolean expression)
{
    statements
}
```

Here the *statements* will be executed only if the *boolean expression* is `true`. If it is `false`, control passes immediately to the first statement following the `if` statement.

THE `if...else` STATEMENT

```
if (boolean expression)
{
    statements
}
else
{
    statements
}
```

Here if the *boolean expression* is `true`, only the *statements* immediately following the test will be executed. If the *boolean expression* is `false`, only the *statements* following the `else` will be executed.

NESTED `if` STATEMENT

If the statement part of an `if` statement is itself an `if` statement, the result is a *nested if statement.*

Example 1

```
if (boolean expr1)
    if (boolean expr2)
        statement;
```

This is equivalent to

```
if (boolean expr1 && boolean expr2)
    statement;
```

Example 2

Beware the dangling `else`! Suppose you want to read in an integer and print it if it's positive and even. Will the following code do the job?

```
int n = IO.readInt();          //read user input
if (n > 0)
    if (n % 2 == 0)
        System.out.println(n);
else
    System.out.println(n + " is not positive");
```

A user enters 7 and is surprised to see the output

```
7 is not positive
```

The reason is that `else` always gets matched with the *nearest* unpaired `if`, not the first `if` as the indenting would suggest.

There are two ways to fix the preceding code. The first is to use {} delimiters to group the statements correctly.

```
int n = IO.readInt();          //read user input
if (n > 0)
{
    if (n % 2 == 0)
        System.out.println(n);
}
else
    System.out.println(n + " is not positive");
```

The second way of fixing the code is to rearrange the statements.

```
int n = IO.readInt();          //read user input
if (n <= 0)
    System.out.println(n + " is not positive");
else
    if (n % 2 == 0)
        System.out.println(n);
```

EXTENDED if STATEMENT

For example,

```
String grade = IO.readString();          //read user input
if (grade.equals("A"))
    System.out.println("Excellent!");
else if (grade.equals("B"))
    System.out.println("Good");
else if (grade.equals("C") || grade.equals("D"))
    System.out.println("Poor");
else if (grade.equals("F"))
    System.out.println("Egregious!");
else
    System.out.println("Invalid grade");
```

If any of A, B, C, D, or F are entered, an appropriate message will be written, and control will go to the statement immediately following the extended if statement. If any other string is entered, the final else is invoked, and the message Invalid grade will be written.

Iteration

Java has three different control structures that allow the computer to perform iterative tasks: the for loop, while loop, and do...while loop. The do...while loop is not in the AP Java subset.

THE for LOOP

The general form of the for loop is

```
for (initialization; termination condition; update statement)
{
    statements          //body of loop
}
```

The termination condition is tested at the top of the loop; the update statement is performed at the bottom.

Example 1

```
//outputs 1 2 3 4
for (i = 1; i < 5; i++)
    System.out.print(i + " ");
```

Here's how it works. The *loop variable* i is initialized to 1, and the termination condition i < 5 is evaluated. If it is true, the body of the loop is executed and then the loop variable i is incremented according to the update statement. As soon as the termination condition is false (i.e., i >= 5), control passes to the first statement following the loop.

Example 2

```
//outputs 20 19 18 17 16 15
for (k = 20; k >= 15; k--)
    System.out.print(k + " ");
```

Example 3

```
//outputs 2 4 6 8 10
for (j = 2; j <= 10; j += 2)
    System.out.print(j + " ");
```

NOTE

1. The loop variable should not have its value changed inside the loop body.
2. The initializing and update statements can use any valid constants, variables, or expressions.
3. The scope (see p. 97) of the loop variable can be restricted to the loop body by combining the loop variable declaration with the initialization. For example,

```
for (int i = 0; i < 3; i++)
{
    ...
}
```

4. The following loop is syntactically valid:

```
for (int i = 1; i <= 0; i++)
{
    ...
}
```

The loop body will not be executed at all, since the exiting condition is true before the first execution.

THE FOR-EACH LOOP

This is used to iterate over an array or collection. The general form of the loop is

```
for (SomeType element : collection)
{
    statements
}
```

(Read the top line as "For each element of type SomeType in collection ...")

Example

```
//Outputs all elements of arr, one per line.
for (int element : arr)
    System.out.println(element);
```

NOTE

1. The for-each loop cannot be used for replacing or removing elements as you traverse.
2. The loop hides the index variable that is used with arrays.

THE while LOOP

The general form of the `while` loop is

```
while (boolean test)
{
    statements          //loop body
}
```

The *boolean test* is performed at the beginning of the loop. If true, the loop body is executed. Otherwise, control passes to the first statement following the loop. After execution of the loop body, the test is performed again. If true, the loop is executed again, and so on.

Example 1

```
int i = 1, mult3 = 3;
while (mult3 < 20)
{
    System.out.print(mult3 + " ");
    i++;
    mult3 *= i;
}                       //outputs 3 6 18
```

NOTE

1. It is possible for the body of a `while` loop never to be executed. This will happen if the test evaluates to `false` the first time.
2. Disaster will strike in the form of an infinite loop if the test can never be false. Don't forget to change the loop variable in the body of the loop in a way that leads to termination!

> The body of a `while` loop must contain a statement that leads to termination.

Example 2

```
int power2 = 1;
while (power2 != 20)
{
    System.out.println(power2);
    power2 *= 2;
}
```

Since `power2` will never exactly equal 20, the loop will grind merrily along eventually causing an integer overflow.

Example 3

```
/* Screen out bad data.
 * The loop won't allow execution to continue until a valid
 * integer is entered. */
System.out.println("Enter a positive integer from 1 to 100");
int num = IO.readInt();          //read user input
while (num < 1 || num > 100)
{
    System.out.println("Number must be from 1 to 100.");
    System.out.println("Please reenter");
    num = IO.readInt();
}
```

Example 4

```
/* Uses a sentinel to terminate data entered at the keyboard.
 * The sentinel is a value that cannot be part of the data.
 * It signals the end of the list. */
final int SENTINEL = -999;
System.out.println("Enter list of positive integers," +
    " end list with " + SENTINEL);
int value = IO.readInt();          //read user input
while (value != SENTINEL)
{
    process the value
    value = IO.readInt();          //read another value
}
```

NESTED LOOPS

You create a *nested loop* when a loop is a statement in the body of another loop.

Example 1

```
for (int k = 1; k <= 3; k++)
{
    for (int i = 1; i <= 4; i++)
        System.out.print("*");
    System.out.println();
}
```

Think:

```
for each of 3 rows
{
    print 4 stars
    go to next line
}
```

Output:

```
****
****
****
```

Example 2

This example has two loops nested in an outer loop.

```
for (int i = 1; i <= 6; i++)
{
    for (int j = 1; j <= i; j++)
        System.out.print("+");
    for (int j = 1; j <= 6 - i; j++)
        System.out.print("*");
    System.out.println();
}
```

Output:

```
+*****
++****
+++***
++++**
+++++*
++++++
```

ERRORS AND EXCEPTIONS

An *exception* is an error condition that occurs during the execution of a Java program. For example, if you divide an integer by zero, an `ArithmeticException` will be thrown. If you use a negative array index, an `ArrayIndexOutOfBoundsException` will be thrown.

An *unchecked exception* is one where you don't provide code to deal with the error. Such exceptions are automatically handled by Java's standard exception-handling methods, which terminate execution. You now need to fix your code!

A *checked exception* is one where you provide code to handle the exception, either a try/catch/finally statement, or an explicit `throw new ...Exception` clause. These exceptions are not necessarily caused by an error in the code. For example, an unexpected end-of-file could be due to a broken network connection. Checked exceptions are not part of the AP Java subset.

The following exceptions are in the AP Java subset:

Exception	Discussed on page
ArithmeticException	this page
NullPointerException	99
ClassCastException	137
ArrayIndexOutOfBoundsException	230
IndexOutOfBoundsException	241
IllegalArgumentException	next page, 362

See also `NoSuchElementException` (pp. 244, 245) and `IllegalStateException` (pp. 244, 245), which refer to iterators, an optional topic.

Java allows you to write code that throws a standard unchecked exception. Here are typical examples:

Example 1

```
if (numScores == 0)
    throw new ArithmeticException("Cannot divide by zero");
else
    findAverageScore();
```

Example 2

```
public void setRadius(int newRadius)
{
    if (newRadius < 0)
        throw new IllegalArgumentException
                ("Radius cannot be negative");
    else
        radius = newRadius;
}
```

NOTE

1. `throw` and `new` are both reserved words.
2. The error message is optional: The line in Example 1 could have read

   ```
   throw new ArithmeticException();
   ```

   The message, however, is useful, since it tells the person running the program what went wrong.
3. An `IllegalArgumentException` is thrown to indicate that a parameter does not satisfy a method's precondition.

Chapter Summary

Be sure that you understand the difference between primitive and user-defined types, and between the following types of operators: arithmetic, relational, logical, and assignment. Know which conditions lead to what types of errors.

You should be able to work with numbers—know how to compare them, and how to convert between decimal, binary, and hexadecimal numbers. Know how integers and floating-point numbers are stored in memory, and be aware of the conditions that can lead to round-off error.

You should know the `Integer` constants `Integer.MIN_VALUE` and `Integer.MAX_VALUE`.

Be familiar with each of the following control structures: conditional statements, `for` loops, `while` loops, and for-each loops.

Be aware of the AP exam expectations concerning input and output.

MULTIPLE-CHOICE QUESTIONS ON INTRODUCTORY JAVA LANGUAGE CONCEPTS

1. Which of the following pairs of declarations will cause an error message?

   I   `double x = 14.7;`
       `int y = x;`

   II   `double x = 14.7;`
       `int y = (int) x;`

   III   `int x = 14;`
       `double y = x;`

   (A) None
   (B) I only
   (C) II only
   (D) III only
   (E) I and III only

2. What output will be produced by

   ```
   System.out.print("\\* This is not\n a comment *\\");
   ```

   (A) `* This is not a comment *`

   (B) `\* This is not a comment *\`

   (C) `* This is not`
       `a comment *`

   (D) `\\* This is not`
       `a comment *\\`

   (E) `\* This is not`
       `a comment *\`

3. Refer to the following code fragment:

```
double answer = 13 / 5;
System.out.println("13 / 5 = " + answer);
```

The output is

```
13 / 5 = 2.0
```

The programmer intends the output to be

```
13 / 5 = 2.6
```

Which of the following replacements for the first line of code will *not* fix the problem?
(A) `double answer = (double) 13 / 5;`
(B) `double answer = 13 / (double) 5;`
(C) `double answer = 13.0 / 5;`
(D) `double answer = 13 / 5.0;`
(E) `double answer = (double) (13 / 5);`

4. What value is stored in `result` if

```
int result = 13 - 3 * 6 / 4 % 3;
```

(A) −5
(B) 0
(C) 13
(D) −1
(E) 12

5. Suppose that addition and subtraction had higher precedence than multiplication and division. Then the expression

```
2 + 3 * 12 / 7 - 4 + 8
```

would evaluate to which of the following?
(A) 11
(B) 12
(C) 5
(D) 9
(E) −4

6. Let `x` be a variable of type `double` that is positive. A program contains the boolean expression `(Math.pow(x,0.5) == Math.sqrt(x))`. Even though $x^{1/2}$ is mathematically equivalent to $\sqrt{x}$, the above expression returns the value `false` in a student's program. Which of the following is the most likely reason?
(A) `Math.pow` returns an `int`, while `Math.sqrt` returns a `double`.
(B) `x` was imprecisely calculated in a previous program statement.
(C) The computer stores floating-point numbers with 32-bit words.
(D) There is round-off error in calculating the `pow` and `sqrt` functions.
(E) There is overflow error in calculating the `pow` function.

7. Consider the following code segment

   ```
   if (n != 0 && x / n > 100)
       statement1;
   else
       statement2;
   ```

   If n is of type int and has a value of 0 when the segment is executed, what will happen?
   (A) An ArithmeticException will be thrown.
   (B) A syntax error will occur.
   (C) *statement1*, but not *statement2*, will be executed.
   (D) *statement2*, but not *statement1*, will be executed.
   (E) Neither *statement1* nor *statement2* will be executed; control will pass to the first statement following the if statement.

8. What will the output be for the following poorly formatted program segment, if the input value for num is 22?

   ```
   int num =  call to a method that reads an integer;
   if (num > 0)
   if (num % 5 == 0)
   System.out.println(num);
   else System.out.println(num + " is negative");
   ```

   (A) 22
   (B) 4
   (C) 2 is negative
   (D) 22 is negative
   (E) Nothing will be output.

9. What values are stored in x and y after execution of the following program segment?

   ```
   int x = 30, y = 40;
   if (x >= 0)
   {
       if (x <= 100)
       {
           y = x * 3;
           if (y < 50)
               x /= 10;
       }
       else
           y = x * 2;
   }
   else
       y = -x;
   ```

   (A) x = 30 y = 90
   (B) x = 30 y = -30
   (C) x = 30 y = 60
   (D) x = 3   y = -3
   (E) x = 30 y = 40

10. Which of the following will evaluate to true only if boolean expressions A, B, and C are all false?
    - (A) `!A && !(B && !C)`
    - (B) `!A || !B || !C`
    - (C) `!(A || B || C)`
    - (D) `!(A && B && C)`
    - (E) `!A || !(B || !C)`

11. Assume that a and b are integers. The boolean expression

    `!(a <= b) && (a * b > 0)`

    a> b →   b > 0

    will always evaluate to true given that
    - (A) `a = b`
    - (B) `a > b`
    - (C) `a < b`
    - (D) `a > b` and `b > 0`
    - (E) `a > b` and `b < 0`

12. Given that a, b, and c are integers, consider the boolean expression

    `(a < b) || !((c == a * b) && (c < a))`

    Which of the following will *guarantee* that the expression is true?
    - (A) `c < a` is false.
    - (B) `c < a` is true.
    - (C) `a < b` is false.
    - (D) `c == a * b` is true.
    - (E) `c == a * b` is true, and `c < a` is true.

13. In the following code segment, you may assume that a, b, and n are all type int.

    ```
    if (a != b && n / (a - b) > 90)
    {
        /* statement 1 */
    }
    else
    {
        /* statement 2 */
    }
    /* statement 3 */
    ```

    What will happen if a == b is false?
    - (A) */* statement 1 */* will be executed.
    - (B) */* statement 2 */* will be executed.
    - (C) Either */* statement 1 */* or */* statement 2 */* will be executed.
    - (D) A compile-time error will occur.
    - (E) An exception will be thrown.

14. Given that n and count are both of type int, which statement is true about the following code segments?

```
I for (count = 1; count <= n; count++)
      System.out.println(count);

II count = 1;
   while (count <= n)
   {
       System.out.println(count);
       count++;
   }
```

(A) I and II are exactly equivalent for all input values n.
(B) I and II are exactly equivalent for all input values $n \geq 1$, but differ when $n \leq 0$.
(C) I and II are exactly equivalent only when $n = 0$.
(D) I and II are exactly equivalent only when n is even.
(E) I and II are not equivalent for any input values of n.

15. The following fragment intends that a user will enter a list of positive integers at the keyboard and terminate the list with a sentinel:

```
int value = 0;
final int SENTINEL = -999;
while (value != SENTINEL)
{
    //code to process value
       ...
    value = IO.readInt();        //read user input
}
```

The fragment is not correct. Which is a true statement?
(A) The sentinel gets processed.
(B) The last nonsentinel value entered in the list fails to get processed.
(C) A poor choice of SENTINEL value causes the loop to terminate before all values have been processed.
(D) The code will always process a value that is not on the list.
(E) Entering the SENTINEL value as the first value causes a run-time error.

16. Suppose that base-2 (binary) numbers and base-16 (hexadecimal) numbers can be denoted with subscripts, as shown below:

$$2A_{hex} = 101010_{bin}$$

Which is equal to $3D_{hex}$?
(A) 111101_{bin}
(B) 101111_{bin}
(C) 10011_{bin}
(D) 110100_{bin}
(E) 101101_{bin}

17. A common use of hexadecimal numerals is to specify colors on web pages. Every color has a red, green, and blue component. In decimal notation, these are denoted with an ordered triple (x, y, z), where x, y, and z are the three components, each an int from 0 to 255. For example, a certain shade of red, whose red, green, and blue components are 238, 9, and 63, is represented as $(238, 9, 63)$.

In hexadecimal, a color is represented in the format #RRGGBB, where RR, GG, and BB are hex values for the red, green, and blue. Using this notation, the color $(238, 9, 63)$ would be coded as #EE093F.

Which of the following hex codes represents the color $(14, 20, 255)$?

(A) #1418FE
(B) #0E20FE
(C) #0E14FF
(D) #0FE5FE
(E) #0D14FF

18. In Java, a variable of type int is represented internally as a 32-bit signed integer. Suppose that one bit stores the sign, and the other 31 bits store the magnitude of the number in base 2. In this scheme, what is the largest value that can be stored as type int?

(A) 2^{32}
(B) $2^{32} - 1$
(C) 2^{31}
(D) $2^{31} - 1$
(E) 2^{30}

19. Consider this code segment:

```
int x = 10, y = 0;
while (x > 5)
{
    y = 3;
    while (y < x)
    {
        y *= 2;
        if (y % x == 1)
            y += x;
    }
    x -= 3;
}
System.out.println(x + " " + y);
```

What will be output after execution of this code segment?

(A) 1   6
(B) 7   12
(C) -3   12
(D) 4   12
(E) -3   6

Questions 20 and 21 refer to the following method, checkNumber, which checks the validity of its four-digit integer parameter.

```
//Precondition:  n is a 4-digit integer.
//Postcondition: Returns true if n is valid, false otherwise.
boolean checkNumber(int n)
{
    int d1,d2,d3,checkDigit,nRemaining,rem;
    //strip off digits
    checkDigit = n % 10;
    nRemaining = n / 10;
    d3 = nRemaining % 10;
    nRemaining /= 10;
    d2 = nRemaining % 10;
    nRemaining /= 10;
    d1 = nRemaining % 10;
    //check validity
    rem = (d1 + d2 + d3) % 7;
    return rem == checkDigit;
}
```

A program invokes method checkNumber with the statement

```
boolean valid = checkNumber(num);
```

20. Which of the following values of num will result in valid having a value of true?
    (A) 6143
    (B) 6144
    (C) 6145
    (D) 6146
    (E) 6147

21. What is the purpose of the local variable nRemaining?
    (A) It is not possible to separate n into digits without the help of a temporary variable.
    (B) nRemaining prevents the parameter num from being altered.
    (C) nRemaining enhances the readability of the algorithm.
    (D) On exiting the method, the value of nRemaining may be reused.
    (E) nRemaining is needed as the left-hand side operand for integer division.

22. What output will be produced by this code segment? (Ignore spacing.)

```
for (int i = 5; i >= 1; i--)
{
    for (int j = i; j >= 1; j--)
        System.out.print(2 * j - 1);
    System.out.println();
}
```

(A) 9 7 5 3 1
    9 7 5 3
    9 7 5
    9 7
    9

(B) 9 7 5 3 1
    7 5 3 1
    5 3 1
    3 1
    1

(C) 9 7 5 3 1
    7 5 3 1 -1
    5 3 1 -1 -3
    3 1 -1 -3 -5
    1 -1 -3 -5 -7

(D) 1
    1 3
    1 3 5
    1 3 5 7
    1 3 5 7 9

(E) 1 3 5 7 9
    1 3 5 7
    1 3 5
    1 3
    1

23. Which of the following program fragments will produce this output? (Ignore spacing.)

```
2 - - - - -
- 4 - - - -
- - 6 - - -
- - - 8 - -
- - - - 10 -
- - - - - 12
```

```
I  for (int i = 1; i <= 6; i++)
   {
       for (int k = 1; k <= 6; k++)
           if (k == i)
               System.out.print(2 * k);
           else
               System.out.print("-");
       System.out.println();
   }
```

```
II  for (int i = 1; i <= 6; i++)
    {
        for (int k = 1; k <= i - 1; k++)
            System.out.print("-");
        System.out.print(2 * i);
        for (int k = 1; k <= 6 - i; k++)
            System.out.print("-");
        System.out.println();
    }
```

```
III  for (int i = 1; i <= 6; i++)
     {
         for (int k = 1; k <= i - 1; k++)
             System.out.print("-");
         System.out.print(2 * i);
         for (int k = i + 1; k <= 6; k++)
             System.out.print("-");
         System.out.println();
     }
```

(A) I only
(B) II only
(C) III only
(D) I and II only
(E) I, II, and III

24. Consider this program segment:

```
int newNum = 0, temp;
int num = k;                //k is some predefined integer value ≥ 0
while (num > 10)
{
    temp = num % 10;
    num /= 10;
    newNum = newNum * 10 + temp;
}
System.out.print(newNum);
```

Which is a true statement about the segment?

I   If $100 \leq$ num ≤ 1000 initially, the final value of newNum must be in the range $10 \leq$ newNum ≤ 100.
II   There is no initial value of num that will cause an infinite while loop.
III   If num ≤ 10 initially, newNum will have a final value of 0.

(A) I only
(B) II only
(C) III only
(D) II and III only
(E) I, II, and III

25. Consider the method reverse:

```
//Precondition:  n > 0.
//Postcondition: returns n with its digits reversed.
//Example: If n = 234, method reverse returns 432.
int reverse(int n)
{
    int rem, revNum = 0;

    /* code segment */

    return revNum;
}
```

Which of the following replacements for /* *code segment* */ would cause the method to work as intended?

```
 I for (int i = 0; i <= n; i++)
   {
       rem = n % 10;
       revNum = revNum * 10 + rem;
       n /= 10;
   }

II while (n != 0)
   {
       rem = n % 10;
       revNum = revNum * 10 + rem;
       n /= 10;
   }

III for (int i = n; i != 0; i /= 10)
    {
        rem = i % 10;
        revNum = revNum * 10 + rem;
    }
```

(A) I only
(B) II only
(C) I and II only
(D) II and III only
(E) I and III only

ANSWER KEY

1. **B**	10. **C**	19. **D**
2. **E**	11. **D**	20. **B**
3. **E**	12. **A**	21. **C**
4. **E**	13. **C**	22. **B**
5. **C**	14. **A**	23. **E**
6. **D**	15. **D**	24. **D**
7. **D**	16. **A**	25. **D**
8. **D**	17. **C**	
9. **A**	18. **D**	

ANSWERS EXPLAINED

1. **(B)** When x is converted to an integer, as in segment I, information is lost. Java requires that an explicit cast to an int be made, as in segment II. Note that segment II will cause x to be truncated: The value stored in y is 14. By requiring the explicit cast, Java doesn't let you do this accidentally. In segment III y will contain the value 14.0. No explicit cast to a double is required since no information is lost.

2. **(E)** The string argument contains two escape sequences: '\\', which means print a backslash (\), and '\n', which means go to a new line. Choice E is the only choice that does both of these.

3. **(E)** For this choice, the integer division 13/5 will be evaluated to 2, which will then be cast to 2.0. The output will be 13/5 = 2.0. The compiler needs a way to recognize that real-valued division is required. All the other options provide a way.

4. **(E)** The operators *, /, and % have equal precedence, all higher than -, and must be performed first, from left to right.

    ```
        13 - 3 * 6 / 4 % 3
      = 13 - 18 / 4 % 3
      = 13 - 4 % 3
      = 13 - 1
      = 12
    ```

5. **(C)** The expression must be evaluated as if parenthesized like this:

    ```
      (2 + 3) * 12 / (7 - 4 + 8)
    ```

    This becomes 5 * 12 / 11 = 60 / 11 = 5.

6. **(D)** Anytime arithmetic operations are done with floating-point numbers, round-off error occurs. The Math class methods (see p. 180) such as pow and sqrt use various approximations to generate their answers to the required accuracy. Since they do different internal arithmetic, however, the round-off will usually not result in exactly the same answers. Note that choice A is not correct because both

Math.pow and Math.sqrt return type double. Choice B is wrong because no matter how x was previously calculated, the same x is input to pow and sqrt. Choice C is wrong since round-off error occurs no matter how many bits are used to represent numbers. Choice E is wrong because if x is representable on the machine (i.e., hasn't overflowed), then its square root, $x^{1/2}$, will not overflow.

7. **(D)** Short-circuit evaluation of the boolean expression will occur. The expression (n != 0) will evaluate to false, which makes the entire boolean expression false. Therefore the expression (x / n > 100) will not be evaluated. Hence no division by zero will occur, causing an ArithmeticException to be thrown. When the boolean expression has a value of false, only the else part of the statement, *statement2*, will be executed.

8. **(D)** Each else gets paired with the nearest unpaired if. Thus when the test (22 % 5 == 0) fails, the else part indicating that 22 is negative will be executed. This is clearly not the intent of the fragment, which can be fixed using delimiters:

```
int num = call to a method that reads an integer;
if (num > 0)
{
    if (num % 5 == 0)
        System.out.println(num);
}
else
    System.out.println(num + " is negative");
```

9. **(A)** Since the first test (x >= 0) is true, the matching else part, y = -x, will not be executed. Since (x <= 100) is true, the matching else part, y = x * 2, will not be executed. The variable y will be set to x * 3 (i.e., 90) and will now fail the test y < 50. Thus x will never be altered in this algorithm. Final values are x = 30 and y = 90.

10. **(C)** In order for !(A || B || C) to be true, (A || B || C) must evaluate to false. This will happen only if A, B, and C are *all* false. Choice A evaluates to true when A and B are false and C is true. In choice B, if any *one* of A, B, or C is false, the boolean expression evaluates to true. In choice D, if any one of A, B, or C is false, the boolean expression evaluates to true since we have !(false). All that's required for choice E to evaluate to true is for A to be false. Since true||(any) evaluates to true, both B and C can be either true or false.

11. **(D)** To evaluate to true, the expression must reduce to true && true. We therefore need !(false) && true. Choice D is the only condition that guarantees this: a > b provides !(false) for the left-hand expression, and a > b and b > 0 implies both a and b positive, which leads to true for the right-hand expression. Choice E, for example, will provide true for the right-hand expression only if a < 0. You have no information about a and can't make assumptions about it.

12. **(A)** If (c < a) is false, ((c == a*b) && (c < a)) evaluates to false irrespective of the value of c == a*b. In this case, !(c == a*b && c < a) evaluates to true. Then (a < b) || true evaluates to true irrespective of the value of the test (a < b). In all the other choices, the given expression *may* be true. There is not enough information given to guarantee this, however.

13. **(C)** If a == b is false, then a != b is true. Thus, the second piece of the compound test must be evaluated before the value of the whole test is known. Since

`a == b` is false, `a - b` is not equal to zero. Thus, there is no division by zero, and no exception will be thrown. Also, since the relative values of a, b, and n are unknown, the value of the test `n / (a - b) > 90` is unknown, and there is insufficient information to determine whether the compound test is true or false. Thus, either /* *statement 1* */ or /* *statement 2* */ will be executed.

14. **(A)** If $n \geq 1$, both segments will print out the integers from 1 through n. If $n \leq 0$, both segments will fail the test immediately and do nothing.

15. **(D)** The (`value != SENTINEL`) test occurs before a value has been read from the list. This will cause 0 to be processed, which may cause an error. The code must be fixed by reading the first value before doing the test:

```
final int SENTINEL = -999;
int value = IO.readInt();
while (value != SENTINEL)
{
    //code to process value
    value = IO.readInt();
}
```

Choices A, B, C, and E are all incorrect because if the program doesn't compile, it won't run! A note, however, about choice C: -999 is a fine choice for the sentinel given that only positive integers are valid input data.

16. **(A)** Quick method: Convert each hex digit to binary.

$$3 \qquad D_{hex}$$
$$= 0011 \qquad 1101 \qquad \text{(where D equals 13 in base 10)}$$
$$= 111101_{bin}$$

Slow method: Convert $3D_{hex}$ to base 10.

$$3D_{hex} = (3)(16^1) + (D)(16^0)$$
$$= 48 + 13$$
$$= 61_{dec}$$

Now convert 61_{dec} to binary. Write 61 as a sum of descending powers of 2:

$$61 = 32 + 16 + 8 + 4 + 1$$
$$= 1(2^5) + 1(2^4) + 1(2^3) + 1(2^2) + 0(2^1) + 1(2^0)$$
$$= 111101_{bin}$$

17. **(C)** Start by converting each of the three numbers to hexadecimal:

$$14 = (0)(16^1) + (14)(16^0) \quad = 0E$$
$$20 = (1)(16^1) + (4)(16^0) \quad = 14$$
$$255 = (15)(16^1) + (15)(16^0) = FF$$

Therefore $(14, 20, 255) = \#0E14FF$.

18. **(D)** Think of the integer as having 31 slots for storage. If there were just one slot, the maximum binary number would be $1 = 2^1 - 1$. If there were just two slots, the maximum binary number would be $11 = 2^2 - 1 = 3$. If there were just eight slots, the maximum binary number would be $11111111 = 2^8 - 1$. So for 31 slots, the maximum value is $2^{31} - 1$.

19. (**D**) Here is a trace of the values of x and y during execution. Note that the condition (y % x == 1) is never true in this example.

x	10				7				4
y		3	6	12		3	6	12	

The while loop terminates when x is 4 since the test while (x > 5) fails.

20. (**B**) The algorithm finds the remainder when the sum of the first three digits of n is divided by 7. If this remainder is equal to the fourth digit, checkDigit, the method returns true, otherwise false. Note that (6+1+4) % 7 equals 4. Thus, only choice B is a valid number.

21. (**C**) As n gets broken down into its digits, nRemaining is the part of n that remains after each digit is stripped off. Thus nRemaining is a self-documenting name that helps describe what is happening. Choice A is false because every digit can be stripped off using some sequence of integer division and mod. Choice B is false because num is passed by value and therefore will not be altered when the method is exited (see p. 100). Eliminate choice D: When the method is exited, all local variables are destroyed. Choice E is nonsense.

22. (**B**) The outer loop produces five rows of output. Each pass through the inner loop goes from i down to 1. Thus five odd numbers starting at 9 are printed in the first row, four odd numbers starting at 7 in the second row, and so on.

23. (**E**) All three algorithms produce the given output. The outer for (int i ...) loop produces six rows, and the inner for (int k ...) loops produce the symbols in each row.

24. (**D**) Statement I is false, since if 100 ≤ num ≤ 109, the body of the while loop will be executed just once. (After this single pass through the loop, the value of num will be 10, and the test if (num > 10) will fail.) With just one pass, newNum will be a one-digit number, equal to temp (which was the original num % 10). Note that statement II is true: There cannot be an infinite loop since num /= 10 guarantees termination of the loop. Statement III is true because if num ≤ 10, the loop will be skipped, and newNum will keep its original value of 0.

25. (**D**) The algorithm works by stripping off the rightmost digit of n (stored in rem), multiplying the current value of revNum by 10, and adding that rightmost digit. When n has been stripped down to no digits (i.e., n == 0 is true), revNum is complete. Both segments II and III work. Segment I fails to produce the right output whenever the input value n has first digit less than (number of digits − 1). For these cases the output has the first digit of the original number missing from the end of the returned number.

Classes and Objects

CHAPTER 2

Work is the curse of the drinking classes.
—Oscar Wilde

Chapter Goals

- Objects and classes
- Encapsulation
- References

- Keywords public, private, and static
- Methods

OBJECTS

Every program that you write involves at least one thing that is being created or manipulated by the program. This thing, together with the operations that manipulate it, is called an *object*.

Consider, for example, a program that must test the validity of a four-digit code number that a person will enter to be able to use a photocopy machine. Rules for validity are provided. The object is a four-digit code number. Some of the operations to manipulate the object could be readNumber, getSeparateDigits, testValidity, and writeNumber.

Any given program can have several different types of objects. For example, a program that maintains a database of all books in a library has at least two objects:

1. A Book object, with operations like getTitle, isOnShelf, isFiction, and goOutOfPrint.
2. A ListOfBooks object, with operations like search, addBook, removeBook, and sortByAuthor.

An object is characterized by its *state* and *behavior*. For example, a book has a state described by its title, author, whether it's on the shelf, and so on. It also has behavior, like going out of print.

Notice that an object is an idea, separate from the concrete details of a programming language. It corresponds to some real-world object that is being represented by the program.

All object-oriented programming languages have a way to represent an object as a variable in a program. In Java, a variable that represents an object is called an *object reference*.

CLASSES

A *class* is a software blueprint for implementing objects of a given type. An object is a single *instance* of the class. In a program there will often be several different instances of a given class type.

The current state of a given object is maintained in its *data fields* or *instance variables*, provided by the class. The *methods* of the class provide both the behaviors exhibited by the object and the operations that manipulate the object. Combining an object's data and methods into a single unit called a class is known as *encapsulation*.

Here is the framework for a simple bank account class:

```
public class BankAccount
{
    private String myPassword;
    private double myBalance;
    public static final double OVERDRAWN_PENALTY = 20.00;

    //constructors
    /* Default constructor.
     * Constructs bank account with default values. */
    public BankAccount()
    { /* implementation code */ }

    /* Constructs bank account with specified password and balance. */
    public BankAccount(String password, double balance)
    { /* implementation code */ }

    //accessor
    /* Returns balance of this account. */
    public double getBalance()
    { /* implementation code */ }

    //mutators
    /* Deposits amount in bank account with given password. */
    public void deposit(String password, double amount)
    { /* implementation code */ }

    /* Withdraws amount from bank account with given password.
     * Assesses penalty if myBalance is less than amount. */
    public void withdraw(String password, double amount)
    { /* implementation code */ }
}
```

PUBLIC, PRIVATE, AND STATIC

The keyword `public` preceding the class declaration signals that the class is usable by all *client programs*. If a class is not public, it can be used only by classes in its own package. In the AP Java subset, all classes are public.

Similarly, *public methods* are accessible to all client programs. Clients, however, are not privy to the class implementation and may not access the private instance variables and private methods of the class. Restriction of access is known as *information hiding*.

In Java, this is implemented by using the keyword `private`. *Private methods and variables in a class can be accessed only by methods of that class.* Even though Java allows public instance variables, in the AP Java subset all instance variables are private.

A *static variable* (class variable) contains a value that is shared by all instances of the class. "Static" means that memory allocation happens once.

Typical uses of a static variable are to

- keep track of statistics for objects of the class

- accumulate a total

- provide a new identity number for each new object of the class.

For example:

```
public class Employee
{
    private String name;
    private static int employeeCount = 0; //number of employees

    public Employee( <parameter list > )
    {
        < initialization of private instance variables >
        employeeCount++; //increment count of all employees
    }
        . . .
}
```

Notice that the static variable was initialized outside the constructor and that its value can be changed.

Static final variables (constants) in a class cannot be changed. They are often declared public (see some examples of `Math` class constants on p. 180). The variable `OVERDRAWN_PENALTY` is an example in the `BankAccount` class. Since the variable is public, it can be used in any client method. The keyword `static` indicates that there is a single value of the variable that applies to the whole class, rather than a new instance for each object of the class. A client method would refer to the variable as `BankAccount.OVERDRAWN_PENALTY`. In its own class it is referred to as simply `OVERDRAWN_PENALTY`.

See p. 95 for static methods.

METHODS

Headers

All method headers, with the exception of constructors (see on the next page) and static methods (p. 95), look like this:

`public`	`void`	`withdraw`	`(String password, double amount)`
access specifier	return type	method name	parameter list

NOTE

1. The *access specifier* tells which other methods can call this method (see Public, Private, and Static on the previous page).

2. A *return type* of void signals that the method does not return a value.

3. Items in the *parameter list* are separated by commas.

The implementation of the method directly follows the header, enclosed in a {} block.

Types of Methods

CONSTRUCTORS

A *constructor* creates an object of the class. You can recognize a constructor by its name—always the same as the class. Also, a constructor has no return type.

Having several constructors provides different ways of initializing class objects. For example, there are two constructors in the BankAccount class.

1. The *default constructor* has no arguments. It provides reasonable initial values for an object. Here is its implementation:

```
/* Default constructor.
 * Constructs a bank account with default values */
public BankAccount()
{
    myPassword = "";
    myBalance = 0.0;
}
```

In a client method, the declaration

```
BankAccount b = new BankAccount();
```

constructs a BankAccount object with a balance of zero and a password equal to the empty string. The new operator returns the address of this newly constructed object. The variable b is assigned the value of this address—we say "b is a *reference* to the object." Picture the setup like this:

2. The constructor with parameters sets the instance variables of a BankAccount object to the values of those parameters.

Here is the implementation:

```
/* Constructor. Constructs a bank account with
 * specified password and balance */
public BankAccount(String password, double balance)
{
    myPassword = password;
    myBalance = balance;
}
```

In a client program a declaration that uses this constructor needs matching parameters:

```
BankAccount c = new BankAccount("KevinC", 800.00);
```

NOTE

b and c are *object variables* that store the *addresses* of their respective BankAccount objects. They do not store the objects themselves (see **References** on p. 98).

ACCESSORS

An *accessor method* accesses a class object without altering the object. An accessor returns some information about the object.

The BankAccount class has a single accessor method, getBalance(). Here is its implementation:

```
/* Returns the  balance of this account */
public double getBalance()
{ return myBalance; }
```

A client program may use this method as follows:

```
BankAccount b1 = new BankAccount("MattW", 500.00);
BankAccount b2 = new BankAccount("DannyB", 650.50);
if (b1.getBalance() > b2.getBalance())
    ...
```

NOTE

The . *operator* (dot operator) indicates that getBalance() is a method of the class to which b1 and b2 belong, namely the BankAccount class.

MUTATORS

A *mutator method* changes the state of an object by modifying at least one of its instance variables.

Here are the implementations of the deposit and withdraw methods, each of which alters the value of myBalance in the BankAccount class:

```
/* Deposits amount in a bank account with the given password. */
public void deposit(String password, double amount)
{
    if (!password.equals(myPassword))
        /* throw an exception */
    else
        myBalance += amount;
}
```

```
/* Withdraws amount from a bank account with the given password.
 * Assesses a penalty if the new balance is negative. */
public void withdraw(String password, double amount)
{
    if (!password.equals(myPassword))
        /* throw an exception */
    else
    {
        myBalance -= amount;        //allows negative balance
        if (myBalance < 0)
            myBalance -= OVERDRAWN_PENALTY;
    }
}
```

A mutator method in a client program is invoked in the same way as an accessor: using an object variable with the dot operator. For example, assuming valid `BankAccount` declarations for `b1` and `b2`:

```
b1.withdraw("MattW", 200.00);
b2.deposit("DannyB", 35.68);
```

STATIC METHODS

Static Methods vs. Instance Methods   The methods discussed in the preceding sections—constructors, accessors, and mutators—all operate on individual objects of a class. They are called *instance methods*. A method that performs an operation for the entire class, not its individual objects, is called a *static method* (sometimes called a *class method*).

The implementation of a static method uses the keyword `static` in its header. There is no implied object in the code (as there is in an instance method). Thus if the code tries to call an instance method or invoke a private instance variable for this nonexistent object, a syntax error will occur. A static method can, however, use a static variable in its code. For example, in the `Employee` example on p. 92, you could add a static method that returns the `employeeCount`:

```
public static int getEmployeeCount()
{ return employeeCount; }
```

Here's an example of a static method that might be used in the `BankAccount` class. Suppose the class has a static variable `intRate`, declared as follows:

```
private static double intRate;
```

The static method `getInterestRate` may be as follows:

```
public static double getInterestRate()
{
    System.out.println("Enter interest rate for bank account");
    System.out.println("Enter in decimal form:");
    intRate = IO.readDouble();          // read user input
    return intRate;
}
```

Since the rate that's read in by this method applies to all bank accounts in the class, not to any particular `BankAccount` object, it's appropriate that the method should be static.

Recall that an instance method is invoked in a client program by using an object variable followed by the dot operator followed by the method name:

```
BankAccount b = new BankAccount();   //invokes the deposit method for
b.deposit(password, amount);          //BankAccount object b
```

A static method, by contrast, is invoked by using the *class name* with the dot operator:

```
double interestRate = BankAccount.getInterestRate();
```

Static Methods in a Driver Class   Often a class that contains the main() method is used as a driver program to test other classes. Usually such a class creates no objects of the class. So all the methods in the class must be static. Note that at the start of program execution, no objects exist yet. So the main() method must *always* be static.

For example, here is a program that tests a class for reading integers entered at the keyboard.

```
import java.util.*;
public class GetListTest
{
    /* Return a list of integers from the keyboard. */
    public static List<Integer> getList()
    {
        List<Integer> a = new ArrayList<Integer>();
        <code to read integers into a>
        return a;
    }

    /* Write contents of List a. */
    public static void writeList(List<Integer> a)
    {
        System.out.println("List is : " + a);
    }

    public static void main(String[] args)
    {
        List<Integer> list = getList();
        writeList(list);
    }
}
```

NOTE

1. The calls to writeList(list) and getList() do not need to be preceded by GetListTest plus a dot because main is not a client program: It is in the same class as getList and writeList.
2. If you omit the keyword static from the getList or writeList header, you get an error message like the following:

   ```
   Can't make static reference to method getList()
   in class GetListTest
   ```

   The compiler has recognized that there was no object variable preceding the method call, which means that the methods were static and should have been declared as such.

Method Overloading

Overloaded methods are two or more methods in the same class that have the same name but different parameter lists. For example,

```
public class DoOperations
{
    public int product(int n) { return n * n; }
    public double product(double x) { return x * x; }
    public double product(int x, int y) { return x * y; }
        ...
```

The compiler figures out which method to call by examining the method's *signature*. The signature of a method consists of the method's name and a list of the parameter types. Thus the signatures of the overloaded product methods are

```
product(int)
product(double)
product(int, int)
```

Note that for overloading purposes, the return type of the method is irrelevant. You can't have two methods with identical signatures but different return types. The compiler will complain that the method call is ambiguous.

Having more than one constructor in the same class is an example of overloading. Overloaded constructors provide a choice of ways to initialize objects of the class.

SCOPE

The *scope* of a variable or method is the region in which that variable or method is visible and can be accessed.

The instance variables, static variables, and methods of a class belong to that class's scope, which extends from the opening brace to the closing brace of the class definition. Within the class all instance variables and methods are accessible and can be referred to simply by name (no dot operator!).

A *local variable* is defined inside a method. It can even be defined inside a statement. Its scope extends from the point where it is declared to the end of the block in which its declaration occurs. A *block* is a piece of code enclosed in a {} pair. When a block is exited, the memory for a local variable is automatically recycled.

Local variables take precedence over instance variables with the same name. (Using the same name, however, creates ambiguity for the programmer, leading to errors. You should avoid the practice.)

The this Keyword

An instance method is always called for a particular object. This object is an *implicit parameter* for the method and is referred to with the keyword this.

In the implementation of instance methods, all instance variables can be written with the prefix this followed by the dot operator.

Example 1

The deposit method of the BankAccount class can refer to myBalance as follows:

```
public void deposit(String password, double amount)
{
    this.myBalance += amount;
}
```

The use of this is unnecessary in the above example.

Example 2

Consider a rational number class called `Rational`, which has two private instance variables:

```
private int num;        //numerator
private int denom;      //denominator
```

Now consider a constructor for the `Rational` class:

```
public Rational(int num, int denom)
{
    this.num = num;
    this.denom = denom;
}
```

It is definitely *not* a good idea to use the same name for the explicit parameters and the private instance variables. But if you do, you can avoid errors by referring to `this.num` and `this.denom` for the current object that is being constructed. (This particular use of `this` will not be tested on the exam.)

REFERENCES

Reference vs. Primitive Data Types

All of the numerical data types, like `double` and `int`, as well as types `char` and `boolean`, are *primitive* data types. All objects are *reference* data types. The difference lies in the way they are stored.

Consider the statements

```
int num1 = 3;
int num2 = num1;
```

The variables `num1` and `num2` can be thought of as memory slots, labeled `num1` and `num2`, respectively:

$$\text{num1} \quad \text{num2}$$
$$\boxed{3} \qquad \boxed{3}$$

If either of the above variables is now changed, the other is not affected. Each has its own memory slot.

Contrast this with the declaration of a reference data type. Recall that an object is created using `new`:

```
Date d = new Date(2, 17, 1948);
```

This declaration creates a reference variable `d` that refers to a `Date` object. The value of `d` is the address in memory of that object:

Suppose the following declaration is now made:

```
Date birthday = d;
```

This statement creates the reference variable `birthday`, which contains the same address as `d`:

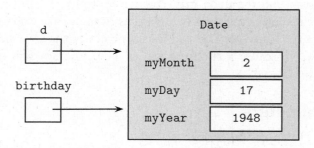

Having two references for the same object is known as *aliasing*. Aliasing can cause unintended problems for the programmer. The statement

```
d.changeDate();
```

will automatically change the object referred to by `birthday` as well.

What the programmer probably intended was to create a second object called `birthday` whose attributes exactly matched those of `d`. This cannot be accomplished without using `new`. For example,

```
Date birthday = new Date(d.getMonth(), d.getDay(), d.getYear());
```

The statement `d.changeDate()` will now leave the `birthday` object unchanged.

The Null Reference

The declaration

```
BankAccount b;
```

defines a reference `b` that is uninitialized. (To construct the object that `b` refers to requires the `new` operator and a `BankAccount` constructor.) An uninitialized object variable is called a *null reference* or *null pointer*. You can test whether a variable refers to an object or is uninitialized by using the keyword `null`:

```
if (b == null)
```

If a reference is not null, it can be set to null with the statement

```
b = null;
```

An attempt to invoke an instance method with a null reference may cause your program to terminate with a `NullPointerException`. For example,

```
public class PersonalFinances
{
    BankAccount b;                //b is a null reference
        ...
    b.withdraw(password, amt);    //throws a NullPointerException
        ...                       //if b not constructed with new
```

NOTE

If you fail to initialize a local variable in a method before you use it, you will get a compile-time error. If you make the same mistake with an instance variable of a class, the compiler provides reasonable default values for primitive variables (0 for numbers, `false` for booleans), and the code may run without error. However, if you don't initialize *reference* instance variables in a class, as in the above example, the compiler will set them to `null`. Any method call for an object of the class that tries to access the null reference will cause a run-time error: The program will terminate with a `NullPointerException`.

> Do not make a method call with an object whose value is `null`.

Method Parameters

FORMAL VS. ACTUAL PARAMETERS

The header of a method defines the *parameters* of that method. For example, consider the `withdraw` method of the `BankAccount` class:

```
public class BankAccount
{   ...
    public void withdraw(String password, double amount)
        ...
```

This method has two explicit parameters, `password` and `amount`. These are *dummy* or *formal parameters*. Think of them as placeholders for the pair of *actual parameters* or *arguments* that will be supplied by a particular method call in a client program.

For example,

```
BankAccount b = new BankAccount("TimB", 1000);
b.withdraw("TimB", 250);
```

Here `"TimB"` and `250` are the actual parameters that match up with `password` and `amount` for the `withdraw` method.

NOTE

1. The number of arguments in the method call must equal the number of parameters in the method header, and the type of each argument must be compatible with the type of each corresponding parameter.
2. In addition to its explicit parameters, the `withdraw` method has an implicit parameter, `this`, the `BankAccount` from which money will be withdrawn. In the method call

   ```
   b.withdraw("TimB", 250);
   ```

   the actual parameter that matches up with `this` is the object reference `b`.

PASSING PRIMITIVE TYPES AS PARAMETERS

Parameters are *passed by value*. For primitive types this means that when a method is called, a new memory slot is allocated for each parameter. The value of each argument is copied into the newly created memory slot corresponding to each parameter.

During execution of the method, the parameters are local to that method. *Any changes made to the parameters will not affect the values of the arguments in the calling program.* When the method is exited, the local memory slots for the parameters are erased.

Here's an example: What will the output be?

```
public class ParamTest
{
    public static void foo(int x, double y)
    {
        x = 3;
        y = 2.5;
    }

    public static void main(String[] args)
    {
        int a = 7;
        double b = 6.5;
        foo(a, b);
        System.out.println(a + "   " + b);
    }
}
```

The output will be

```
7  6.5
```

The arguments a and b remain unchanged, despite the method call!

This can be understood by picturing the state of the memory slots during execution of the program.

Just before the foo(a, b) method call:

```
   a          b
┌─────┐    ┌─────┐
│  7  │    │ 6.5 │
└─────┘    └─────┘
```

At the time of the foo(a, b) method call:

```
   a          b
┌─────┐    ┌─────┐
│  7  │    │ 6.5 │
└─────┘    └─────┘

   x          y
┌─────┐    ┌─────┐
│  7  │    │ 6.5 │
└─────┘    └─────┘
```

Just before exiting the method: Note that the values of x and y have been changed.

```
   a          b
┌─────┐    ┌─────┐
│  7  │    │ 6.5 │
└─────┘    └─────┘

   x          y
┌─────┐    ┌─────┐
│  3  │    │ 2.5 │
└─────┘    └─────┘
```

After exiting the method: Note that the memory slots for x and y have been reclaimed. The values of a and b remain unchanged.

```
   a          b
┌─────┐    ┌─────┐
│  7  │    │ 6.5 │
└─────┘    └─────┘
```

PASSING OBJECTS AS PARAMETERS

In Java both primitive types and object references are passed by value. When an object's reference is a parameter, the same mechanism of copying into local memory is used. The key difference is that the *address* (reference) is copied, not the values of the individual instance variables. As with primitive types, changes made to the parameters will not change the values of the matching arguments. What this means in practice is that it is not possible for a method to replace an object with another one—you can't change the reference that was passed. It is, however, possible to change the state of the object to which the parameter refers through methods that act on the object.

Example 1

A method that changes the state of an object.

```
/* Subtracts fee from balance in b if current balance too low. */
public static void chargeFee(BankAccount b, String password,
        double fee)
{
    final double MIN_BALANCE = 10.00;
    if (b.getBalance() < MIN_BALANCE)
        b.withdraw(password, fee);
}

public static void main(String[] args)
{
    final double FEE = 5.00;
    BankAccount andysAccount = new BankAccount("AndyS", 7.00);
    chargeFee(andysAccount, "AndyS", FEE);
        ...
}
```

Here are the memory slots before the `chargeFee` method call:

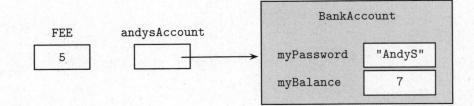

At the time of the `chargeFee` method call, copies of the matching parameters are made:

Just before exiting the method: The `myBalance` field of the `BankAccount` object has been changed.

After exiting the method: All parameter memory slots have been erased, but the object remains altered.

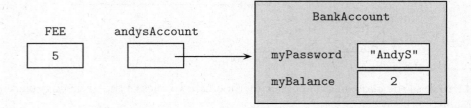

NOTE

The `andysAccount` reference is unchanged throughout the program segment. The object to which it refers, however, has been changed. This is significant. Contrast this with Example 2 below in which an attempt is made to replace the object itself.

Example 2

A `chooseBestAccount` method attempts—erroneously—to set its `betterFund` parameter to the `BankAccount` with the higher balance:

```
public static void chooseBestAccount(BankAccount better,
            BankAccount b1, BankAccount b2)
{
    if (b1.getBalance() > b2.getBalance())
        better = b1;
    else
        better = b2;
}

public static void main(String[] args)
{
    BankAccount briansFund = new BankAccount("BrianL", 10000);
    BankAccount paulsFund = new BankAccount("PaulM", 90000);
    BankAccount betterFund = null;

    chooseBestAccount(betterFund, briansFund, paulsFund);
        ...
}
```

The intent is that `betterFund` will be a reference to the `paulsFund` object after execution of the `chooseBestAccount` statement. A look at the memory slots illustrates why this fails.

Before the `chooseBestAccount` method call:

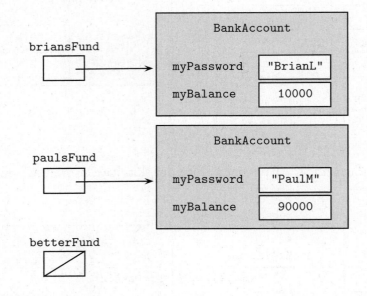

At the time of the `chooseBestAccount` method call: Copies of the matching references are made.

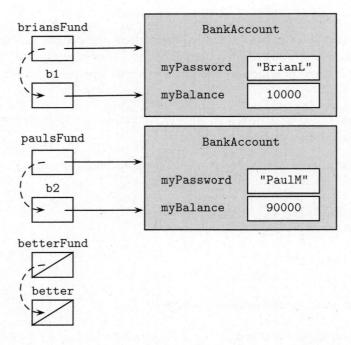

Just before exiting the method: The value of `better` has been changed; `betterFund`, however, remains unchanged.

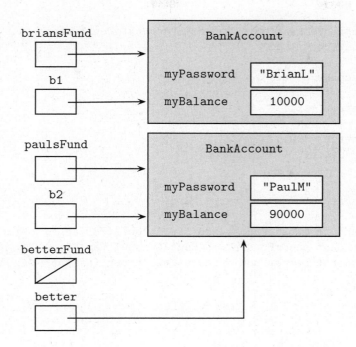

After exiting the method: All parameter slots have been erased.

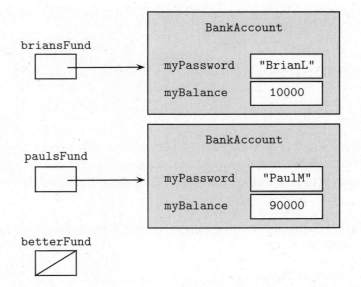

Note that the betterFund reference continues to be null, contrary to the programmer's intent.

The way to fix the problem is to modify the method so that it returns the better account. Returning an object from a method means that you are returning the address of the object.

```
public static BankAccount chooseBestAccount(BankAccount b1,
        BankAccount b2)
{
    BankAccount better;
    if (b1.getBalance() > b2.getBalance())
        better = b1;
    else
        better = b2;
    return better;
}

public static void main(String[] args)
{
    BankAccount briansFund = new BankAccount("BrianL", 10000);
    BankAccount paulsFund = new BankAccount("PaulM", 90000);
    BankAccount betterFund = chooseBestAccount(briansFund, paulsFund);
        ...
}
```

NOTE

The effect of this is to create the betterFund reference, which refers to the same object as paulsFund:

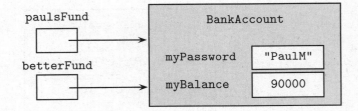

What the method does *not* do is create a new object to which betterFund refers. To do that would require the keyword new and use of a BankAccount constructor. Assuming that a getPassword() accessor has been added to the BankAccount class, the code would look like this:

```
public static BankAccount chooseBestAccount(BankAccount b1,
        BankAccount b2)
{
    BankAccount better;
    if (b1.getBalance() > b2.getBalance())
        better = new BankAccount(b1.getPassword(), b1.getBalance());
    else
        better = new BankAccount(b2.getPassword(), b2.getBalance());
    return better;
}
```

Using this modified method with the same main() method above has the following effect:

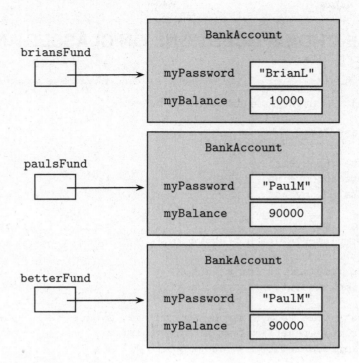

Modifying more than one object in a method can be accomplished using a *wrapper class* (see p. 177).

Chapter Summary

By now you should be able to write code for any given object, with its private data fields and methods encapsulated in a class. Be sure that you know the various types of methods—static, instance, and overloaded.

You should also understand the difference between storage of primitive types and the references used for objects.

MULTIPLE-CHOICE QUESTIONS ON CLASSES AND OBJECTS

Questions 1–3 refer to the Time class declared below:

```java
public class Time
{
    private int myHrs;
    private int myMins;
    private int mySecs;

    public Time()
    { /* implementation not shown */ }

    public Time(int h, int m, int s)
    { /* implementation not shown */ }

    //Resets time to myHrs = h, myMins = m, mySecs = s.
    public void resetTime(int h, int m, int s)
    { /* implementation not shown */ }

    //Advances time by one second.
    public void increment()
    { /* implementation not shown */ }

    //Returns true if this time equals t, false otherwise.
    public boolean equals(Time t)
    { /* implementation not shown */ }

    //Returns true if this time is earlier than t, false otherwise.
    public boolean lessThan(Time t)
    { /* implementation not shown */ }

    //Returns time as a String in the form hrs:mins:secs.
    public String toString()
    { /* implementation not shown */ }
}
```

1. Which of the following is a *false* statement about the methods?
   (A) equals, lessThan, and toString are all accessor methods.
   (B) increment is a mutator method.
   (C) Time() is the default constructor.
   (D) The Time class has three constructors.
   (E) There are no static methods in this class.

2. Which of the following represents correct *implementation code* for the constructor with parameters?

  (A)
```
myHrs = 0;
myMins = 0;
mySecs = 0;
```

  (B)
```
myHrs = h;
myMins = m;
mySecs = s;
```

  (C) `resetTime(myHrs, myMins, mySecs);`

  (D)
```
h = myHrs;
m = myMins;
s = mySecs;
```

  (E) `Time = new Time(h, m, s);`

3. A client class has a `display` method that writes the time represented by its parameter:

```
//Outputs time t in the form hrs:mins:secs.
public void display (Time t)
{
    /* method body */
}
```

  Which of the following are correct replacements for /* *method body* */?

  I
```
Time T = new Time(h, m, s);
System.out.println(T);
```

  II `System.out.println(t.myHrs + ":" + t.myMins + ":" + t.mySecs);`

  III `System.out.println(t);`

  (A) I only
  (B) II only
  (C) III only
  (D) II and III only
  (E) I, II, and III

4. Which statement about parameters is *false*?
  (A) The scope of parameters is the method in which they are defined.
  (B) Static methods have no implicit parameter `this`.
  (C) Two overloaded methods in the same class must have parameters with different names.
  (D) All parameters in Java are passed by value.
  (E) Two different constructors in a given class can have the same number of parameters.

Questions 5–11 refer to the following Date class declaration:

```
public class Date
{
    private int myDay;
    private int myMonth;
    private int myYear;

    public Date()                          //default constructor
    {
        ...
    }

    public Date(int mo, int day, int yr)   //constructor
    {
        ...
    }

    public int month()      //returns month of Date
    {
        ...
    }

    public int day()        //returns day of Date
    {
        ...
    }

    public int year()       //returns year of Date
    {
        ...
    }

    //Returns String representation of Date as "m/d/y", e.g. 4/18/1985.
    public String toString()
    {
        ...
    }
}
```

5. Which of the following correctly constructs a Date object?

    (A) Date d = new (2, 13, 1947);

    (B) Date d = new Date(2, 13, 1947);

    (C) Date d;
        d = new (2, 13, 1947);

    (D) Date d;
        d = Date(2, 13, 1947);

    (E) Date d = Date(2, 13, 1947);

6. Which of the following will cause an error message?

    I   `Date d1 = new Date(8, 2, 1947);`
          `Date d2 = d1;`

    II `Date d1 = null;`
          `Date d2 = d1;`

    III `Date d = null;`
          `int x = d.year();`

    (A) I only
    (B) II only
    (C) III only
    (D) II and III only
    (E) I, II, and III

7. A client program creates a `Date` object as follows:

    ```
    Date d = new Date(1, 13, 2002);
    ```

    Which of the following subsequent code segments will cause an error?
    (A) `String s = d.toString();`
    (B) `int x = d.day();`
    (C) `Date e = d;`
    (D) `Date e = new Date(1, 13, 2002);`
    (E) `int y = d.myYear;`

8. Consider the implementation of a `write()` method that is added to the `Date` class:

    ```
    //Write the date in the form m/d/y, for example 2/17/1948.
    public void write()
    {
        /* implementation code */
    }
    ```

    Which of the following could be used as /* *implementation code* */?

    I   `System.out.println(myMonth + "/" + myDay + "/" + myYear);`

    II `System.out.println(month() + "/" + day() + "/" + year());`

    III `System.out.println(this);`

    (A) I only
    (B) II only
    (C) III only
    (D) II and III only
    (E) I, II, and III

9. Here is a client program that uses `Date` objects:

```
public class BirthdayStuff
{
    public static Date findBirthdate()
    {
        /* code to get birthDate */
        return birthDate;
    }

    public static void main(String[] args)
    {
        Date d = findBirthdate();
            ...
    }
}
```

Which of the following is a correct replacement for
/* *code to get* `birthDate` */?

```
 I  System.out.println("Enter birthdate: mo, day, yr: ");
    int m = IO.readInt();                      //read user input
    int d = IO.readInt();                      //read user input
    int y = IO.readInt();                      //read user input
    Date birthDate = new Date(m, d, y);
```

```
II  System.out.println("Enter birthdate: mo, day, yr: ");
    int birthDate.month() = IO.readInt();      //read user input
    int birthDate.day() = IO.readInt();        //read user input
    int birthDate.year() = IO.readInt();       //read user input
    Date birthDate = new Date(birthDate.month(), birthDate.day(),
        birthDate.year());
```

```
III System.out.println("Enter birthdate: mo, day, yr: ");
    int birthDate.myMonth = IO.readInt();      //read user input
    int birthDate.myDay = IO.readInt();        //read user input
    int birthDate.myYear = IO.readInt();       //read user input
    Date birthDate = new Date(birthDate.myMonth, birthDate.myDay,
        birthDate.myYear);
```

(A) I only
(B) II only
(C) III only
(D) I and II only
(E) I and III only

10. A method in a client program for the Date class has this declaration:

    ```
    Date d1 = new Date(month, day, year);
    ```

    where month, day, and year are previously defined integer variables. The same method now creates a second Date object d2 that is an exact copy of the object d1 refers to. Which of the following code segments will *not* do this correctly?

    I Date d2 = d1;

    II Date d2 = new Date(month, day, year);

    III Date d2 = new Date(d1.month(), d1.day(), d1.year());

    (A) I only
    (B) II only
    (C) III only
    (D) II and III only
    (E) I, II, and III

11. The Date class is modified by adding the following mutator method:

    ```
    public void addYears(int n)     //add n years to date
    ```

    Here is part of a poorly coded client program that uses the Date class:

    ```
    public static void addCentury(Date recent, Date old)
    {
        old.addYears(100);
        recent = old;
    }

    public static void main(String[] args)
    {
        Date oldDate = new Date(1, 13, 1900);
        Date recentDate = null;
        addCentury(recentDate, oldDate);
            . . .
    }
    ```

    Which will be true after executing this code?
    (A) A NullPointerException is thrown.
    (B) The oldDate object remains unchanged.
    (C) recentDate is a null reference.
    (D) recentDate refers to the same object as oldDate.
    (E) recentDate refers to a separate object whose contents are the same as those of oldDate.

Questions 12–15 refer to the following definition of the Rational class:

```
public class Rational
{
    private int myNum;        //numerator
    private int myDenom;      //denominator

    //constructors
    /* default constructor */
    Rational()
    { /* implementation not shown */ }

    /* Constructs a Rational with numerator n and
     * denominator 1. */
    Rational(int n)
    { /* implementation not shown */ }

    /* Constructs a Rational with specified numerator and
     * denominator. */
    Rational(int numer, int denom)
    { /* implementation not shown */ }

    //accessors
    /* Returns numerator. */
    int numerator()
    { /* implementation not shown */ }

    /* Returns denominator. */
    int denominator()
    { /* implementation not shown */ }

    //arithmetic operations
    /* Returns (this + r).
     * Leaves this unchanged. */
    public Rational plus(Rational r)
    { /* implementation not shown */ }

    //Similarly for times, minus, divide
           . . .
    /* Ensures myDenom > 0. */
    private void fixSigns()
    { /* implementation not shown */ }

    /* Ensures lowest terms. */
    private void reduce()
    { /* implementation not shown */ }
}
```

12. The method reduce() is not a public method because
    (A) methods whose return type is void cannot be public.
    (B) methods that change this cannot be public.
    (C) the reduce() method is not intended for use by clients of the Rational class.
    (D) the reduce() method is intended for use only by clients of the Rational class.
    (E) the reduce() method uses only the private data fields of the Rational class.

13. The constructors in the `Rational` class allow initialization of `Rational` objects in several different ways. Which of the following will cause an error?
    (A) `Rational r1 = new Rational();`
    (B) `Rational r2 = r1;`
    (C) `Rational r3 = new Rational(2,-3);`
    (D) `Rational r4 = new Rational(3.5);`
    (E) `Rational r5 = new Rational(10);`

14. Here is the implementation code for the `plus` method:

    ```
    /* Returns (this + r) in reduced form. Leaves this unchanged. */
    public Rational plus(Rational r)
    {
        fixSigns();
        r.fixSigns();
        int denom = myDenom * r.myDenom;
        int num = myNum * r.myDenom + r.myNum * myDenom;
        /* some more code */
    }
    ```

    Which of the following is a correct replacement for /* *some more code* */?

    (A) `Rational rat(num, denom);`
        `rat.reduce();`
        `return rat;`

    (B) `return new Rational(num, denom);`

    (C) `reduce();`
        `Rational rat = new Rational(num, denom);`
        `return rat;`

    (D) `Rational rat = new Rational(num, denom);`
        `Rational.reduce();`
        `return rat;`

    (E) `Rational rat = new Rational(num, denom);`
        `rat.reduce();`
        `return rat;`

15. Assume these declarations:

    ```
    Rational a = new Rational();
    Rational r = new Rational(num, denom);
    int n = value;
    //num, denom, and value are valid integer values
    ```

    Which of the following will cause a compile-time error?
    (A) `r = a.plus(r);`
    (B) `a = r.plus(new Rational(n));`
    (C) `r = r.plus(r);`
    (D) `a = n.plus(r);`
    (E) `r = r.plus(new Rational(n));`

16. Here are the private instance variables for a Frog object:

```
public class Frog
{
    private String mySpecies;
    private int myAge;
    private double myWeight;
    private Position myPosition;      //position (x,y) in pond
    private boolean amAlive;
    ...
```

Which of the following methods in the Frog class is the best candidate for being a static method?

(A) swim   //frog swims to new position in pond

(B) getPondTemperature   //returns temperature of pond

(C) eat   //frog eats and gains weight

(D) getWeight   //returns weight of frog

(E) die   //frog dies with some probability based
                    //on frog's age and pond temperature

17. What output will be produced by this program?

```
public class Mystery
{
    public static void strangeMethod(int x, int y)
    {
        x += y;
        y *= x;
        System.out.println(x + " " + y);
    }

    public static void main(String[] args)
    {
        int a = 6, b = 3;
        strangeMethod(a, b);
        System.out.println(a + " " + b);
    }
}
```

(A) 36
    9

(B) 3 6
    9

(C) 9 27
    9 27

(D) 6 3
    9 27

(E) 9 27
    6 3

Questions 18–20 refer to the `Temperature` class shown below:

```
public class Temperature
{
    private String myScale;  //valid values are "F" or "C"
    private double myDegrees;

    //constructors
    /* default constructor */
    public Temperature()
    { /* implementation not shown */ }

    /* constructor with specified degrees and scale */
    public Temperature(double degrees, String scale)
    { /* implementation not shown */ }

    //accessors
    /* Returns degrees for this temperature. */
    public double getDegrees()
    { /* implementation not shown */ }

    /* Returns scale for this temperature. */
    public String getScale()
    { /* implementation not shown */ }

    //mutators
    /* Precondition:  Temperature is a valid temperature
     *                in degrees Celsius.
     * Postcondition: Returns this temperature, which has been
     *                converted to degrees Fahrenheit. */
    public Temperature toFahrenheit()
    { /* implementation not shown */ }

    /* Precondition:  Temperature is a valid temperature
     *                in degrees Fahrenheit.
     * Postcondition: Returns this temperature, which has been
     *                converted to degrees Celsius. */
    public Temperature toCelsius()
    { /* implementation not shown */ }

    /* Raise this temperature by amt degrees and return it. */
    public Temperature raise(double amt)
    { /* implementation not shown */ }

    /* Lower this temperature by amt degrees and return it. */
    public Temperature lower(double amt)
    { /* implementation not shown */ }

    /* Returns true if the number of degrees is a valid
     * temperature in the given scale, false otherwise. */
    public static boolean isValidTemp(double degrees, String scale)
    { /* implementation not shown */ }

    //other methods not shown ...
}
```

18. A client method contains this code segment:

```
Temperature t1 = new Temperature(40, "C");
Temperature t2 = t1;
Temperature t3 = t2.lower(20);
Temperature t4 = t1.toFahrenheit();
```

Which statement is *true* following execution of this segment?
(A) t1, t2, t3, and t4 all represent the identical temperature, in degrees Celsius.
(B) t1, t2, t3, and t4 all represent the identical temperature, in degrees Fahrenheit.
(C) t4 represents a Fahrenheit temperature, while t1, t2, and t3 all represent degrees Celsius.
(D) t1 and t2 refer to the same Temperature object; t3 refers to a Temperature object that is 20 degrees lower than t1 and t2, while t4 refers to an object that is t1 converted to Fahrenheit.
(E) A NullPointerException was thrown.

19. Consider the following code:

```
public class TempTest
{
    public static void main(String[] args)
    {
        System.out.println("Enter temperature scale: ");
        String scale = IO.readString();      //read user input
        System.out.println("Enter number of degrees: ");
        double degrees = IO.readDouble();     //read user input
        /* code to construct a valid temperature from user input */
    }
}
```

Which is a correct replacement for /* *code to construct... */*?

```
  I  Temperature t = new Temperature(degrees, scale);
     if (!t.isValidTemp(degrees,scale))
```
/* *error message and exit program* */

```
 II  if (isValidTemp(degrees,scale))
         Temperature t = new Temperature(degrees, scale);
     else
```
/* *error message and exit program* */

```
III  if (Temperature.isValidTemp(degrees,scale))
         Temperature t = new Temperature(degrees, scale);
     else
```
/* *error message and exit program* */

(A) I only
(B) II only
(C) III only
(D) I and II only
(E) I and III only

20. The formula to convert degrees Celsius C to Fahrenheit F is

$$F = 1.8C + 32$$

For example, 30°C is equivalent to 86°F.

An `inFahrenheit()` accessor method is added to the `Temperature` class. Here is its implementation:

```
/* Precondition:  temperature is a valid temperature in
 *                degrees Celsius
 * Postcondition: an equivalent temperature in degrees
 *                Fahrenheit has been returned. Original
 *                temperature remains unchanged */
public Temperature inFahrenheit()
{
    Temperature result;
    /* more code */
    return result;
}
```

Which of the following correctly replaces /* *more code* */ so that the postcondition is achieved?

```
  I  result = new Temperature(myDegrees*1.8 + 32, "F");

 II  result = new Temperature(myDegrees*1.8, "F");
     result = result.raise(32);

III  myDegrees *= 1.8;
     this = this.raise(32);
     result = new Temperature(myDegrees, "F");
```

(A) I only
(B) II only
(C) III only
(D) I and II only
(E) I, II, and III

21. Consider this program:

```
public class CountStuff
{
    public static void doSomething()
    {
        int count = 0;
            ...
        //code to do something - no screen output produced
        count++;
    }

    public static void main(String[] args)
    {
        int count = 0;
        System.out.println("How many iterations?");
        int n = IO.readInt();     //read user input
        for (int  i = 1; i <= n; i++)
        {
            doSomething();
            System.out.println(count);
        }
    }
}
```

If the input value for n is 3, what screen output will this program subsequently produce?

(A) 0
     0
     0

(B) 1
     2
     3

(C) 3
     3
     3

(D) ?
     ?
     ?
    where ? is some undefined value.

(E) No output will be produced.

22. This question refers to the following class:

```
public class IntObject
{
    private int myInt;

    public IntObject()       //default constructor
    { myInt = 0; }
    public IntObject(int n)  //constructor
    { myInt = n; }
    public void increment()  //increment by 1
    { myInt++; }
}
```

Here is a client program that uses this class:

```
public class IntObjectTest
{
    public static IntObject someMethod(IntObject obj)
    {
        IntObject ans = obj;
        ans.increment();
        return ans;
    }

    public static void main(String[] args)
    {
        IntObject x = new IntObject(2);
        IntObject y = new IntObject(7);
        IntObject a = y;
        x = someMethod(y);
        a = someMethod(x);
    }
}
```

Just before exiting this program, what are the object values of x, y, and a, respectively?

(A) 9, 9, 9
(B) 2, 9, 9
(C) 2, 8, 9
(D) 3, 8, 9
(E) 7, 8, 9

23. Consider the following program:

```
public class Tester
{
    public void someMethod(int a, int b)
    {
        int temp = a;
        a = b;
        b = temp;
    }
}

public class TesterMain
{
    public static void main(String[] args)
    {
        int x = 6, y = 8;
        Tester tester = new Tester();
        tester.someMethod(x, y);
    }
}
```

Just before the end of execution of this program, what are the values of x, y, and temp, respectively?

(A) 6, 8, 6
(B) 8, 6, 6
(C) 6, 8, ?, where ? means undefined
(D) 8, 6, ?, where ? means undefined
(E) 8, 6, 8

ANSWER KEY

1. **D**	9. **A**	17. **E**
2. **B**	10. **A**	18. **B**
3. **C**	11. **C**	19. **C**
4. **C**	12. **C**	20. **D**
5. **B**	13. **D**	21. **A**
6. **C**	14. **E**	22. **A**
7. **E**	15. **D**	23. **C**
8. **E**	16. **B**	

ANSWERS EXPLAINED

1. **(D)** There are just two constructors. Constructors are recognizable by having the same name as the class, and no return type.

2. **(B)** Each of the private instance variables should be assigned the value of the matching parameter. Choice B is the only choice that does this. Choice D confuses the order of the assignment statements. Choice A gives the code for the *default* constructor, ignoring the parameters. Choice C would be correct if it were resetTime(h, m, s). As written, it doesn't assign the parameter values h, m, and s to myHrs, myMins, and mySecs. Choice E is wrong because the keyword new should be used to create a new object, not to implement the constructor!

3. **(C)** Replacement III will automatically print time t in the required form since a toString method was defined for the Time class. Replacement I is wrong because it doesn't refer to the parameter, t, of the method. Replacement II is wrong because a client program may not access private data of the class.

4. **(C)** The parameter names can be the same—the *signatures* must be different. For example,

```
public void print(int x)      //prints x
public void print(double x)   //prints x
```

The signatures (method name plus parameter types) here are print(int) and print(double), respectively. The parameter name x is irrelevant. Choice A is true: All local variables and parameters go out of scope (are erased) when the method is exited. Choice B is true: Static methods apply to the whole class. Only instance methods have an implicit this parameter. Choice D is true even for object parameters: Their references are passed by value. Note that choice E is true because it's possible to have two different constructors with different signatures but the same number of parameters (e.g., one for an int argument and one for a double).

5. **(B)** Constructing an object requires the keyword new and a constructor of the Date class. Eliminate choices D and E since they omit new. The class name Date should appear on the right-hand side of the assignment statement, immediately following the keyword new. This eliminates choices A and C.

6. **(C)** Segment III will cause a `NullPointerException` to be thrown since `d` is a null reference. You cannot invoke a method for a null reference. Segment II has the effect of assigning `null` to both `d1` and `d2`—obscure but not incorrect. Segment I creates the object reference `d1` and then declares a second reference `d2` that refers to the same object as `d1`.

7. **(E)** A client program cannot access a private instance variable.

8. **(E)** All are correct. Since `write()` is a `Date` instance method, it is OK to use the private data members in its implementation code. Segment III prints `this`, the current `Date` object. This usage is correct since `write()` is part of the `Date` class. The `toString()` method guarantees that the date will be printed in the required format (see p. 172).

9. **(A)** The idea here is to read in three separate variables for month, day, and year and then to construct the required date using `new` and the `Date` class constructor with three parameters. Code segment II won't work because `month()`, `day()`, and `year()` are accessor methods that access existing values and may not be used to read new values into `bDate`. Segment III is wrong because it tries to access private instance variables from a client program.

10. **(A)** Segment I will not create a second object. It will simply cause `d2` to refer to the *same* object as `d1`, which is not what was required. The keyword `new` *must* be used to create a new object.

11. **(C)** When `recentDate` is declared in `main()`, its value is null. Recall that a method is not able to replace an object reference, so `recentDate` remains null. Note that the intent of the program is to change `recentDate` to refer to the updated `oldDate` object. The code, however, doesn't do this. Choice A is false: No methods are invoked with a null reference. Choice B is false because `addYears()` is a mutator method. Even though a method doesn't change the address of its object parameter, it can change the contents of the object, which is what happens here. Choices D and E are wrong because the `addCentury()` method cannot change the value of its `recentDate` argument.

12. **(C)** The `reduce()` method will be used only in the implementation of the instance methods of the `Rational` class.

13. **(D)** None of the constructors in the `Rational` class takes a real-valued parameter. Thus, the real-valued parameter in choice D will need to be converted to an integer. Since in general truncating a real value to an integer involves a loss of precision, it is not done automatically—you have to do it explicitly with a cast. Omitting the cast causes a compile-time error.

14. **(E)** A new `Rational` object must be created using the newly calculated `num` and `denom`. Then it must be reduced before being returned. Choice A is wrong because it doesn't correctly create the new object. Choice B returns a correctly constructed object, but one that has not been reduced. Choice C reduces the current object, `this`, instead of the new object, `rat`. Choice D is wrong because it invokes `reduce()` for the `Rational` class instead of the specific `rat` object.

15. **(D)** The `plus` method of the `Rational` class can only be invoked by `Rational` objects. Since `n` is an `int`, the statement in choice D will cause an error.

16. **(B)** The method `getPondTemperature` is the only method that applies to more than one frog. It should therefore be static. All of the other methods relate directly to one particular `Frog` object. So `f.swim()`, `f.die()`, `f.getWeight()`,

and `f.eat()` are all reasonable methods for a single instance `f` of a `Frog`. On the other hand, it doesn't make sense to say `f.getPondTemperature()`. It makes more sense to say `Frog.getPondTemperature()`, since the same value will apply to all frogs in the class.

17. **(E)** Here are the memory slots at the start of `strangeMethod(a, b)`:

Before exiting `strangeMethod(a, b)`:

Note that 9 27 is output before exiting. After exiting `strangeMethod(a, b)`, the memory slots are

The next step outputs 6 3.

18. **(B)** This is an example of *aliasing*. The keyword `new` is used just once, which means that just one object is constructed. Here are the memory slots after each declaration:

After declaration for t1   After declaration for t2

After declaration for t3   After declaration for t4

19. **(C)** Notice that `isValidTemp` is a static method for the `Temperature` class, which means that it cannot be invoked with a `Temperature` object. Thus segment I is incorrect: `t.isValidTemp` is wrong. Segment II fails because `isValidTemp` is not a method of the `TempTest` class. It therefore must be invoked with its class name, which is what happens (correctly) in segment III: `Temperature.isValidTemp`.

20. **(D)** A new `Temperature` object must be constructed to prevent the current `Temperature` from being changed. Segment I, which applies the conversion formula directly to `myDegrees`, is the best way to do this. Segment II, while not the best algorithm, does work. The statement

    ```
    result = result.raise(32);
    ```

    has the effect of raising the `result` temperature by 32 degrees, and completing the conversion. Segment III fails because

    ```
    myDegrees *= 1.8;
    ```

    alters the `myDegrees` instance variable of the current object, as does

    ```
    this = this.raise(32);
    ```

    To be correct, these operations must be applied to the `result` object.

21. **(A)** This is a question about the scope of variables. The scope of the `count` variable that is declared in `main()` extends up to the closing brace of `main()`. In `doSomething()`, `count` is a local variable. After the method call in the `for` loop, the local variable `count` goes out of scope, and the value that's being printed is the value of the `count` in `main()`, which is unchanged from 0.

22. **(A)** Here are the memory slots before the first `someMethod` call:

Just before exiting `x = someMethod(y)`:

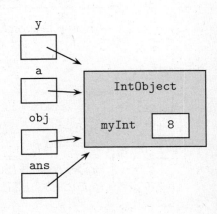

After exiting

```
x = someMethod(y);
```

x has been reassigned, so the object with `myInt = 2` has been recycled:

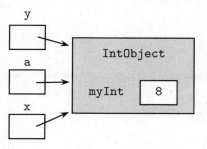

After exiting `a = someMethod(x)`:

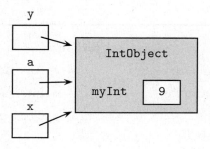

23. **(C)** Recall that when primitive types are passed as parameters, copies are made of the actual arguments. All manipulations in the method are performed on the copies, and the arguments remain unchanged. Thus x and y retain their values of 6 and 8. The local variable `temp` goes out of scope as soon as `someMethod` is exited and is therefore undefined just before the end of execution of the program.

Inheritance and Polymorphism

CHAPTER 3

Say not you know another entirely,
till you have divided an inheritance with him.
—*Johann Kaspar Lavatar,* Aphorisms on Man

Chapter Goals

- Superclasses and subclasses
- Inheritance hierarchy
- Polymorphism
- Type compatibility
- Abstract classes
- Interfaces
- The `Comparable` interface

INHERITANCE

Superclass and Subclass

Inheritance defines a relationship between objects that share characteristics. Specifically it is the mechanism whereby a new class, called a *subclass*, is created from an existing class, called a *superclass*, by absorbing its state and behavior and augmenting these with features unique to the new class. We say that the subclass *inherits* characteristics of its superclass.

Don't get confused by the names: a subclass is bigger than a superclass—it contains more data and more methods!

Inheritance provides an effective mechanism for code reuse. Suppose the code for a superclass has been tested and debugged. Since a subclass object shares features of a superclass object, the only new code required is for the additional characteristics of the subclass.

Inheritance Hierarchy

A subclass can itself be a superclass for another subclass, leading to an *inheritance hierarchy* of classes.

For example, consider the relationship between these objects: `Person`, `Employee`, `Student`, `GradStudent`, and `UnderGrad`.

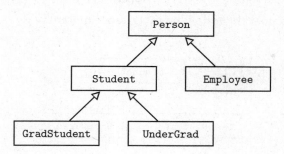

For any of these classes, an arrow points to its superclass. The arrow designates the *is-a* relationship. Thus, an `Employee` *is-a* `Person`; a `Student` *is-a* `Person`; a `GradStudent` *is-a* `Student`; an `UnderGrad` *is-a* `Student`. Notice that the opposite is not necessarily true: A `Person` may not be a `Student`, nor is a `Student` necessarily an `UnderGrad`.

Note that the *is-a* relationship is transitive: If a `GradStudent` *is-a* `Student` and a `Student` *is-a* `Person`, then a `GradStudent` *is-a* `Person`.

Suppose the `Person` class has instance variables `name`, `socialSecurityNumber`, and `age`, and instance methods `getName`, `getSocSecNum`, `getAge`, and `printName`. Then every one of the derived classes shown inherits these variables and methods. The `Student` class may have additional instance variables `studentID` and `gpa`, plus a method `computeGrade`. All of these additional features are inherited by the subclasses `GradStudent` and `UnderGrad`. Suppose `GradStudent` and `UnderGrad` use different algorithms for computing the course grade. Then the `computeGrade` implementation can be redefined in these classes. This is called *method overriding*. If part of the original method implementation from the superclass is retained, we refer to the rewrite as *partial overriding*.

Implementing Subclasses

THE extends KEYWORD

The inheritance relationship between a subclass and a superclass is specified in the declaration of the subclass, using the keyword extends. The general format looks like this:

```
public class Superclass
{
    //private instance variables
    //other data members
    //constructors
    //public methods
    //private methods
}

public class Subclass extends Superclass
{
    //additional private instance variables
    //additional data members
    //constructors   (Not inherited!)
    //additional public methods
    //inherited public methods whose implementation is overridden
    //additional private methods
}
```

For example, consider the following inheritance hierarchy:

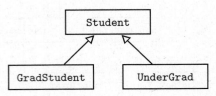

The implementation of the classes may look something like this (discussion follows the code):

```java
public class Student
{
    //data members
    public final static int NUM_TESTS = 3;
    private String myName;
    private int[] myTests;
    private String myGrade;

    //constructors
    public Student()
    {
        myName = "";
        myTests = new int[NUM_TESTS];
        myGrade = "";
    }

    public Student(String name, int[] tests, String grade)
    {
        myName = name;
        myTests = tests;
        myGrade = grade;
    }

    public String getName()
    { return myName; }

    public String getGrade()
    { return myGrade; }

    public void setGrade(String newGrade)
    { myGrade = newGrade; }

    public void computeGrade()
    {
        if (myName.equals(""))
            myGrade = "No grade";
        else if (getTestAverage() >= 65)
            myGrade = "Pass";
        else
            myGrade = "Fail";
    }
```

```
    public double getTestAverage()
    {
        double total = 0;
        for (int score : myTests)
            total += score;
        return total/NUM_TESTS;
    }
}

public class UnderGrad extends Student
{
    public UnderGrad()    //default constructor
    { super(); }

    //constructor
    public UnderGrad(String name, int[] tests, String grade)
    { super(name, tests, grade); }

    public void computeGrade()
    {
        if (getTestAverage() >= 70)
            setGrade("Pass");
        else
            setGrade("Fail");
    }
}

public class GradStudent extends Student
{
    private int myGradID;

    public GradStudent()        //default constructor
    {
        super();
        myGradID = 0;
    }

    //constructor
    public GradStudent(String name, int[] tests, String grade,
            int gradID)
    {
        super(name, tests, grade);
        myGradID = gradID;
    }

    public int getID()
    { return myGradID; }

    public void computeGrade()
    {
        //invokes computeGrade in Student superclass
        super.computeGrade();
        if (getTestAverage() >= 90)
            setGrade("Pass with distinction");
    }
}
```

INHERITING INSTANCE METHODS AND VARIABLES

The UnderGrad and GradStudent subclasses inherit all of the methods and variables of the Student superclass. Notice, however, that the Student instance variables myName, myTests, and myGrade are private, and are therefore not directly accessible to the methods in the UnderGrad and GradStudent subclasses. A subclass can, however, directly invoke the public accessor and mutator methods of the superclass. Thus, both UnderGrad and GradStudent use getTestAverage. Additionally, both UnderGrad and GradStudent use setGrade to access indirectly—and modify—myGrade.

If, instead of private, the access specifier for the instance variables in Student were protected, then the subclasses could directly access these variables. The keyword protected is not part of the AP Java subset.

Classes on the same level in a hierarchy diagram do not inherit anything from each other (for example, UnderGrad and GradStudent). All they have in common is the identical code they inherit from their superclass.

METHOD OVERRIDING AND THE super KEYWORD

A method in a superclass is overridden in a subclass by defining a method with the same return type and signature (name and parameter types). For example, the computeGrade method in the UnderGrad subclass overrides the computeGrade method in the Student superclass.

Sometimes the code for overriding a method includes a call to the superclass method. This is called *partial overriding*. Typically this occurs when the subclass method wants to do what the superclass does, plus something extra. This is achieved by using the keyword super in the implementation. The computeGrade method in the GradStudent subclass partially overrides the matching method in the Student class. The statement

```
super.computeGrade();
```

signals that the computeGrade method in the superclass should be invoked here. The additional test

```
if (getTestAverage() >= 90)
    ...
```

allows a GradStudent to have a grade Pass with distinction. Note that this option is open to GradStudents only.

CONSTRUCTORS AND super

Be sure to provide at least one constructor when you write a subclass. Constructors are never inherited from the superclass.

Constructors are never inherited! If no constructor is written for a subclass, the superclass default constructor with no parameters is generated. If the superclass does not have a default (zero-parameter) constructor, but only a constructor with parameters, a compiler error will occur. If there is a default constructor in the superclass, inherited data members will be initialized as for the superclass. Additional instance variables in the subclass will get a default initialization—0 for primitive types and null for reference types.

A subclass constructor can be implemented with a call to the super method, which invokes the superclass constructor. For example, the default constructor in the UnderGrad class is identical to that of the Student class. This is implemented with the statement

```
super();
```

The second constructor in the UnderGrad class is called with parameters that match those in the constructor of the Student superclass.

```
public UnderGrad(String name, int[] tests, String grade)
{ super(name, tests, grade); }
```

For each constructor, the call to super has the effect of initializing the inherited instance variables myName, myTests, and myGrade exactly as they are initialized in the Student class.

Contrast this with the constructors in GradStudent. In each case, the inherited instance variables myName, myTests, and myGrade are initialized as for the Student class. Then the new instance variable, myGradID, must be explicitly initialized.

```
public GradStudent()
{
    super();
    myGradID = 0;
}

public GradStudent(String name, int[] tests, String grade,
            int gradID)
{
    super(name, tests, grade);
    myGradID = gradID;
}
```

NOTE

1. If super is used in the implementation of a subclass constructor, it *must* be used in the first line of the constructor body.
2. If no constructor is provided in a subclass, the compiler provides the following default constructor:

    ```
    public SubClass()
    {
        super();       //calls default constructor of superclass
    }
    ```

Rules for Subclasses

- A subclass can add new private instance variables.
- A subclass can add new public, private, or static methods.
- A subclass can override inherited methods.
- A subclass may not redefine a public method as private.
- A subclass may not override static methods of the superclass.
- A subclass should define its own constructors.
- A subclass cannot directly access the private members of its superclass. It must use accessor or mutator methods.

Declaring Subclass Objects

When a variable of a superclass is declared in a client program, that reference can refer not only to an object of the superclass, but also to objects of any of its subclasses. Thus, each of the following is legal:

```
Student s = new Student();
Student g = new GradStudent();
Student u = new UnderGrad();
```

This works because a GradStudent *is-a* Student, and an UnderGrad *is-a* Student.

Note that since a Student is not necessarily a GradStudent nor an UnderGrad, the following declarations are *not* valid:

```
GradStudent g = new Student();
UnderGrad u = new Student();
```

Consider these valid declarations:

```
Student s = new Student("Brian Lorenzen", new int[] {90,94,99},
        "none");
Student u = new UnderGrad("Tim Broder", new int[] {90,90,100},
        "none");
Student g = new GradStudent("Kevin Cristella",
        new int[] {85,70,90}, "none", 1234);
```

Suppose you make the method call

```
s.setGrade("Pass");
```

The appropriate method in Student is found and the new grade assigned. The method calls

```
g.setGrade("Pass");
```

and

```
u.setGrade("Pass");
```

achieve the same effect on g and u since GradStudent and UnderGrad both inherit the setGrade method from Student. The following method calls, however, won't work:

```
int studentNum = s.getID();
int underGradNum = u.getID();
```

Neither Student s nor UnderGrad u inherit the getID method from the GradStudent class: A superclass does not inherit from a subclass.

Now consider the following valid method calls:

```
s.computeGrade();
g.computeGrade();
u.computeGrade();
```

Since s, g, and u have all been declared to be of type Student, will the appropriate method be executed in each case? That is the topic of the next section, *polymorphism*.

NOTE

The initializer list syntax used in constructing the array parameters—for example, `new int[] {90,90,100}`— will not be tested on the AP exam.

POLYMORPHISM

A method that has been overridden in at least one subclass is said to be *polymorphic*. An example is `computeGrade`, which is redefined for both `GradStudent` and `UnderGrad`.

Polymorphism is the mechanism of selecting the appropriate method for a particular object in a class hierarchy. The correct method is chosen because, in Java, method calls are always determined by the type of the *actual object*, not the type of the object reference. For example, even though s, g, and u are all declared as type `Student`, `s.computeGrade()`, `g.computeGrade()`, and `u.computeGrade()` will all perform the correct operations for their particular instances. In Java, the selection of the correct method occurs *during the run of the program*.

Dynamic Binding (Late Binding)

Making a run-time decision about which instance method to call is known as *dynamic binding* or *late binding*. Contrast this with selecting the correct method when methods are *overloaded* (see p. 96) rather than overridden. The compiler selects the correct overloaded method at compile time by comparing the methods' signatures. This is known as *static binding*, or *early binding*. In polymorphism, the actual method that will be called is not determined by the compiler. Think of it this way: The compiler determines *if* a method can be called (i.e., is it legal?), while the run-time environment determines *how* it will be called (i.e., which overridden form should be used?).

Example 1

```
Student s = null;
Student u = new UnderGrad("Tim Broder", new int[] {90,90,100},
        "none");
Student g = new GradStudent("Kevin Cristella",
        new int[] {85,70,90}, "none", 1234);
System.out.print("Enter student status: ");
System.out.println("Grad (G), Undergrad (U), Neither (N)");
String str = IO.readString();        //read user input
if (str.equals("G"))
    s = g;
else if (str.equals("U"))
    s = u;
else
    s = new Student();
s.computeGrade();
```

When this code fragment is run, the `computeGrade` method used will depend on the type of the actual object s refers to, which in turn depends on the user input.

Example 2

```java
public class StudentTest
{
    public static void computeAllGrades(Student[] studentList)
    {
        for (Student s : studentList)
            if (s != null)
                s.computeGrade();
    }

    public static void main(String[] args)
    {
        Student[] stu = new Student[5];
        stu[0] = new Student("Brian Lorenzen",
                    new int[] {90,94,99}, "none");
        stu[1] = new UnderGrad("Tim Broder",
                    new int[] {90,90,100}, "none");
        stu[2] = new GradStudent("Kevin Cristella",
                    new int[] {85,70,90}, "none", 1234);
        computeAllGrades(stu);
    }
}
```

> Polymorphism applies only to overridden methods in subclasses.

Here an array of five `Student` references is created, all of them initially null. Three of these references, `stu[0]`, `stu[1]`, and `stu[2]`, are then assigned to actual objects. The `computeAllGrades` method steps through the array invoking for each of the objects the appropriate `computeGrade` method, using dynamic binding in each case. The null test in `computeAllGrades` is necessary because some of the array references could be null.

TYPE COMPATIBILITY

Downcasting

Consider the statements

```java
Student s = new GradStudent();
GradStudent g = new GradStudent();
int x = s.getID();          //compile-time error
int y = g.getID();          //legal
```

Both `s` and `g` represent `GradStudent` objects, so why does `s.getID()` cause an error? The reason is that `s` is of type `Student`, and the `Student` class doesn't have a `getID` method. At compile time, only nonprivate methods of the `Student` class can appear to the right of the dot operator when applied to `s`. Don't confuse this with polymorphism: `getID` is not a polymorphic method. It occurs in just the `GradStudent` class and can therefore be called only by a `GradStudent` object.

The error shown above can be fixed by casting `s` to the correct type:

```java
int x = ((GradStudent) s).getID();
```

Since `s` (of type `Student`) is actually representing a `GradStudent` object, such a cast can be carried out. Casting a superclass to a subclass type is called a *downcast*.

NOTE

1. The outer parentheses are necessary:

   ```
   int x = (GradStudent) s.getID();
   ```

   will still cause an error, despite the cast. This is because the dot operator has higher precedence than casting, so `s.getID()` is invoked before `s` is cast to `GradStudent`.

2. The statement

   ```
   int y = g.getID();
   ```

   compiles without problem because `g` is declared to be of type `GradStudent`, and this is the class that contains `getID`. No cast is required.

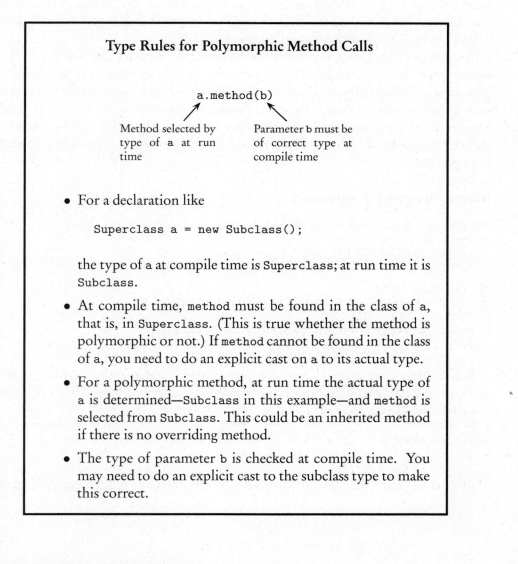

Type Rules for Polymorphic Method Calls

```
a.method(b)
```

Method selected by type of `a` at run time

Parameter `b` must be of correct type at compile time

- For a declaration like

  ```
  Superclass a = new Subclass();
  ```

  the type of `a` at compile time is `Superclass`; at run time it is `Subclass`.

- At compile time, `method` must be found in the class of `a`, that is, in `Superclass`. (This is true whether the method is polymorphic or not.) If `method` cannot be found in the class of `a`, you need to do an explicit cast on `a` to its actual type.

- For a polymorphic method, at run time the actual type of `a` is determined—`Subclass` in this example—and `method` is selected from `Subclass`. This could be an inherited method if there is no overriding method.

- The type of parameter `b` is checked at compile time. You may need to do an explicit cast to the subclass type to make this correct.

The `ClassCastException`

The `ClassCastException` is a run-time exception thrown to signal an attempt to cast an object to a class of which it is not an instance.

```
Student u = new UnderGrad();
System.out.println((String) u);   //ClassCastException
                              //u is not an instance of String
int x = ((GradStudent) u).getID(); //ClassCastException
                           //u is not an instance of GradStudent
```

ABSTRACT CLASSES

Abstract Class

An *abstract class* is a superclass that represents an abstract concept, and therefore should not be instantiated. For example, a maze program could have several different maze components—paths, walls, entrances, and exits. All of these share certain features (e.g., location, and a way of displaying). They can therefore all be declared as subclasses of the abstract class MazeComponent. The program will create path objects, wall objects, and so on, but no instances of MazeComponent.

An abstract class may contain *abstract methods*. An abstract method has no implementation code, just a header. The rationale for an abstract method is that there is no good default code for the method. Every subclass will need to override this method, so why bother with a meaningless implementation in the superclass? The method appears in the abstract class as a placeholder. The implementation for the method occurs in the subclasses. If a class contains any abstract methods, it *must* be declared an abstract class.

The abstract Keyword

An abstract class is declared with the keyword abstract in the header:

```
public abstract class AbstractClass
{    ...
```

The keyword extends is used as before to declare a subclass:

```
public class SubClass extends AbstractClass
{    ...
```

If a subclass of an abstract class does not provide implementation code for all the abstract methods of its superclass, it too becomes an abstract class and must be declared as such to avoid a compile-time error:

```
public abstract class SubClass extends AbstractClass
{    ...
```

Here is an example of an abstract class, with two concrete (nonabstract) subclasses.

```
public abstract class Shape
{
    private String myName;

    //constructor
    public Shape(String name)
    { myName = name; }
```

```
    public String getName()
    { return myName; }

    public abstract double area();
    public abstract double perimeter();

    public double semiPerimeter()
    { return perimeter() / 2; }
}

public class Circle extends Shape
{
    private double myRadius;

    //constructor
    public Circle(double radius, String name)
    {
        super(name);
        myRadius = radius;
    }

    public double perimeter()
    { return 2 * Math.PI * myRadius; }

    public double area()
    { return Math.PI * myRadius * myRadius; }
}

public class Square extends Shape
{
    private double mySide;

    //constructor
    public Square(double side, String name)
    {
        super(name);
        mySide = side;
    }

    public double perimeter()
    { return 4 * mySide; }

    public double area()
    { return mySide * mySide; }
}
```

NOTE

1. It is meaningless to define `perimeter` and `area` methods for `Shape`—thus, these are declared as abstract methods.

2. An abstract class can have both instance variables and concrete (nonabstract) methods. See, for example, `myName`, `getName`, and `semiPerimeter` in the `Shape` class.

3. Abstract methods are declared with the keyword `abstract`. There is no method body. The header is terminated with a semicolon.

4. It is possible for an abstract class to have no abstract methods.
5. An abstract class may or may not have constructors.
6. No instances can be created for an abstract class:

```
Shape a = new Shape("blob");  //Illegal.
                    //Can't create instance of abstract class.
Shape c = new Circle(1.5, "small circle");  //legal
```

7. Polymorphism works with abstract classes as it does with concrete classes:

```
Shape circ = new Circle(10, "circle");
Shape sq = new Square(9.4, "square");
Shape s = null;
System.out.println("Which shape?");
String str = IO.readString();       //read user input
if (str.equals("circle"))
    s = circ;
else
    s = sq;
System.out.println("Area of " + s.getName() + " is "
        + s.area());
```

INTERFACES

Interface

An *interface* is a collection of related methods whose headers are provided without implementations. All of the methods are both public and abstract—no need to explicitly include these keywords. As such, they provide a framework of behavior for any class.

The classes that implement a given interface may represent objects that are vastly different. They all, however, have in common a capability or feature expressed in the methods of the interface. An interface called FlyingObject, for example, may have the methods fly and isFlying. Some classes that implement FlyingObject could be Bird, Airplane, Missile, Butterfly, and Witch. A class called Turtle would be unlikely to implement FlyingObject because turtles don't fly.

An interface called Computable may have just three methods: add, subtract, and multiply. Classes that implement Computable could be Fraction, Matrix, LongInteger, and ComplexNumber. It would not be meaningful, however, for a TelevisionSet to implement Computable—what does it mean, for example, to multiply two TelevisionSet objects?

A class that implements an interface can define any number of methods. In particular, it contracts to provide implementations for *all* the methods declared in the interface. If it fails to implement any of the methods, the class must be declared abstract.

> A nonabstract class that implements an interface must implement every method of the interface.

Defining an Interface

An interface is declared with the interface keyword. For example,

```
public interface FlyingObject
{
    void fly();        //method that simulates flight of object
    boolean isFlying();  //true if object is in flight,
                         //false otherwise
}
```

The `implements` Keyword

Interfaces are implemented using the `implements` keyword. For example,

```
public class Bird implements FlyingObject
{
    ...
```

This declaration means that two of the methods in the `Bird` class must be `fly` and `isFlying`. Note that any subclass of `Bird` will automatically implement the interface `FlyingObject`, since `fly` and `isFlying` will be inherited by the subclass.

A class that extends a superclass can also *directly* implement an interface. For example,

```
public class Mosquito extends Insect implements FlyingObject
{
    ...
```

NOTE

1. The `extends` clause must precede the `implements` clause.
2. A class can have just one superclass, but it can implement any number of interfaces:

```
public class SubClass extends SuperClass
        implements Interface1, Interface2, ...
```

The `Comparable` Interface

The standard `java.lang` package contains the `Comparable` interface, which provides a useful method for comparing objects. Note that the AP Java subset uses the raw `Comparable` interface, not the generic `Comparable<E>` of Java 5.0.

> Classes written for objects that need to be compared should implement `Comparable`.

```
public interface Comparable
{
    int compareTo(Object obj);
}
```

Any class that implements `Comparable` must provide a `compareTo` method. This method compares the implicit object (`this`) with the parameter object (`obj`) and returns a negative integer, zero, or a positive integer depending on whether the implicit object is less than, equal to, or greater than the parameter. If the two objects being compared are not type compatible, a `ClassCastException` is thrown by the method.

Example

The abstract `Shape` class defined previously (p. 138) is modified to implement the `Comparable` interface:

```
public abstract class Shape implements Comparable
{
    private String myName;

    //constructor
    public Shape(String name)
    { myName = name; }

    public String getName()
    { return myName; }

    public abstract double area();
    public abstract double perimeter();

    public double semiPerimeter()
    { return perimeter() / 2; }

    public int compareTo(Object obj)
    {
        final double EPSILON = 1.0e-15;    //slightly bigger than
                                           //machine precision
        Shape rhs = (Shape) obj;
        double diff = area() - rhs.area();
        if (Math.abs(diff) <= EPSILON * Math.abs(area()))
            return 0;  //area of this shape equals area of obj
        else if (diff < 0)
            return -1; //area of this shape less than area of obj
        else
            return 1;  //area of this shape greater than area of obj
    }
}
```

NOTE

1. The `Circle`, `Square`, and other subclasses of `Shape` will all automatically implement `Comparable` and inherit the `compareTo` method.

2. It is tempting to use a simpler test for equality of areas, namely

```
if (diff == 0)
    return 0;
```

But recall that real numbers can have round-off errors in their storage (Box p. 63). This means that the simple test may return false even though the two areas are essentially equal. A more robust test is implemented in the code given, namely to test if the relative error in `diff` is small enough to be considered zero.

3. The `Object` class is a universal superclass (see p. 171). This means that the `compareTo` method can take as a parameter any object reference that implements `Comparable`.

4. The first step of a `compareTo` method must cast the `Object` argument to the class type, in this case `Shape`. If this is not done, the compiler won't find the `area` method—remember, an `Object` is not necessarily a `Shape`.

5. The algorithm one chooses in `compareTo` should in general be consistent with the `equals` method (see p. 173): Whenever `object1.equals(object2)` returns `true`, `object1.compareTo(object2)` returns 0.

Here is a program that finds the larger of two `Comparable` objects.

```
public class FindMaxTest
{
    /* Return the larger of two objects a and b. */
    public static Comparable max(Comparable a, Comparable b)
    {
        if (a.compareTo(b) > 0) //if a > b ...
            return a;
        else
            return b;
    }

    /* Test max on two Shape objects. */
    public static void main(String[] args)
    {
        Shape s1 = new Circle(3.0, "circle");
        Shape s2 = new Square(4.5, "square");
        System.out.println("Area of " + s1.getName() + " is " +
                s1.area());
        System.out.println("Area of " + s2.getName() + " is " +
                s2.area());
        Shape s3 = (Shape) max(s1, s2);
        System.out.println("The larger shape is the " +
                s3.getName());
    }
}
```

Here is the output:

```
Area of circle is 28.27
Area of square is 20.25
The larger shape is the circle
```

NOTE

1. The `max` method takes parameters of type `Comparable`. Since `s1` *is-a* `Comparable` object and `s2` *is-a* `Comparable` object, no casting is necessary in the method call.
2. The `max` method can be called with any two `Comparable` objects, for example, two `String` objects or two `Integer` objects (see Chapter 4).
3. The objects must be type compatible (i.e., it must make sense to compare them). For example, in the program shown, if `s1` *is-a* `Shape` and `s2` *is-a* `String`, the `compareTo` method will throw a `ClassCastException` at the line

   ```
   Shape rhs = (Shape) obj;
   ```

4. The cast is needed in the line

   ```
   Shape s3 = (Shape) max(s1, s2);
   ```

   since `max(s1, s2)` returns a `Comparable`.
5. A primitive type is not an object and therefore cannot be passed as `Comparable`. You can, however, use a wrapper class and in this way convert a primitive type to a `Comparable` (see p. 177).

ABSTRACT CLASS VS. INTERFACE

Consider writing a program that simulates a game of Battleships. The program may have a `Ship` class with subclasses `Submarine`, `Cruiser`, `Destroyer`, and so on. The various ships will be placed in a two-dimensional grid that represents a part of the ocean, much like the grid in the GridWorld Case Study.

An abstract class `Ship` is a good design choice. There will not be any instances of `Ship` objects because the specific features of the subclasses must be known in order to place these ships in the grid. A `Grid` interface like that in the case study suggests itself for the two-dimensional grid.

Notice that the abstract `Ship` class is specific to the Battleships application, whereas the `Grid` interface is not. You could use the `Grid` interface in any program that has a two-dimensional grid.

Interface vs. Abstract Class

- Use an abstract class for an object that is application-specific, but incomplete without its subclasses.

- Consider using an interface when its methods are suitable for your program, but could be equally applicable in a variety of programs.

- An interface cannot provide implementations for any of its methods, whereas an abstract class can.

- An interface cannot contain instance variables, whereas an abstract class can.

- An interface and an abstract class can both declare constants.

- It is not possible to create an instance of an interface object or an abstract class object.

Sample Free-Response Question

Consider the hierarchy of classes shown for a small part of a bird sanctuary.

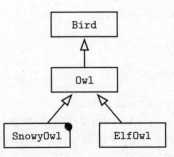

Notice that an `Owl` *is-a* `Bird`, a `SnowyOwl` *is-a* `Owl`, and an `ElfOwl` *is-a* `Owl`.

The class `Bird` is specified as an abstract class as shown in the following declaration. Each `Bird` has a name and a noise that are specified when it is constructed.

```
public abstract class Bird
{
    private String myName;
    private String myNoise;

    /** Constructor for objects of class Bird */
    public Bird(String name, String noise)
    {
        myName = name;
        myNoise = noise;
    }

    public String getName()
    { return myName; }

    public String getNoise()
    { return myNoise; }

    public abstract String getFood();
}
```

(a) An `Owl` is a `Bird` whose noise is `"hoot"`. The food it eats depends on the type of `Owl`, which means that getFood cannot be implemented in the `Owl` class.
Given the hierarchy shown above, write a complete class declaration for the class `Owl`, including its constructor and any method(s).

(b) A `SnowyOwl` is an `Owl` whose name is always `"Snowy owl"`. A `SnowyOwl` will randomly eat a hare, a lemming, or a small bird (depending on what's available!), where each type of food is equally likely. The `SnowyOwl` class should use a random number to determine which food the `SnowyOwl` will eat. Assuming that the `Owl` class has been correctly defined, and given the class hierarchy shown previously, write a complete declaration of the class `SnowyOwl`, including implementation of its constructor and method(s).

(c) Consider the following partial declaration of class `BirdSanctuary`.

```
public class BirdSanctuary
{
    /** The list of birds */
    private Bird[] birdList;

    /**
     * Precondition:  Each Bird in birdList has a getFood
     *                method implemented for it.
     * Postcondition: For each Bird in the birdList array, its
     *                name followed by the result of a call to
     *                its getFood method has been printed, one
     *                line per Bird.  */
    public void allEat()
    { /* to be implemented in this part */ }

    //The constructor and other methods are not shown.
}
```

Write the `BirdSanctuary` method `allEat`. For each `Bird` in `BirdSanctuary`, `allEat` prints a line with the name of the `Bird` followed by the result of a call to its `getFood` method, one line per `Bird`.

Complete method `allEat` below.

```
/**
 * Precondition:  Each Bird in birdList has a getFood
 *                method implemented for it.
 * Postcondition: For each Bird in the birdList array, its
 *                name followed by the result of a call to
 *                its getFood method has been printed, one
 *                line per Bird.
 */
public void allEat()
```

Solution

(a)
```
public abstract class Owl extends Bird
{
    //Constructor
    public Owl(String name)
    { super(name, "hoot"); }
}
```

(b)
```
public class SnowyOwl extends Owl
{
    //Constructor
    public SnowyOwl()
    { super ("Snowy owl"); }

    //Returns type of food for this SnowyOwl
    public String getFood()
    {
        int num = (int)(Math.random()*3);
        if (num == 0)
            return "hare";
        else if (num == 1)
            return "lemming";
        else
            return "small bird";
    }
}
```

(c)
```
public void allEat()
{
    for (Bird b: birdList)
        System.out.println(b.getName() + " " + b.getFood());
}
```

NOTE

- The `Owl` class inherits the abstract `getFood` method. Since the food type for an `Owl` depends on the type of `Owl`, the `Owl` class does not provide implementation code for `getFood`. Therefore, the `Owl` class must be an abstract class.

- In parts (a) and (b), super must be used in the constructors because there is no direct access to the private instance variables of the Bird class.
- Note that the noise for Owl will always be "hoot". Thus, noise does not need to be provided as a parameter in the Owl constructor. The statement super(name, "hoot") will use the superclass—namely Bird—constructor to automatically assign "hoot" as an Owl's noise. Similarly, the SnowyOwl does not need any parameters in its constructor: using the superclass (Owl) constructor will automatically provide it with its name through the statement super("Snowy owl").
- In part (c), polymorphism will determine which getFood method to print for the actual instance of each Bird in birdList.

Chapter Summary

You should be able to write your own subclasses, given any superclass, and should be able to use the compareTo method to compare objects.

Be sure you can explain what polymorphism is: Recall that it only operates when methods have been overridden in at least one subclass. You should also be able to explain the difference between the following concepts:

- An abstract class and an interface.
- An overloaded method and an overridden method.
- Dynamic binding (late binding) and static binding (early binding).

MULTIPLE-CHOICE QUESTIONS ON INHERITANCE AND POLYMORPHISM

Questions 1–10 refer to the BankAccount, SavingsAccount, and CheckingAccount classes defined below:

```java
public class BankAccount
{
    private double myBalance;

    public BankAccount()
    { myBalance = 0; }

    public BankAccount(double balance)
    { myBalance = balance; }

    public void deposit(double amount)
    { myBalance += amount; }

    public void withdraw(double amount)
    { myBalance -= amount; }

    public double getBalance()
    { return myBalance; }
}

public class SavingsAccount extends BankAccount
{
    private double myInterestRate;

    public SavingsAccount()
    { /* implementation not shown */ }

    public SavingsAccount(double balance, double rate)
    { /* implementation not shown */ }

    public void addInterest()    //Add interest to balance
    { /* implementation not shown */ }
}

public class CheckingAccount extends BankAccount
{
    private static final double FEE = 2.0;
    private static final double MIN_BALANCE = 50.0;

    public CheckingAccount(double balance)
    { /* implementation not shown */ }

    /* FEE of $2 deducted if withdrawal leaves balance less
     * than MIN_BALANCE. Allows for negative balance. */
    public void withdraw(double amount)
    { /* implementation not shown */ }
}
```

1. Of the methods shown, how many different nonconstructor methods can be invoked by a `SavingsAccount` object?
   (A) 1
   (B) 2
   (C) 3
   (D) 4
   (E) 5

2. Which of the following correctly implements the default constructor of the `SavingsAccount` class?

   ```
    I myInterestRate = 0;
      super();
   ```

   ```
   II super();
      myInterestRate = 0;
   ```

   ```
   III super();
   ```

   (A) II only
   (B) I and II only
   (C) II and III only
   (D) III only
   (E) I, II, and III

3. Which is a correct implementation of the constructor with parameters in the `SavingsAccount` class?

   (A)
   ```
   myBalance = balance;
   myInterestRate = rate;
   ```

   (B)
   ```
   getBalance() =  balance;
   myInterestRate = rate;
   ```

   (C)
   ```
   super();
   myInterestRate = rate;
   ```

   (D)
   ```
   super(balance);
   myInterestRate = rate;
   ```

   (E)
   ```
   super(balance, rate);
   ```

4. Which is a correct implementation of the `CheckingAccount` constructor?

   ```
    I super(balance);
   ```

   ```
   II super();
      deposit(balance);
   ```

   ```
   III deposit(balance);
   ```

   (A) I only
   (B) II only
   (C) III only
   (D) II and III only
   (E) I, II, and III

5. Which is correct implementation code for the `withdraw` method in the `CheckingAccount` class?

   (A) ```
       super.withdraw(amount);
       if (myBalance < MIN_BALANCE)
           super.withdraw(FEE);
       ```

   (B) ```
       withdraw(amount);
       if (myBalance < MIN_BALANCE)
           withdraw(FEE);
       ```

   (C) ```
       super.withdraw(amount);
       if (getBalance() < MIN_BALANCE)
           super.withdraw(FEE);
       ```

   (D) ```
       withdraw(amount);
       if (getBalance() < MIN_BALANCE)
           withdraw(FEE);
       ```

   (E) ```
       myBalance -= amount;
       if (myBalance < MIN_BALANCE)
           myBalance -= FEE;
       ```

6. Redefining the `withdraw` method in the `CheckingAccount` class is an example of
   (A) method overloading.
   (B) method overriding.
   (C) downcasting.
   (D) dynamic binding (late binding).
   (E) static binding (early binding).

Use the following for Questions 7–9.
A program to test the `BankAccount`, `SavingsAccount`, and `CheckingAccount` classes has these declarations:

```
BankAccount b = new BankAccount(1400);
BankAccount s = new SavingsAccount(1000, 0.04);
BankAccount c = new CheckingAccount(500);
```

7. Which method call will cause an error?
   (A) `b.deposit(200);`
   (B) `s.withdraw(500);`
   (C) `c.withdraw(500);`
   (D) `s.deposit(10000);`
   (E) `s.addInterest();`

8. In order to test polymorphism, which method must be used in the program?
   (A) Either a `SavingsAccount` constructor or a `CheckingAccount` constructor
   (B) `addInterest`
   (C) `deposit`
   (D) `withdraw`
   (E) `getBalance`
```

9. Which of the following will *not* cause a `ClassCastException` to be thrown?
   (A) `((SavingsAccount) b).addInterest();`
   (B) `((CheckingAccount) b).withdraw(200);`
   (C) `((CheckingAccount) c).deposit(800);`
   (D) `((CheckingAccount) s).withdraw(150);`
   (E) `((SavingsAccount) c).addInterest();`

10. A new method is added to the `BankAccount` class.

```
/* Transfer amount from this BankAccount to another BankAccount.
 * Precondition: myBalance > amount */
public void transfer(BankAccount another, double amount)
{
    withdraw(amount);
    another.deposit(amount);
}
```

A program has these declarations:

```
BankAccount b = new BankAccount(650);
SavingsAccount timsSavings = new SavingsAccount(1500, 0.03);
CheckingAccount daynasChecking = new CheckingAccount(2000);
```

Which of the following will transfer money from one account to another without error?

I `b.transfer(timsSavings, 50);`

II `timsSavings.transfer(daynasChecking, 30);`

III `daynasChecking.transfer(b, 55);`

(A) I only
(B) II only
(C) III only
(D) I, II, and III
(E) None

11. Consider these class declarations:

```
public class Person
{
    ...
}

public class Teacher extends Person
{
    ...
}
```

Which is a true statement?

    I Teacher inherits the constructors of Person.

    II Teacher can add new methods and private instance variables.

  III Teacher can override existing private methods of Person.

(A) I only

(B) II only

(C) III only

(D) I and II only

(E) II and III only

12. Which statement about abstract classes and interfaces is *false*?

(A) An interface cannot implement any methods, whereas an abstract class can.

(B) A class can implement many interfaces but can have only one superclass.

(C) An unlimited number of unrelated classes can implement the same interface.

(D) It is not possible to construct either an abstract class object or an interface object.

(E) All of the methods in both an abstract class and an interface are public.

13. Consider the following hierarchy of classes:

A program is written to print data about various birds:

```
public class BirdStuff
{
    public static void printName(Bird b)
    { /* implementation not shown */ }

    public static void printBirdCall(Parrot p)
    { /* implementation not shown */ }

    //several more Bird methods

    public static void main(String[] args)
    {
        Bird bird1 = new Bird();
        Bird bird2 = new Parrot();
        Parrot parrot1 = new Parrot();
        Parrot parrot2 = new Parakeet();
        /* more code */
    }
}
```

Assuming that none of the given classes is abstract and all have default constructors, which of the following segments of /* *more code* */ will *not* cause an error?

(A) printName(parrot2);
     printBirdCall((Parrot) bird2);

(B) printName((Parrot) bird1);
     printBirdCall(bird2);

(C) printName(bird2);
     printBirdCall(bird2);

(D) printName((Parakeet) parrot1);
     printBirdCall(parrot2);

(E) printName((Owl) parrot2);
     printBirdCall((Parakeet) parrot2);

Refer to the classes below for Questions 14 and 15.

```
public class ClassA
{
    //default constructor not shown ...

    public void method1()
    { /* implementation of method1 */ }
}

public class ClassB extends ClassA
{
    //default constructor not shown ...

    public void method1()
    { /* different implementation from method1 in ClassA*/ }


    public void method2()
    { /* implementation of method2 */ }
}
```

14. The `method1` method in `ClassB` is an example of
     (A) method overloading.
     (B) method overriding.
     (C) polymorphism.
     (D) information hiding.
     (E) procedural abstraction.

15. Consider the following declarations in a client class.

```
ClassA ob1 = new ClassA();
ClassA ob2 = new ClassB();
```

     Which of the following method calls will cause an error?

     I `ob1.method2();`

     II `ob2.method2();`

     III `((ClassB) ob1).method2();`

     (A) I only
     (B) II only
     (C) III only
     (D) I and III only
     (E) I, II, and III

Use the declarations below for Questions 16–18.

```
public abstract class Solid
{
    private String myName;

    //constructor
    public Solid(String name)
    { myName = name; }

    public String getName()
    { return myName; }

    public abstract double volume();
}

public class Sphere extends Solid
{
    private double myRadius;

    //constructor
    public Sphere(String name, double radius)
    {
        super(name);
        myRadius = radius;
    }

    public double volume()
    { return (4.0/3.0) * Math.PI * myRadius * myRadius * myRadius; }
}

public class RectangularPrism extends Solid
{
    private double myLength;
    private double myWidth;
    private double myHeight;

    //constructor
    public RectangularPrism(String name, double l, double w,
            double h)
    {
        super(name);
        myLength = l;
        myWidth = w;
        myHeight = h;
    }

    public double volume()
    { return myLength * myWidth * myHeight; }
}
```

16. A program that tests these classes has the following declarations and assignments:

```
Solid s1, s2, s3, s4;
s1 = new Solid("blob");
s2 = new Sphere("sphere", 3.8);
s3 = new RectangularPrism("box", 2, 4, 6.5);
s4 = null;
```

How many of the above lines of code are incorrect?
(A) 1
(B) 2
(C) 3
(D) 4
(E) 5

17. Which is *false*?
(A) If a program has several objects declared as type `Solid`, the decision about which `volume` method to call will be resolved at run time.
(B) If the `Solid` class were modified to provide a default implementation for the `volume` method, it would no longer need to be an abstract class.
(C) If the `Sphere` and `RectangularPrism` classes failed to provide an implementation for the `volume` method, they would need to be declared as abstract classes.
(D) The fact that there is no reasonable default implementation for the `volume` method in the `Solid` class suggests that it should be an abstract method.
(E) Since `Solid` is abstract and its subclasses are nonabstract, polymorphism no longer applies when these classes are used in a program.

18. Here is a program that prints the volume of a solid:

```
public class SolidMain
{
    /* Output volume of Solid s. */
    public static void printVolume(Solid s)
    {
        System.out.println("Volume = " + s.volume() +
                " cubic units");
    }

    public static void main(String[] args)
    {
        Solid sol;
        Solid sph = new Sphere("sphere", 4);
        Solid rec = new RectangularPrism("box", 3, 6, 9);
        int flipCoin = (int) (Math.random() * 2);   //0 or 1
        if (flipCoin == 0)
            sol = sph;
        else
            sol = rec;
        printVolume(sol);
    }
}
```

Which is a true statement about this program?

(A) It will output the volume of the sphere or box, as intended.

(B) It will output the volume of the default `Solid` s, which is neither a sphere nor a box.

(C) A `ClassCastException` will be thrown.

(D) A compile-time error will occur because there is no implementation code for `volume` in the `Solid` class.

(E) A run-time error will occur because of parameter type mismatch in the method call `printVolume(sol)`.

19. Consider the `Computable` interface below for performing simple calculator operations:

```
public interface Computable
{
    //Return this Object + y.
    Object add(Object y);

    //Return this Object - y.
    Object subtract(Object y);

    //Return this Object * y.
    Object multiply(Object y);
}
```

Which of the following is the *least* suitable class for implementing `Computable`?

(A) `LargeInteger`   //integers with 100 digits or more

(B) `Fraction`   //implemented with numerator and
            //denominator of type int

(C) `IrrationalNumber` //nonrepeating, nonterminating decimal

(D) `Length`   //implemented with different units, such
            //as inches, centimeters, etc.

(E) `BankAccount`   //implemented with myBalance

Refer to the `Player` interface shown below for Questions 20–23.

```
public interface Player
{
    /* Return an integer that represents a move in a game. */
    int getMove();

    /* Display the status of the game for this Player after
     * implementing the next move. */
    void updateDisplay();
}
```

20. `HumanPlayer` is a class that implements the `Player` interface. Another class, `SmartPlayer`, is a subclass of `HumanPlayer`. Which statement is *false*?
    (A) `SmartPlayer` automatically implements the `Player` interface.
    (B) `HumanPlayer` must contain implementations of both the `updateDisplay` and `getMove` methods.
    (C) It is not possible to declare a reference of type `Player`.
    (D) The `SmartPlayer` class can override the methods `updateDisplay` and `getMove` of the `HumanPlayer` class.
    (E) A method in a client program can have `Player` as a parameter type.

21. A programmer plans to write programs that simulate various games. In each case he will have several classes, each representing a different kind of competitor in the game, such as ExpertPlayer, ComputerPlayer, RecklessPlayer, CheatingPlayer, Beginner, IntermediatePlayer, and so on. It may or may not be suitable for these classes to implement the Player interface, depending on the particular game being simulated. In the games described below, which is the *least* suitable for having the competitor classes implement the given Player interface?

   (A) High-Low Guessing Game: The computer thinks of a number and the competitor who guesses it with the least number of guesses wins. After each guess, the computer tells whether its number is higher or lower than the guess.

   (B) Chips: Start with a pile of chips. Each player in turn removes some number of chips. The winner is the one who removes the final chip. The first player may remove any number of chips, but not all of them. Each subsequent player must remove at least one chip and at most twice the number removed by the preceding player.

   (C) Chess: Played on a square board of 64 squares of alternating colors. There are just two players, called White and Black, the colors of their respective pieces. The players each have a set of pieces on the board that can move according to a set of rules. The players alternate moves, where a move consists of moving any one piece to another square. If that square is occupied by an opponent's piece, the piece is captured and removed from the board.

   (D) Tic-Tac-Toe: Two players alternate placing "X" or "O" on a 3 × 3 grid. The first player to get three in a row, where a row can be vertical, horizontal, or diagonal, wins.

   (E) Battleships: There are two players, each with a 10 × 10 grid hidden from his opponent. Various "ships" are placed on the grid. A move consists of calling out a grid location, trying to "hit" an opponent's ship. Players alternate moves. The first player to sink his opponent's fleet wins.

Consider these declarations for Questions 22 and 23:

```
public class HumanPlayer implements Player
{
    private String myName;

    //constructors not shown ...

    //code to implement getMove and updateDisplay not shown ...

    public String getName()
    { /* implementation not shown */ }
}

public class ExpertPlayer extends HumanPlayer implements Comparable
{
    private int myRating;

    //constructors not shown ...

    public int compareTo(Object obj)
    { /* implementation not shown */ }
}
```

22. Which code segment in a client program will cause an error?

    I   ```
        Player p1 = new HumanPlayer();
        Player p2 = new ExpertPlayer();
        int x1 = p1.getMove();
        int x2 = p2.getMove();
        ```

    II  ```
        int x;
        Comparable c1 = new ExpertPlayer(/* correct parameter list */);
        Comparable c2 = new ExpertPlayer(/* correct parameter list */);
        if (c1.compareTo(c2) < 0)
            x = c1.getMove();
        else
            x = c2.getMove();
        ```

    III ```
        int x;
        HumanPlayer h1 = new HumanPlayer(/* correct parameter list */);
        HumanPlayer h2 = new HumanPlayer(/* correct parameter list */);
        if (h1.compareTo(h2) < 0)
            x = h1.getMove();
        else
            x = h2.getMove();
        ```

    (A) II only
    (B) III only
    (C) II and III only
    (D) I, II, and III
    (E) None
        ```

23. Which of the following is correct implementation code for the compareTo method in the ExpertPlayer class?

```
  I ExpertPlayer rhs = (ExpertPlayer) obj;
    if (myRating == rhs.myRating)
        return 0;
    else if (myRating < rhs.myRating)
        return -1;
    else
        return 1;

 II ExpertPlayer rhs = (ExpertPlayer) obj;
    return myRating - rhs.myRating;

III ExpertPlayer rhs = (ExpertPlayer) obj;
    if (getName().equals(rhs.getName()))
        return 0;
    else if (getName().compareTo(rhs.getName()) < 0)
        return -1;
    else
        return 1;
```

(A) I only
(B) II only
(C) III only
(D) I and II only
(E) I, II, and III

24. Which statement about interfaces is true?

   I An interface contains only public abstract methods and public static final fields.
   II If a class implements an interface and then fails to implement any methods in that interface, then the class *must* be declared abstract.
   III While a class may implement just one interface, it may extend more than one class.

(A) I only
(B) I and II only
(C) I and III only
(D) II and III only
(E) I, II, and III

25. Which of the following classes is the least suitable candidate for implementing the Comparable interface?

    (A) ```
        public class Point
        {
                private double x;
                private double y;

                //various methods follow
                    ...
        }
        ```

    (B) ```
        public class Name
        {
                private String firstName;
                private String lastName;

                //various methods follow
                    ...
        }
        ```

    (C) ```
        public class Car
        {
                private int modelNumber;
                private int year;
                private double price;

                //various methods follow
                    ...
        }
        ```

    (D) ```
        public class Student
        {
                private String name;
                private double gpa;

                //various methods follow
                    ...
        }
        ```

    (E) ```
        public class Employee
        {
                private String name;
                private int hireDate;
                private double salary;

                //various methods follow
                    ...
        }
        ```
        ```

26. A programmer has the task of maintaining a database of students of a large university. There are two types of students, undergraduates and graduate students. About a third of the graduate students are doctoral candidates.

   All of the students have the same personal information stored, like name, address, and phone number, and also student information like courses taken and grades. Each student's GPA is computed, but differently for undergraduates and graduates. The doctoral candidates have information about their dissertations and faculty advisors.

   The programmer will write a Java program to handle all the student information. Which of the following is the best design, in terms of programmer efficiency and code reusability? Note: { ... } denotes class code.

   (A)
```
public interface Student { ...}
public class Undergraduate implements Student { ... }
public class Graduate implements Student { ... }
public class DocStudent extends Graduate { ... }
```

   (B)
```
public abstract class Student { ...}
public class Undergraduate extends Student { ... }
public class Graduate extends Student { ... }
public class DocStudent extends Graduate { ... }
```

   (C)
```
public class Student { ...}
public class Undergraduate extends Student { ... }
public class Graduate extends Student { ... }
public class DocStudent extends Graduate { ... }
```

   (D)
```
public abstract class Student { ...}
public class Undergraduate extends Student { ... }
public class Graduate extends Student { ... }
public class DocStudent extends Student { ... }
```

   (E)
```
public interface PersonalInformation { ... }
public class Student implements PersonalInformation { ...}
public class Undergraduate extends Student { ... }
public abstract class Graduate extends Student { ... }
public class DocStudent extends Graduate { ... }
```

27. A certain interface provided by a Java package contains just a single method:

```
public interface SomeName
{
    int method1(Object o);
}
```

A programmer adds some functionality to this interface by adding another method to it, method2:

```
public interface SomeName
{
    int method1(Object ob1);
    void method2(Object ob2);
}
```

As a result of this addition, which of the following is true?

(A) A ClassCastException will occur if ob1 and ob2 are not compatible.

(B) All classes that implement the original SomeName interface will need to be rewritten because they no longer implement SomeName.

(C) A class that implements the original SomeName interface will need to modify its declaration as follows:

```
public class ClassName implements SomeName extends method2
{    ...
```

(D) SomeName will need to be changed to an abstract class and provide implementation code for method2, so that the original and upgraded versions of SomeName are compatible.

(E) Any new class that implements the upgraded version of SomeName will not compile.

28. Consider the Temperature class defined below:

```
public class Temperature implements Comparable
{
    private String myScale;
    private double myDegrees;

    //default constructor
    public Temperature ()
    { /* implementation not shown */ }

    //constructor
    public Temperature(String scale, double degrees)
    { /* implementation not shown */ }

    public int compareTo(Object obj)
    { /* implementation not shown */ }

    public String toString()
    { /* implementation not shown */ }
}
```

Here is a program that finds the lowest of three temperatures:

```
public class TemperatureMain
{
    /* Find smaller of objects a and b. */
    public static Comparable min(Comparable a, Comparable b)
    {
        if (a.compareTo(b) < 0)
            return a;
        else
            return b;
    }

    /* Find smallest of objects a, b, and c */
    public static Comparable minThree(Comparable a,
            Comparable b, Comparable c)
    {
        return min(min(a, b), c);
    }

    public static void main(String[] args)
    {
        /* code to test minThree method */
    }
}
```

Which are correct replacements for /* *code to test* minThree *method* */?

```
 I Temperature t1 = new Temperature("C", 85);
   Temperature t2 = new Temperature("F", 45);
   Temperature t3 = new Temperature("F", 120);
   System.out.println("The lowest temperature is " +
           minThree(t1, t2, t3));

II Comparable c1 = new Temperature("C", 85);
   Comparable c2 = new Temperature("F", 45);
   Comparable c3 = new Temperature("F", 120);
   System.out.println("The lowest temperature is " +
           minThree(c1, c2, c3));

III Comparable c1 = new Comparable("C", 85);
    Comparable c2 = new Comparable("F", 45);
    Comparable c3 = new Comparable("F", 120);
    System.out.println("The lowest temperature is " +
            minThree(c1, c2, c3));
```

(A) II only
(B) I and II only
(C) II and III only
(D) I and III only
(E) I, II, and III

ANSWER KEY

1. D	11. E	21. C
2. C	12. E	22. C
3. D	13. A	23. E
4. E	14. B	24. B
5. C	15. E	25. A
6. B	16. A	26. B
7. E	17. E	27. B
8. D	18. A	28. B
9. C	19. E	
10. D	20. C	

ANSWERS EXPLAINED

1. **(D)** The methods are `deposit`, `withdraw`, and `getBalance`, all inherited from the `BankAccount` class, plus `addInterest`, which was defined just for the class `SavingsAccount`.

2. **(C)** Implementation I fails because `super()` *must* be the first line of the implementation whenever it is used in a constructor. Implementation III may appear to be incorrect because it doesn't initialize `myInterestRate`. Since `myInterestRate`, however, is a primitive type—`double`—the compiler will provide a default initialization of `0`, which was required.

3. **(D)** First, the statement `super(balance)` initializes the inherited private variable `myBalance` as for the `BankAccount` superclass. Then the statement `myInterestRate = rate` initializes `myInterestRate`, which belongs uniquely to the `SavingsAccount` class. Choice E fails because `myInterestRate` does not belong to the `BankAccount` class and therefore cannot be initialized by a `super` method. Choice A is wrong because the `SavingsAccount` class cannot directly access the private instance variables of its superclass. Choice B assigns a value to an accessor method, which is meaningless. Choice C is incorrect because `super()` invokes the *default* constructor of the superclass. This will cause `myBalance` of the `SavingsAccount` object to be initialized to `0`, rather than `balance`, the parameter value.

4. **(E)** The constructor must initialize the inherited instance variable `myBalance` to the value of the `balance` parameter. All three segments achieve this. Implementation I does it by invoking `super(balance)`, the constructor in the superclass. Implementation II first initializes `myBalance` to `0` by invoking the *default* constructor of the superclass. Then it calls the inherited `deposit` method of the superclass to add `balance` to the account. Implementation III works because `super()` is automatically called as the first line of the constructor code if there is no explicit call to `super`.

5. **(C)** First the withdraw method of the BankAccount superclass is used to withdraw amount. A prefix of super must be used to invoke this method, which eliminates choices B and D. Then the balance must be tested using the accessor method getBalance, which is inherited. You can't test myBalance directly since it is private to the BankAccount class. This eliminates choices A and E, and provides another reason for eliminating choice B.

6. **(B)** When a superclass method is redefined in a subclass, the process is called *method overriding*. Which method to call is determined at run time. This is called *dynamic binding* (p. 135). *Method overloading* is two or more methods with different signatures in the same class (p. 96). The compiler recognizes at compile time which method to call. This is *early binding*. The process of *downcasting* is unrelated to these principles (p. 136).

7. **(E)** The addInterest method is defined only in the SavingsAccount class. It therefore cannot be invoked by a BankAccount object. The error can be fixed by casting s to the correct type:

```
((SavingsAccount) s).addInterest();
```

The other method calls do not cause a problem because withdraw and deposit are both methods of the BankAccount class.

8. **(D)** The withdraw method is the only method that has one implementation in the superclass and a *different* implementation in a subclass. Polymorphism is the mechanism of selecting the correct method from the different possibilities in the class hierarchy. Notice that the deposit method, for example, is available to objects of all three bank account classes, but it's the *same* code in all three cases. So polymorphism isn't tested.

9. **(C)** You will get a ClassCastException whenever you try to cast an object to a class of which it is not an instance. Choice C is the only statement that doesn't attempt to do this. Look at the other choices: In choice A, b is not an instance of SavingsAccount. In choice B, b is not an instance of CheckingAccount. In choice D, s is not an instance of CheckingAccount. In choice E, c is not an instance of SavingsAccount.

10. **(D)** It is OK to use timsSavings and daynasChecking as parameters since each of these *is-a* BankAccount object. It is also OK for timsSavings and daynasChecking to call the transfer method (statements II and III), since they inherit this method from the BankAccount superclass.

11. **(E)** Statement I is false: A subclass must specify its own constructors. Otherwise the default constructor of the superclass will automatically be invoked. Note that statement III is true: It is OK to override private instance methods—they can even be declared public in the subclass implementation. What is *not* OK is to make the access more restrictive, for example, to override a public method and declare it private.

12. **(E)** All of the methods in an interface are by default public (the public keyword isn't needed). An abstract class can have both private and public methods.

13. **(A)** There are two quick tests you can do to find the answer to this question:

   (1) Test the *is-a* relationship, namely the parameter for printName *is-a* Bird? and the parameter for printBirdCall *is-a* Parrot?
   (2) A reference cannot be cast to something it's not an instance of.

Choice A passes both of these tests: `parrot2` *is-a* `Bird`, and `(Parrot) bird2` *is-a* `Parrot`. Also `bird2` is an instance of a `Parrot` (as you can see by looking at the right-hand side of the assignment), so the casting is correct. In choice B `printBirdCall(bird2)` is wrong because `bird2` *is-a* `Bird` and the `printBirdCall` method is expecting a `Parrot`. Therefore `bird2` must be downcast to a `Parrot`. Also, the method call `printName((Parrot) bird1)` fails because `bird1` is an instance of a `Bird` and therefore cannot be cast to a `Parrot`. In choice C, `printName(bird2)` is correct: `bird2` *is-a* `Bird`. However, `printBirdCall(bird2)` fails as already discussed. In choice D, `(Parakeet) parrot1` is an incorrect cast: `parrot1` is an instance of a `Parrot`. Note that `printBirdCall(parrot2)` is OK since `parrot2` *is-a* `Parrot`. In choice E, `(Owl) parrot2` is an incorrect cast: `parrot2` is an instance of `Parakeet`. Note that `printBirdCall((Parakeet) parrot2)` is correct: A `Parakeet` *is-a* `Parrot`, and `parrot2` is an instance of a `Parakeet`.

14. **(B)** Method overriding occurs whenever a method in a superclass is redefined in a subclass. Method overloading is a method in the same class that has the same name but different parameter types. Polymorphism is when the correct overridden method is called for a particular subclass object during run time. Information hiding is the use of `private` to restrict access. Procedural abstraction is the use of helper methods.

15. **(E)** All will cause an error!
I: An object of a superclass does not have access to a new method of its subclass.
II: `ob2` is declared to be of type `ClassA`, so a compile-time error will occur with a message indicating that there is no `method2` in `ClassA`. Casting `ob2` to `ClassB` would correct the problem.
III: A `ClassCastException` will be thrown, since `ob1` is of type `ClassA`, and therefore cannot be cast to `ClassB`.

16. **(A)** The only incorrect line is `s1 = new Solid("blob")`: You can't create an instance of an abstract class. Abstract class references can, however, refer to objects of concrete (nonabstract) subclasses. Thus, the assignments for `s2` and `s3` are OK. Note that an abstract class reference can also be null, so the final assignment, though redundant, is correct.

17. **(E)** The point of having an abstract method is to postpone until run time the decision about which subclass version to call. This is what polymorphism is—calling the appropriate method at run time based on the type of the object.

18. **(A)** This is an example of polymorphism: The correct `volume` method is selected at run time. The parameter expected for `printVolume` is a `Solid` reference, which is what it gets in `main()`. The reference `sol` will refer either to a `Sphere` or a `RectangularPrism` object depending on the outcome of the coin flip. Since a `Sphere` is a `Solid` and a `RectangularPrism` is a `Solid`, there will be no type mismatch when these are the actual parameters in the `printVolume` method. (Note: The `Math.random` method is discussed in Chapter 4.)

19. **(E)** Each of choices A though D represent `Computable` objects: It makes sense to add, subtract, or multiply two large integers, two fractions, two irrational numbers, and two lengths. (One can multiply lengths to get an area, for example.) While it may make sense under certain circumstances to add or subtract two bank accounts, it does not make sense to multiply them!

20. **(C)** You can *declare a reference* of type `Player`. What you cannot do is *construct*

an object of type `Player`. The following declarations are therefore legal:
```
SmartPlayer s = new SmartPlayer();
Player p1 = s;
Player p2 = new HumanPlayer();
```

21. **(C)** Remember, to implement the `Player` interface a class must provide implementations for `getMove` and `updateDisplay`. The `updateDisplay` method is suitable for all five games described. The `getMove` method returns a single integer, which works well for the High-Low game of choice A and the Chips game of choice B. In Tic-Tac-Toe (choice D) and Battleships (choice E) a move consists of giving a grid location. This can be provided by a single integer if the grid locations are numbered in a unique way. It's not ideal, but certainly doable. In the Chess game, however, a move cannot be described by a single integer. The player needs to specify both the grid location he is moving the piece to *and* which piece he is moving. The `getMove` method would need to be altered in a way that changes its return type. This makes the `Player` interface unsuitable.

22. **(C)** Segment II has an error in the `getMove` calls. References `c1` and `c2` are of type `Comparable`, which doesn't contain a `getMove` method. To correct these statements a cast is necessary:
```
x = ((ExpertPlayer) c1).getMove();
```
and similarly for the `c2` call. Note that `c1.compareTo(c2)` is fine, since `Comparable` does contain the `compareTo` method and `ExpertPlayer` implements `Comparable`. Segment III fails because `HumanPlayer` does not implement `Comparable` and therefore does not have a `compareTo` method. Note that in segment I the `getMove` calls are fine and require no downcasting, since `p1` and `p2` are of type `Player` and `Player` has the `getMove` method.

23. **(E)** All implementations are correct. This is *not* a question about whether it is better to compare `ExpertPlayers` based on their ratings or their names! One might need an alphabetized list of players, or one might need a list according to ranking. In practice, the program specification will instruct the programmer which to use. Note that segment II is correct because `compareTo` doesn't need to return 1 or −1. Any positive or negative integer is OK. Note also that in segments I and II it is OK to use `rhs.myRating`, since `rhs` is of type `ExpertPlayer`, the current class being written. Normally, a parameter of some class type cannot access the private instance variables of another class.

24. **(B)** Statement III would be correct if it read as follows: While a class may extend just one class, it may implement more than one interface.

25. **(A)** There is no good way to write a `compareTo` method for a `Point` class. Two points (x_1, y_1) and (x_2, y_2) are equal if and only if $x_1 = x_2$ and $y_1 = y_2$. But if points P_1 and P_2 are not equal, what will determine if $P_1 < P_2$ or $P_1 > P_2$? You could try using the distance from the origin. Define $P_1 > P_2$ if and only if $OP_1 > OP_2$, and $P_1 < P_2$ if and only if $OP_1 < OP_2$, where O is $(0,0)$. This definition means that points (a, b) and (b, a) are equal, which violates the definition of equals! The problem is that there is no way to map the two-dimensional set of points to a one-dimensional distance function and still be consistent with the definition of equals. The objects in each of the other classes can be compared without a problem. In choice B, two `Name` objects can be ordered alphabetically. In choice C, two `Car` objects can be ordered by year or by price. In choice D, two `Student` objects can be ordered by name or GPA. In choice E, two `Employee` objects can be ordered by name or seniority (date of hire).

26. **(B)** Here is the hierarchy of classes:

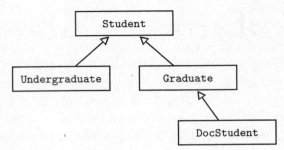

Eliminate choice D which fails to make `DocStudent` a subclass of `Graduate`. This is a poor design choice since a `DocStudent` *is-a* `Graduate`. Making `Student` an abstract class is desirable since the methods that are common to all students can go in there with implementations provided. The method to calculate the GPA, which differs among student types, will be declared in `Student` as an abstract method. Then unique implementations will be provided in both the `Graduate` and `Undergraduate` classes. Choice A is a poor design because making `Student` an interface means that all of its methods will need to be implemented in both the `Undergraduate` and `Graduate` classes. Many of these methods will have the same implementations. As far as possible, you want to arrange for classes to inherit common methods and to avoid repeated code. Choice C is slightly inferior to choice B because you are told that all students are either graduates or undergraduates. Having the `Student` class abstract guarantees that you won't create an instance of a `Student` (who is neither a graduate nor an undergraduate). Choice E has a major design flaw: making `Graduate` an abstract class means that you can't create any instances of `Graduate` objects. Disaster! If the keyword `abstract` is removed from choice E, it becomes a fine design, as good as that in choice B. Once `Student` has implemented all the common `PersonalInformation` methods, these are inherited by each of the subclasses.

27. **(B)** Classes that implement an interface must provide implementation code for all methods in the interface. Adding `method2` to the `SomeName` interface means that all of those classes need to be rewritten with implementation code for `method2`. (This is not good—it violates the sacred principle of code reusability, and programmers relying on the interface will squeal.) Choices A, C, and D are all meaningless garbage. Choice E *may* be true if there is some other error in the new class. Otherwise, as long as the new class provides implementation code for both `method1` and `method2`, the class will compile.

28. **(B)** Segment III is wrong because you can't construct an interface object. (Remember, `Comparable` is an interface!) Segments I and II both work because the `minThree` method is expecting three parameters, each of which is a `Comparable`. Since `Temperature` implements `Comparable`, each of the `Temperature` objects is a `Comparable` and can be used as a parameter in this method. Note that the program assumes that the `compareTo` method is able to compare `Temperature` objects with different scales. This is an internal detail that would be dealt with in the `compareTo` method, and hidden from the client. When a class implements `Comparable` there is always an assumption that the `compareTo` method will be implemented in a reasonable way.

Some Standard Classes

*Anyone who considers arithmetical methods of producing
random digits is, of course, in a state of sin.*
—*John von Neumann (1951)*

Chapter Goals

- The `Object` class
- The `String` class
- Wrapper classes
- The `Math` class
- Random numbers

THE `Object` CLASS

The Universal Superclass

Think of `Object` as the superclass of the universe. Every class automatically extends
`Object`, which means that `Object` is a direct or indirect superclass of every other class.
In a class hierarchy tree, `Object` is at the top:

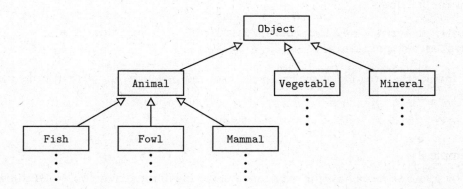

Methods in `Object`

There are many methods in `Object`, all of them inherited by every other class. Since
`Object` is not an abstract class, all of its methods have implementations. The expectation is that these methods will be overridden in any class where the default implementation is not suitable. The required methods in the AP Java subset are `toString` and
`equals`.

THE toString METHOD

`public String toString()`

This method returns a version of your object in `String` form.

When you attempt to print an object, the inherited default `toString` method is invoked, and what you will see is the class name followed by an @ followed by a meaningless number (the address in memory of the object). For example,

```
SavingsAccount s = new SavingsAccount(500);
System.out.println(s);
```

produces something like

```
SavingsAccount@fea485c4
```

To have more meaningful output, you need to override the `toString` method for your own classes. Even if your final program doesn't need to output any objects, you should define a `toString` method for each class to help in debugging.

Example 1

```
public class OrderedPair
{
    private double x;
    private double y;

    //constructors and other methods ...

    /* Returns this OrderedPair in String form. */
    public String toString()
    {
        return "(" + x + "," + y + ")";
    }
}
```

Now the statements

```
OrderedPair p = new OrderedPair(7,10);
System.out.println(p);
```

will invoke the overridden `toString` method and produce output that looks like an ordered pair:

```
(7,10)
```

Example 2

For a `BankAccount` class the overridden `toString` method may look something like this:

```
/* Returns this  BankAccount in String form. */
public String toString()
{
    return "Bank Account: balance = $" + myBalance;
}
```

The statements

```
BankAccount b = new BankAccount(600);
System.out.println(b);
```

will produce output that looks like this:

```
Bank Account: balance = $600
```

NOTE

1. The + sign is a concatenation operator for strings (see p. 175).
2. Array objects are unusual in that they do not have a toString method. To print the elements of an array, the array must be traversed and each element must explicitly be printed.

THE equals METHOD

```
public boolean equals(Object other)
```

All classes inherit this method from the Object class. It returns true if this object and other are the same object, false otherwise. Being the same object means referencing the same memory slot. For example,

```
Date d1 = new Date("January", 14, 2001);
Date d2 = d1;
Date d3 = new Date("January", 14, 2001);
```

The test if (d1.equals(d2)) returns true, but the test if (d1.equals(d3)) returns false, since d1 and d3 do not refer to the same object. Often, as in this example, you may want two objects to be considered equal if their *contents* are the same. In that case, you have to override the equals method in your class to achieve this. Some of the standard classes described later in this chapter have overridden equals in this way. You will not be required to write code that overrides equals on the AP exam.

Do not use == to test objects for equality. Use the equals method.

NOTE

1. The default implementation of equals is equivalent to the == relation for objects: In the Date example above, the test if (d1 == d2) returns true; the test if (d1 == d3) returns false.
2. The operators <, >, and so on, are not overloaded in Java. To compare objects, one must use either the equals method or the compareTo method if the class implements the Comparable interface (see p. 141).

THE hashCode METHOD

Optional topic

Every class inherits the hashCode method from Object. The value returned by hashCode is an integer produced by some formula that maps your object to an address in a hash table. A given object must always produce the same hash code. Also, two objects that are equal should produce the same hash code; that is, if obj1.equals(obj2) is true, then obj1 and obj2 should have the same hash code. Note that the opposite is not necessarily true. Hash codes do not have to be unique—two objects with the same hash code are not necessarily equal.

To maintain the condition that obj1.equals(obj2) is true implies that obj1 and obj2 have the same hash code, overriding equals means that you should override hashCode at the same time. You will not be required to do this on the AP exam.

(continued)

You should, however, understand that every object is associated with an integer value called its hash code, and that objects that are equal have the same hash code.

THE `String` CLASS

`String` Objects

An object of type `String` is a sequence of characters. All *string literals*, such as `"yikes!"`, are implemented as instances of this class. A string literal consists of zero or more characters, including escape sequences, surrounded by double quotes. (The quotes are not part of the `String` object.) Thus, each of the following is a valid string literal:

```
""               //empty string
"2468"
"I must\n go home"
```

`String` objects are *immutable*, which means that there are no methods to change them after they've been constructed. You can, however, always create a new `String` that is a mutated form of an existing `String`.

Constructing `String` Objects

A `String` object is unusual in that it can be initialized like a primitive type:

```
String s = "abc";
```

This is equivalent to

```
String s = new String("abc");
```

in the sense that in both cases s is a reference to a `String` object with contents `"abc"` (see Box on p. 176).

It is possible to reassign a `String` reference:

```
String s = "John";
s = "Harry";
```

This is equivalent to

```
String s = new String("John");
s = new String("Harry");
```

Notice that this is consistent with the immutable feature of `String` objects. `"John"` has not been changed; he has merely been discarded! The fickle reference s now refers to a new `String`, `"Harry"`. It is also OK to reassign s as follows:

```
s = s + " Windsor";
```

s now refers to the object `"Harry Windsor"`.

Here are other ways to initialize `String` objects:

```
String s1 = null;         //s1 is a null reference
String s2 = new String();   //s2 is an empty character sequence

String state = "Alaska";
String dessert = "baked " + state;  //dessert has value "baked Alaska"
```

The Concatenation Operator

The dessert declaration above uses the *concatenation operator*, +, which operates on String objects. Given two String operands lhs and rhs, lhs + rhs produces a single String consisting of lhs followed by rhs. If either lhs or rhs is an object other than a String, the toString method of the object is invoked, and lhs and rhs are concatenated as before. If one of the operands is a String and the other is a primitive type, then the non-String operand is converted to a String, and concatenation occurs as before. If neither lhs nor rhs is a String object, an error occurs. Here are some examples:

```
int five = 5;
String state = "Hawaii-";
String tvShow = state + five + "-0";  //tvShow has value
                                      //"Hawaii-5-0"
int x = 3, y = 4;
String sum = x + y;          //error: can't assign int 7 to String
```

Suppose a Date class has a toString method that outputs dates that look like this: 2/17/1948.

```
Date d1 = new Date(8, 2, 1947);
Date d2 = new Date(2, 17, 1948);
String s = "My birthday is " + d2;  //s has value
                                    //"My birthday is 2/17/1948"
String s2 = d1 + d2;    //error: + not defined for objects
String s3 = d1.toString() + d2.toString();  //s3 has value
                                            //8/2/19472/17/1948
```

Comparison of String Objects

There are two ways to compare String objects:

1. Use the equals method that is inherited from the Object class and overridden to do the correct thing:

   ```
   if (string1.equals(string2)) ...
   ```

   This returns true if string1 and string2 are identical strings, false otherwise.

2. Use the compareTo method. The String class implements Comparable, which means that the compareTo method is provided in String. This method compares strings in dictionary (lexicographical) order:

   - If string1.compareTo(string2) < 0, then string1 precedes string2 in the dictionary.
   - If string1.compareTo(string2) > 0, then string1 follows string2 in the dictionary.
   - If string1.compareTo(string2) == 0, then string1 and string2 are identical. (This test is an alternative to string1.equals(string2).)

Be aware that Java is case-sensitive. Thus, if s1 is "cat" and s2 is "Cat", s1.equals(s2) will return false.

Characters are compared according to their position in the ASCII chart. All you need to know is that all digits precede all capital letters, which precede all lowercase letters. Thus "5" comes before "R", which comes before "a". Two strings are compared as follows: Start at the left end of each string and do a character-by-character comparison until you reach the first character in which the strings differ, the kth character, say. If the kth character of s1 comes before the kth character of s2, then s1 will come before s2, and vice versa. If the strings have identical characters, except that s1 terminates before s2, then s1 comes before s2. Here are some examples:

```
String s1 = "HOT", s2 = "HOTEL", s3 = "dog";
if (s1.compareTo(s2) < 0))      //true, s1 terminates first
    ...
if (s1.compareTo(s3) > 0))      //false, "H" comes before "d"
```

Don't Use == to Test Strings!

The expression `if(string1 == string2)` tests whether `string1` and `string2` are the same reference. It does not test the actual strings. Using `==` to compare strings may lead to unexpected results.

Example 1

```
String s = "oh no!";
String t = "oh no!";
if (s == t) ...
```

The test returns `true` even though it appears that s and t are different references. The reason is that for efficiency Java makes only one `String` object for equivalent string literals. This is safe in that a `String` cannot be altered.

Example 2

```
String s = "oh no!";
String t = new String("oh no!");
if (s == t) ...
```

The test returns `false` because use of `new` creates a new object, and s and t *are* different references in this example!

The moral of the story? Use `equals` not `==` to test strings. It always does the right thing.

Other String Methods

The Java `String` class provides many methods, only a small number of which are in the AP Java subset. In addition to the constructors, comparison methods, and concatenation operator + discussed so far, you should know the following methods:

```
int length()
```

Returns the length of this string.

```
String substring(int startIndex)
```

Returns a new string that is a substring of this string. The substring starts with the character at startIndex and extends to the end of the string. The first character is at index zero. The method throws a StringIndexOutOfBoundsException if startIndex is negative or larger than the length of the string.

```
String substring(int startIndex, int endIndex)
```

Returns a new string that is a substring of this string. The substring starts at index startIndex and extends to the character at endIndex-1. (Think of it this way: startIndex is the first character that you want; endIndex is the first character that you *don't* want.) The method throws a StringIndexOutOfBoundsException if startIndex is negative, or endIndex is larger than the length of the string, or startIndex is larger than endIndex.

```
int indexOf(String str)
```

Returns the index of the first occurrence of str within this string. If str is not a substring of this string, -1 is returned. The method throws a NullPointerException if str is null.

Here are some examples:

```
"unhappy".substring(2)        //returns "happy"
"cold".substring(4)           //returns "" (empty string)
"cold".substring(5)           //StringIndexOutOfBoundsException
"strawberry".substring(5,7)   //returns "be"
"crayfish".substring(4,8)     //returns "fish"
"crayfish".substring(4,9)     //StringIndexOutOfBoundsException
"crayfish".substring(5,4)     //StringIndexOutOfBoundsException

String s = "funnyfarm";
int x = s.indexOf("farm");    //x has value 5
x = s.indexOf("farmer");      //x has value -1
int y = s.length();           //y has value 9
```

WRAPPER CLASSES

A *wrapper class* takes either an existing object or a value of primitive type, "wraps" or "boxes" it in an object, and provides a new set of methods for that type. The point of a wrapper class is to provide extended capabilities for the boxed quantity:

- It can be used in generic Java methods that require objects as parameters.
- It can be used in Java container classes that require the items be objects (see p. 239).

In each case, the wrapper class allows

1. Construction of an object from a single value (wrapping or boxing the primitive in a wrapper object).
2. Retrieval of the primitive value (unwrapping or unboxing from the wrapper object).

Java provides a wrapper class for each of its primitive types. The two that you should know for the AP exam are the `Integer` and `Double` classes.

The Integer Class

The `Integer` class wraps a value of type `int` in an object. An object of type `Integer` contains just one instance variable whose type is `int`.

Here are the `Integer` methods you should know for the AP exam:

```
Integer(int value)
```

Constructs an `Integer` object from an `int`. (Boxing.)

```
int compareTo(Object other)
```

If `other` is an `Integer`, `compareTo` returns 0 if the value of this `Integer` is equal to the value of `other`, a negative integer if it is less than the value of `other`, and a positive integer if it is greater than the value of `other`.

NOTE

1. The `Integer` class implements `Comparable`.
2. The `compareTo` method throws a `ClassCastException` if the argument `other` is not an `Integer`.

```
int intValue()
```

Returns the value of this `Integer` as an `int`. (Unboxing.)

```
boolean equals(Object obj)
```

Returns `true` if and only if this `Integer` has the same `int` value as `obj`.

NOTE

1. This method overrides `equals` in class `Object`.
2. This method throws a `ClassCastException` if `obj` is not an `Integer`.

```
String toString()
```

Returns a `String` representing the value of this `Integer`.

Here are some examples to illustrate the `Integer` methods:

```
Integer intObj = new Integer(6);  //boxes 6 in Integer object
int j = intObj.intValue();        //unboxes 6 from Integer object

System.out.println("Integer value is " + intObj);
//calls toString() for intObj
//output is
//Integer value is 6
```

```
Object object = new Integer(5);    //Integer is a subclass of Object

Integer intObj2 = new Integer(3);
int k = intObj2.intValue();
if (intObj.equals(intObj2))        //OK, evaluates to false
   ...
if (intObj.intValue() == intObj2.intValue())
   ...                 //OK, since comparing primitive types

if (k.equals(j))       //error, k and j not objects
   ...
if ((intObj.intValue()).compareTo(intObj2.intValue()) < 0)
   ...                 //error, can't use compareTo on primitive types

if (intObj.compareTo(object) < 0)  //OK
   ...
if (object.compareTo(intObj) < 0)  //error, no compareTo in Object
   ...
if (((Integer) object).compareTo(intObj) < 0)  //OK
   ...
```

The Double Class

The Double class wraps a value of type double in an object. An object of type Double contains just one instance variable whose type is double.

The methods you should know for the AP exam are analogous to those for type Integer.

`Double(double value)`

Constructs a Double object from a double. (Boxing.)

`double doubleValue()`

Returns the value of this Double as a double. (Unboxing.)

`int compareTo(Object other)`

The Double class implements Comparable. If the argument other is not a Double, the compareTo method will throw a ClassCastException. If other is a Double, compareTo returns 0 if the value of this Double is equal to the value of other, a negative integer if it is less than the value of other, and a positive integer if it is greater than the value of other.

`boolean equals(Object obj)`

This method overrides equals in class Object and throws a ClassCastException if obj is not a Double. Otherwise it returns true if and only if this Double has the same double value as obj.

`String toString()`

Returns a String representing the value of this Double.

Remember:
`Integer`, `Double`, and `String` are all `Comparable`.

Here are some examples:

```
Double dObj = new Double(2.5);        //boxes 2.5 in Double object
double d = dObj.doubleValue();        //unboxes 2.5 from Double object

Object object = new Double(7.3);      //Double is a subclass of Object
Object intObj = new Integer(4);
if (dObj.compareTo(object) > 0)       //OK
    ...
if (dObj.compareTo(intObj) > 0)       //ClassCastException
    ...                               //can't compare Integer to Double
```

NOTE

1. `Integer` and `Double` objects are immutable: There are no mutator methods in the classes.
2. See p. 239 for a discussion of auto-boxing and -unboxing. This is a new feature in Java 5.0 that is very useful and convenient. It will *not*, however, be tested on the AP exam.

THE `Math` CLASS

This class implements standard mathematical functions such as absolute value, square root, trigonometric functions, the log function, the power function, and so on. It also contains mathematical constants such as π and e.

Here are the functions you should know for the AP exam:

`static int abs(int x)`

Returns the absolute value of integer x.

`static double abs(double x)`

Returns the absolute value of real number x.

`static double pow(double base, double exp)`

Returns base^{exp}. Assumes base > 0, or base $= 0$ and exp > 0, or base < 0 and exp is an integer.

`static double sqrt(double x)`

Returns $\sqrt{x}$, $x \geq 0$.

`static double random()`

Returns a random number r, where $0.0 \leq r < 1.0$. (See the next section, Random Numbers.)

All of the functions and constants are implemented as static methods and variables, which means that there are no instances of `Math` objects. The methods are invoked using the class name, `Math`, followed by the dot operator.

Here are some examples of mathematical formulas and the equivalent Java statements.

1. The relationship between the radius and area of a circle:

$$r = \sqrt{A/\pi}$$

In code:

```
radius = Math.sqrt(area / Math.PI);
```

2. The amount of money A in an account after ten years, given an original deposit of P and an interest rate of 5% compounded annually, is

$$A = P(1.05)^{10}$$

In code:

```
a = p * Math.pow(1.05, 10);
```

3. The distance D between two points $P(x_P, y)$ and $Q(x_Q, y)$ on the same horizontal line is

$$D = |x_P - x_Q|$$

In code:

```
d = Math.abs(xp - xq);
```

NOTE

A new feature of Java 5.0, the static import construct, allows you to use the static members of a class without the class name prefix. For example, the statement

```
import static java.lang.Math.*;
```

allows use of all `Math` methods and constants without the `Math` prefix. Thus, the statement in formula 1 above could be written

```
radius = sqrt(area / PI);
```

Static imports are not part of the AP subset.

Random Numbers

RANDOM REALS

The statement

```
double r = Math.random();
```

produces a random real number in the range 0.0 to 1.0, where 0.0 is included and 1.0 is not.

This range can be scaled and shifted. On the AP exam you will be expected to write algebraic expressions involving `Math.random()` that represent linear transformations of the original interval $0.0 \leq x < 1.0$.

Example 1

Produce a random real value x in the range $0.0 \le x < 6.0$.

```
double x = 6 * Math.random();
```

Example 2

Produce a random real value x in the range $2.0 \le x < 3.0$.

```
double x = Math.random() + 2;
```

Example 3

Produce a random real value x in the range $4.0 \le x < 6.0$.

```
double x = 2 * Math.random() + 4;
```

In general, to produce a random real value in the range `lowValue` $\le x <$ `highValue`:

```
double x = (highValue - lowValue) * Math.random() + lowValue;
```

RANDOM INTEGERS

Using a cast to `int`, a scaling factor, and a shifting value, `Math.random()` can be used to produce random integers in any range.

Example 1

Produce a random integer, from 0 to 99.

```
int num = (int) (Math.random() * 100);
```

In general, the expression

```
(int) (Math.random() * k)
```

produces a random `int` in the range $0, 1, \ldots, k - 1$, where k is called the scaling factor. Note that the cast to `int` truncates the real number `Math.random() * k`.

Example 2

Produce a random integer, from 1 to 100.

```
int num = (int) (Math.random() * 100) + 1;
```

In general, if k is a scaling factor, and p is a shifting value, the statement

```
int n = (int) (Math.random() * k) + p;
```

produces a random integer n in the range $p, p + 1, \ldots, p + (k - 1)$.

Example 3

Produce a random integer from 5 to 24.

```
int num = (int) (Math.random() * 20) + 5;
```

NOTE

There are 20 possible integers from 5 to 24, inclusive.

Chapter Summary

All students should know about overriding the `equals` and `toString` methods of the `Object` class, and should be familiar with the `Integer` and `Double` wrapper classes.

Know the AP subset methods of both the `String` and `Math` classes, especially the use of `Math.random()` for generating both random reals and random integers. Be sure to check where exceptions are thrown in the `String` methods.

MULTIPLE-CHOICE QUESTIONS ON STANDARD CLASSES

1. Here is a program segment to find the quantity base^{exp}. Both base and exp are entered at the keyboard.

```
System.out.println("Enter base and exponent: ");
double base = IO.readDouble();   //read user input
double exp = IO.readDouble();    //read user input
/* code to find power, which equals base^exp */
System.out.print(base + " raised to the power " + exp);
System.out.println(" equals " + power);
}
```

Which is a correct replacement for
/* *code to find* power, *which equals* base^{exp} */?

```
  I double power;
    Math m = new Math();
    power = m.pow(base, exp);

 II double power;
    power = Math.pow(base, exp);

III int power;
    power = Math.pow(base, exp);
```

(A) I only
(B) II only
(C) III only
(D) I and II only
(E) I and III only

2. Consider the `squareRoot` method defined below:

```
public Double squareRoot(Double d)
//Precondition:  value of d >= 0.
//Postcondition: Returns a Double whose value is the square
//               root of the value represented by d.
{
    /* implementation code */
}
```

Which /* *implementation code* */ satisfies the postcondition?

```
 I double x = d.doubleValue();
   x = Math.sqrt(x);
   return new Double(x);

II return new Double(Math.sqrt(d.doubleValue()));

III return ((Double) Math).sqrt(d.doubleValue());
```

(A) I only
(B) I and II only
(C) I and III only
(D) II and III only
(E) I, II, and III

3. Here are some examples of negative numbers rounded to the nearest integer.

Negative real number	Rounded to nearest integer
−3.5	−4
−8.97	−9
−5.0	−5
−2.487	−2
−0.2	0

Refer to the declaration

```
double d = -4.67;
```

Which of the following correctly rounds d to the nearest integer?

(A) `int rounded = Math.abs(d);`

(B) `int rounded = (int) (Math.random() * d);`

(C) `int rounded = (int) (d - 0.5);`

(D) `int rounded = (int) (d + 0.5);`

(E) `int rounded = Math.abs((int) (d - 0.5));`

4. A program is to simulate plant life under harsh conditions. In the program, plants die randomly according to some probability. Here is part of a `Plant` class defined in the program.

```
public class Plant
{
    private double myProbDeath;  //probability that plant dies,
                                 //real number between 0 and 1
    // other private instance variables
            ...

    public Plant(double probDeath, <other parameters>)
    {
        myProbDeath = probDeath;
        <initialization of other instance variables>
    }

    //plant dies
    public void die()
    {
        /* statement to generate random number */
        if (/* test to determine if plant dies */)
            <code to implement plant's death>
        else
            <code to make plant continue living>
    }

    //other methods
        ...
}
```

Which of the following are correct replacements for
(1) /* *statement to generate random number* */ and
(2) /* *test to determine if plant dies* */?

(A)   (1) `double x = Math.random();`
         (2) `x == myProbDeath`

(B)   (1) `double x = (int) (Math.random());`
         (2) `x > myProbDeath`

(C)   (1) `double x = Math.random();`
         (2) `x < myProbDeath`

(D)   (1) `int x = (int) (Math.random() * 100);`
         (2) `x < (int) myProbDeath`

(E)   (1) `int x = (int) (Math.random() * 100) + 1;`
         (2) `x == (int) myProbDeath`

5. A program simulates fifty slips of paper, numbered 1 through 50, placed in a bowl for a raffle drawing. Which of the following statements stores in `winner` a random integer from 1 to 50?
   (A) `int winner = (int) (Math.random() * 50) + 1;`
   (B) `int winner = (int) (Math.random() * 50);`
   (C) `int winner = (int) (Math.random() * 51);`
   (D) `int winner = (int) (Math.random() * 51) + 1;`
   (E) `int winner = (int) (1 + Math.random() * 49);`

6. Consider the code segment

   ```
   Integer i = new Integer(20);
   /* more code */
   ```

   Which of the following replacements for /* *more code* */ correctly sets `i` to have an integer value of 25?

   I `i = new Integer(25);`

   II `i.intValue() = 25;`

   III `Integer j = new Integer(25);`
   `   i = j;`

   (A) I only
   (B) II only
   (C) III only
   (D) I and III only
   (E) II and III only

7. Consider these declarations:

   ```
   Integer intOb = new Integer(3);
   Object ob = new Integer(4);
   Double doubOb = new Double(3.0);
   ```

   Which of the following will *not* cause an error?
   (A) `if ((Integer) ob.compareTo(intOb) < 0) ...`
   (B) `if (ob.compareTo(intOb) < 0) ...`
   (C) `if (intOb.compareTo(doubOb) < 0) ...`
   (D) `if (intOb.compareTo(ob) < 0) ...`
   (E) `if (intOb.compareTo((Integer) ob) < 0) ...`

8. Refer to these declarations:

```
Integer k = new Integer(8);
Integer m = new Integer(4);
```

Which test will *not* generate an error?

  I if (k.intValue() == m.intValue())...

  II if ((k.intValue()).equals(m.intValue()))...

  III if ((k.toString()).equals(m.toString()))...

(A) I only
(B) II only
(C) III only
(D) I and III only
(E) I, II, and III

9. Consider the code fragment

```
Object intObj = new Integer(9);
System.out.println((String) intObj);
```

What will be output as a result of running the fragment?
(A) No output. A ClassCastException will be thrown.
(B) No output. An ArithmeticException will be thrown.
(C) 9
(D) "9"
(E) nine

10. Consider these declarations:

```
String s1 = "crab";
String s2 = new String("crab");
String s3 = s1;
```

Which expression involving these strings evaluates to true?

  I s1 == s2

  II s1.equals(s2)

  III s3.equals(s2)

(A) I only
(B) II only
(C) II and III only
(D) I and II only
(E) I, II, and III

11. Suppose that `strA` = `"TOMATO"`, `strB` = `"tomato"`, and `strC` = `"tom"`. Given that `"A"` comes before `"a"` in dictionary order, which is true?

   (A) `strA.compareTo(strB) < 0 && strB.compareTo(strC) < 0`

   (B) `strB.compareTo(strA) < 0 || strC.compareTo(strA) < 0`

   (C) `strC.compareTo(strA) < 0 && strA.compareTo(strB) < 0`

   (D) `!(strA.equals(strB)) && strC.compareTo(strB) < 0`

   (E) `!(strA.equals(strB)) && strC.compareTo(strA) < 0`

12. This question refers to the following declaration:

```
String line = "Some more silly stuff on strings!";
//the words are separated by a single space
```

   What string will `str` refer to after execution of the following?

```
int x = line.indexOf("m");
String str = line.substring(10, 15) + line.substring(25, 25 + x);
```

   (A) `"sillyst"`
   (B) `"sillystr"`
   (C) `"silly st"`
   (D) `"silly str"`
   (E) `"sillystrin"`

13. A program has a `String` variable `fullName` that stores a first name, followed by a space, followed by a last name. There are no spaces in either the first or last names. Here are some examples of `fullName` values: `"Anthony Coppola"`, `"Jimmy Carroll"`, and `"Tom DeWire"`. Consider this code segment that extracts the last name from a `fullName` variable, and stores it in `lastName` with no surrounding blanks:

```
int k = fullName.indexOf(" ");    //find index of blank
String lastName = /* expression */
```

   Which is a correct replacement for /* *expression* */?

   I `fullName.substring(k);`

   II `fullName.substring(k + 1);`

   III `fullName.substring(k + 1, fullName.length());`

   (A) I only
   (B) II only
   (C) III only
   (D) II and III only
   (E) I and III only

14. One of the rules for converting English to Pig Latin states: If a word begins with a consonant, move the consonant to the end of the word and add "ay". Thus "dog" becomes "ogday," and "crisp" becomes "rispcay". Suppose s is a String containing an English word that begins with a consonant. Which of the following creates the correct corresponding word in Pig Latin? Assume the declarations

```
String ayString = "ay";
String pigString;
```

(A) `pigString = s.substring(0, s.length()) + s.substring(0,1)`
`          + ayString;`

(B) `pigString = s.substring(1, s.length()) + s.substring(0,0)`
`          + ayString;`

(C) `pigString = s.substring(0, s.length()-1) + s.substring(0,1)`
`          + ayString;`

(D) `pigString = s.substring(1, s.length()-1) + s.substring(0,0)`
`          + ayString;`

(E) `pigString = s.substring(1, s.length()) + s.substring(0,1)`
`          + ayString;`

15. This question refers to the getString method shown below:

```
public static String getString(String s1, String s2)
{
    int index = s1.indexOf(s2);
    return s1.substring(index, index + s2.length());
}
```

Which is true about getString? It may return a string that

   I Is equal to s2.
  II Has no characters in common with s2.
 III Is equal to s1.

(A) I and III only
(B) II and III only
(C) I and II only
(D) I, II, and III
(E) None is true.

16. Consider this method:

```
public static String doSomething(String s)
{
    final String BLANK = " ";    //BLANK contains a single space
    String str = "";             //empty string
    String temp;
    for (int i = 0; i < s.length(); i++)
    {
        temp = s.substring(i, i + 1);
        if (!(temp.equals(BLANK)))
            str += temp;
    }
    return str;
}
```

Which of the following is the most precise description of what doSomething does?
(A) It returns s unchanged.
(B) It returns s with all its blanks removed.
(C) It returns a String that is equivalent to s with all its blanks removed.
(D) It returns a String that is an exact copy of s.
(E) It returns a String that contains s.length() blanks.

Questions 17 and 18 refer to the classes `Position` and `PositionTest` below.

```
public class Position implements Comparable
{
    private int myRow, myCol;
    /* myRow and myCol are both >= 0 except in
     * the default constructor where they are initialized to -1 */

    public Position()           //constructor
    {
        myRow = -1;
        myCol = -1;
    }

    public Position(int r, int c)        //constructor
    {
        myRow = r;
        myCol = c;
    }

    /* Returns row of Position. */
    public int getRow()
    { return myRow; }

    /* Returns column of Position. */
    public int getCol()
    { return myCol; }

    /* Returns Position north of (up from) this position. */
    public Position north()
    { return new Position(myRow - 1, myCol); }

    //Similar methods south, east, and west
           ...

    /* Compares this Position to another Position object.
     * Returns -1 (less than), 0 (equals), or 1 (greater than). */
    public int compareTo(Object o)
    {
        Position p = (Position) o;
        if (this.getRow() < p.getRow() || this.getRow() == p.getRow()
            && this.getCol() < p.getCol())
                return -1;
        if (this.getRow() > p.getRow() || this.getRow() == p.getRow()
            && this.getCol() > p.getCol())
                return 1;
        return 0;             //row and col both equal
    }

    /* Returns string form of Position. */
    public String toString()
    { return "(" + myRow + "," + myCol + ")"; }
}
```

```
public class PositionTest
{
    public static void main(String[] args)
    {
        Position p1 = new Position(2, 3);
        Position p2 = new Position(4, 1);
        Position p3 = new Position(2, 3);

        //tests to compare positions
            ...
    }
}
```

17. Which is true about the value of p1.compareTo(p2)?
    (A) It equals true.
    (B) It equals false.
    (C) It equals 0.
    (D) It equals 1.
    (E) It equals -1.

18. Which boolean expression about p1 and p3 is true?

    I p1 == p3

    II p1.equals(p3)

    III p1.compareTo(p3) == 0

    (A) I only
    (B) II only
    (C) III only
    (D) II and III only
    (E) I, II, and III

Questions 19 and 20 deal with the problem of swapping two integer values. Three methods are proposed to solve the problem, using primitive `int` types, `Integer` objects, and `IntPair` objects, where `IntPair` is defined as follows:

```java
public class IntPair
{
    private int firstValue;
    private int secondValue;

    public IntPair(int first, int second)
    {
        firstValue = first;
        secondValue = second;
    }

    public int getFirst()
    { return firstValue; }

    public int getSecond()
    { return secondValue; }

    public void setFirst(int a)
    { firstValue = a; }

    public void setSecond(int b)
    { secondValue = b;}
}
```

19. Here are three different swap methods, each intended for use in a client program.

```
 I public static void swap(int a, int b)
   {
       int temp = a;
       a = b;
       b = temp;
   }

II public static void swap(Integer obj_a, Integer obj_b)
   {
       Integer temp = new Integer(obj_a.intValue());
       obj_a = obj_b;
       obj_b = temp;
   }

III public static void swap(IntPair pair)
   {
       int temp = pair.getFirst();
       pair.setFirst(pair.getSecond());
       pair.setSecond(temp);
   }
```

When correctly used in a client program with appropriate parameters, which method will swap two integers, as intended?
(A) I only
(B) II only
(C) III only
(D) II and III only
(E) I, II, and III

20. Consider the following program that uses the `IntPair` class:

```
public class TestSwap
{
    public static void swap(IntPair pair)
    {
        int temp = pair.getFirst();
        pair.setFirst(pair.getSecond());
        pair.setSecond(temp);
    }

    public static void main(String[] args)
    {
        int x = 8, y = 6;
        /* code to swap x and y */
    }
}
```

Which is a correct replacement for /* *code to swap* x *and* y */?

```
 I  IntPair iPair = new IntPair(x, y);
    swap(x, y);
    x = iPair.getFirst();
    y = iPair.getSecond();

 II IntPair iPair = new IntPair(x, y);
    swap(iPair);
    x = iPair.getFirst();
    y = iPair.getSecond();

III IntPair iPair = new IntPair(x, y);
    swap(iPair);
    x = iPair.setFirst();
    y = iPair.setSecond();
```

(A) I only
(B) II only
(C) III only
(D) II and III only
(E) None is correct.

Refer to the Name class below for Questions 21 and 22.

```java
public class Name implements Comparable
{
    private String firstName;
    private String lastName;

    public Name(String first, String last)  //constructor
    {
        firstName = first;
        lastName = last;
    }

    public String toString()
    { return firstName + " " + lastName; }

    public boolean equals(Object obj)
    {
        Name n = (Name) obj;
        return n.firstName.equals(firstName) &&
                n.lastName.equals(lastName);
    }

    public int hashCode()
    { /* implementation not shown */ }

    public int compareTo(Object obj)
    {
        Name n = (Name) obj;
        /* more code */
    }
}
```

21. The `compareTo` method implements the standard name-ordering algorithm where last names take precedence over first names. Lexicographic or dictionary ordering of `Strings` is used. For example, the name Scott Dentes comes before Nick Elser, and Adam Cooper comes before Sara Cooper.

    Which of the following is a correct replacement for /* *more code* */?

    ```
    I  int lastComp = lastName.compareTo(n.lastName);
       if (lastComp != 0)
           return lastComp;
       else
           return firstName.compareTo(n.firstName);

    II  if (lastName.equals(n.lastName))
            return firstName.compareTo(n.firstName);
        else
            return 0;

    III  if (!(lastName.equals(n.lastName)))
             return firstName.compareTo(n.firstName);
         else
             return lastName.compareTo(n.lastName);
    ```

    (A) I only
    (B) II only
    (C) III only
    (D) I and II only
    (E) I, II, and III

22. Which statement about the `Name` class is *false*?
    (A) `Name` objects are immutable.
    (B) It is possible for the methods in `Name` to throw a `NullPointerException`.
    (C) If `n1` and `n2` are `Name` objects in a client class, then the expressions `n1.equals(n2)` and `n1.compareTo(n2) == 0` must have the same value.
    (D) The `compareTo` method throws a run-time exception if the parameter is null or the parameter is incompatible with `Name` objects.
    (E) Since the `Name` class implements `Comparable`, it *must* provide an implementation for an `equals` method.

ANSWER KEY

1. B	9. A	17. E
2. B	10. C	18. C
3. C	11. D	19. C
4. C	12. A	20. B
5. A	13. D	21. A
6. D	14. E	22. E
7. E	15. A	
8. D	16. C	

ANSWERS EXPLAINED

1. **(B)** All the Math class methods are static methods, which means there is no instance of a Math object that calls the method. The method is invoked using the class name, Math, followed by the dot operator. Thus segment II is correct, and segment I is incorrect. Segment III will cause an error: Since the parameters of pow are of type double, the result should be stored in a double.

2. **(B)** The Math.sqrt method must be invoked on a primitive type double, which is the reason d.doubleValue() is needed. A correct segment must create a Double object using new, which eliminates segment III. Segment III is egregiously bad: It tries to cast Math to Double. But Math is not an object! Math.sqrt is a static method.

3. **(C)** The value −4.67 must be rounded to −5. Subtracting 0.5 gives a value of −5.17. Casting to int truncates the number (chops off the decimal part) and leaves a value of −5. None of the other choices produces −5. Choice A gives the absolute value of d: 4.67. Choice B is an incorrect use of Random. The parameter for nextInt should be an integer n, $n \geq 2$. The method then returns a random int k, where $0 \leq k < n$. Choice D is the way to round a *positive* real number to the nearest integer. In the actual case it produces −4. Choice E gives the absolute value of −5, namely 5.

4. **(C)** The statement double x = Math.random(); generates a random double in the range $0 \leq x < 1$. Suppose myProbDeath is 0.67, or 67%. Assuming that random doubles are uniformly distributed in the interval, one can expect that 67% of the time x will be in the range $0 \leq x < 0.67$. You can therefore simulate the probability of death by testing if x is between 0 and 0.67, that is, if x < 0.67. Thus, x < myProbDeath is the desired condition for plant death, eliminating choices A and B. Choices D and E fail because (int) myProbDeath truncates myProbDeath to 0. The test x < 0 will always be false, and the test x == 0 will only be true if the random number generator returned exactly 0, an extremely unlikely occurrence! Neither of these choices correctly simulates the probability of death.

5. **(A)** The expression

```
(int) (Math.random() * 50);
```

returns an `int` from 0 to 49. Therefore, adding 1 shifts the range to be 1 to 50, which was required.

6. **(D)** The `Integer` class has no methods that can change the contents of `i`. However, `i` can be reassigned so that it refers to another object. This happens in both segments I and III. Segment II is wrong because `intValue` is an *accessor*—it cannot be used to change the value of object `i`.

7. **(E)** Choice D fails because you can't compare an `Integer` to an `Object`. You need to cast `ob` to `Integer`, as is done in choice E, the correct answer. Choice D will give the error message

    ```
    compareTo(java.lang.Integer) in java.lang.Integer cannot
    be applied to (java.lang.Object)
    ```

    Choice C will cause a `ClassCastException` since the calling and parameter objects are incompatible types. The `compareTo` method will try erroneously to cast its parameter to the type of the object calling the method. Choice A *almost* works: It fails because the dot operator has higher precedence than casting, which means that `ob.compareTo` is parsed before `ob` is cast to `Integer`, generating a message that the `compareTo` method is not in class `Object`. Choice A can be fixed with an extra pair of parentheses:

    ```
    if (((Integer) ob).compareTo(intOb) < 0) ...
    ```

    Choice B causes the same error message as choice A: no `compareTo` method in class `Object`.

8. **(D)** Test I is correct because it's OK to compare primitive types (in this case `int` values) using `==`. Test III works because `k.toString()` and `m.toString()` are `String`s, which should be compared with `equals`. Test II is wrong because you can't invoke a method (in this case `equals`) on an `int`.

9. **(A)** An `Integer` cannot be cast to a `String`. Don't confuse this with

    ```
    System.out.println(intObj.toString());    //outputs 9
    ```

    Note that if the first line of the code fragment were

    ```
    Integer intObj = new Integer(9);
    ```

    then the error would be detected at compile time.

10. **(C)** Here are the memory slots:

    Statements II and III are true because the contents of `s1` and `s2` are the same, and the contents of `s3` and `s2` are the same. Statement I is false because `s1` and `s2` are not the same reference. Note that the expression `s1 == s3` would be true since `s1` and `s3` *are* the same reference.

11. **(D)** Note that `"TOMATO"` precedes both `"tomato"` and `"tom"`, since `"T"` precedes `"t"`. Also, `"tom"` precedes `"tomato"` since the length of `"tom"` is less than the length of `"tomato"`. Therefore each of the following is true:

```
strA.compareTo(strB) < 0
strA.compareTo(strC) < 0
strC.compareTo(strB) < 0
```

So

   Choice A is T and F which evaluates to F
   Choice B is F or F which evaluates to F
   Choice C is F and T which evaluates to F
   Choice D is T and T which evaluates to T
   Choice E is T and F which evaluates to F

12. **(A)** x contains the index of the first occurrence of "m" in `line`, namely 2. (Remember that "S" is at index 0.) The method call `line.substring(10,15)` returns "silly", the substring starting at index 10 and extending though index 14. The method call `line.substring(25,27)` returns "st" (don't include the character at index 27!). The concatenation operator, +, joins these.

13. **(D)** The first character of the last name starts at the first character after the space. Thus, `startIndex` for `substring` must be `k+1`. This eliminates expression I. Expression II takes all the characters from position `k+1` to the end of the `fullName` string, which is correct. Expression III takes all the characters from position `k+1` to position `fullName.length()-1`, which is also correct.

14. **(E)** Suppose s contains "cat". You want `pigString = "at" + "c" + "ay"`. Now the string "at" is the substring of s starting at position 1 and ending at position `s.length()-1`. The correct substring call for this piece of the word is `s.substring(1,s.length())`, which eliminates choices A, C, and, D. (Recall that the first parameter is the starting position and the second parameter is one position past the last index of the substring.) The first letter of the word—"c" in the example—starts at position 0 and ends at position 0. The correct expression is `s.substring(0,1)`, which eliminates choice B.

15. **(A)** Statement I is true whenever s2 occurs in s1. For example, if strings s1 = "catastrophe" and s2 = "cat", then `getString` returns "cat". Statement II will never happen. If s2 is not contained in s1, the `indexOf` call will return -1. Using a negative integer as the first parameter of `substring` will cause a `StringIndexOutOfBoundsException`. Statement III will be true whenever s1 equals s2.

16. **(C)** The `String temp` represents a single-character substring of s. The method examines each character in s and, if it is a nonblank, appends it to `str`, which is initially empty. Each assignment `str += temp` assigns a new reference to `str`. Thus, `str` ends up as a copy of s but without the blanks. A reference to the final `str` object is returned. Choice A is correct in that s is left unchanged, but it is not the *best* characterization of what the method does. Choice B is not precise because an object parameter is never modified: Changes, if any, are performed on a copy. Choices D and E are wrong because the method removes blanks.

17. **(E)** The `compareTo` method returns an int, so eliminate choices A and B. In the implementation of `compareTo`, the code segment that applies to the particular example is

```
if (this.getRow() < p.getRow() || ...
    return -1;
```

Since 2 < 4, the value -1 is returned.

18. **(C)** Expression III is true: The `compareTo` method is implemented to return `0` if two `Position` objects have the same row and column. Expression I is false because `object1 == object2` returns `true` only if `object1` and `object2` are the *same reference*. Expression II is tricky. One would like `p1` and `p3` to be equal since they have the same row and column values. This is not going to happen automatically, however. The `equals` method must explicitly be overridden for the `Position` class. If this hasn't been done, the default `equals` method, which is inherited from class `Object`, will return true only if `p1` and `p3` are the same reference, which is not true.

19. **(C)** Recall that primitive types and object references are passed by value. This means that copies are made of the actual arguments. Any changes that are made are made to the *copies*. The actual parameters remain unchanged. Thus, in methods I and II, the parameters will retain their original values and remain unswapped.

    To illustrate, for example, why method II fails, consider this piece of code that tests it:

```
public static void main(String[] args)
{
    int x = 8, y = 6;
    Integer xObject = new Integer(x);
    Integer yObject = new Integer(y);
    swap(xObject, yObject);
    x = xObject.intValue();      //surprise! still has value 8
    y = yObject.intValue();      //surprise! still has value 6
        ...
}
```

Here are the memory slots before swap is called:

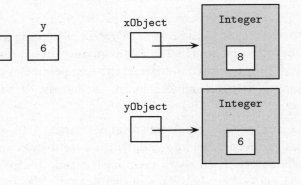

Here they are when swap is invoked:

Just before exiting the swap method:

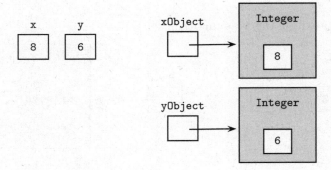

After exiting, xObject and yObject have retained their original values:

The reason method III works is that instead of the object references being changed, the object *contents* are changed. Thus, after exiting the method, the IntPair reference is as it was, but the first and second values have been interchanged. (See explanation to next question for diagrams of the memory slots.) In this question, IntPair is used as a wrapper class for a pair of integers whose values need to be swapped.

20. **(B)** The swap method has just a single IntPair parameter, which eliminates segment I. Segment III fails because setFirst and setSecond are used incorrectly. These are mutator methods that change an IntPair object. What is desired is to return the (newly swapped) first and second values of the pair: Accessor methods

getFirst and getSecond do the trick. To see why this swap method works, look at the memory slots.

Before the swap method is called:

Just after the swap method is called:

Just before exiting the swap method:

Just after exiting the swap method:

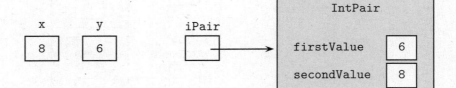

After the statements:

```
x = iPair.getFirst();
y = iPair.getSecond();
```

Notice that x and y have been swapped!

21. **(A)** The first statement of segment I compares last names. If these are different, the method returns the `int` value `lastComp`, which is negative if `lastName` precedes `n.lastName`, positive otherwise. If last names are the same, the method returns the `int` result of comparing first names. Segments II and III use incorrect algorithms for comparing names. Segment II would be correct if the `else` part were

    ```
    return lastName.compareTo(n.lastName);
    ```

    Segment III would be correct if the two `return` statements were interchanged.

22. **(E)** The `Comparable` interface has just one method, `compareTo`. Choice E would be true if `equals` were replaced by `compareTo`. Choice A is true. You know this because the `Name` class has no mutator methods. Thus, `Name` objects can never be changed. Choice B is true: If a `Name` is initialized with null references, each of the methods will throw a `NullPointerException`. Choice C is true: If `n1.equals(n2)` is true, then `n1.compareTo(n2) == 0` is true, because both are conditions for equality of `n1` and `n2` and should therefore be consistent. Choice D is true: If the parameter is null, the `compareTo` method will throw a `NullPointerException`. If the parameter is incompatible with `Name` objects, its first statement will throw a `ClassCastException`.

Program Design and Analysis

Weeks of coding can save you hours of planning.
—Anonymous

Chapter Goals

- Program development, including design and testing
- Object-oriented program design
- Relationships between classes
- Program analysis
- Efficiency

Students of introductory computer science typically see themselves as programmers. They no sooner have a new programming project in their heads than they're at the computer, typing madly to get some code up and running. (Is this you?)

To succeed as a programmer, however, you have to combine the practical skills of a software engineer with the analytical mindset of a computer scientist. A software engineer oversees the life cycle of software development: initiation of the project, analysis of the specification, and design of the program, as well as implementation, testing, and maintenance of the final product. A computer scientist (among other things!) analyzes the implementation, correctness, and efficiency of algorithms. All these topics are tested on the APCS exam.

THE SOFTWARE DEVELOPMENT LIFE CYCLE

The Waterfall Model

The waterfall model of software development came about in the 1960s in order to bring structure and efficiency into the process of creating large programs.

Each step in the process flows into the next: The picture resembles a waterfall.

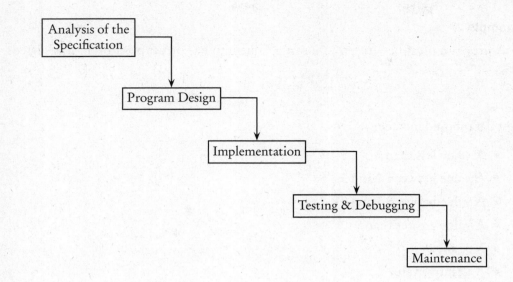

Program Specification

The *specification* is a written description of the project. Typically it is based on a customer's requirements. The first step in writing a program is to analyze the specification, make sure you understand it, and clarify with the customer anything that is unclear.

Program Design

Even for a small-scale program a good design can save programming time and enhance the reliability of the final program. The design is a fairly detailed plan for solving the problem outlined in the specification. It should include all objects that will be used in the solution, the data structures that will implement them, plus a detailed list of the tasks to be performed by the program.

A good design provides a fairly detailed overall plan at a glance, without including the minutiae of Java code.

Program Implementation

Program implementation is the coding phase. Design and implementation are discussed in more detail on p. 209.

Testing and Debugging

TEST DATA

Not every possible input value can be tested, so a programmer should be diligent in selecting a representative set of *test data*. Typical values in each part of a domain of the program should be selected, as well as endpoint values and out-of-range values. If only positive input is required, your test data should include a negative value just to check that your program handles it appropriately.

Example

A program must be written to insert a value into its correct position in this sorted list:

> 2   5   9

Test data should include

- A value less than 2
- A value between 2 and 5
- A value between 5 and 9
- A value greater than 9
- 2, 5, and 9
- A negative value

TYPES OF ERRORS (BUGS)

- A *compile-time error* occurs during compilation of the program. The compiler is unable to translate the program into bytecode and prints an appropriate error message. A *syntax error* is a compile-time error caused by violating the rules of the programming language. Some examples are omitting semicolons or braces, using undeclared identifiers, using keywords inappropriately, having parameters that don't match in type and number, and invoking a method for an object whose class definition doesn't contain that method.

- A *run-time error* occurs during execution of the program. The Java run-time environment *throws an exception*, which means that it stops execution and prints an error message. Typical causes of run-time errors include attempting to divide an integer by zero, using an array index that is out of bounds, attempting to open a file that cannot be found, and so on. An error that causes a program to run forever ("infinite loop") can also be regarded as a run-time error. (See also Errors and Exceptions, p. 73.)

- An *intent* or *logic error* is one that fails to carry out the specification of the program. The program compiles and runs but does not do the job. These are sometimes the hardest types of errors to fix.

ROBUSTNESS

Always assume that any user of your program is not as smart as you are. You must therefore aim to write a *robust* program, namely one that

- Won't give inaccurate answers for some input data.
- Won't crash if the input data are invalid.
- Won't allow execution to proceed if invalid data are entered.

Examples of bad input data include out-of-range numbers, characters instead of numerical data, and a response of "maybe" when "yes" or "no" was asked for.

Note that bad input data that invalidates a computation won't be detected by Java. Your program should include code that catches the error, allows the error to be fixed, and allows program execution to resume.

Program Maintenance

Program maintenance involves upgrading the code as circumstances change. New features may be added. New programmers may come on board. To make their task easier, the original program must have clear and precise documentation.

OBJECT-ORIENTED PROGRAM DESIGN

Object-oriented programming has been the dominant programming methodology since the mid 1990s. It uses an approach that blurs the lines of the waterfall model. Analysis of the problem, development of the design, and pieces of the implementation all overlap and influence one another.

Here are the steps in object-oriented design:

- Identify classes to be written.
- Identify behaviors (i.e., methods) for each class.
- Determine the relationships between classes.
- Write the interface (public method headers) for each class.
- Implement the methods.

Identifying Classes

Identify the objects in the program by picking out the nouns in the program specification. Ignore pronouns and nouns that refer to the user. Select those nouns that seem suitable as classes, the "big-picture" nouns that describe the major objects in the application. Some of the other nouns may end up as attributes of the classes.

Many applications have similar object types: a low-level basic component; a collection of low-level components; a controlling object that puts everything together; and a display object that could be a GUI (graphical user interface) but doesn't have to be.

Example 1

Write a program that maintains an inventory of stock items for a small store.

Nouns to consider: inventory, item, store.

Basic Object:	`StockItem`
Collection:	`Inventory` (a list of `StockItems`)
Controller:	`Store` (has an `Inventory`, uses a `StoreDisplay`)
Display:	`StoreDisplay` (could be a GUI)

Example 2

Write a program that simulates a game of bingo. There should be at least two players, each of whom has a bingo card, and a caller who calls the numbers.

Nouns to consider: game, players, bingo card, caller.

Basic Objects:	`BingoCard`, `Caller`
Collection:	`Players` (each has a `BingoCard`)
Controller:	`GameMaster` (sets up the `Players` and `Caller`)
Display:	`BingoDisplay` (shows each player's card and displays winners, etc.)

Example 3

Write a program that creates random bridge deals and displays them in a specified format. (The specification defines a "deal" as consisting of four hands. It also describes a deck of cards, and shows how each card should be displayed.)

Nouns to consider: deal, hand, format, deck, card.

Basic Object:	`Card`
Collection:	`Deck` (has an array of `Cards`)
	`Hand` (has an array of `Cards`)
	`Deal` (has an array of `Hands`)
	`Dealer` (has a `Deck`, or several `Decks`)
Controller:	`Formatter` (has a `Deal` and a `TableDisplay`)
Display:	`TableDisplay` (could be a GUI)

Identifying Behaviors

Find all verbs in the program description that help lead to the solution of the programming task. These are likely behaviors that will probably become the methods of the classes. Now decide which methods belong in which classes. Recall that the process of bundling a group of methods and data fields into a class is called *encapsulation*.

Think carefully about who should do what. Do not ask a basic object to perform operations for the group. For example, a `StockItem` should keep track of its own details (price, description, how many on the shelf, etc.) but should not be required to search for another item. A `Card` should know its value and suit, but should not be responsible for keeping track of how many cards are left in a deck. A `Caller` in a bingo game should be responsible for keeping track of the numbers called so far and for producing the next number, but not for checking whether a player has bingo: That is the job of an individual player (element of `Players`) and his `BingoCard`.

You will also need to decide which data fields each class will need and which data structures should store them. For example, if an object represents a list of items, consider an array or `ArrayList` as the data structure.

Determining Relationships Between Classes

INHERITANCE RELATIONSHIPS

Look for classes with common behaviors. This will help identify *inheritance relationships*. Recall the *is-a* relationship—if object1 *is-a* object2, then object2 is a candidate for a superclass.

COMPOSITION RELATIONSHIPS

Composition relationships are defined by the *has-a* relationship. For example, a `Nurse` *has-a* `Uniform`. Typically, if two classes have a composition relationship, one of them contains an instance variable whose type is the other class.

Note that a wrapper class always implements a *has-a* relationship with any objects that it wraps.

UML Diagrams

An excellent way to keep track of the relationships between classes and show the inheritance hierarchy in your programs is with a UML (Unified Modeling Language) diagram. This is a standard graphical scheme used by object-oriented programmers. Although it is not part of the AP subset, on the AP exam you may be expected to interpret simple UML diagrams and inheritance hierarchies.

Here is a simplified version of the UML rules:

- Represent classes with rectangles.
- Use angle brackets with the word "abstract" or "interface" to indicate either an abstract class or interface.
- Show the *is-a* relationship between classes with an open up-arrow.
- Show the *is-a* relationship that involves an interface with an open, dotted up-arrow.
- Show the *has-a* relationship with a down arrow or sideways arrow (indicates composition).

Example

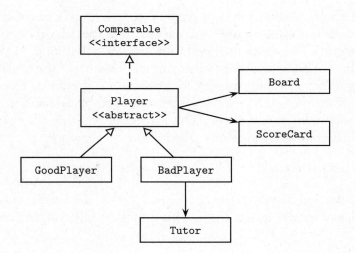

From this diagram you can see at a glance that GoodPlayer and BadPlayer are subclasses of an abstract class Player, and that each Player implements the Comparable interface. Every Player has a Board and a ScoreCard, while only the BadPlayer has a Tutor.

Implementing Classes

BOTTOM-UP DEVELOPMENT

For each method in a class, list all of the other classes needed to implement that particular method. These classes are called *collaborators*. A class that has no collaborators is *independent*.

To implement the classes, often an incremental, *bottom-up* approach is used. This means that independent classes are fully implemented and tested before being incorporated into the overall project. Typically, these are the basic objects of the program, like StockItem, Card, and BingoCard. Unrelated classes in a programming project can be implemented by different programmers.

Note that a class can be tested using a dummy `Tester` class that will be discarded when the methods of the class are working. Constructors, then methods, should be added, and tested, one at a time. A *driver class* that contains a `main` method can be used to test the program as you go. The purpose of the driver is to test the class fully before incorporating it as an object in a new class.

When each of the independent classes is working, classes that depend on just one other class are implemented and tested, and so on. This may lead to a working, bare bones version of the project. New features and enhancements can be added later.

Design flaws can be corrected at each stage of development. Remember, a design is never set in stone: It simply guides the implementation.

TOP-DOWN DEVELOPMENT

In a top-down design, the programmer starts with an overview of the program, selecting the highest-level controlling object and the tasks needed. During development of the program, subsidiary classes may be added to simplify existing classes.

Implementing Methods

PROCEDURAL ABSTRACTION

A good programmer avoids chunks of repeated code wherever possible. To this end, if several methods in a class require the same task, like a search or a swap, you should use *helper methods*. The `reduce` method in the `Rational` class on p. 114 is an example of such a method. Also, wherever possible you should enhance the readability of your code by using helper methods to break long methods into smaller tasks. The use of helper methods within a class is known as *procedural abstraction* and is an example of top-down development within a class. This process of breaking a long method into a sequence of smaller tasks is sometimes called *stepwise refinement*.

INFORMATION HIDING

Instance variables and helper methods are generally declared as `private`, which prevents client classes from accessing them. This strategy is called *information hiding*.

STUB METHOD

Sometimes it makes more sense in the development of a class to test a calling method before testing a method it invokes. A *stub* is a dummy method that stands in for a method until the actual method has been written and tested. A stub typically has an output statement to show that it was called in the correct place, or it may return some reasonable values if necessary.

ALGORITHM

An *algorithm* is a precise step-by-step procedure that solves a problem or achieves a goal. Don't write any code for an algorithm in a method until the steps are completely clear to you.

Example 1

A program must test the validity of a four-digit code number that a person will enter to be able to use a photocopy machine. The number is valid if the fourth digit equals the remainder when the sum of the first three digits is divided by seven.

Classes in the program may include an `IDNumber`, the four-digit code; `Display`, which would handle input and output; and `IDMain`, the driver for the program. The data structure used to implement an `IDNumber` could be an instance variable of type `int`, or an instance variable of type `String`, or four instance variables of type `int`—one per digit, and so on.

A top-down design for the program that tests the validity of the number is reflected in the steps of the `main` method of `IDMain`:

Create `Display`
Read in `IDNumber`
Check validity
Print message

Each method in this design is tested before the next method is added to `main`. If the display will be handled in a GUI (graphical user interface), stepwise refinement of the design might look like this:

Create `Display`
    Construct a `Display`
    Create window panels
    Set up text fields
    Add panels and fields to window

Read in `IDNumber`
    Prompt and read

Check validity of `IDNumber`
    Check input
        Check characters
        Check range
    Separate into digits
    Check validity property

Print message
    Write number
    State if valid

NOTE

1. The `IDNumber` class, which contains the four-digit code, is responsible for the following operations:
    Split value into separate objects
    Check condition for validity
The `Display` class, which contains objects to read and display, must also contain an `IDNumber` object. It is responsible for the following operations:
    Set up display
    Read in code number
    Display validity message
Creating these two classes with their data fields and operations (methods) is an example of encapsulation.

2. The `Display` method `readCodeNumber` needs private helper methods to check the input: `checkCharacters` and `checkRange`. This is an example of procedu-

ral abstraction (use of helper methods) and information hiding (making them private).

3. Initially the programmer had just an IDNumber class and a driver class. The Display class was added as a refinement, when it was realized that handling the input and message display was separate from checking the validity of the IDNumber. This is an example of top-down development (adding an auxiliary class to clarify the code).

4. The IDNumber class contains no data fields that are objects. It is therefore an independent class. The Display class, which contains an IDNumber data member, has a composition relationship with IDNumber (Display *has-a* IDNumber).

5. When testing the final program, the programmer should be sure to include each of the following as a user-entered code number: a valid four-digit number, an invalid four-digit number, an n-digit number, where $n \neq 4$, and a "number" that contains a nondigit character. A robust program should be able to deal with all these cases.

Example 2

A program must create a teacher's grade book. The program should maintain a class list of students for any number of classes in the teacher's schedule. A menu should be provided that allows the teacher to

- Create a new class of students.

- Enter a set of scores for any class.

- Correct any data that's been entered.

- Display the record of any student.

- Calculate the final average and grade for all students in a class.

- Print a class list, with or without grades.

- Add a student, delete a student, or transfer a student to another class.

- Save all the data in a file.

IDENTIFYING CLASSES

Use nouns in the specification to identify possible classes.

Use the nouns in the specification as a starting point for identifying classes in the program. The nouns are: program, teacher, grade book, class list, class, student, schedule, menu, set of scores, data, record, average, grade, and file.

Eliminate each of the following:

program	(Always eliminate "program" when used in this context.)
teacher	(Eliminate, because he or she is the user.)
schedule	(This will be reflected in the name of the external file for each class, e.g., apcs_period3.dat.)
data, record	(These are synonymous with student name, scores, grades, etc., and will be covered by these features.)
class	(This is synonymous with class list.)

The following seem to be excellent candidates for classes: GradeBook, ClassList, Student, and FileHandler. Other possibilities are Menu, ScoreList, and a GUI_Display.

On further thought: Basic independent objects are Student, Menu, Score, and File-Handler. Group objects are ClassList (collection of students), ScoreList (collection of scores), and `AllClasses` (collection of `ClassLists`). The controlling class is the `GradeBook`. A `Display` class is essential for many of the grade book operations, like showing a class list or displaying information for a single student.

RELATIONSHIPS BETWEEN CLASSES

There are no inheritance relationships. There are many composition relationships between objects, however. The `GradeBook` *has-a* Menu, the `ClassList` *has-a* `Student` (several, in fact!), a `Student` *has-a* name, average, grade, `list_of_scores`, etc. The programmer must decide whether to code these attributes as classes or data fields.

IDENTIFYING BEHAVIORS

Use the verbs in the specification to identify required operations in the program. The verbs are: maintain <list>, provide <menu>, allow <user>, create <list>, enter <scores>, correct <data>, display <record>, calculate <average>, calculate <grade>, print <list>, add <student>, delete <student>, transfer <student>, and save <data>.

> Use verbs in the specification to identify possible methods.

You must make some design decisions about which class is responsible for which behavior. For example, will a `ClassList` display the record of a single `Student`, or will a `Student` display his or her own record? Who will enter scores—the `GradeBook`, a `ClassList`, or a `Student`? Is it desirable for a `Student` to enter scores of other `Students`? Probably not!

DECISIONS

Here are some preliminary decisions. The `GradeBook` will provideMenu. The menu selection will send execution to the relevant object.

The `ClassList` will maintain an updated list of each class. It will have these public methods: `addStudent`, `deleteStudent`, `transferStudent`, `createNewClass`, `printClassList`, `printScores`, and `updateList`. A good candidate for a helper method in this class is search for a given student.

Each `Student` will have complete personal and grade information. Public methods will include `setName`, `getName`, `enterScore`, `correctData`, `findAverage`, `getAverage`, `getGrade`, and `displayRecord`.

Saving and retrieving information is crucial to this program. The `FileHandler` will take care of `openFileForReading`, `openFileForWriting`, `closeFiles`, `loadClass`, and `saveClass`. The `FileHandler` class should be written and tested right at the beginning, using a small dummy class list.

`Score`, `ScoreList`, and `Student` are easy classes to implement. When these are working, the programmer can go on to `ClassList`. Finally the `Display` GUI class, which will have the `GradeBook`, can be developed. This is an example of bottom-up development.

Vocabulary Summary

Know these terms for the AP exam:

Vocabulary	Meaning
software development	Writing a program
object-oriented program	Uses interacting objects
program specification	Description of a task
program design	A written plan, an overview of the solution
program implementation	The code
test data	Input to test the program
program maintenance	Keeping the program working and up to date
top-down development	Implement main classes first, subsidiary classes later
independent class	Doesn't use other classes of the program in its code
bottom-up development	Implement lowest level, independent classes first
driver class	Used to test other classes; contains `main` method
inheritance relationship	*is-a* relationship between classes
composition relationship	*has-a* relationship between classes
inheritance hierarchy	Inheritance relationship shown in a tree-like diagram
UML diagram	Graphical representation of relationship between classes
data structure	Java construct for storing a data field (e.g., array)
encapsulation	Combining data fields and methods in a class
information hiding	Using `private` to restrict access
stepwise refinement	Breaking methods into smaller methods
procedural abstraction	Using helper methods
algorithm	Step-by-step process that solves a problem
stub method	Dummy method called by another method being tested
debugging	Fixing errors
robust program	Screens out bad input
compile-time error	Usually a syntax error; prevents program from compiling
syntax error	Bad language usage (e.g., missing brace)
run-time error	Occurs during execution (e.g., `int` division by 0)
exception	Run-time error thrown by Java method
logic error	Program runs but does the wrong thing

PROGRAM ANALYSIS

Program Correctness

Testing that a program works does not prove that the program is correct. After all, you can hardly expect to test programs for every conceivable set of input data. Computer scientists have developed mathematical techniques to prove correctness in certain cases, but these are beyond the scope of the APCS course. Nevertheless, you are expected to be able to make assertions about the state of a program at various points during its execution.

Assertions

An *assertion* is a precise statement about a program at any given point. The idea is that if an assertion is proved to be true, then the program is working correctly at that point.

An informal step on the way to writing correct algorithms is to be able to make different kinds of assertions about your code.

PRECONDITION

The *precondition* for any piece of code, whether it is a method, loop, or block, is a statement of what is true immediately before execution of that code.

POSTCONDITION

The *postcondition* for a piece of code is a statement of what is true immediately after execution of that code.

Efficiency

An efficient algorithm is one that is economical in the use of

- CPU time. This refers to the number of machine operations required to carry out the algorithm (arithmetic operations, comparisons, data movements, etc.).
- Memory. This refers to the number and complexity of the variables used.

Some factors that affect run-time efficiency include unnecessary tests, excessive movement of data elements, and redundant computations, especially in loops.

Always aim for early detection of output conditions: Your sorting algorithm should halt when the list is sorted; your search should stop if the key element has been found.

In discussing efficiency of an algorithm, we refer to the *best case*, *worst case*, and *average case*. The best case is a configuration of the data that causes the algorithm to run in the least possible amount of time. The worst case is a configuration that leads to the greatest possible run time. Typical configurations (i.e., not specially chosen data) give the average case. It is possible that best, worst, and average cases don't differ much in their run times.

For example, suppose that a list of distinct random numbers must be searched for a given key value. The algorithm used is a sequential search starting at the beginning of the list. In the best case, the key will be found in the first position examined. In the worst case, it will be in the last position or not in the list at all. On average, the key will be somewhere in the middle of the list.

Chapter Summary

There's a lot of vocabulary that you are expected to know in this chapter. Learn the words!

Never make assumptions about a program specification, and always write a design before starting to write code. Even if you don't do this for your own programs, these are the answers you will be expected to give on the AP exam. You are certain to get questions about program design. Know the procedures and terminology involved in developing an object-oriented program.

Be sure you understand what is meant by best case, worst case, and average case for an algorithm. There will be questions about efficiency on the AP exam.

By now you should know what a precondition and postcondition are.

MULTIPLE-CHOICE QUESTIONS ON PROGRAM DESIGN AND ANALYSIS

1. A program that reads in a five-digit identification number is to be written. The specification does not state whether zero can be entered as a first digit. The programmer should
   (A) write the code to accept zero as a first digit since zero is a valid digit.
   (B) write the code to reject zero as a first digit since five-digit integers do not start with zero.
   (C) eliminate zero as a possibility for any of the digits.
   (D) treat the identification number as a four-digit number if the user enters a number starting with zero.
   (E) check with the writer of the specification whether zero is acceptable as a first digit.

2. Refer to the following three program descriptions:

   I Test whether there exists at least one three-digit integer whose value equals the sum of the squares of its digits.
   II Read in a three-digit code number and check if it is valid according to some given formula.
   III Passwords consist of three digits and three capital letters in any order. Read in a password, and check if there are any repeated characters.

   For which of the preceding program descriptions would a `ThreeDigitNumber` class be suitable?
   (A) I only
   (B) II only
   (C) III only
   (D) I and II only
   (E) I, II, and III

3. Top-down programming is illustrated by which of the following?
   (A) Writing a program from top to bottom in Java
   (B) Writing an essay describing how the program will work, without including any Java code
   (C) Using driver programs to test all methods in the order that they're called in the program
   (D) Writing and testing the lowest level methods first and then combining them to form appropriate abstract operations
   (E) Writing the program in terms of the operations to be performed and then refining these operations by adding more detail

4. Which of the following should influence your choice of a particular algorithm?

    I The run time of the algorithm
    II The memory requirements of the algorithm
    III The ease with which the logic of the algorithm can be understood

  (A) I only
  (B) III only
  (C) I and III only
  (D) I and II only
  (E) I, II, and III

5. A list of numbers is stored in a sorted array. It is required that the list be maintained in sorted order. This requirement leads to inefficient execution for which of the following processes?

    I Summing the five smallest numbers in the list
    II Finding the maximum value in the list
    III Inserting and deleting numbers

  (A) I only
  (B) III only
  (C) II and III only
  (D) I and III only
  (E) I, II, and III

6. Which of the following is *not* necessarily a feature of a robust program?
  (A) Does not allow execution to proceed with invalid data
  (B) Uses algorithms that give correct answers for extreme data values
  (C) Will run on any computer without modification
  (D) Will not allow division by zero
  (E) Will anticipate the types of errors that users of the program may make

7. A certain freight company charges its customers for shipping overseas according to this scale:

    $80 per ton for a weight of 10 tons or less
    $40 per ton for each additional ton over 10 tons but
        not exceeding 25 tons
    $30 per ton for each additional ton over 25 tons

For example, to ship a weight of 12 tons will cost $10(80) + 2(40) = \$880$. To ship 26 tons will cost $10(80) + 15(40) + 1(30) = \$1430$.

    A method takes as parameter an integer that represents a valid shipping weight and outputs the charge for the shipment. Which of the following is the smallest set of input values for shipping weights that will adequately test this method?
  (A) 10, 25
  (B) 5, 15, 30
  (C) 5, 10, 15, 25, 30
  (D) 0, 5, 10, 15, 25, 30
  (E) 5, 10, 15, 20, 25, 30

8. A code segment calculates the mean of values stored in integers n1, n2, n3, and n4 and stores the result in average, which is of type double. What kind of error is caused with this statement?

   ```
   double average = n1 + n2 + n3 + n4 / (double) 4;
   ```

   (A) Logic
   (B) Run-time
   (C) Overflow
   (D) Syntax
   (E) Type mismatch

9. A program evaluates binary arithmetic expressions that are read from an input file. All of the operands are integers, and the only operators are +, -, *, and /. In writing the program, the programmer forgot to include a test that checks whether the right-hand operand in a division expression equals zero. When will this oversight be detected?
   (A) At compile time
   (B) While editing the program
   (C) As soon as the data from the input file is read
   (D) During evaluation of the expressions
   (E) When at least one incorrect value for the expressions is output

10. Which best describes the precondition of a method? It is an assertion that
    (A) describes precisely the conditions that must be true at the time the method is called.
    (B) initializes the parameters of the method.
    (C) describes the effect of the method on its postcondition.
    (D) explains what the method does.
    (E) states what the initial values of the local variables in the method must be.

11. Consider the following code fragment:

```
//Precondition:  a1, a2, a3 contain 3 distinct integers.
//Postcondition: max contains the largest of a1, a2, a3.

//first set max equal to larger of a1 and a2
if (a1 > a2)
    max = a1;
else
    max = a2;
//set max equal to larger of max and a3
if (max < a3)
    max = a3;
```

For this algorithm, which of the following initial setups for a1, a2, and a3 will cause
    (1) the least number of computer operations (best case) and
    (2) the greatest number of computer operations (worst case)?

  (A)   (1) largest value in a1 or a2   (2) largest value in a3
  (B)   (1) largest value in a2 or a3   (2) largest value in a1
  (C)   (1) smallest value in a1   (2) largest value in a2
  (D)   (1) largest value in a2   (2) smallest value in a3
  (E)   (1) smallest value in a1 or a2   (2) largest value in a3

12. Refer to the following code segment.

```
//Compute the mean of integers 1 .. N.
//N is an integer >= 1 and has been initialized.
int k = 1;
double mean, sum = 1.0;
while (k < N)
{
    /* loop body */
}
mean = sum / N;
```

What is the precondition for the while loop?
  (A) k $\geq$ N,   sum = 1.0
  (B) sum = 1 + 2 + 3 + ... + k
  (C) k < N,   sum = 1.0
  (D) N $\geq$ 1,   k = 1,   sum = 1.0
  (E) mean = sum / N

13. The sequence of Fibonacci numbers is 1, 1, 2, 3, 5, 8, 13, 21, ... The first two Fibonacci numbers are each 1. Each subsequent number is obtained by adding the previous two. Consider this method:

```
//Precondition:  n >= 1.
//Postcondition: The nth Fibonacci number has been returned.
public static int fib(int n)
{
    int prev = 1, next = 1, sum = 1;
    for (int i = 3; i <= n; i++)
    {
        /* assertion */
        sum = next + prev;
        prev = next;
        next = sum;
    }
    return sum;
}
```

Which of the following is a correct /* assertion */ about the loop variable i?
(A) $1 \leq i \leq n$
(B) $0 \leq i \leq n$
(C) $3 \leq i \leq n$
(D) $3 < i \leq n$
(E) $3 < i < n+1$

14. Refer to the following method.

```
//Precondition: a and b are initialized integers.
public static int mystery(int a, int b)
{
    int total = 0, count = 1;
    while (count <= b)
    {
        total += a;
        count++;
    }
    return total;
}
```

What is the postcondition for method mystery?
(A) $total = a + b$
(B) $total = a^b$
(C) $total = b^a$
(D) $total = a * b$
(E) $total = a/b$

15. A program is to be written that prints an invoice for a small store. A copy of the invoice will be given to the customer and will display

    - A list of items purchased.
    - The quantity, unit price, and total price for each item.
    - The amount due.

    Three candidate classes for this program are `Invoice`, `Item`, and `ItemList`, where an `Item` is a single item purchased and `ItemList` is the list of all items purchased. Which class is a reasonable choice to be responsible for the `amountDue` method, which returns the amount the customer must pay?

      I `Item`

      II `ItemList`

      III `Invoice`

    (A) I only
    (B) III only
    (C) I and II only
    (D) II and III only
    (E) I, II, and III

16. Which is a *false* statement about classes in object-oriented program design?
    (A) If a class `C1` has an instance variable whose type is another class, `C2`, then `C1` *has-a* `C2`.
    (B) If a class `C1` is associated with another class, `C2`, then `C1` depends on `C2` for its implementation.
    (C) If classes `C1` and `C2` are related such that `C1` *is-a* `C2`, then `C2` *has-a* `C1`.
    (D) If class `C1` is independent, then none of its methods will have parameters that are objects of other classes.
    (E) Classes that have common methods do not necessarily define an inheritance relationship.

17. A Java program maintains a large database of vehicles and parts for a car dealership. Some of the classes in the program are `Vehicle`, `Car`, `Truck`, `Tire`, `Circle`, `SteeringWheel`, and `AirBag`. The declarations below show the relationships between classes. Which is a poor choice?

    (A)
    ```
    public class Vehicle
    {   ...
        private Tire[] tires;
        private SteeringWheel sw;
        ...
    }
    ```

    (B)
    ```
    public class Tire extends Circle
    {   ...
        //inherits methods that compute circumference
        //and center point
    }
    ```

    (C)
    ```
    public class Car extends Vehicle
    {   ...
        //inherits private Tire[] tires from Vehicle class
        //inherits private SteeringWheel sw from Vehicle class
        ...
    }
    ```

    (D)
    ```
    public class Tire
    {   ...
        private String rating;      //speed rating of tire
        private Circle boundary;
    }
    ```

    (E)
    ```
    public class SteeringWheel
    {   ...
        private AirBag ab;  //AirBag is stored in SteeringWheel
        private Circle boundary;
    }
    ```

18. A Java programmer has completed a preliminary design for a large program. The programmer has developed a list of classes, determined the methods for each class, established the relationships between classes, and written an interface for each class. Which class(es) should be implemented first?
    (A) Any superclasses
    (B) Any subclasses
    (C) All collaborator classes (classes that will be used to implement other classes)
    (D) The class that represents the dominant object in the program
    (E) All independent classes (classes that have no references to other classes)

Use the program description below for Questions 19–21.

A program is to be written that simulates bumper cars in a video game. The cars move on a square grid and are located on grid points (x, y), where x and y are integers between -20 and 20. A bumper car moves in a random direction, either left, right, up, or down. If it reaches a boundary (i.e., x or y is ± 20), then it reverses direction. If it is about to collide with another bumper car, it reverses direction. Your program should be able to add bumper cars and run the simulation. One step of the simulation allows each car in the grid to move. After a bumper car has reversed direction twice, its turn is over and the next car gets to move.

19. To identify classes in the program, the nouns in the specification are listed:

    program, bumper car, grid, grid point, integer, direction, boundary, simulation

    How many nouns in the list should immediately be discarded because they are unsuitable as classes for the program?
    (A) 0
    (B) 1
    (C) 2
    (D) 3
    (E) 4

A programmer decides to include the following classes in the program. Refer to them for Questions 20 and 21.

- `Simulation` will run the simulation.
- `Display` will show the state of the game.
- `BumperCar` will know its identification number, position in the grid, and current direction when moving.
- `GridPoint` will be a position in the grid. It will be represented by two integer fields, `x_coord` and `y_coord`.
- `Grid` will keep track of all bumper cars in the game, the number of cars, and their positions in the grid. It will update the grid each time a car moves. It will be implemented with a two-dimensional array of `BumperCar`.

20. Which operation should not be the responsibility of the `GridPoint` class?

    (A) `isEmpty`   returns false if grid point contains a `BumperCar`, true otherwise

    (B) `atBoundary`   returns true if x or y coordinate $= \pm 20$, false otherwise

    (C) `left`   if not at left boundary, change grid point to 1 unit left of current point

    (D) `up`   if not at top of grid, change grid point to 1 unit above current point

    (E) `get_x`   return x-coordinate of this point

21. Which method is not suitable for the `BumperCar` class?

    (A) `public boolean atBoundary()`
         `//Returns true if BumperCar at boundary, false otherwise.`

    (B) `public void selectRandomDirection()`
         `//Select random direction (up, down, left, or right)`
         `// at start of turn.`

    (C) `public void reverseDirection()`
         `//Move to grid position that is in direction opposite to`
         `// current direction.`

    (D) `public void move()`
         `//Take turn to move. Stop move after two changes`
         `// of direction.`

    (E) `public void update()`
         `//Modify Grid to reflect new position after each stage`
         `// of move.`

ANSWER KEY

1. E	8. A	15. D
2. D	9. D	16. C
3. E	10. A	17. B
4. E	11. A	18. E
5. B	12. D	19. C
6. C	13. C	20. A
7. C	14. D	21. E

ANSWERS EXPLAINED

1. **(E)** A programmer should never make unilateral decisions about a program specification. When in doubt, check with the person who wrote the specification.

2. **(D)** In I and II a three-digit number is the object being manipulated. For III, however, the object is a six-character string, which suggests a class other than a `ThreeDigitNumber`.

3. **(E)** Top-down programming consists of listing the methods for the main object and then using stepwise refinement to break each method into a list of subtasks. Eliminate choices A, C, and D: Top-down programming refers to the design and planning stage and does not involve any actual writing of code. Choice B is closer to the mark, but "top-down" implies a list of operations, not an essay describing the methods.

4. **(E)** All three considerations are valid when choosing an algorithm. III is especially important if your code will be part of a larger project created by several programmers. Yet even if you are the sole writer of a piece of software, be aware that your code may one day need to be modified by others.

5. **(B)** A process that causes excessive data movement is inefficient. Inserting an element into its correct (sorted) position involves moving elements to create a slot for this element. In the worst case, the new element must be inserted into the first slot, which involves moving every element up one slot. Similarly, deleting an element involves moving elements down a slot to close the "gap." In the worst case, where the first element is deleted, all elements in the array will need to be moved. Summing the five smallest elements in the list means summing the first five elements. This requires no testing of elements and no excessive data movement, so it is efficient. Finding the maximum value in a sorted list is very fast—just select the element at the appropriate end of the list.

6. **(C)** "Robustness" implies the ability to handle all data input by the user and to give correct answers even for extreme values of data. A program that is not robust may well run on another computer without modification, and a robust program may need modification before it can run on another computer.

7. **(C)** Eliminate choice D because 0 is an invalid weight, and you may infer from the method description that invalid data have already been screened out. Eliminate

choice E because it tests two values in the range 10–25. (This is not wrong, but choice C is better.) Eliminate choice A since it tests only the endpoint values. Eliminate B because it tests *no* endpoint values.

8. **(A)** The statement is syntactically correct, but as written it will not find the mean of the integers. The bug is therefore an intent or logic error. To execute as intended, the statement needs parentheses:

```
double average = (n1 + n2 + n3 + n4) / (double) 4;
```

9. **(D)** The error that occurs is a run-time error caused by an attempt to divide by zero (`ArithmeticException`). Don't be fooled by choice C. Simply reading an expression 8/0 from the input file won't cause the error. Note that if the operands were of type `double`, the correct answer would be E. In this case, dividing by zero does not cause an exception; it gives an answer of `Infinity`. Only on inspecting the output would it be clear that something was wrong.

10. **(A)** A precondition does not concern itself with the action of the method, the local variables, the algorithm, or the postcondition. Nor does it initialize the parameters. It simply asserts what must be true directly before execution of the method.

11. **(A)** The best case causes the fewest computer operations, and the worst case leads to the maximum number of operations. In the given algorithm, the initial test `if (a1 > a2)` and the assignment to `max` will occur irrespective of which value is the largest. The second test, `if (max < a3)`, will also always occur. The final statement, `max = a3`, will occur only if the largest value is in `a3`; thus, this represents the worst case. So the best case must have the biggest value in `a1` or `a2`.

12. **(D)** The precondition is an assertion about the variables in the loop just before the loop is executed. Variables `N`, `k`, and `sum` have all been initialized to the values shown in choice D. Choice C is wrong because `k` may equal `N`. Choice A is wrong because `k` may be less than `N`. Choice E is wrong because `mean` is not defined until the loop has been exited. Choice B is wrong because it omits the assertions about `N` and `k`.

13. **(C)** Eliminate choices A and B, since `i` is initialized to 3 in the `for` loop. Choices D and E are wrong because `i` is equal to 3 the first time through the loop.

14. **(D)** `a` is being added to `total` `b` times, which means that at the end of execution `total = a*b`.

15. **(D)** It makes sense for an `Item` to be responsible for its name, unit price, quantity, and total price. It is *not* reasonable for it to be responsible for other `Items`. Since an `ItemList`, however, will contain information for all the `Items` purchased, it is reasonable to have it also compute the total `amountDue`. It makes just as much sense to give an `Invoice` the responsibility for displaying information for the items purchased, as well as providing a final total, `amountDue`.

16. **(C)** The *is-a* relationship defines inheritance, while the *has-a* relationship defines association. These types of relationship are mutually exclusive. For example, a graduate student *is-a* student. It doesn't make sense to say a student *has-a* graduate student!

17. **(B)** Even though it's convenient for a `Tire` object to inherit `Circle` methods, an inheritance relationship between a `Tire` and a `Circle` is incorrect: It is false to say

that a Tire *is-a* Circle. A Tire is a car part, while a Circle is a geometric shape. Notice that there is an *association* relationship between a Tire and a Circle: A Tire *has-a* Circle as its boundary.

18. **(E)** Independent classes do not have relationships with other classes and can therefore be more easily coded and tested.

19. **(C)** The word "program" is never included when it's used in this context. The word "integer" describes the type of coordinates x and y and has no further use in the specification. While words like "direction," "boundary," and "simulation" may later be removed from consideration as classes, it is not unreasonable to keep them as candidates while you ponder the design.

20. **(A)** A GridPoint object knows only its x and y coordinates. It has no information about whether a BumperCar is at that point. Notice that operations in all of the other choices depend on the x and y coordinates of a GridPoint object. An isEmpty method should be the responsibility of the Grid class that keeps track of the status of each position in the grid.

21. **(E)** A BumperCar is responsible for itself—keeping track of its own position, selecting an initial direction, making a move, and reversing direction. It is not, however, responsible for maintaining and updating the grid. That should be done by the Grid class.

Arrays and Array Lists

Should array indices start at 0 or 1?
My compromise of 0.5 was rejected,
without, I thought, proper consideration.
—S. Kelly-Bootle

Chapter Goals

- One-dimensional arrays
- The `ArrayList<E>` class
- Two-dimensional arrays
- The `List<E>` interface

ONE-DIMENSIONAL ARRAYS

An array is a data structure used to implement a list object, where the elements in the list are of the same type; for example, a class list of 25 test scores, a membership list of 100 names, or a store inventory of 500 items.

For an array of N elements in Java, index values ("subscripts") go from 0 to $N - 1$. Individual elements are accessed as follows: If arr is the name of the array, the elements are `arr[0]`, `arr[1]`, ..., `arr[N-1]`. If a negative subscript is used, or a subscript k where $k \geq N$, an `ArrayIndexOutOfBoundsException` is thrown.

Initialization

In Java, an array is an object; therefore, the keyword `new` must be used in its creation. The size of an array remains fixed once it has been created. As with `String` objects, however, an array reference may be reassigned to a new array of a different size.

Example

All of the following are equivalent. Each creates an array of 25 `double` values and assigns the reference `data` to this array.

1. ```
   double[] data = new double[25];
   ```

2. ```
   double data[] = new double[25];
   ```

3. ```
   double[] data;
   data = new double[25];
   ```

A subsequent statement like
   ```

```
data = new double[40];
```

reassigns data to a new array of length 40. The memory allocated for the previous data array is recycled by Java's automatic garbage collection system.

When arrays are declared, the elements are automatically initialized to zero for the primitive numeric data types (int and double), to false for boolean variables, or to null for object references.

It is possible to declare several arrays in a single statement. For example,

```
int[] intList1, intList2;   //declares intList1 and intList2 to
                            //contain int values
int[] arr1 = new int[15], arr2 = new int[30];  //reserves 15 slots
                                     //for arr1, 30 for arr2
```

INITIALIZER LIST

Small arrays whose values are known can be declared with an *initializer list*. For example, instead of writing

```
int[] coins = new int[4];
coins[0] = 1;
coins[1] = 5;
coins[2] = 10;
coins[3] = 25;
```

you can write

```
int[] coins = {1, 5, 10, 25};
```

This construction is the one case where new is not required to create an array.

Length of Array

A Java array has a final public instance variable (i.e., a constant), length, which can be accessed when you need the number of elements in the array. For example,

```
String[] names = new String[25];
< code to initialize names >

//loop to process all names in array
for (int i = 0; i < names.length; i++)
     < process names >
```

NOTE

1. The array subscripts go from 0 to names.length-1; therefore, the test on i in the for loop must be strictly less than names.length.
2. length is not a method and therefore is not followed by parentheses. Contrast this with String objects, where length *is* a method and *must* be followed by parentheses. For example,

```
String s = "Confusing syntax!";
int size = s.length();    //assigns 17 to size
```

Traversing an Array

Do not use a for-each loop to remove or replace elements of an array.

Use a for-each loop whenever you need access to every element in an array without replacing or removing any elements. Use a for loop in all other cases: to access the index of any element, to replace or remove elements, or to access just some of the elements.

Note that if you have an array of objects (not primitive types), you can use the for-each loop and mutator methods of the object to modify the fields of any instance (see the shuffleAll method on p. 236).

Example 1

```
//Return the number of even integers in array arr of integers.
public static int countEven(int[] arr)
{
    int count = 0;
    for (int num : arr)
        if ( num % 2 == 0)    //num is even
            count++;
    return count;
}
```

Example 2

```
//Change each even-indexed element in array arr to 0.
//Precondition:  arr contains integers.
//Postcondition: arr[0], arr[2], arr[4], ... have value 0.
public static void changeEven(int[] arr)
{
    for (int i = 0; i < arr.length; i += 2)
        arr[i] = 0;
}
```

Arrays as Parameters

Since arrays are treated as objects, passing an array as a parameter means passing its object reference. No copy is made of the array. *Thus, the elements of the actual array can be accessed—and modified.*

Example 1

Array elements accessed but not modified:

```
//Return index of smallest element in array arr of integers.
public static int findMin (int[] arr)
{
    int min = arr[0];
    int minIndex = 0;
    for (int i = 1; i < arr.length; i++)
        if (arr[i] < min)    //found a smaller element
        {
            min = arr[i];
            minIndex = i;
        }
    return minIndex;
}
```

To call this method (in the same class that it's defined):

```
int[] array;
< code to initialize array >
int min = findMin(array);
```

NOTE

An alternative header for the method is

```
public static int findMin(int arr[])
```

Example 2

Array elements modified:

```
//Add 3 to each element of array b.
public static void changeArray(int[] b)
{
    for (int i = 0; i < b.length; i++)
        b[i] += 3;
}
```

To call this method (in the same class):

```
int[] list = {1, 2, 3, 4};
changeArray(list);
System.out.print("The changed list is ");
for (int num : list)
    System.out.print(num + " ");
```

The output produced is

```
The changed list is 4 5 6 7
```

> When an array is passed as a parameter, it is possible to alter the contents of the array.

Look at the memory slots to see how this happens:

Before the method call:

At the start of the method call:

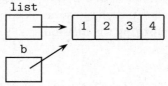

Just before exiting the method:

After exiting the method:

Example 3

Contrast the changeArray method with the following attempt to modify one array element:

```
//Add 3 to an element.
public static void changeElement(int n)
{ n += 3; }
```

Here is some code that invokes this method:

```
int[] list = {1, 2, 3, 4};
System.out.print("Original array: ");
for (int num : list)
    System.out.print(num + " ");
changeElement(list[0]);
System.out.print("\nModified array: ");
for (int num : list)
    System.out.print(num + " ");
```

Contrary to the programmer's expectation, the output is

```
Original array: 1 2 3 4
Modified array: 1 2 3 4
```

A look at the memory slots shows why the list remains unchanged.

The point of this is that primitive types—including single array elements of type `int` or `double`—are passed by value. A copy is made of the actual parameter, and the copy is erased on exiting the method.

Example 4

```
//Swap arr[i] and arr[j] in array arr.
public static void swap(int[] arr, int i, int j)
{
    int temp = arr[i];
    arr[i] = arr[j];
    arr[j] = temp;
}
```

To call the `swap` method:

```
int[] list = {1, 2, 3, 4};
swap(list, 0, 3);
System.out.print("The changed list is: ");
for (int num : list)
    System.out.print(num + " ");
```

The output shows that the program worked as intended:

```
The changed list is: 4 2 3 1
```

Example 5

```
//Precondition:  Array undefined.
//Postcondition: Returns array containing NUM_ELEMENTS integers
//                read from the keyboard.
public int[] getIntegers()
{
    int[] arr = new int[NUM_ELEMENTS];
    for (int i = 0; i < arr.length; i++)
    {
        System.out.println("Enter integer: ");
        arr[i] = IO.readInt();         //read user input
    }
    return arr;
}
```

To call this method:

```
int[] list = getIntegers();
```

Array Variables in a Class

Consider a simple Deck class in which a deck of cards is represented by the integers 0 to 51.

```
public class Deck
{
    private int[] myDeck;
    public static final int NUMCARDS = 52;

    //constructor
    public Deck()
    {
        myDeck = new int[NUMCARDS];
        for (int i = 0; i < NUMCARDS; i++)
            myDeck[i] = i;
    }

    //Write contents of Deck.
    public void writeDeck()
    {
        for (int card : myDeck)
            System.out.print(card + " ");
        System.out.println();
        System.out.println();
    }

    //Swap arr[i] and arr[j] in array arr.
    private void swap(int[] arr, int i, int j)
    {
        int temp = arr[i];
        arr[i] = arr[j];
        arr[j] = temp;
    }
```

```
//Shuffle Deck: Generate a random permutation by picking a
//   random card from those remaining and putting it in the
//   next slot, starting from the right.
public void shuffle()
{
    int index;
    for (int i = NUMCARDS - 1; i > 0; i--)
    {
        //generate an int from 0 to i
        index = (int) (Math.random() * (i + 1));
        swap(myDeck, i, index);
    }
}
```

Here is a simple driver class that tests the Deck class:

```
public class DeckMain
{
    public static void main(String args[])
    {
        Deck d = new Deck();
        d.shuffle();
        d.writeDeck();
    }
}
```

NOTE

There is no evidence of the array that holds the deck of cards—myDeck is a private instance variable and is therefore invisible to clients of the Deck class.

Array of Class Objects

Suppose a large card tournament needs to keep track of many decks. The code to do this could be implemented with an array of Deck:

```
public class ManyDecks
{
    private Deck[] allDecks;
    public static final int NUMDECKS = 500;

    //constructor
    public ManyDecks()
    {
        allDecks = new Deck[NUMDECKS];
        for (int i = 0; i < NUMDECKS; i++)
            allDecks[i] = new Deck();
    }

    //Shuffle the Decks.
    public void shuffleAll()
    {
        for (Deck d : allDecks)
            d.shuffle();
    }
```

```
    //Write contents of all the Decks.
    public void printDecks()
    {
        for (Deck d : allDecks)
            d.writeDeck();
    }
}
```

NOTE

The statement

```
allDecks = new Deck[NUMDECKS];
```

creates an array, `allDecks`, of 500 `Deck` objects. The default initialization for these `Deck` objects is null. In order to initialize them with actual decks, the `Deck` constructor must be called for each array element. This is achieved with the `for` loop of the `ManyDecks` constructor.

Analyzing Array Algorithms

Example 1

Discuss the efficiency of the `countNegs` method below. What are the best and worst case configurations of the data?

```
//Precondition:  arr[0],...,arr[arr.length-1] contain integers.
//Postcondition: Number of negative values in arr has been returned.
public static int countNegs(int[] arr)
{
    int count = 0;
    for (int num : arr)
        if (num < 0)
            count++;
    return count;
}
```

Solution:
This algorithm sequentially examines each element in the array. In the best case, there are no negative elements, and `count++` is never executed. In the worst case, all the elements are negative, and `count++` is executed in each pass of the `for` loop.

Example 2

The code fragment below inserts a value, `num`, into its correct position in a sorted array of integers. Discuss the efficiency of the algorithm.

```
//Precondition:  arr[0],...,arr[n-1] contain integers sorted in
//               increasing order. n < arr.length.
//Postcondition: num has been inserted in its correct position.
{
    //find insertion point
    int i = 0;
    while (i < n && num > arr[i])
        i++;
```

```
    //if necessary, move elements arr[i]...arr[n-1] up 1 slot
    for (int j = n; j >= i + 1; j--)
        arr[j] = arr[j-1];
    //insert num in i-th slot and update n
    arr[i] = num;
    n++;
}
```

Solution:

In the best case, num is greater than all the elements in the array: Because it gets inserted at the end of the list, no elements must be moved to create a slot for it. The worst case has num less than all the elements in the array. In this case, num must be inserted in the first slot, arr[0], and every element in the array must be moved up one position to create a slot.

This algorithm illustrates a disadvantage of arrays: Insertion and deletion of an element in an ordered list is inefficient, since, in the worst case, it may involve moving all the elements in the list.

ARRAY LISTS

An ArrayList provides an alternative way of storing a list of objects and has the following advantages over an array:

- An ArrayList shrinks and grows as needed in a program, whereas an array has a fixed length that is set when the array is created.

- In an ArrayList list, the last slot is always list.size()-1, whereas in a partially filled array, you, the programmer, must keep track of the last slot currently in use.

- For an ArrayList, you can do insertion or deletion with just a single statement. Any shifting of elements is handled automatically. In an array, however, insertion or deletion requires you to write the code that shifts the elements.

The Collections API

The ArrayList class is in the Collections API (Application Programming Interface), which is a library provided by Java. Most of the API is in java.util. This library gives the programmer access to prepackaged data structures and the methods to manipulate them. The implementations of these *container classes* are invisible and should not be of concern to the programmer. The code works. And it is reusable.

All of the collections classes, including ArrayList, have the following features in common:

- They are designed to be both memory and run-time efficient.

- They provide methods for insertion and removal of items (i.e., they can grow and shrink).

- They provide for iteration over the entire collection.

The Collections Hierarchy

Inheritance is a defining feature of the Collections API. The interfaces that are used to manipulate the collections specify the operations that must be defined for any container class that implements that interface.

The diagram below shows that the `ArrayList` class implements the `List` interface.

Collections and Generics

The collections classes are generic, with type parameters. Thus, `List<E>` and `ArrayList<E>` contain elements of type `E`.

When a generic class is declared, the type parameter is replaced by an actual object type. For example,

```
private ArrayList<Clown> clowns;
```

NOTE

1. The `clowns` list must contain only `Clown` objects. An attempt to add an `Acrobat` to the list, for example, will cause a compile-time error.
2. Since the type of objects in a generic class is restricted, the elements can be accessed without casting.
3. All of the type information in a program with generic classes is examined at compile time. After compilation the type information is erased. This feature of generic classes is known as *erasure*. During execution of the program, any attempt at incorrect casting will lead to a `ClassCastException`.

Auto-Boxing and -Unboxing

There are no primitive types in collections classes. An `ArrayList` must contain *objects*, not types like `double` and `int`. Numbers must therefore be boxed—placed in wrapper classes like `Integer` and `Double`—before insertion into an `ArrayList`.

Auto-boxing is the automatic wrapping of primitive types in their wrapper classes.

To retrieve the numerical value of an `Integer` (or `Double`) stored in an `ArrayList`, the `intValue()` (or `doubleValue()`) method must be invoked (unwrapping). *Auto-unboxing* is the automatic conversion of a wrapper class to its corresponding primitive type. This means that you don't need to explicitly call the `intValue()` or `doubleValue()` methods. Be aware that if a program tries to auto-unbox `null`, the method will throw a `NullPointerException`.

Note that while auto-boxing and -unboxing cut down on code clutter, these operations must still be performed behind the scenes, leading to decreased run-time efficiency. It is much more efficient to assign and access primitive types in an array than an `ArrayList`. You should therefore consider using an array for a program that manipulates sequences of numbers and does not need to use objects.

NOTE

Auto-boxing and -unboxing is a new feature in Java 5.0 and later versions, and will not be tested on the AP exam. It is OK, however, to use this convenient feature in code that you write in the free-response questions.

THE `List<E>` INTERFACE

A class that implements the `List<E>` interface—`ArrayList<E>`, for example—is a list of elements of type `E`. In a list, duplicate elements are allowed. The elements of the list are indexed, with 0 being the index of the first element.

A list allows you to

- Access an element at any position in the list using its integer index.
- Insert an element anywhere in the list.
- Iterate over all elements using `ListIterator` or `Iterator` (not in the AP subset).

The Methods of `List<E>`

Here are the methods you should know.

```
boolean add(E obj)
```

Appends `obj` to the end of the list. Always returns `true`. If the specified element is not of type `E`, throws a `ClassCastException`.

```
int size()
```

Returns the number of elements in the list.

```
E get(int index)
```

Returns the element at the specified `index` in the list.

```
E set(int index, E element)
```

Replaces item at specified `index` in the list with specified `element`. Returns the element that was previously at `index`. Throws a `ClassCastException` if the specified element is not of type `E`.

```
void add(int index, E element)
```

Inserts `element` at specified `index`. Elements from position `index` and higher have 1 added to their indices. Size of list is incremented by 1.

```
E remove(int index)
```

Removes and returns the element at the specified `index`. Elements to the right of position `index` have 1 subtracted from their indices. Size of list is decreased by 1.

```
Iterator<E> iterator()
```

Returns an iterator over the elements in the list, in proper sequence, starting at the first element.

The `ArrayList<E>` Class

This is an array implementation of the List<E> interface. The main difference between an array and an ArrayList is that an ArrayList is resizable during run time, whereas an array has a fixed size at construction.

Shifting of elements, if any, caused by insertion or deletion, is handled automatically by ArrayList. Operations to insert or delete at the end of the list are very efficient. Be aware, however, that at some point there will be a resizing; but, on average, over time, an insertion at the end of the list is a single, quick operation. In general, insertion or deletion in the middle of an ArrayList requires elements to be shifted to accommodate a new element (add), or to close a "hole" (remove).

THE METHODS OF `ArrayList<E>`

In addition to the two add methods, and size, get, set, and remove, you must know the following constructor.

```
ArrayList()
```

Constructs an empty list.

NOTE

Each method above that has an index parameter—add, get, remove, and set—throws an IndexOutOfBoundsException if index is out of range. For get, remove, and set, index is out of range if

```
index < 0 || index >= size()
```

For add, however, it is OK to add an element at the end of the list. Therefore index is out of range if

```
index < 0 || index > size()
```

Using `ArrayList<E>`

Example 1

```
//Create an ArrayList containing 0 1 4 9.
List<Integer> list = new ArrayList<Integer>(); //An ArrayList is-a List
for (int i = 0; i < 4; i++)
    list.add(i * i);  //example of auto-boxing
                      //i*i wrapped in an Integer before insertion
Integer intOb = list.get(2); //assigns Integer with value 4 to intOb.
                             //Leaves list unchanged.
int n = list.get(3);  //example of auto-unboxing
                      //Integer is retrieved and converted to int
                      //n contains 9
Integer x = list.set(3, 5);  //list is 0 1 4 5
                             //x contains Integer with value 9
```

```
x = list.remove(2);              //list is 0 1 5
                                 //x contains Integer with value 4
list.add(1, 7);                  //list is 0 7 1 5
list.add(2, 8);                  //list is 0 7 8 1 5
```

Example 2

```
//Traversing an ArrayList of Integer.
//Print the elements of list, one per line.
for (Integer num : list)
    System.out.println(num);
```

Example 3

```
/* Precondition:  List list is an ArrayList that contains Integer
 *                values sorted in increasing order.
 * Postcondition: value inserted in its correct position in list. */
public static void insert(List<Integer> list, Integer value)
{
    int index = 0;
    //find insertion point
    while (index < list.size() &&
            value.compareTo(list.get(index)) > 0)
        index++;
    //insert value
    list.add(index, value);
}
```

NOTE

Suppose value is larger than all the elements in list. Then the insert method will throw an IndexOutOfBoundsException if the first part of the test is omitted, namely index < list.size().

Example 4

```
//Return an ArrayList of random integers from 0 to 100.
public static List<Integer> getRandomIntList()
{
    List<Integer> list = new ArrayList<Integer>();
    System.out.print("How many integers? ");
    int length = IO.readInt();       //read user input
    for (int i = 0; i < length; i++)
    {
        int newNum = (int) (Math.random() * 101);
        list.add(new Integer(newNum));
    }
    return list;
}
```

NOTE

1. The variable list is declared to be of type List<Integer> (the interface) but is instantiated as type ArrayList<Integer> (the implementation).
2. The add method in getRandomIntList is the List method that appends its parameter to the end of the list.

Example 5

```
//Swap two values in list, indexed at i and j.
public static void swap(List<E> list, int i, int j)
{
    E temp = list.get(i);
    list.set(i, list.get(j));
    list.set(j, temp);
}
```

Example 6

```
//Print all negatives in list a.
//Precondition: a contains Integer values.
public static void printNegs(List<Integer> a)
{
    System.out.println("The negative values in the list are: ");
    for (Integer i : a)
        if (i.intValue() < 0)
            System.out.println(i);
}
```

Example 7

```
//Change every even-indexed element of strList to the empty string.
//Precondition: strList contains String values.
public static void changeEvenToEmpty(List<String> strList)
{
    boolean even = true;
    int index = 0;
    while (index < strList.size())
    {
        if (even)
            strList.set(index, "");
        index++;
        even = !even;
    }
}
```

Optional topic

COLLECTIONS AND ITERATORS

Definition of an Iterator

An *iterator* is an object whose sole purpose is to traverse a collection, one element at a time. During iteration, the iterator object maintains a current position in the collection, and is the controlling object in manipulating the elements of the collection.

The `Iterator<E>` Interface

The package `java.util` provides a generic interface, `Iterator<E>`, whose methods are `hasNext`, `next`, and `remove`. The Java Collections API allows iteration over each of its collections classes.

(continued)

THE METHODS OF Iterator<E>

```
boolean hasNext()
```

Returns true if there's at least one more element to be examined, false otherwise.

```
E next()
```

Returns the next element in the iteration. If no elements remain, the method throws a NoSuchElementException.

```
void remove()
```

Deletes from the collection the last element that was returned by next. This method can be called only once per call to next. It throws an IllegalStateException if the next method has not yet been called, or if the remove method has already been called after the last call to next.

Using a Generic Iterator

To iterate over a parameterized collection, you must use a parameterized iterator whose parameter is the same type.

Example 1

```
List<String> list = new ArrayList<String>();
< code to initialize list with strings>
//Print strings in list, one per line.
Iterator<String> itr = list.iterator();
while (itr.hasNext())
    System.out.println(itr.next());
```

NOTE

1. Only classes that allow iteration can use the for-each loop. This is because the loop operates by using an iterator. Thus, the loop in the above example is equivalent to

```
for (String str : list)    //no iterator in sight!
    System.out.println(str);
```

2. Recall, however, that a for-each loop cannot be used to remove elements from the list. The easiest way to "remove all occurrences of ..." from an ArrayList is to use an iterator.

Example 2

```
//Remove all 2-character strings from strList.
//Precondition: strList initialized with String objects.
public static void removeTwos(List<String> strList)
{
    Iterator<String> itr = strList.iterator();
    while (itr.hasNext())
        if (itr.next().length() == 2)
            itr.remove();
}
```

(continued)

Example 3

```
//Assume a list of integer strings.
//Remove all occurrences of "6" from the list.
Iterator<String> itr = list.iterator();
while (itr.hasNext())
{
    String num = itr.next();
    if (num.equals("6"))
    {
        itr.remove();
        System.out.println(list);
    }
}
```

If the original list is 2 6 6 3 5 6 the output will be

```
[2, 6, 3, 5, 6]
[2, 3, 5, 6]
[2, 3, 5]
```

Example 4

```
//Illustrate NoSuchElementException.
Iterator<SomeType> itr = list.iterator();
while (true)
    System.out.println(itr.next());
```

The list elements will be printed, one per line. Then an attempt will be made to move past the end of the list, causing a NoSuchElementException to be thrown. The loop can be corrected by replacing true with itr.hasNext().

Example 5

```
//Illustrate IllegalStateException.
Iterator<SomeType> itr = list.iterator();
SomeType ob = itr.next();
itr.remove();
itr.remove();
```

Every remove call must be preceded by a next. The second itr.remove() statement will therefore cause an IllegalStateException to be thrown.

NOTE

In a given program, the declaration

```
Iterator<SomeType> itr = list.iterator();
```

must be made every time you need to initialize the iterator to the beginning of the list.

Example 6

```
//Remove all negatives from intList.
//Precondition: intList contains Integer objects.
public static void removeNegs(List<Integer> intList)
{
    Iterator<Integer> itr = intList.iterator();
    while (itr.hasNext())
        if (itr.next().intValue() < 0)
            itr.remove();
}
```

(continued)

Every call to
remove must be
preceded by next.

NOTE

1. In Example 6 on p. 243 a for-each loop is used because each element is accessed without changing the list. An iterator operates unseen in the background. Contrast this with Example 6 on the previous page, where the list is changed by removing elements. Here you cannot use a for-each loop.
2. To test for a negative value, you could use

```
if (itr.next() < 0)
```

because of auto-unboxing.
3. Use a for-each loop for accessing and modifying objects in a list. Use an iterator for removal of objects.

TWO-DIMENSIONAL ARRAYS

A two-dimensional array (matrix) is often the data structure of choice for objects like board games, tables of values, theater seats, and mazes.

Look at the following 3×4 matrix:

$$
\begin{array}{cccc}
2 & 6 & 8 & 7 \\
1 & 5 & 4 & 0 \\
9 & 3 & 2 & 8
\end{array}
$$

If `mat` is the matrix variable, the row subscripts go from 0 to 2 and the column subscripts go from 0 to 3. The element `mat[1][2]` is 4, whereas `mat[0][2]` and `mat[2][3]` are both 8. As with one-dimensional arrays, if the subscripts are out of range, an `ArrayIndexOutOfBoundsException` is thrown.

Declarations

Each of the following declares a two-dimensional array:

```
int[][] table;       //table can reference a 2-D array of integers
                     //table is currently a null reference
double[][] matrix = new double[3][4];  //matrix references a 3 × 4
                                       //array of real numbers.
                                       //Each element has value 0.0
String[][] strs = new String[2][5]; //strs references a 2 × 5
                                    //array of String objects.
                                    //Each element is null
```

An *initializer list* can be used to specify a two-dimensional array:

```
int[][] mat = { {3, 4, 5},        //row 0
                {6, 7, 8} };      //row 1
```

This defines a 2×3 *rectangular* array (i.e., one in which each row has the same number of elements).

The initializer list is a list of lists in which each inside list represents a row of the matrix. Since a matrix is implemented as an array of rows (where each row is a one-dimensional array of elements), the quantity `mat.length` represents the number of rows. For any given row k, the quantity `mat[k].length` represents the number of elements in that row, namely the number of columns. (Java allows a variable number of elements in each row. Since these "jagged arrays" are not part of the AP Java subset, you can assume that `mat[k].length` is the same for all rows k of the matrix, i.e., that the matrix is rectangular.)

Processing a Two-Dimensional Array

Example 1

Find the sum of all elements in a matrix mat.

```
//Precondition: mat is initialized with integer values.
int sum = 0;
for (int r = 0; r < mat.length; r++)
    for (int c = 0; c < mat[r].length; c++)
        sum += mat[r][c];
```

NOTE

1. `mat[r][c]` represents the rth row and the cth column.
2. Rows are numbered from 0 to `mat.length-1`, and columns are numbered from 0 to `mat[r].length-1`. Any index that is outside these bounds will generate an `ArrayIndexOutOfBoundsException`.
3. Since elements are not being replaced, nested for-each loops can be used instead:

   ```
   for (int[] row : mat)        //for each row array in mat
       for (int element : row)  //for each element in this row
           sum += element;
   ```

   Optional topic

4. The AP Java subset does not include nested for-each loops for two-dimensional arrays. You can, however, use this construct in free-response questions where applicable—use it for accessing each element, but not for replacing or removing elements.

Example 2

Add 10 to each element in row 2 of matrix mat.

```
for (int c = 0; c < mat[2].length; c++)
    mat[2][c] += 10;
```

NOTE

1. In the for loop, you can use `c < mat[k].length`, where $0 \le k < \text{mat.length}$, since each row has the same number of elements.
2. You cannot use a for-each loop here because elements are being replaced.

Example 3

The major and minor diagonals of a square matrix are shown below:

Major diagonal

Minor diagonal

You can process the diagonals as follows:

```
int[][] mat = new int[SIZE][SIZE];  //SIZE is a constant int value

for (int i = 0; i < SIZE; i++)
    Process mat[i][i];              //major diagonal
        OR
    Process mat[i][SIZE - i - 1];   //minor diagonal
```

Two-Dimensional Array as Parameter

Example 1

Here is a method that counts the number of negative values in a matrix.

```
//Precondition: mat is initialized with integers.
//Postcondition: Returns count of negative values in mat.
public static int countNegs (int[][] mat)
{
    int count = 0;
    for (int r = 0; r < mat.length; r++)
        for (int c = 0; c < mat[0].length; c++)
            if (mat[r][c] < 0)
                count++;
    return count;
}
```

A method in the same class can invoke this method with a statement such as

```
int negs = countNegs(mat);
```

Example 2

Reading elements into a matrix:

```
//Precondition: Number of rows and columns known.
//Returns matrix containing rows × cols integers
//         read from the keyboard.
public static int[][] getMatrix(int rows, int cols)
{
    int[][] mat = new int[rows][cols];   //initialize slots
    System.out.println("Enter matrix, one row per line:");
    System.out.println();

    //read user input and fill slots
    for (int r = 0; r < rows; r++)
        for (int c = 0; c < cols; c++)
            mat[r][c] = IO.readInt();   //read user input
    return mat;
}
```

To call this method:

```
//prompt for number of rows and columns
int rows = IO.readInt();      //read user input
int cols = IO.readInt();      //read user input
int[][] mat = getMatrix(rows, cols);
```

Chapter Summary

Manipulation of one-dimensional arrays, two-dimensional arrays, and array lists should be second nature to you by now. Know the Java subset methods for the `List<E>` class. You must also know when these methods throw an `IndexOutOfBoundsException` and when an `ArrayIndexOutOfBoundsException` can occur.

When traversing an `ArrayList`:

- Use a for-each loop to access each element without changing it, or to modify each object in the list using a mutator method.

- Use an `Iterator` to remove elements. (This is not in the AP subset, but it is the easiest way to remove elements from an `ArrayList`.)

MULTIPLE-CHOICE QUESTIONS ON ARRAYS AND ARRAY LISTS

1. Which of the following correctly initializes an array `arr` to contain four elements each with value 0?

   I `int[] arr = {0, 0, 0, 0};`

   II `int[] arr = new int[4];`

   III `int[] arr = new int[4];`
   ```
   for (int i = 0; i < arr.length; i++)
       arr[i] = 0;
   ```

   (A) I only
   (B) III only
   (C) I and III only
   (D) II and III only
   (E) I, II, and III

2. The following program segment is intended to find the index of the first negative integer in `arr[0] ... arr[N-1]`, where `arr` is an array of `N` integers.

   ```
   int i = 0;
   while (arr[i] >= 0)
   {
       i++;
   }
   location = i;
   ```

   This segment will work as intended
   (A) always.
   (B) never.
   (C) whenever arr contains at least one negative integer.
   (D) whenever arr contains at least one nonnegative integer.
   (E) whenever arr contains no negative integers.

3. Refer to the following code segment. You may assume that `arr` is an array of `int` values.

   ```
   int sum = arr[0], i = 0;
   while (i < arr.length)
   {
       i++;
       sum += arr[i];
   }
   ```

   Which of the following will be the result of executing the segment?
   (A) Sum of `arr[0], arr[1], ..., arr[arr.length-1]` will be stored in `sum`.
   (B) Sum of `arr[1], arr[2], ..., arr[arr.length-1]` will be stored in `sum`.
   (C) Sum of `arr[0], arr[1], ..., arr[arr.length]` will be stored in `sum`.
   (D) An infinite loop will occur.
   (E) A run-time error will occur.

4. The following code fragment is intended to find the smallest value in
   `arr[0] ... arr[n-1]`.

```
//Precondition:  arr[0]...arr[n-1] initialized with integers.
//               arr is an array, arr.length = n.
//Postcondition: min = smallest value in arr[0]...arr[n-1].
int min = arr[0];
int i = 1;
while (i < n)
{
    i++;
    if (arr[i] < min)
        min = arr[i];
}
```

This code is incorrect. For the segment to work as intended, which of the following modifications could be made?

I Change the line

```
int i = 1;
```

to

```
int i = 0;
```

Make no other changes.

II Change the body of the while loop to

```
{
    if (arr[i] < min)
        min = arr[i];
    i++;
}
```

Make no other changes.

III Change the test for the while loop as follows:

```
while (i <= n)
```

Make no other changes.

(A) I only
(B) II only
(C) III only
(D) I and II only
(E) I, II, and III

5. Refer to the following code segment. You may assume that array `arr1` contains elements `arr1[0]`, `arr1[1]`, ..., `arr1[N-1]`, where N = `arr1.length`.

```
int count = 0;
for (int i = 0; i < N; i++)
    if (arr1[i] != 0)
    {
        arr1[count] = arr1[i];
        count++;
    }
int[] arr2 = new int[count];
for (int i = 0; i < count; i++)
    arr2[i] = arr1[i];
```

If array `arr1` initially contains the elements 0, 6, 0, 4, 0, 0, 2 in this order, what will `arr2` contain after execution of the code segment?

(A) 6, 4, 2
(B) 0, 0, 0, 0, 6, 4, 2
(C) 6, 4, 2, 4, 0, 0, 2
(D) 0, 6, 0, 4, 0, 0, 2
(E) 6, 4, 2, 0, 0, 0, 0

6. Consider this program segment:

```
for (int i = 2; i <= k; i++)
    if (arr[i] < someValue)
        System.out.print("SMALL");
```

What is the maximum number of times that SMALL can be printed?

(A) 0
(B) 1
(C) k - 1
(D) k - 2
(E) k

7. What will be output from the following code segment, assuming it is in the same class as the doSomething method?

    ```
    int[] arr = {1, 2, 3, 4};
    doSomething(arr);
    System.out.print(arr[1] + " ");
    System.out.print(arr[3]);
        ...
    public void doSomething(int[] list)
    {
        int[] b = list;
        for (int i = 0; i < b.length; i++)
            b[i] = i;
    }
    ```

    (A) 0 0
    (B) 2 4
    (C) 1 3
    (D) 0 2
    (E) 0 3

8. Consider writing a program that reads the lines of any text file into a sequential list of lines. Which of the following is a good reason to implement the list with an ArrayList of String objects rather than an array of String objects?
    (A) The get and set methods of ArrayList are more convenient than the [] notation for arrays.
    (B) The size method of ArrayList provides instant access to the length of the list.
    (C) An ArrayList can contain objects of any type, which leads to greater generality.
    (D) If any particular text file is unexpectedly long, the ArrayList will automatically be resized. The array, by contrast, may go out of bounds.
    (E) The String methods are easier to use with an ArrayList than with an array.

9. Consider writing a program that produces statistics for long lists of numerical data. Which of the following is the best reason to implement each list with an array of int (or double), rather than an ArrayList of Integer (or Double) objects?
    (A) An array of primitive number types is more efficient to manipulate than an ArrayList of wrapper objects that contain numbers.
    (B) Insertion of new elements into a list is easier to code for an array than for an ArrayList.
    (C) Removal of elements from a list is easier to code for an array than for an ArrayList.
    (D) Accessing individual elements in the middle of a list is easier for an array than for an ArrayList.
    (E) Accessing all the elements is more efficient in an array than in an ArrayList.

Refer to the following classes for Questions 10–13.

```
public class Address
{
    private String myName;
    private String myStreet;
    private String myCity;
    private String myState;
    private String myZip;

    //constructors
        ...

    //accessors
    public String getName()
    { return myName; }
    public String getStreet()
    { return myStreet; }
    public String getCity()
    { return myCity; }
    public String getState()
    { return myState; }
    public String getZip()
    { return myZip; }
}

public class Student
{
    private int idNum;
    private double gpa;
    private Address myAddress;

    //constructors
        ...

    //accessors
    public Address getAddress()
    { return myAddress; }
    public int getIdNum()
    { return idNum; }
    public double getGpa()
    { return gpa; }
}
```

10. A client method has this declaration, followed by code to initialize the list:

    ```
    Address[] list = new Address[100];
    ```

    Here is a code segment to generate a list of *names only*.

    ```
    for (Address a : list)
        /* line of code */
    ```

    Which is a correct /* *line of code* */?
    (A) `System.out.println(Address[i].getName());`
    (B) `System.out.println(list[i].getName());`
    (C) `System.out.println(a[i].getName());`
    (D) `System.out.println(a.getName());`
    (E) `System.out.println(list.getName());`

11. The following code segment is to print out a list of addresses:

    ```
    for (Address addr : list)
    {
        /* more code */
    }
    ```

    Which is a correct replacement for /* *more code* */?

    ```
      I System.out.println(list[i].getName());
        System.out.println(list[i].getStreet());
        System.out.print(list[i].getCity() + ", ");
        System.out.print(list[i].getState() + " ");
        System.out.println(list[i].getZip());

     II System.out.println(addr.getName());
        System.out.println(addr.getStreet());
        System.out.print(addr.getCity() + ", ");
        System.out.print(addr.getState() + " ");
        System.out.println(addr.getZip());

    III System.out.println(addr);
    ```

    (A) I only
    (B) II only
    (C) III only
    (D) I and II only
    (E) I, II, and III

12. A client method has this declaration:

```
Student[] allStudents = new Student[NUM_STUDS]; //NUM_STUDS is
                                                //an int constant
```

Here is a code segment to generate a list of Student names only. (You may assume that allStudents has been initialized.)

```
for (Student student : allStudents)
    /* code to print list of names */
```

Which is a correct replacement for /* *code to print list of names* */?
(A) System.out.println(allStudents.getName());
(B) System.out.println(student.getName());
(C) System.out.println(student.getAddress().getName());
(D) System.out.println(allStudents.getAddress().getName());
(E) System.out.println(student[i].getAddress().getName());

13. Here is a method that locates the Student with the highest idNum:

```
//Precondition:  Array stuArr of Student is initialized.
//Postcondition: Student with highest idNum has been returned.
public static Student locate(Student[] stuArr)
{
    /* method body */
}
```

Which of the following could replace /* *method body* */ so that the method works as intended?

```
I   int max = stuArr[0].getIdNum();
    for (Student student : stuArr)
        if (student.getIdNum() > max)
        {
            max = student.getIdNum();
            return student;
        }
    return stuArr[0];
```

```
II  Student highestSoFar = stuArr[0];
    int max = stuArr[0].getIdNum();
    for (Student student : stuArr)
        if(student.getIdNum() > max)
        {
            max = student.getIdNum();
            highestSoFar = student;
        }
    return highestSoFar;
```

```
III int maxPos = 0;
    for(int i = 1; i < stuArr.length; i++)
        if(stuArr[i].getIdNum() > stuArr[maxPos].getIdNum())
            maxPos = i;
    return stuArr[maxPos];
```

(A) I only
(B) II only
(C) III only
(D) I and III only
(E) II and III only

Questions 14–16 refer to the `Ticket` and `Transaction` classes below.

```java
public class Ticket
{
    private String myRow;
    private int mySeat;
    private double myPrice;

    //constructor
    public Ticket(String row, int seat, double price)
    {
        myRow = row;
        mySeat = seat;
        myPrice = price;
    }

    //accessors getRow(), getSeat(), and getPrice()
        ...
}

public class Transaction
{
    private int myNumTickets;
    private Ticket[] tickList;

    //constructor
    public Transaction(int numTicks)
    {
        myNumTickets = numTicks;
        tickList = new Ticket[numTicks];
        String row;
        int seat;
        double price;
        for (int i = 0; i < numTicks; i++)
        {
            < read user input for row, seat, and price >
                ...

            /* more code */
        }
    }

    //Returns total amount paid for this transaction.
    public double totalPaid()
    {
        double total = 0.0;
        /* code to calculate amount */
        return total;
    }
}
```

14. Which of the following correctly replaces /* *more code* */ in the `Transaction` constructor to initialize the `tickList` array?

    (A) `tickList[i] = new Ticket(getRow(), getSeat(), getPrice());`

    (B) `tickList[i] = new Ticket(row, seat, price);`

    (C) `tickList[i] = new tickList(getRow(), getSeat(), getPrice());`

    (D) `tickList[i] = new tickList(row, seat, price);`

    (E) `tickList[i] = new tickList(numTicks);`

15. Which represents correct /* *code to calculate amount* */ in the `totalPaid` method?

    (A) ```
    for (Ticket t : tickList)
        total += t.myPrice;
    ```

    (B) ```
    for (Ticket t : tickList)
        total += tickList.getPrice();
    ```

    (C) ```
    for (Ticket t : tickList)
        total += t.getPrice();
    ```

    (D) ```
    Transaction T;
    for (Ticket t : T)
        total += t.getPrice();
    ```

    (E) ```
    Transaction T;
    for (Ticket t : T)
        total += t.myPrice;
    ```

16. Suppose it is necessary to keep a list of all ticket transactions. A suitable declaration would be

    (A) `Transaction[] listOfSales = new Transaction[NUMSALES];`

    (B) `Transaction[] listOfSales = new Ticket[NUMSALES];`

    (C) `Ticket[] listOfSales = new Transaction[NUMSALES];`

    (D) `Ticket[] listOfSales = new Ticket[NUMSALES];`

    (E) `Transaction[] Ticket = new listOfSales[NUMSALES];`
    ```

17. Refer to method `match` below:

```
//Precondition:  v[0]..v[N-1] and w[0]..w[M-1] initialized with
//               integers. v[0] < v[1] < .. < v[N-1] and
//               w[0] < w[1] < .. < w[M-1].
//Postcondition: Returns true if there is an integer k that occurs
//               in both arrays, otherwise returns false.
public static boolean match(int[] v, int[] w, int N, int M)
{
    int vIndex = 0, wIndex = 0;
    while (vIndex < N && wIndex < M)
    {
        if (v[vIndex] == w[wIndex])
            return true;
        else if (v[vIndex] < w[wIndex])
            vIndex++;
        else
            wIndex++;
    }
    return false;
}
```

Assuming that the method has not been exited, which assertion is true at the end of every execution of the `while` loop?

(A) `v[0]..v[vIndex-1]` and `w[0]..w[wIndex-1]` contain no common value,
    `vIndex` ≤ `N` and `wIndex` ≤ `M`.

(B) `v[0]..v[vIndex]` and `w[0]..w[wIndex]` contain no common value,
    `vIndex` ≤ `N` and `wIndex` ≤ `M`.

(C) `v[0]..v[vIndex-1]` and `w[0]..w[wIndex-1]` contain no common value,
    `vIndex` ≤ `N-1` and `wIndex` ≤ `M-1`.

(D) `v[0]..v[vIndex]` and `w[0]..w[wIndex]` contain no common value,
    `vIndex` ≤ `N-1` and `wIndex` ≤ `M-1`.

(E) `v[0]..v[N-1]` and `w[0]..w[M-1]` contain no common value,
    `vIndex` ≤ `N` and `wIndex` ≤ `M`.

18. Consider this class:

```
public class Book
{
    private String myTitle;
    private String myAuthor;
    private boolean myCheckoutStatus;

    //constructor
    public Book(String title, String author)
    {
        myTitle = title;
        myAuthor = author;
        myCheckoutStatus = false;
    }

    //Change checkout status.
    public void changeStatus()
    { myCheckoutStatus = !myCheckoutStatus; }

    //other methods not shown ...
}
```

A client program has this declaration:

```
Book[] bookList = new Book[SOME_NUMBER];
```

Suppose bookList is initialized so that each Book in the list has a title, author, and checkout status. The following piece of code is written, whose intent is to change the checkout status of each book in bookList.

```
for (Book b : bookList)
    b.changeStatus();
```

Which is *true* about this code?
(A) The bookList array will remain unchanged after execution.
(B) Each book in the bookList array will have its checkout status changed, as intended.
(C) A NullPointerException may occur.
(D) A run-time error will occur because it is not possible to modify objects using the for-each loop.
(E) A logic error will occur because it is not possible to modify objects in an array without accessing the indexes of the objects.

Consider this class for Questions 19 and 20:

```
public class BingoCard
{
    private int[] myCard;

    /* Default constructor: Creates BingoCard with
     * 20 random digits in the range 1 - 90. */
    public BingoCard()
    { /* implementation not shown */ }

    /* Display BingoCard. */
    public void display()
    { /* implementation not shown */ }
        ...
}
```

A program that simulates a bingo game declares an array of BingoCard. The array has NUMPLAYERS elements, where each element represents the card of a different player. Here is a code segment that creates all the bingo cards in the game:

```
/* declare array of BingoCard */
/* construct each BingoCard */
```

19. Which of the following is a correct replacement for

    /* *declare array of* BingoCard */?

    (A) int[] BingoCard = new BingoCard[NUMPLAYERS];

    (B) BingoCard[] players = new int[NUMPLAYERS];

    (C) BingoCard[] players = new BingoCard[20];

    (D) BingoCard[] players = new BingoCard[NUMPLAYERS];

    (E) int[] players = new BingoCard[NUMPLAYERS];

20. Assuming that players has been declared as an array of BingoCard, which of the following is a correct replacement for
    /* *construct each* BingoCard */

    I for (BingoCard card : players)
           card = new BingoCard();

    II for (BingoCard card : players)
           players[card] = new BingoCard();

    III for (int i = 0; i < players.length; i++)
           players[i] = new BingoCard();

    (A) I only
    (B) II only
    (C) III only
    (D) I and III only
    (E) I, II, and III

21. Which declaration will cause an error?

    I `List<String> stringList = new ArrayList<String>();`

    II `List<int> intList = new ArrayList<int>();`

    III `ArrayList<Comparable> compList = new ArrayList<Comparable>();`

    (A) I only
    (B) II only
    (C) III only
    (D) I and III only
    (E) II and III only

22. Consider these declarations:

    ```
    List<String> strList = new ArrayList<String>();
    String ch = " ";
    Integer intOb = new Integer(5);
    ```

    Which statement will cause an error?
    (A) `strList.add(ch);`
    (B) `strList.add(new String("handy andy"));`
    (C) `strList.add(intOb.toString());`
    (D) `strList.add(ch + 8);`
    (E) `strList.add(intOb + 8);`

23. Let `list` be an `ArrayList<Integer>` containing these elements:

    `2 5 7 6 0 1`

    Which of the following statements would *not* cause an error to occur? Assume that each statement applies to the given list, independent of the other statements.
    (A) `Object ob = list.get(6);`
    (B) `Integer intOb = list.add(3.4);`
    (C) `list.add(6, 9);`
    (D) `Object x = list.remove(6);`
    (E) `Object y = list.set(6, 8);`

24. Refer to method `insert` below:

```
/* Precondition:  List list is an ArrayList that contains
 *                Comparable values sorted in decreasing order.
 * Postcondition: Element inserted in its correct position
 *                in list. */
public void insert(List<Comparable> list, Comparable element)
{
    int index = 0;
    while (element.compareTo(list.get(index)) < 0)
        index++;
    list.add(index, element);
}
```

Assuming that the type of `element` is compatible with the objects in the list, which is a *true* statement about the `insert` method?
(A) It works as intended for all values of `element`.
(B) It fails for all values of `element`.
(C) It fails if `element` is greater than the first item in `list` and works in all other cases.
(D) It fails if `element` is smaller than the last item in `list` and works in all other cases.
(E) It fails if `element` is either greater than the first item or smaller than the last item in `list` and works in all other cases.

25. Consider the following code segment, applied to `list`, an `ArrayList` of `Integer` values.

```
int len = list.size();
for (int i = 0; i < len; i++)
{
    list.add(i + 1, new Integer(i));
    Object x = list.set(i, new Integer(i + 2));
}
```

If `list` is initially 6 1 8, what will it be following execution of the code segment?
(A) 2 3 4 2 1 8
(B) 2 3 4 6 2 2 0 1 8
(C) 2 3 4 0 1 2
(D) 2 3 4 6 1 8
(E) 2 3 3 2

Questions 26 and 27 are based on the `Coin` and `Purse` classes given below:

```
/* A simple coin class */
public class Coin
{
    private double myValue;
    private String myName;

    //constructor
    public Coin(double value, String name)
    {
        myValue = value;
        myName = name;
    }

    //Return the value and name of this coin.

    public double getValue()
    { return myValue; }

    public String getName()
    { return myName; }

    //Define equals method for Coin objects.
    public boolean equals(Object obj)
    { /* implementation not shown */ }

    //Other methods not shown.
        ...
}


/* A purse holds a collection of coins */
public class Purse
{
    private List<Coin> coins;

    //constructor
    //Creates an empty purse.
    public Purse()
    { coins = new ArrayList<Coin>(); }

    //Adds aCoin to the purse.
    public void add(Coin aCoin)
    { coins.add(aCoin); }

    //Returns total value of coins in purse.
    public double getTotal()
    { /* implementation not shown */}

}
```

26. Here is the getTotal method from the Purse class:

```
//Returns total value of coins in purse.
public double getTotal()
{
    double total = 0;
    /* more code */
    return total;
}
```

Which of the following is a correct replacement for /* *more code* */?

(A)
```
for (Coin c : coins)
{
    c = coins.get(i);
    total += c.getValue();
}
```

(B)
```
for (Coin c : coins)
{
    Coin value = c.getValue();
    total += value;
}
```

(C)
```
for (Coin c : coins)
{
    Coin c = coins.get(i);
    total += c.getValue();
}
```

(D)
```
for (Coin c : coins)
{
    total += coins.getValue();
}
```

(E)
```
for (Coin c : coins)
{
    total += c.getValue();
}
```

27. A boolean method `find` is added to the `Purse` class:

```
/* Returns true if the purse has a coin that matches aCoin,
 * false otherwise.  */
public boolean find(Coin aCoin)
{
    for (Coin c : coins)
    {
        /* code to find match */
    }
    return false;
}
```

Which is a correct replacement for /* *code to find match* */?

```
 I if (c.equals(aCoin))
        return true;

 II if ((c.getName()).equals(aCoin.getName()))
        return true;

III if ((c.getValue()).equals(aCoin.getValue()))
        return true;
```

(A) I only
(B) II only
(C) III only
(D) I and II only
(E) I, II, and III

28. Which of the following initializes an 8 × 10 matrix with integer values that are perfect squares? (0 is a perfect square.)

```
  I int[][] mat = new int[8][10];

 II int[][] mat = new int[8][10];
    for (int r = 0; r < mat.length; r++)
        for (int c = 0; c < mat[r].length; c++)
            mat[r][c] = r * r;

III int[][] mat = new int[8][10];
    for (int c = 0; c < mat[r].length; c++)
        for (int r = 0; r < mat.length; r++)
            mat[r][c] = c * c;
```

(A) I only
(B) II only
(C) III only
(D) I and II only
(E) I, II, and III

29. Consider a class that has this private instance variable:

```
private int[][] mat;
```

The class has the following method, `alter`.

```
public void alter(int c)
{
    for (int i = 0; i < mat.length; i++)
        for (int j = c + 1; j < mat[0].length; j++)
            mat[i][j-1] = mat[i][j];
}
```

If a 3 × 4 matrix mat is

```
1 3 5 7
2 4 6 8
3 5 7 9
```

then `alter(1)` will change mat to

(A) 1 5 7 7
     2 6 8 8
     3 7 9 9

(B) 1 5 7
     2 6 8
     3 7 9

(C) 1 3 5 7
     3 5 7 9

(D) 1 3 5 7
     3 5 7 9
     3 5 7 9

(E) 1 7 7 7
     2 8 8 8
     3 9 9 9

30. Consider the following method that will alter the matrix mat:

```
//Precondition: mat is initialized.
public static void matStuff(int[][] mat, int row)
{
    int numCols = mat[0].length;
    for (int col = 0; col < numCols; col++)
        mat[row][col] = row;
}
```

Suppose mat is originally

```
1   4   9   0
2   7   8   6
5   1   4   3
```

After the method call matStuff(mat,2), matrix mat will be

(A) 1   4   9   0
     2   7   8   6
     2   2   2   2

(B) 1   4   9   0
     2   2   2   2
     5   1   4   3

(C) 2   2   2   2
     2   2   2   2
     2   2   2   2

(D) 1   4   2   0
     2   7   2   6
     5   1   2   3

(E) 1   2   9   0
     2   2   8   6
     5   2   4   3

31. Assume that a square matrix mat is defined by

```
int[][] mat = new int[SIZE][SIZE];
//SIZE is an integer constant >= 2
```

What does the following code segment do?

```
for (int i = 0; i < SIZE - 1; i++)
    for (int j = 0; j < SIZE - i - 1; j++)
        swap(mat, i, j, SIZE - j - 1, SIZE - i - 1);
```

You may assume the existence of this swap method:

```
//Interchange mat[a][b] and mat[c][d].
public void swap(int[][] mat, int a, int b, int c, int d)
```

(A) Reflects mat through its major diagonal. For example,

$$
\begin{matrix} 2 & 6 \\ 4 & 3 \end{matrix} \longrightarrow \begin{matrix} 2 & 4 \\ 6 & 3 \end{matrix}
$$

(B) Reflects mat through its minor diagonal. For example,

$$
\begin{matrix} 2 & 6 \\ 4 & 3 \end{matrix} \longrightarrow \begin{matrix} 3 & 6 \\ 4 & 2 \end{matrix}
$$

(C) Reflects mat through a horizontal line of symmetry. For example,

$$
\begin{matrix} 2 & 6 \\ 4 & 3 \end{matrix} \longrightarrow \begin{matrix} 4 & 3 \\ 2 & 6 \end{matrix}
$$

(D) Reflects mat through a vertical line of symmetry. For example,

$$
\begin{matrix} 2 & 6 \\ 4 & 3 \end{matrix} \longrightarrow \begin{matrix} 6 & 2 \\ 3 & 4 \end{matrix}
$$

(E) Leaves mat unchanged.

32. Consider a class `MatrixStuff` that has a private instance variable:

    ```
    private int[][] mat;
    ```

    Refer to method `alter` below that occurs in the `MatrixStuff` class. (The lines are numbered for reference.)

    ```
    1   //Precondition:  mat is initialized with integers.
    2   //Postcondition: column c has been removed and the last column
    3   //               is filled with zeros.
    4   public void alter(int[][] mat, int c)
    5   {
    6       for (int i = 0; i < mat.length; i++)
    7           for (int j = c; j < mat[0].length; j++)
    8               mat[i][j] = mat[i][j+1];
    9       //code to insert zeros in rightmost column
    10          ...
    11  }
    ```

    The intent of the method `alter` is to remove column c. Thus, if the input matrix `mat` is

    ```
    2   6   8   9
    1   5   4   3
    0   7   3   2
    ```

    the method call `alter(mat, 1)` should change `mat` to

    ```
    2   8   9   0
    1   4   3   0
    0   3   2   0
    ```

    The method does not work as intended. Which of the following changes will correct the problem?

    I Change line 7 to

    ```
    for (int j = c; j < mat[0].length - 1; j++)
    ```

    and make no other changes.

    II Change lines 7 and 8 to

    ```
    for (int j = c + 1; j < mat[0].length; j++)
        mat[i][j-1] = mat[i][j];
    ```

    and make no other changes.

    III Change lines 7 and 8 to

    ```
    for (int j = mat[0].length - 1; j > c; j--)
        mat[i][j-1] = mat[i][j];
    ```

    and make no other changes.

    (A) I only
    (B) II only
    (C) III only
    (D) I and II only
    (E) I, II, and III

33. This question refers to the following method:

```
public static boolean isThere(String[][] mat, int row, int col,
    String symbol)
{
    boolean yes;
    int i, count = 0;
    for (i = 0; i < SIZE; i++)
        if (mat[i][col].equals(symbol))
            count++;
    yes = (count == SIZE);
    count = 0;
    for (i = 0; i < SIZE; i++)
        if (mat[row][i].equals(symbol))
            count++;
    return (yes || count == SIZE);
}
```

Now consider this code segment:

```
public final int SIZE = 8;
String[][] mat = new String[SIZE][SIZE];
```

Which of the following conditions on a matrix mat of the type declared in the code segment will by itself guarantee that

```
isThere(mat, 2, 2, "$")
```

will have the value true when evaluated?

   I The element in row 2 and column 2 is "$"
  II All elements in both diagonals are "$"
 III All elements in column 2 are "$"

(A) I only
(B) III only
(C) I and II only
(D) I and III only
(E) II and III only

Questions 34–37 use the nested for-each loop for two-dimensional arrays.

34. The method `changeNegs` below should replace every occurrence of a negative integer in its matrix parameter with 0.

```
//Precondition: mat is initialized with integers.
//Postcondition: All negative values in mat replaced with 0.
public static void changeNegs(int[][] mat)
{
    /* code */
}
```

Which is correct replacement for */* code */?*

```
 I for (int r = 0; r < mat.length; r++)
        for (int c = 0; c < mat[r].length; c++)
            if (mat[r][c] < 0)
                mat[r][c] = 0;

 II for (int c = 0; c < mat[0].length; c++)
        for (int r = 0; r < mat.length; r++)
            if (mat[r][c] < 0)
                mat[r][c] = 0;

III for (int[] row : mat)
        for (int element : row)
            if (element < 0)
                element = 0;
```

(A) I only
(B) II only
(C) III only
(D) I and II only
(E) I, II, and III

(continued)

35. This question is based on the `Point` class below:

```
public class Point
{
    private int x;
    private int y;

    //constructor
    public Point (int x, int y)
    {
        this.x = x;
        this.y = y;
    }

    //accessors
    public int getx()
    { return x; }

    public int gety()
    { return y; }

    //Set x and y to new_x and new_y.
    public void setPoint(int new_x, int new_y)
    {
        x = new_x;
        y = new_y;
    }

    //Return Point in String form.
    public String toString()
    {
        return "(" + x + "," + y + ")";
    }

    //other methods not shown
        ...
}
```

The method `changeNegs` below takes a matrix of `Point` objects as parameter and replaces every `Point` that has as least one negative coordinate with the `Point` (0,0).

```
/* Precondition:  pointMat is initialized with Point objects.
 * Postcondition: Every point with at least one negative
 *                coordinate has been changed to have both
 *                coordinates equal to zero.  */
public static void changeNegs (Point [][] pointMat)
{
    /* code */
}
```

Which is a correct replacement for /* *code* */?

(continued)

```
 I  for (int r = 0; r < pointMat.length; r++)
        for (int c = 0; c < pointMat[r].length; c++)
            if (pointMat[r][c].getx() < 0
                || pointMat[r][c].gety() < 0)
                    pointMat[r][c].setPoint(0, 0);

II  for (int c = 0; c < pointMat[0].length; c++)
        for (int r = 0; r < pointMat.length; r++)
            if (pointMat[r][c].getx() < 0
                || pointMat[r][c].gety() < 0)
                    pointMat[r][c].setPoint(0, 0);

III for (Point[] row : pointMat)
        for (Point p : row)
            if (p.getx() < 0 || p.gety() < 0)
                    p.setPoint(0, 0);
```

(A) I only
(B) II only
(C) III only
(D) I and II only
(E) I, II, and III

36. A simple Tic-Tac-Toe board is a 3 × 3 array filled with either X's, O's, or blanks. Here is a class for a game of Tic-Tac-Toe:

```java
public class TicTacToe
{
    private String[][] board;
    private static final int ROWS = 3;
    private static final int COLS = 3;

    //constructor. constructs empty board
    public TicTacToe()
    {
        board = new String[ROWS][COLS];
        for (int r = 0; r < ROWS; r++)
            for (int c = 0; c < COLS; c++)
                board[r][c] = " ";
    }

    /* Precondition:  square on Tic-Tac-Toe board is empty.
     * Postcondition: symbol placed in that square. */
    public void makeMove(int r, int c, String symbol)
    {
        board[r][c] = symbol;
    }

    /* Creates a string representation of the board, e.g.
     *    |o  |
     *    |xx |
     *    |  o|
     * Postcondition: returns the string representation. */
    public String toString()
    {
        String s = "";      //empty string
        < more code >
        return s;
    }
}
```

Which segment represents a correct replacement for *< more code >* for the toString method?

```java
(A) for (int r = 0; r < ROWS; r++)
    {
        for (int c = 0; c < COLS; c++)
        {
            s = s + "|";
            s = s + board[r][c];
            s = s + "|\n";
        }
    }
```

(B)
```
    for (int r = 0; r < ROWS; r++)
    {
        s = s + "|";
        for (int c = 0; c < COLS; c++)
        {
            s = s + board[r][c];
            s = s + "|\n";
        }
    }
```

(C)
```
    for (int r = 0; r < ROWS; r++)
    {
        s = s + "|";
        for (int c = 0; c < COLS; c++)
            s = s + board[r][c];
    }
    s = s + "|\n";
```

(D)
```
    for (int r = 0; r < ROWS; r++)
        s = s + "|";
    for (int c = 0; c < COLS; c++)
    {
        s = s + board[r][c];
        s = s + "|\n";
    }
```

(E)
```
    for (int r = 0; r < ROWS; r++)
    {
        s = s + "|";
        for (int c = 0; c < COLS; c++)
            s = s + board[r][c];
        s = s + "|\n";
    }
```

37. A two-dimensional array of `double`, `rainfall`, will be used to represent the daily rainfall for a given year. In this scheme, `rainfall[month][day]` represents the amount of rain on the given day and month. For example,

    `rainfall[1][15]`   is the amount of rain on Jan. 15
    `rainfall[12][25]`   is the amount of rain on Dec. 25

The array can be declared as follows:

`double[][] rainfall = new double[13][32];`

This creates 13 rows indexed from 0 to 12 and 32 columns indexed from 0 to 31, all initialized to 0.0. Row 0 and column 0 will be ignored. Column 31 in row 4 will be ignored, since April 31 is not a valid day. In years that are not leap years, columns 29, 30, and 31 in row 2 will be ignored since Feb. 29, 30, and 31 are not valid days.

Consider the method `averageRainfall` below:

```
/* Precondition:  rainfall is initialized with values
 *                representing amounts of rain on all valid
 *                days. Invalid days are initialized to 0.0.
 *                Feb 29 is not a valid day.
 * Postcondition: Returns average rainfall for the year. */
public double averageRainfall(double rainfall[][])
{
    double total = 0.0;
    /* more code */
}
```

Which of the following is a correct replacement for /* *more code* */ so that the postcondition for the method is satisfied?

```
 I for (int month = 1; month < rainfall.length; month++)
        for (int day = 1; day < rainfall[month].length; day++)
            total += rainfall[month][day];
    return total / (13 * 32);
```

```
 II for (int month = 1; month < rainfall.length; month++)
        for (int day = 1; day < rainfall[month].length; day++)
            total += rainfall[month][day];
    return total / 365;
```

```
III for (double[] month : rainfall)
        for (double rainAmt : month)
            total += rainAmt;
    return total / 365;
```

(A) None
(B) I only
(C) II only
(D) III only
(E) II and III only

ANSWER KEY

1. E	14. B	27. D
2. C	15. C	28. D
3. E	16. A	29. A
4. B	17. A	30. A
5. A	18. B	31. B
6. C	19. D	32. D
7. C	20. C	33. B
8. D	21. B	34. D
9. A	22. E	35. E
10. D	23. C	36. E
11. B	24. D	37. E
12. C	25. A	
13. E	26. E	

ANSWERS EXPLAINED

1. **(E)** Segment I is an initializer list which is equivalent to

```
int[] arr = new int[4];
arr[0] = 0;
arr[1] = 0;
arr[2] = 0;
arr[3] = 0;
```

   Segment II creates four slots for integers, which by default are initialized to 0. The for loop in segment III is therefore unnecessary. It is not, however, incorrect.

2. **(C)** If arr contains no negative integers, the value of i will eventually exceed N-1, and arr[i] will cause an ArrayIndexOutOfBoundsException to be thrown.

3. **(E)** The intent is to sum elements arr[0], arr[1], ..., arr[arr.length-1]. Notice, however, that when i has the value arr.length-1, it is incremented to arr.length in the loop, so the statement sum += arr[i] uses arr[arr.length], which is out of range.

4. **(B)** There are two problems with the segment as given:

   1. arr[1] is not tested.
   2. When i has a value of n-1, incrementing i will lead to an out-of-range error for the if(arr[i] < min) test.

   Modification II corrects both these errors. The change suggested in III corrects neither of these errors. The change in I corrects (1) but not (2).

5. **(A)** The code segment has the effect of removing all occurrences of 0 from array arr1. Then the nonzero elements are transferred to array arr2.

6. **(C)** If `arr[i]` < `someValue` for all `i` from 2 to `k`, `SMALL` will be printed on each iteration of the `for` loop. Since there are `k - 1` iterations, the maximum number of times that `SMALL` can be printed is `k - 1`.

7. **(C)** Array `arr` is changed by `doSomething`. Here are the memory slots:

Just before `doSomething` is called:

Just after `doSomething` is called,
but before the `for` loop is executed:

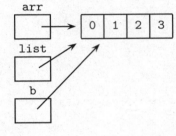

Just before exiting `doSomething`:

Just after exiting `doSomething`:

8. **(D)** Arrays are of fixed length and do not shrink or grow if the size of the data set varies. An `ArrayList` automatically resizes the list. Choice A is false: The `[]` notation is compact and easy to use. Choice B is not a valid reason because an array `arr` also provides instant access to its length with the quantity `arr.length`. Choice C is invalid because an array can also contain objects. Also, generality is beside the point in the given program: The list *must* hold `String` objects. Choice E is false: Whether a `String` object is `arr[i]` or `list.get(i)`, the `String` methods are equally easy to invoke.

9. **(A)** In order for numerical elements to be added to an `ArrayList`, each element must be wrapped in a wrapper class before insertion into the list. Then, to retrieve a numerical value from the `ArrayList`, the element must be unboxed using the `intValue` or `doubleValue` methods. Even though these operations can be taken care of with auto-boxing and -unboxing, there are efficiency costs. In an array, you simply use the `[]` notation for assignment (as in `arr[i] = num`) or retrieval (`value = arr[i]`). Note that choices B and C are false statements: Both insertion and deletion for an array involve writing code to shift elements. An `ArrayList` automatically takes care of this through its `add` and `remove` methods. Choice D is a poor reason for choosing an array. While the `get` and `set` methods of `ArrayList` might be slightly more awkward than using the `[]` notation, both mechanisms work pretty easily. Choice E is false: Efficiency of access is roughly the same.

10. **(D)** For each `Address` object `a` in `list`, access the name of the object with `a.getName()`.

11. **(B)** Since the `Address` class does not have a `toString` method, each data field must explicitly be printed. Segment III would work if there *were* a `toString` method

for the class (but there isn't, so it doesn't!). Segment I fails because of incorrect use of the for-each loop: The array index should not be accessed.

12. **(C)** Each `Student` name must be accessed through the `Address` class accessor `getName()`. The expression `student.getAddress()` accesses the entire address of that student. The `myName` field is then accessed using the `getName()` accessor of the `Address` class.

13. **(E)** Both correct solutions are careful not to lose the student who has the highest `idNum` so far. Segment II does it by storing a reference to the student, `highestSoFar`. Segment III does it by storing the array index of that student. Code segment I is incorrect because it returns the first student whose `idNum` is greater than `max`, not necessarily the student with the highest `idNum` in the list.

14. **(B)** For each `i`, `tickList[i]` is a new `Ticket` object that must be constructed using the `Ticket` constructor. Therefore eliminate choices C, D, and E. Choice A is wrong because `getRow()`, `getSeat()`, and `getPrice()` are accessors for values *that already exist* for some `Ticket` object. Note also the absence of the dot member construct.

15. **(C)** To access the price for each `Ticket` in the `tickList` array, the `getPrice()` accessor in the `Ticket` class must be used, since `myPrice` is private to that class. This eliminates choices A and E. Choice B uses the array name incorrectly. Choices D and E incorrectly declare a `Transaction` object. (The method applies to an existing `Transaction` object.)

16. **(A)** An array of type `Transaction` is required. This eliminates choices C and D. Additionally, choices B and D incorrectly use type `Ticket` on the right-hand side. Choice E puts the identifier `listOfSales` in the wrong place.

17. **(A)** Notice that either `vIndex` or `wIndex` is incremented at the end of the loop. This means that, when the loop is exited, the current values of `v[vIndex]` and `w[wIndex]` have not been compared. Therefore, you can only make an assertion for values `v[0]..v[vIndex-1]` and `w[0]..w[wIndex-1]`. Also, notice that if there is no common value in the arrays, the exiting condition for the `while` loop will be that the end of one of the arrays has been reached, namely `vIndex` equals `N` or `wIndex` equals `M`.

18. **(B)** Objects in an array can be changed in a for-each loop by using mutator methods of the objects' class. The `changeStatus` method, a mutator in the `Book` class, will work as intended in the given code. Choice C would be true if it were not given that each `Book` in `bookList` was initialized. If any given `b` had a value of `null`, then a `NullPointerException` would be thrown.

19. **(D)** The declaration must start with the type of value in the array, namely `BingoCard`. This eliminates choices A and E. Eliminate choice B: The type on the right of the assignment should be `BingoCard`. Choice C is wrong because the number of slots in the array should be `NUMPLAYERS`, not 20.

20. **(C)** Segment III is the only segment that works, since the for-each loop cannot be used to replace elements in an array. After the declaration

```
BingoCard[] players = new BingoCard[NUMPLAYERS];
```

each element in the `players` array is `null`. The intent in the given code is to replace each null reference with a newly constructed `BingoCard`.

21. **(B)** The type parameter in a generic `ArrayList` must be a class type, not a primitive.

22. **(E)** All elements added to `strList` must be of type `String`. Each choice satisfies this except choice E. Note that in choice D, the expression `ch + 8` becomes a `String` since `ch` is a `String` (just one of the operands needs to be a `String` to convert the whole expression to a `String`). In choice E, neither `intOb` nor 8 is a `String`.

23. **(C)** The effect of choice C is to adjust the size of the list to 7 and to add the `Integer` 9 to the last slot (i.e., the slot with index 6). Choices A, D, and E will all cause an `IndexOutOfBoundsException` because there is no slot with index 6: the last slot has index 5. Choice B will cause a compile-time error, since it is attempting to add an element of type `Double` to a list of type `Integer`.

24. **(D)** If `element` is smaller than the last item in the list, it will be compared with every item in the list. Eventually `index` will be incremented to a value that is out of bounds. To avoid this error, the test in the `while` loop should be

```
while(index < list.size() &&
        element.compareTo(list.get(index)) < 0)
```

Notice that if `element` is greater than or equal to at least one item in `list`, the test as given in the problem will eventually be false, preventing an out-of-range error.

25. **(A)** Recall that `add(index, obj)` shifts all elements, starting at `index`, one unit to the right, then inserts `obj` at position `index`. The `set(index, obj)` method replaces the element in position `index` with `obj`. So here is the state of `list` after each change:

```
i = 0    6 0 1 8
         2 0 1 8
i = 1    2 0 1 1 8
         2 3 1 1 8
i = 2    2 3 1 2 1 8
         2 3 4 2 1 8
```

26. **(E)** The value of each `Coin` c in `coins` must be accessed with `c.getValue()`. This eliminates choice D. Eliminate choices A and B: The loop accesses each `Coin` in the `coins` `ArrayList`, which means that there should not be any statements attempting to get the next `Coin`. Choice B would be correct if the first statement in the loop body were

```
double value = c.getValue();
```

27. **(D)** The `equals` method is defined for objects only. Since `getValue` returns a `double`, the quantities `c.getValue()` and `aCoin.getValue()` must be compared either using `==`, or as described in the box on p. 63 (better).

28. **(D)** Segment II is the straightforward solution. Segment I is correct because it initializes all slots of the matrix to 0, a perfect square. (By default, all arrays of `int` or `double` are initialized to 0.) Segment III fails because r is undefined in the condition `c < mat[r].length`. In order to do a column-by-column traversal, you need to get the number of columns in each row. The outer `for` loop could be

```
for (int c = 0; c < mat[0].length; c++)
```

Now segment III works. Note that since the array is rectangular, you can use any index k in the conditional `c < mat[k].length`, provided that k satisfies $0 \le k < $ `mat.length`.

29. **(A)** Method `alter` shifts all the columns, starting at column `c+1`, one column to the left. Also, it does it in a way that overwrites column `c`. Here are the replacements for the method call `alter(1)`:

```
mat[0][1] = mat[0][2]
mat[0][2] = mat[0][3]
mat[1][1] = mat[1][2]
mat[1][2] = mat[1][3]
mat[2][1] = mat[2][2]
mat[2][2] = mat[2][3]
```

30. **(A)** `matStuff` processes the row selected by the row parameter, 2 in the method call. The row value, 2, overwrites each element in row 2. Don't make the mistake of selecting choice B—the row labels are 0, 1, 2.

31. **(B)** Hand execute this for a 2 × 2 matrix. `i` goes from 0 to 0, `j` goes from 0 to 0, so the only interchange is swap `mat[0][0]` with `mat[1][1]`, which suggests choice B. Check with a 3 × 3 matrix:

```
i = 0   j = 0   swap mat[0][0] with mat[2][2]
        j = 1   swap mat[0][1] with mat[1][2]
i = 1   j = 0   swap mat[1][0] with mat[2][1]
```

The elements to be interchanged are shown paired in the following figure. The result will be a reflection through the minor diagonal.

32. **(D)** The method as given will throw an `ArrayIndexOutOfBoundsException`. For the matrix in the example, `mat[0].length` is 4. The call `mat.alter(1)` gives `c` a value of 1. Thus, in the inner `for` loop, `j` goes from 1 to 3. When `j` is 3, the line `mat[i][j] = mat[i][j+1]` becomes `mat[i][3] = mat[i][4]`. Since columns go from 0 to 3, `mat[i][4]` is out of range. The changes in segments I and II both fix this problem. In each case, the correct replacements are made for each row `i`: `mat[i][1] = mat[i][2]` and `mat[i][2] = mat[i][3]`. Segment III makes the following incorrect replacements as `j` goes from 3 to 2: `mat[i][2] = mat[i][3]` and `mat[i][1] = mat[i][2]`. This will cause both columns 1 and 2 to be overwritten. Before inserting zeros in the last column, `mat` will be

$$
\begin{array}{cccc}
2 & 9 & 9 & 9 \\
1 & 3 & 3 & 3 \\
0 & 2 & 2 & 2
\end{array}
$$

This does not achieve the intended postcondition of the method.

33. **(B)** For the method call `isThere(mat, 2, 2, "$")`, the code counts how many times `"$"` appears in row 2 and how many times in column 2. The method returns `true` only if `count == SIZE` for either the row or column pass (i.e., the whole of row 2 or the whole of column 2 contains the symbol `"$"`). This eliminates choices I and II.

34. **(D)** Segment I is a row-by-row traversal; segment II is a column-by-column traversal. Each achieves the correct postcondition. Segment III traverses the matrix but

Optional topic

(continued)

does not alter it. All that is changed is the local variable `element`. You cannot use this kind of loop to replace elements in an array.

35. **(E)** This is similar to the previous question, but in this case segment III is also correct. This is because instead of *replacing* a matrix element, you are *modifying* it using a mutator method.

36. **(E)** There are three things that must be done in each row:

   - Add an opening boundary line:

   ```
   s = s + "|";
   ```

   - Add the symbol in each square:

   ```
   for (int c = 0; c < COLS; c++)
       s = s + board[r][c];
   ```

   - Add a closing boundary line and go to the next line:

   ```
   s = s + "|\n";
   ```

   All of these statements must therefore be enclosed in the outer `for` loop, that is,

   ```
   for (int r = ...)
   ```

Optional topic

37. **(E)** Since there are 365 valid days in a year, the divisor in calculating the average must be 365. It may appear that segments II and III are incorrect because they include rainfall for invalid days in `total`. Since these values are initialized to `0.0`, however, including them in the total won't affect the final result.

Recursion

> recursion *n*. *See* recursion.
> —*Eric S. Raymond*, The New Hacker's Dictionary *(1991)*

Chapter Goals

- Recursive methods
- Recursion in two-dimensional grids
- Recursive helper methods
- Analysis of recursive algorithms

RECURSIVE METHODS

A *recursive method* is a method that calls itself. For example, here is a program that calls a recursive method stackWords.

```
public class WordPlay
{
    public static void stackWords()
    {
        String word = IO.readString();      //read user input
        if (word.equals("."))
            System.out.println();
        else
            stackWords();
        System.out.println(word);
    }

    public static void main(String args[])
    {
        System.out.println("Enter list of words, one per line.");
        System.out.println("Final word should be a period (.)");
        stackWords();
    }
}
```

Here is the output if you enter

```
hold
my
hand
.
```

You get

```
.
hand
my
hold
```

The program reads in a list of words terminated with a period, and prints the list in reverse order, starting with the period. How does this happen?

Each time the recursive call to stackWords() is made, execution goes back to the start of a new method call. The computer must remember to complete all the pending calls to the method. It does this by stacking the statements that must still be executed as follows: The first time stackWords() is called, the word "hold" is read and tested for being a period. No it's not, so stackWords() is called again. The statement to output "hold" (which has not yet been executed) goes on a stack, and execution goes to the start of the method. The word "my" is read. No, it's not a period, so the command to output "my" goes on the stack. And so on. The stack looks something like this before the recursive call in which the period is read:

```
┌─────────────────────────────────┐
│                                 │
│                                 │
│                                 │
├─────────────────────────────────┤
│ System.out.println("hand");     │
│  System.out.println("my");      │
│ System.out.println("hold");     │
└─────────────────────────────────┘
```

Imagine that these statements are stacked like plates. In the final stackWords() call, word has the value ".". Yes, it *is* a period, so the stackWords() line is skipped, the period is printed on the screen, and the method call terminates. The computer now completes each of the previous method calls in turn by "popping" the statements off the top of the stack. It prints "hand", then "my", then "hold", and execution of method stackWords() is complete.[1]

NOTE

1. Each time stackWords() is called, a new local variable word is created.
2. The first time the method actually terminates, the program returns to complete the most recently invoked previous call. That's why the words get reversed in this example.

GENERAL FORM OF SIMPLE RECURSIVE METHODS

Every recursive method has two distinct parts:

- A base case or termination condition that causes the method to end.
- A nonbase case whose actions move the algorithm toward the base case and termination.

---

[1] Actually, the computer stacks the pending statements in a recursive method call more efficiently than the way described. But *conceptually* this is how it is done.

Here is the framework for a simple recursive method that has no specific return type.

```
public void recursiveMeth( ... )
{
    if (base case)
        < Perform some action >
    else
    {
        < Perform some other action >
        recursiveMeth( ... );    //recursive method call
    }
}
```

The base case typically occurs for the simplest case of the problem, such as when an integer has a value of 0 or 1. Other examples of base cases are when some key is found, or an end-of-file is reached. A recursive algorithm can have more than one base case.

In the `else` or nonbase case of the framework shown, the code fragment < *Perform some other action* > and the method call `recursiveMeth` can sometimes be interchanged without altering the net effect of the algorithm. Be careful though, because what *does* change is the order of executing statements. This can sometimes be disastrous. (See the `eraseBlob` example on p. 294.)

Example 1

```
public void drawLine(int n)
{
    if (n == 0)
        System.out.println("That's all, folks!");
    else
    {
        for (int i = 1; i <= n; i++)
            System.out.print("*");
        System.out.println();
        drawLine(n - 1);
    }
}
```

The method call `drawLine(3)` produces this output:

```
***
**
*
That's all, folks!
```

NOTE

1. A method that has no pending statements following the recursive call is an example of *tail recursion*. Method `drawLine` is such a case, but `stackWords` is not.
2. The base case in the `drawLine` example is `n == 0`. Notice that each subsequent call, `drawLine(n - 1)`, makes progress toward termination of the method. If your method has no base case, or if you never reach the base case, you will create *infinite recursion*. This is a catastrophic error that will cause your computer eventually to run out of memory and give you heart-stopping messages like `java.lang.StackOverflowError ...` .

Example 2

```
//Illustrates infinite recursion.
public void catastrophe(int n)
{
    System.out.println(n);
    catastrophe(n);
}
```

> A recursive method must have a base case.

Try running the case `catastrophe(1)` if you have lots of time to waste!

WRITING RECURSIVE METHODS

> Optional topic

To come up with a recursive algorithm, you have to be able to frame a process *recursively* (i.e., in terms of a simpler case of itself). This is different from framing it *iteratively*, which repeats a process until a final condition is met. A good strategy for writing recursive methods is to first state the algorithm recursively in words.

Example 1

Write a method that returns *n*! (*n* factorial).

n! defined iteratively	*n*! defined recursively
0! = 1	0! = 1
1! = 1	1! = (1)(0!)
2! = (2)(1)	2! = (2)(1!)
3! = (3)(2)(1)	3! = (3)(2!)
...	...

The general recursive definition for *n*! is

$$n! = \begin{cases} 1 & n = 0 \\ n(n-1)! & n > 0 \end{cases}$$

The definition seems to be circular until you realize that if 0! is defined, all higher factorials are defined. Code for the recursive method follows directly from the recursive definition:

```
/* Compute n! recursively.
 * Precondition:  n >= 0.
 * Postcondition: returns n! */
public static int factorial(int n)
{
    if (n == 0)      //base case
        return 1;
    else
        return n * factorial(n - 1);
}
```

Example 2

Write a recursive method `revDigs` that outputs its integer parameter with the digits reversed. For example,

(continued)

```
revDigs(147)   outputs   741
revDigs(4)     outputs   4
```

First, describe the process recursively: Output the rightmost digit. Then, if there are still digits left in the remaining number n/10, reverse its digits. Repeat this until n/10 is 0. Here is the method:

```
/* Precondition:  n >= 0.
 * Postcondition: Outputs n with digits reversed. */
public static void revDigs(int n)
{
    System.out.print(n % 10);  //rightmost digit
    if (n / 10 != 0)           //base case
        revDigs(n / 10);
}
```

NOTE

On the AP exam, you are expected to "understand and evaluate" recursive methods. This means that you would not be asked to come up with the code for methods such as factorial and revDigs (as shown above). You could, however, be asked to identify output for any given call to factorial or revDigs.

ANALYSIS OF RECURSIVE METHODS

Recall the Fibonacci sequence 1, 1, 2, 3, 5, 8, 13, ... The *n*th Fibonacci number equals the sum of the previous two numbers if $n \geq 3$. Recursively,

$$\text{Fib}(n) = \begin{cases} 1, & n = 1, 2 \\ \text{Fib}(n-1) + \text{Fib}(n-2), & n \geq 3 \end{cases}$$

Here is the method:

```
/* Precondition:  n >= 1.
 * Postcondition: Returns the nth Fibonacci number. */
public static int fib(int n)
{
    if (n == 1 || n == 2)
        return 1;
    else
        return fib(n - 1) + fib(n - 2);
}
```

Notice that there are two recursive calls in the last line of the method. So to find Fib(5), for example, takes eight recursive calls to fib!

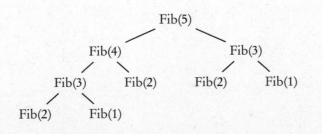

In general, each call to `fib` makes two more calls, which is the tipoff for an exponential algorithm (i.e., one that is *very* inefficient). This is *much* slower than the run time of the corresponding iterative algorithm (see Chapter 5, Question 13).

You may ask: Since every recursive algorithm can be written iteratively, when should programmers use recursion? Bear in mind that recursive algorithms can incur extra run time and memory. Their major plus is elegance and simplicity of code.

General Rules for Recursion

1. Avoid recursion for algorithms that involve large local arrays—too many recursive calls can cause memory overflow.
2. Use recursion when it significantly simplifies code.
3. Avoid recursion for simple iterative methods like factorial, Fibonacci, and the linear search on the next page.
4. Recursion is especially useful for

   - Branching processes like traversing trees or directories.
   - Divide-and-conquer algorithms like mergesort and binary search.

SORTING ALGORITHMS THAT USE RECURSION

Mergesort and quicksort are discussed in Chapter 8.

RECURSIVE HELPER METHODS

Optional topic

A common technique in designing recursive algorithms is to have a public nonrecursive driver method that calls a private *recursive helper method* to carry out the task. The main reasons for doing this are

- To hide the implementation details of the recursion from the user.
- To enhance the efficiency of the program.

(continued)

Example 1

Consider the simple example of recursively finding the sum of the first *n* positive integers.

```
//Returns 1 + 2 + 3 + ... + n.
public static int sum(int n)
{
    if (n == 1)
        return 1;
    else
        return n + sum(n - 1);
}
```

Notice that you get infinite recursion if $n \leq 0$. Suppose you want to include a test for $n > 0$ before you execute the algorithm. Placing this test in the recursive method is inefficient because if *n* is initially positive, it will remain positive in subsequent recursive calls. You can avoid this problem by using a driver method called getSum, which does the test on *n just once*. The recursive method sum becomes a private helper method.

```
public class FindSum
{
    /* Private recursive helper method.
     * Finds 1 + 2 + 3 + ... + n.
     * Precondition:  n > 0. */
    private static int sum(int n)
    {
        if (n == 1)
            return 1;
        else
            return n + sum(n - 1);
    }

    /* Driver method */
    public static int getSum(int n)
    {
        if (n > 0)
            return sum(n);
        else
        {
            throw new IllegalArgumentException
                    ("Error: n must be positive");
        }
    }
}
```

NOTE

This is a trivial method used to illustrate a private recursive helper method. In practice, you would never use recursion to find a simple sum!

Example 2

Consider a recursive solution to the problem of doing a sequential search for a key in an array of elements that are Comparable. If the key is found, the method returns true, otherwise it returns false.

(continued)

The solution can be stated recursively as follows:

- If the key is in a[0], then the key is found.

- If not, recursively search the array starting at a[1].

- If you are past the end of the array, then the key wasn't found.

Here is a straightforward (but inefficient) implementation:

```
public class Searcher
{
    /* Recursively search array a for key.
     * Postcondition: If a[k] equals key for 0 <= k < a.length
     *                returns true, otherwise returns false.  */
    public boolean search(Comparable[] a, Comparable key)
    {
        if (a.length == 0)  //base case. key not found
            return false;
        else if (a[0].compareTo(key) == 0) //base case
            return true;                   //key found
        else
        {
            Comparable[] shorter = new Comparable[a.length-1];
            for (int i = 0; i < shorter.length; i++)
                shorter[i] = a[i+1];
            return search(shorter, key);
        }
    }

    public static void main(String[] args)
    {
        String[] list = {"Mary", "Joe", "Lee", "Jake"};
        Searcher s = new Searcher();
        System.out.println("Enter key: Mary, Joe, Lee or Jake.");
        String key = IO.readString();  //read user input
        boolean result = s.search(list, key);
        if (!result)
            System.out.println(key + " was not found.");
        else
            System.out.println(key + " was found.");
    }
}
```

Notice how horribly inefficient the search method is: For each recursive call, a new array shorter has to be created! It is much better to use a parameter, startIndex, to keep track of where you are in the array. Replace the search method above with the following one, which calls the private helper method recurSearch:

```
/* Driver method. Searches array a for key.
 * Precondition:  a contains at least one element.
 * Postcondition: If a[k] equals key for 0 <= k < a.length
 *                returns true, otherwise returns false. */
public boolean search(Comparable[] a, Comparable key)
{
    return recurSearch(a, 0, key);
}
```

(continued)

```
/* Recursively search array a for key, starting at startIndex.
 * Precondition:  a contains at least one element and
 *                0 <= startIndex <= a.length.
 * Postcondition: If a[k] equals key for 0 <= k < a.length
 *                returns true, otherwise returns false. */
private boolean recurSearch(Comparable[] a, int startIndex,
    Comparable key)
{
    if(startIndex == a.length)   //base case. key not found
        return false;
    else if(a[startIndex].compareTo(key) == 0) //base case
        return true;                           //key found
    else
        return recurSearch(a, startIndex+1, key);
}
```

NOTE

1. Using the parameter `startIndex` avoids having to create a new array object for each recursive call. Making `startIndex` a parameter of a helper method hides implementation details from the user.
2. Since `String` implements `Comparable`, it is OK to use an array of `String`. It would also have been OK to test with an array of `Integer` or `Double`, since they too implement `Comparable`.
3. The helper method is private because it is called only by `search` within the `Searcher` class.
4. It's easy to modify the `search` method to return the index in the array where the key is found: Make the return type `int` and return `startIndex` if the key is found, -1 (say) if it isn't.

> Use a recursive helper method to hide private coding details from a client.

RECURSION IN TWO-DIMENSIONAL GRIDS

Here is a commonly-used technique: using recursion to traverse a two-dimensional array. The problem comes in several different guises, for example,

1. A game board from which you must remove pieces.
2. A maze with walls and paths from which you must try to escape.
3. White "containers" enclosed by black "walls" into which you must "pour paint."

In each case, you will be given a starting position (row, col) and instructions on what to do. The recursive solution typically involves these steps:

> *Check that the starting position is not out of range:*
> *If (starting position satisfies some requirement)*
> *Perform some action to solve problem*
> *RecursiveCall(row + 1, col)*
> *RecursiveCall(row − 1, col)*
> *RecursiveCall(row, col + 1)*
> *RecursiveCall(row, col − 1)*

(continued)

Example

On the right is an image represented as a square grid of black and white cells. Two cells in an image are part of the same "blob" if each is black and there is a sequence of moves from one cell to the other, where each move is either horizontal or vertical to an adjacent black cell. For example, the diagram represents an image that contains two blobs, one of them consisting of a single cell.

Assuming the following Image class declaration, you are to write the body of the eraseBlob method, using a recursive algorithm.

```java
public class Image
{
    private final int BLACK = 1;
    private final int WHITE = 0;
    private int[][] image;    //square grid
    private int size;         //number of rows and columns

    public Image()   //constructor
    { /* implementation not shown */ }

    public void display()   //displays Image
    { /* implementation not shown */ }

    /* Precondition:  Image is defined with either BLACK or WHITE
                      cells.
     * Postcondition: If 0 <= row < size, 0 <= col < size,
     *                and image[row][col] is BLACK, set all cells
     *                in the same blob to WHITE. Otherwise image
     *                is unchanged. */
    public void eraseBlob(int row, int col)
    /* your code goes here */
}
```

Solution:

```java
public void eraseBlob(int row, int col)
{
    if (row >= 0 && row < size && col >= 0 && col < size)
        if (image[row][col] == BLACK)
        {
            image[row][col] = WHITE;
            eraseBlob(row - 1, col);
            eraseBlob(row + 1, col);
            eraseBlob(row, col - 1);
            eraseBlob(row, col + 1);
        }
}
```

NOTE

1. The ordering of the four recursive calls is irrelevant.

(continued)

2. The test

```
if (image[row][col] == BLACK)
```

can be included as the last piece of the test in the first line:

```
if (row >= 0 && ...
```

If `row` or `col` is out of range, the test will short-circuit, avoiding the dreaded `ArrayIndexOutOfBoundsException`.

3. If you put the statement

```
image[row][col] = WHITE;
```

after the four recursive calls, you get infinite recursion if your blob has more than one cell. This is because, when you visit an adjacent cell, one of its recursive calls visits the original cell. If this cell is still `BLACK`, yet more recursive calls are generated, *ad infinitum*.

A final thought: Recursive algorithms can be tricky. Try to state the solution recursively *in words* before you launch into code. Oh, and don't forget the base case!

Sample Free-Response Question 1

Here is a sample free-response question that uses recursion in a two-dimensional array. See if you can answer it before looking at the solution.

A *color grid* is defined as a two-dimensional array whose elements are character strings having values "b" (blue), "r" (red), "g" (green), or "y" (yellow). The elements are called pixels because they represent pixel locations on a computer screen. For example,

```
              y g r
b b g r       b y g
g r g r   r r r r   g r b
              b b g
```

A *connected region* for any pixel is the set of all pixels of the same color that can be reached through a direct path along horizontal or vertical moves starting at that pixel. A connected region can consist of just a single pixel or the entire color grid. For example, if the two-dimensional array is called `pixels`, the connected region for `pixels[1][0]` is as shown here for three different arrays.

```
b b g r    y g r b    b b
g r g r    g g y g    b b
           b g r g
```

The class `ColorGrid`, whose declaration is shown below, is used for storing, displaying, and changing the colors in a color grid.

(continued)

```
public class ColorGrid
{
    private String[][] myPixels;
    private int myRows;
    private int myCols;

    /**
     * Creates numRows × numCols ColorGrid from String s.
     * @param s the string containing colors of the ColorGrid
     * @param numRows the number of rows in the ColorGrid
     * @param numCols the number of columns in the ColorGrid
     */
    public ColorGrid(String s, int numRows, int numCols)
    { /* to be implemented in part (a) */ }

    /**
     * Precondition:  myPixels[row][col] is oldColor, one of "r",
     *                "b","g", or "y".
     *                newColor is one of "r","b","g", or "y".
     * Postcondition: if 0 <= row < myRows and 0 <= col < myCols,
     *                paints the connected region of
     *                myPixels[row][col] the newColor.
     *                Does nothing if oldColor is the same as
     *                newColor.
     * @param row the given row
     * @param col the given column
     * @param newColor the new color for painting
     * @param oldColor the current color of myPixels[row][col]
     */
    public void paintRegion(int row, int col, String newColor,
        String oldColor)
    { /* to be implemented in part (b) */ }

    //other methods not shown
        ...
}
```

(a) Write the implementation code for the ColorGrid constructor. The constructor should initialize the myPixels matrix of the ColorGrid as follows: The dimensions of myPixels are numRows × numCols. String s contains numRows × numCols characters, where each character is one of the colors of the grid—"r", "g", "b", or "y". The characters are contained in s row by row from top to bottom and left to right. For example, given that numRows is 3, and numCols is 4, if s is "brrygrggyyyr", myPixels should be initialized to be

```
b r r y
g r g g
y y y r
```

(continued)

Complete the constructor below:

```
/**
 * Creates numRows × numCols ColorGrid from String s.
 * @param s the string containing colors of the ColorGrid
 * @param numRows the number of rows in the ColorGrid
 * @param numCols the number of columns in the ColorGrid
 */
public ColorGrid(String s, int numRows, int numCols)
```

(b) Write the implementation of the `paintRegion` method as started below. **Note: You must write a recursive solution.** The `paintRegion` paints the connected region of the given pixel, specified by `row` and `col`, a different color specified by the `newColor` parameter. If `newColor` is the same as `oldColor`, the color of the given pixel, `paintRegion` does nothing. To visualize what `paintRegion` does, imagine that the different colors surrounding the connected region of a given pixel form a boundary. When paint is poured onto the given pixel, the new color will fill the connected region up to the boundary.

For example, the effect of the method call `c.paintRegion(2, 3, "b", "r")` on the `ColorGrid` c is shown here. (The starting pixel is shown in a frame, and its connected region is shaded.)

before	after
r r b g y y	r r b g y y
b r b y r r	b r b y b b
g g r r r b	g g b b b b
y r r y r b	y b b y b b

Complete the method `paintRegion` below. **Note: Only a recursive solution will be accepted.**

```
/**
 * Precondition:  myPixels[row][col] is oldColor, one of "r",
 *                "b","g", or "y".
 *                newColor is one of "r","b","g", or "y".
 * Postcondition: if 0 <= row < myRows and 0 <= col < myCols,
 *                paints the connected region of
 *                myPixels[row][col] the newColor.
 *                Does nothing if oldColor is the same as
 *                newColor.
 * @param row the given row
 * @param col the given column
 * @param newColor the new color for painting
 * @param oldColor the current color of myPixels[row][col]
 */
public void paintRegion(int row, int col, String newColor,
    String oldColor)
```

(continued)

Solution

```
(a) public ColorGrid(String s, int numRows, int numCols)
    {
        myRows = numRows;
        myCols = numCols;
        myPixels = new String[numRows][numCols];
        int stringIndex = 0;
        for (int r = 0; r < numRows; r++)
            for (int c = 0; c < numCols; c++)
            {
                myPixels[r][c] = s.substring(stringIndex,
                    stringIndex + 1);
                stringIndex++;
            }
    }


(b) public void paintRegion(int row, int col, String newColor,
        String oldColor)
    {
        if (row >= 0 && row < myRows && col >= 0 && col < myCols)
            if (!myPixels[row][col].equals(newColor) &&
                myPixels[row][col].equals(oldColor))
            {
                myPixels[row][col] = newColor;
                paintRegion(row + 1, col, newColor, oldColor);
                paintRegion(row - 1, col, newColor, oldColor);
                paintRegion(row, col + 1, newColor, oldColor);
                paintRegion(row, col - 1, newColor, oldColor);
            }
    }
```

NOTE

- In part (a), you don't need to test if `stringIndex` is in range: The precondition states that the number of characters in s is numRows × numCols.
- In part (b), each recursive call must test whether `row` and `col` are in the correct range for the `myPixels` array; otherwise, your algorithm may sail right off the edge!
- Don't forget to test if `newColor` is different from that of the starting pixel. Method `paintRegion` does nothing if the colors are the same.
- Also, don't forget to test if the current pixel is `oldColor`—you don't want to overwrite *all* the colors, just the connected region of `oldColor`!
- The color-change assignment `myPixels[row][col] = newColor` must precede the recursive calls to avoid infinite recursion.

Sample Free-Response Question 2

Here is another sample free-response question that uses recursion.

This question refers to the `Sentence` class below. Note: A *word* is a string of consecutive nonblank (and nonwhitespace) characters. For example, the sentence

(continued)

"Hello there!" she said.

consists of the four words

```
    "Hello      there!"      she      said.
```

```java
public class Sentence
{
    private String mySentence;
    private int myNumWords;

    /**
     * Constructor.  Creates sentence from String str.
     *               Finds the number of words in sentence.
     * Precondition: Words in str separated by exactly one blank.
     * @param str the string containing a sentence
     */
    public Sentence(String str)
    { /* to be implemented in part (a) */ }

    public int getNumWords()
    { return myNumWords; }

    public String getSentence()
    { return mySentence; }

    /**
     * @param s the specified string
     * @return a copy of String s with all blanks removed
     * Postcondition: Returned string contains just one word.
     */
    private static String removeBlanks(String s)
    { /* implementation not shown */ }

    /**
     * @param s the specified string
     * @return a copy of String s with all letters in lowercase
     * Postcondition: Number of words in returned string equals
     *                number of words in s.
     */
    private static String lowerCase(String s)
    { /* implementation not shown */ }

    /**
     * @param s the specified string
     * @return a copy of String s with all punctuation removed
     * Postcondition: Number of words in returned string equals
     *                number of words in s.
     */
    private static String removePunctuation(String s)
    { /* implementation not shown */ }
}
```

(a) Complete the Sentence constructor as started below. The constructor assigns
str to mySentence. You should write the subsequent code that assigns a value to
myNumWords, the number of words in mySentence.

(continued)

Complete the constructor below:

```
/**
 * Constructor.  Creates sentence from String str.
 *              Finds the number of words in sentence.
 * Precondition: Words in str separated by exactly one blank.
 * @param str the string containing a sentence
 */
public Sentence(String str)
{
    mySentence = str;
}
```

(b) Consider the problem of testing whether a string is a palindrome. A *palindrome* reads the same from left to right and right to left, ignoring spaces, punctuation, and capitalization. For example,

> A Santa lived as a devil at NASA.
>
> Flo, gin is a sin! I golf.
>
> Eva, can I stab bats in a cave?

A public method isPalindrome is added to the Sentence class. Here is the method and its implementation:

```
/**
 * @return true if mySentence is a palindrome, false otherwise
 */
public boolean isPalindrome()
{
    String temp = removeBlanks(mySentence);
    temp = removePunctuation(temp);
    temp = lowerCase(temp);
    return isPalindrome(temp, 0, temp.length() - 1);
}
```

The overloaded isPalindrome method contained in the code is a private recursive helper method, also added to the Sentence class. You are to write the implementation of this method. It takes a "purified" string as a parameter, namely one that has been stripped of blanks and punctuation and is all lowercase letters. It also takes as parameters the first and last index of the string. It returns true if this "purified" string is a palindrome, false otherwise.

A recursive algorithm for testing if a string is a palindrome is as follows:

- If the string has length 0 or 1, it's a palindrome.
- Remove the first and last letters.
- If those two letters are the same, and the remaining string is a palindrome, then the original string is a palindrome. Otherwise it's not.

(continued)

Complete the `isPalindrome` method below:

```
/* Private recursive helper method that tests whether a substring
 * of string s is a palindrome.
 * @param s the given string
 * @param start the index of the first character of the substring
 * @param end the index of the last character of the substring
 * Precondition: s contains no spaces, punctuation, or capitals.
 * @return true if the substring is a palindrome, false otherwise
 */
private static boolean isPalindrome(String s, int start, int end)
```

Solution

(a)
```
public Sentence(String str)
{
    mySentence = str;
    myNumWords = 1;
    int k = str.indexOf(" ");
    while (k != -1)    //while there are still blanks in str
    {
        myNumWords++;
        str = str.substring(k + 1); //substring after blank
        k = str.indexOf(" ");        //get index of next blank
    }
}
```

(b)
```
private static boolean isPalindrome(String s, int start,
        int end)
{
    if (start >= end)  //substring has length 0 or 1
        return true;
    else
    {
        String first = s.substring(start, start + 1);
        String last = s.substring(end, end + 1);
        if (first.equals(last))
            return isPalindrome(s, start + 1, end - 1);
        else
            return false;
    }
}
```

NOTE

- In part (a), for every occurrence of a blank in `mySentence`, `myNumWords` must be incremented. (Be sure to initialize `myNumWords` to 1!)
- In part (a), the code locates all the blanks in `mySentence` by replacing `str` with the substring that consists of the piece of `str` directly following the most recently located blank.
- Recall that `indexOf` returns -1 if its `String` parameter does not occur as a substring in its `String` calling object.
- In part (b), the `start` and `end` indexes move toward each other with each subsequent recursive call. This shortens the string to be tested in each call. When `start` and `end` meet, the base case has been reached.

(continued)

- Notice the private static methods in the Sentence class, including the helper method you were asked to write. They are static because they are not invoked by a Sentence object (no dot member construct). The only use of these methods is to help achieve the postconditions of other methods in the class.

Chapter Summary

On the AP exam you will be expected to calculate the results of recursive method calls. Recursion becomes second nature when you practice a lot of examples. For the more difficult questions, untangle the statements with either repeated method calls (like that shown in the solution to Question 5 on p. 314), or box diagrams (as shown in the solution to Question 12 on p. 315).

You should understand that recursive algorithms can be *very* inefficient.

MULTIPLE-CHOICE QUESTIONS ON RECURSION

1. Which of the following statements about recursion are true?

    I Every recursive algorithm can be written iteratively.
    II Tail recursion is always used in "divide-and-conquer" algorithms.
    III In a recursive definition, an object is defined in terms of a simpler case of itself.

    (A) I only
    (B) III only
    (C) I and II only
    (D) I and III only
    (E) II and III only

2. Which of the following, when used as the /* *body* */ of method sum, will enable that method to compute $1 + 2 + \cdots + n$ correctly for any $n > 0$?

    ```
    public int sum(int n)
    //Precondition:  n > 0.
    //Postcondition: 1 + 2 + ... + n has been returned.
    {
         /* body */
    }
    ```

    I
    ```
    return n + sum(n - 1);
    ```

    II
    ```
    if (n == 1)
        return 1;
    else
        return n + sum(n - 1);
    ```

    III
    ```
    if (n == 1)
        return 1;
    else
        return sum(n) + sum(n - 1);
    ```

    (A) I only
    (B) II only
    (C) III only
    (D) I and II only
    (E) I, II, and III

3. Refer to the method `stringRecur`:

```
public void stringRecur(String s)
{
    if (s.length() < 15)
        System.out.println(s);
    stringRecur(s + "*");
}
```

When will method `stringRecur` terminate without error?
(A) Only when the length of the input string is less than 15
(B) Only when the length of the input string is greater than or equal to 15
(C) Only when an empty string is input
(D) For all string inputs
(E) For no string inputs

4. Refer to method `strRecur`:

```
public void strRecur(String s)
{
    if (s.length() < 15)
    {
        System.out.println(s);
        strRecur(s + "*");
    }
}
```

When will method `strRecur` terminate without error?
(A) Only when the length of the input string is less than 15
(B) Only when the length of the input string is greater than or equal to 15
(C) Only when an empty string is input
(D) For all string inputs
(E) For no string inputs

Questions 5 and 6 refer to method `result`:

```
public int result(int n)
{
    if (n == 1)
        return 2;
    else
        return 2 * result(n - 1);
}
```

5. What value does `result(5)` return?
(A) 64
(B) 32
(C) 16
(D) 8
(E) 2

6. If $n > 0$, how many times will `result` be called to evaluate `result(n)` (including the initial call)?

    (A) 2

    (B) 2^n

    (C) n

    (D) $2n$

    (E) n^2

7. Refer to method `mystery`:

```
public int mystery(int n, int a, int d)
{
    if (n == 1)
        return a;
    else
        return d + mystery(n - 1, a, d);
}
```

What value is returned by the call `mystery(3, 2, 6)`?

    (A) 20

    (B) 14

    (C) 10

    (D) 8

    (E) 2

8. Refer to method `f`:

```
public int f(int k, int n)
{
    if (n == k)
        return k;
    else
        if (n > k)
            return f(k, n - k);
        else
            return f(k - n, n);
}
```

What value is returned by the call `f(6, 8)`?

    (A) 8

    (B) 4

    (C) 3

    (D) 2

    (E) 1

9. What does method recur do?

```
//Precondition: x is an array of n integers.
public int recur(int[] x, int n)
{
    int t;
    if (n == 1)
        return x[0];
    else
    {
        t = recur(x, n - 1);
        if (x[n-1] > t)
            return x[n-1];
        else
            return t;
    }
}
```

(A) It finds the largest value in x and leaves x unchanged.
(B) It finds the smallest value in x and leaves x unchanged.
(C) It sorts x in ascending order and returns the largest value in x.
(D) It sorts x in descending order and returns the largest value in x.
(E) It returns x[0] or x[n-1], whichever is larger.

10. Which best describes what the printString method below does?

```
public void printString(String s)
{
    if (s.length() > 0)
    {
        printString(s.substring(1));
        System.out.print(s.substring(0, 1));
    }
}
```

(A) It prints string s.
(B) It prints string s in reverse order.
(C) It prints only the first character of string s.
(D) It prints only the first two characters of string s.
(E) It prints only the last character of string s.

11. Refer to the method power:

```
//Precondition:  expo is any integer, base is not zero.
//Postcondition: base raised to expo power returned.
public double power(double base, int expo)
{
    if (expo == 0)
        return 1;
    else if (expo > 0)
        return base * power(base, expo - 1);
    else
        return /* code */;
}
```

Which /* *code* */ correctly completes method power?
(Recall that $a^{-n} = 1/a^n$, $a \neq 0$; for example, $2^{-3} = 1/2^3 = 1/8$.)
(A) `(1 / base) * power(base, expo + 1)`
(B) `(1 / base) * power(base, expo - 1)`
(C) `base * power(base, expo + 1)`
(D) `base * power(base, expo - 1)`
(E) `(1 / base) * power(base, expo)`

12. Consider the following method:

```
public void doSomething(int n)
{
    if (n > 0)
    {
        doSomething(n - 1);
        System.out.print(n);
        doSomething(n - 1);
    }
}
```

What would be output following the call doSomething(3)?
(A) `3211211`
(B) `1121213`
(C) `1213121`
(D) `1211213`
(E) `1123211`

13. A user enters several positive integers at the keyboard and terminates the list with a sentinel (-999). A `writeEven` method reads those integers and outputs the even integers only, in the reverse order that they are read. Thus, if the user enters

    ```
    3 5 14 6 1 8 -999
    ```

    the output for the `writeEven` method will be

    ```
    8 6 14
    ```

    Here is the method:

    ```
    /* Assume user enters at least one positive integer,
     * and terminates the list with -999.
     * Postcondition: All even integers in the list are
     *                output in reverse order. */
    public static void writeEven()
    {
        int num = IO.readInt();    //read user input
        if (num != -999)
        {
            /* code */
        }
    }
    ```

    Which /* *code* */ satisfies the postcondition of method `writeEven`?

    I   ```
    if (num % 2 == 0)
        System.out.print(num + " ");
    writeEven();
    ```

    II   ```
    if (num % 2 == 0)
        writeEven();
    System.out.print(num + " ");
    ```

    III ```
    writeEven();
    if (num % 2 == 0)
        System.out.print(num + " ");
    ```

    (A) I only
    (B) II only
    (C) III only
    (D) I and II only
    (E) I, II, and III
    ```

14. Refer to the following recursive method.

```
public int mystery(int n)
{
    if (n < 0)
        return 2;
    else
        return mystery(n - 1) + mystery(n - 3);
}
```

What value is returned by the call mystery(3)?
(A) 12
(B) 10
(C) 8
(D) 6
(E) 4

Questions 15 and 16 refer to method t:

```
//Precondition: n >= 1.
public int t(int n)
{
    if (n == 1 || n == 2)
        return 2 * n;
    else
        return t(n - 1) - t(n - 2);
}
```

15. What will be returned by t(5)?
    (A) 4
    (B) 2
    (C) 0
    (D) −2
    (E) −4

16. For the method call t(6), how many calls to t will be made, including the origi-nal call?
    (A) 6
    (B) 7
    (C) 11
    (D) 15
    (E) 25

17. This question refers to methods f1 and f2 that are in the same class:

```
public int f1(int a, int b)
{
    if (a == b)
        return b;
    else
        return a + f2(a - 1, b);
}

public int f2(int p, int q)
{
    if (p < q)
        return p + q;
    else
        return p + f1(p - 2, q);
}
```

What value will be returned by a call to f1(5, 3)?
    (A) 5
    (B) 6
    (C) 7
    (D) 12
    (E) 15

18. Consider method `foo`:

```
public int foo(int x)
{
    if (x == 1 || x == 3)
        return x;
    else
        return x * foo(x - 1);
}
```

Assuming no possibility of integer overflow, what will be the value of z after execution of the following statement?

```
int z = foo(foo(3) + foo(4));
```

(A) (15!)/(2!)
(B) 3! + 4!
(C) (7!)!
(D) (3! + 4!)!
(E) 15

Questions 19 and 20 refer to the `IntFormatter` class below.

```
public class IntFormatter
{
    //Write 3 digits adjacent to each other.
    public static void writeThreeDigits(int n)
    {
        System.out.print(n / 100);
        System.out.print((n / 10) % 10);
        System.out.print(n % 10);
    }

    //Insert commas in n, every 3 digits starting at the right.
    //Precondition: n >= 0.
    public static void writeWithCommas(int n)
    {
        if (n < 1000)
            System.out.print(n);
        else
        {
            writeThreeDigits(n % 1000);
            System.out.print(",");
            writeWithCommas(n / 1000);
        }
    }
}
```

19. The method `writeWithCommas` is supposed to print its nonnegative int argument with commas properly inserted (every three digits, starting at the right). For example, the integer 27048621 should be printed as 27,048,621. Method `writeWithCommas` does not always work as intended, however. Assuming no integer overflow, which of the following integer arguments will *not* be printed correctly?
    (A) 896
    (B) 251462251
    (C) 365051
    (D) 278278
    (E) 4

20. Which change in the code of the given methods will cause method `writeWithCommas` to work as intended?
    (A) Interchange the lines `System.out.print(n / 100)` and `System.out.print(n % 10)` in method `writeThreeDigits`.
    (B) Interchange the lines `writeThreeDigits(n % 1000)` and `writeWithCommas(n / 1000)` in method `writeWithCommas`.
    (C) Change the test in `writeWithCommas` to `if (n > 1000)`.
    (D) In the method `writeWithCommas`, change the line `writeThreeDigits(n % 1000)` to `writeThreeDigits(n / 1000)`.
    (E) In the method `writeWithCommas`, change the recursive call `writeWithCommas(n / 1000)` to `writeWithCommas(n % 1000)`.

21. Consider the following method:

```
public static void sketch(int x1, int y1, int x2, int y2, int n)
{
    if (n <= 0)
        drawLine(x1, y1, x2, y2);
    else
    {
        int xm = (x1 + x2 + y1 - y2) / 2;
        int ym = (y1 + y2 + x2 - x1) / 2;
        sketch(x1, y1, xm, ym, n - 1);
        sketch(xm, ym, x2, y2, n - 1);
    }
}
```

Assume that the screen looks like a Cartesian coordinate system with the origin at the center, and that drawLine connects (x1,y1) to (x2,y2). Assume also that x1, y1, x2, and y2 are never too large or too small to cause errors. Which picture best represents the sketch drawn by the method call

```
sketch(a, 0, -a, 0, 2)
```

where a is a positive integer?

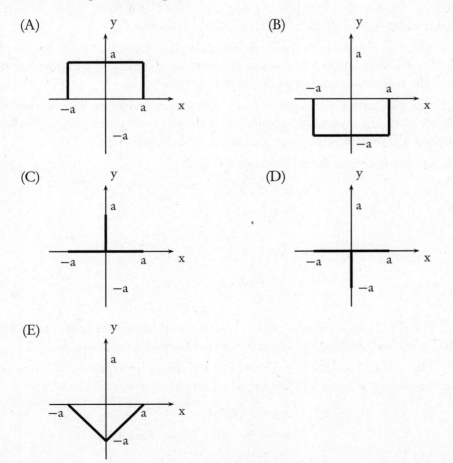

ANSWER KEY

1. **D**	8. **D**	15. **E**
2. **B**	9. **A**	16. **D**
3. **E**	10. **B**	17. **E**
4. **D**	11. **A**	18. **A**
5. **B**	12. **C**	19. **C**
6. **C**	13. **C**	20. **B**
7. **B**	14. **A**	21. **B**

ANSWERS EXPLAINED

1. **(D)** Tail recursion is when the recursive call of a method is made as the last executable step of the method. Divide-and-conquer algorithms like those used in mergesort or quicksort have recursive calls *before* the last step. Thus, statement II is false.

2. **(B)** Code segment I is wrong because there is no base case. Code segment III is wrong because, besides anything else, sum(n) prevents the method from terminating—the base case n == 1 will not be reached.

3. **(E)** When stringRecur is invoked, it calls itself irrespective of the length of s. Since there is no action that leads to termination, the method will not terminate until the computer runs out of memory (run-time error).

4. **(D)** The base case is s.length() $\geq$ 15. Since s gets longer on each method call, the method will eventually terminate. If the original length of s is $\geq$ 15, the method will terminate without output on the first call.

5. **(B)** Letting R denote the method result, we have

$$\begin{aligned} R(5) &= 2 * R(4) \\ &= 2 * (2 * (R(3))) \\ &= \cdots \\ &= 2 * (2 * (2 * (2 * R(1)))) \\ &= 2^5 \\ &= 32 \end{aligned}$$

6. **(C)** For result(n) there will be $(n-1)$ recursive calls before result(1), the base case, is reached. Adding the initial call gives a total of n method calls.

7. **(B)** This method returns the nth term of an arithmetic sequence with first term a and common difference d. Letting M denote method mystery, we have

$$\begin{aligned} M(3,2,6) &= 6 + M(2,2,6) \\ &= 6 + (6 + M(1,2,6)) \quad \text{(base case)} \\ &= 6 + 6 + 2 \\ &= 14 \end{aligned}$$

8. **(D)** Here are the recursive calls that are made, in order: $f(6,8) \rightarrow f(6,2) \rightarrow f(4,2) \rightarrow f(2,2)$, base case. Thus, 2 is returned.

9. **(A)** If there is only one element in x, then `recur` returns that element. Having the recursive call at the beginning of the `else` part of the algorithm causes the `if` part for each method call to be stacked until `t` eventually gets assigned to `x[0]`. The pending `if` statements are then executed, and `t` is compared to each element in x. The largest value in x is returned.

10. **(B)** Since the recursive call is made directly following the base case, the `System.out.print...` statements are stacked up. If `printString("cat")` is called, here is the sequence of recursive calls and pending statements on the stack:

Execution stack

When `printString("")`, the base case, is called, the `print` statements are then popped off the stack in reverse order, which means that the characters of the string will be printed in reverse order.

11. **(A)** The required code is for a negative `expo`. For example, `power(2, -3)` should return $2^{-3} = 1/8$. Notice that

$$2^{-3} = \tfrac{1}{2}\left(2^{-2}\right)$$
$$2^{-2} = \tfrac{1}{2}\left(2^{-1}\right)$$
$$2^{-1} = \tfrac{1}{2}\left(2^{0}\right)$$

In general:

$$2^{n} = \tfrac{1}{2}(2^{n+1}) \quad \text{whenever} \quad n < 0$$

This is equivalent to `(1 / base) * power(base, expo + 1)`.

12. **(C)** Each box in the diagram below represents a recursive call to `doSomething`. The numbers to the right of the boxes show the order of execution of the statements. Let D denote `doSomething`.

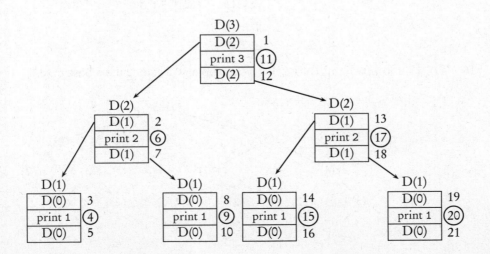

The numbers in each box refer to that method call only. D(0) is the base case, so the statement immediately following it is executed next. When all statements in a given box (method call) have been executed, backtrack along the arrow to find the statement that gets executed next. The circled numbers represent the statements that produce output. Following them in order, statements 4, 6, 9, 11, 15, 17, and 20 produce the output in choice C.

13. **(C)** Since even numbers are printed *before* the recursive call in segment I, they will be printed in the order in which they are read from the keyboard. Contrast this with the correct choice, segment III, in which the recursive call is made before the test for evenness. These tests will be stacked until the last number is read. Recall that the pending statements are removed from the stack in reverse order (most recent recursive call first), which leads to even numbers being printed in reverse order. Segment II is wrong because all numbers entered will be printed, irrespective of whether they are even or not. Note that segment II would work if the input list contained only even numbers.

14. **(A)** Let mystery(3) be denoted $m(3)$. Picture the execution of the method as follows:

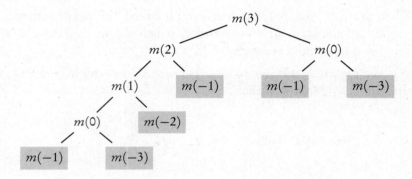

The base cases are shaded. Note that each of the six base case calls returns 2, resulting in a total of 12.

15. **(E)** The method generates a sequence. The first two terms, $t(1)$ and $t(2)$, are 2 and 4. Each subsequent term is generated by subtracting the previous two terms. This is the sequence: 2, 4, 2, −2, −4, −2, 2, 4, ... Thus, $t(5) = -4$. Alternatively,

$$t(5) = t(4) - t(3)$$
$$= [t(3) - t(2)] - t(3)$$
$$= -t(2)$$
$$= -4$$

16. **(D)** 15. Count them! (Note that you stop at $t(2)$ since it's a base case.)

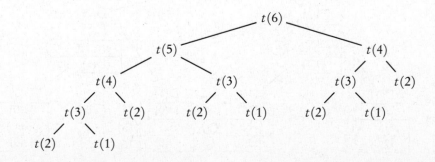

17. **(E)** This is an example of *mutual recursion*, where two methods call each other.

$$\begin{aligned}
f_1(5,3) &= 5 + f_2(4,3) \\
&= 5 + (4 + f_1(2,3)) \\
&= 5 + (4 + (2 + f_2(1,3))) \\
&= 5 + (4 + (2 + 4)) \\
&= 15
\end{aligned}$$

Note that $f_2(1,3)$ is a base case.

18. **(A)** foo(3) = 3 (This is a base case). Also, foo(4) = 4 × foo(3) = 12. So you need to find foo(foo(3) + foo(4)) = foo(15).

$$\begin{aligned}
\text{foo}(15) &= 15 \times \text{foo}(14) \\
&= 15 \times (14 \times \text{foo}(13)) \\
&= \cdots \\
&= 15 \times 14 \times \cdots \times 4 \times \text{foo}(3) \\
&= 15 \times 14 \times \cdots \times 4 \times 3 \\
&= (15)!/(2!)
\end{aligned}$$

19. **(C)** Suppose that $n = 365051$. The method call `writeWithCommas(365051)` will write `051` and then execute the call `writeWithCommas(365)`. This is a base case, so 365 will be written out, resulting in `051,365`. A number like 278278 (two sets of three identical digits) will be written out correctly, as will a "symmetrical" number like 251462251. Also, any $n < 1000$ is a base case and the number will be written out correctly as is.

20. **(B)** The cause of the problem is that the numbers are being written out with the sets of three digits in the wrong order. The problem is fixed by interchanging `writeThreeDigits(n % 1000)` and `writeWithCommas(n / 1000)`. For example, here is the order of execution for `writeWithCommas(365051)`.

   `writeWithCommas(365)` → Base case. Writes 365
   `System.out.print(",");` → 365,
   `writeThreeDigits(051)` → 365,051 which is correct

21. **(B)** Here is the "box diagram" for the recursive method calls, showing the order of execution of statements. Notice that the circled statements are the base case calls, the only statements that actually draw a line. Note also that the first time you reach a base case (see circled statement 6), you can get the answer: The picture in choice B is the only one that has a line segment joining `(a,0)` to `(a,-a)`.

Sorting and Searching

*Critics search for ages for the wrong word, which,
to give them credit, they eventually find.*
—*Peter Ustinov (1952)*

Chapter Goals

- Java implementation of sorting algorithms

- Selection and insertion sorts

- Recursive sorts: mergesort and quicksort

- Sequential search and binary search

In each of the following sorting algorithms, assume that an array of *n* elements, a[0], a[1], ..., a[n-1], is to be sorted in ascending order.

SORTS: SELECTION AND INSERTION SORTS

Selection Sort

This is a "search-and-swap" algorithm. Here's how it works.

Find the smallest element in the array and exchange it with a[0], the first element. Now find the smallest element in the subarray a[1]...a[n-1] and swap it with a[1], the second element in the array. Continue this process until just the last two elements remain to be sorted, a[n-2] and a[n-1]. The smaller of these two elements is placed in a[n-2]; the larger, in a[n-1]; and the sort is complete.

Trace these steps with a small array of four elements. The unshaded part is the subarray still to be searched.

8	1	4	6	
1	8	4	6	after first pass
1	4	8	6	after second pass
1	4	6	8	after third pass

NOTE

1. For an array of *n* elements, the array is sorted after $n - 1$ passes.
2. After the *k*th pass, the first *k* elements are in their final sorted position.

Insertion Sort

Think of the first element in the array, a[0], as being sorted with respect to itself. The array can now be thought of as consisting of two parts, a sorted list followed by an unsorted list. The idea of insertion sort is to move elements from the unsorted list to the sorted list one at a time; as each item is moved, it is inserted into its correct position in the sorted list. In order to place the new item, some elements may need to be moved down to create a slot.

Here is the array of four elements. In each case, the boxed element is "it," the next element to be inserted into the sorted part of the list. The shaded area is the part of the list sorted so far.

NOTE

1. For an array of *n* elements, the array is sorted after $n - 1$ passes.
2. After the *k*th pass, a[0], a[1], ..., a[k] are sorted with respect to each other but not necessarily in their final sorted positions.
3. The worst case for insertion sort occurs if the array is initially sorted in reverse order, since this will lead to the maximum possible number of comparisons and moves.
4. The best case for insertion sort occurs if the array is already sorted in increasing order. In this case, each pass through the array will involve just one comparison, which will indicate that "it" is in its correct position with respect to the sorted list. Therefore, no elements will need to be moved.

> Both insertion and selection sorts are inefficient for large *n*.

RECURSIVE SORTS: MERGESORT AND QUICKSORT

Selection and insertion sorts are inefficient for large *n*, requiring approximately *n* passes through a list of *n* elements. More efficient algorithms can be devised using a "divide-and-conquer" approach, which is used in both the sorting algorithms that follow.

Mergesort

Here is a recursive description of how mergesort works:

If there is more than one element in the array
      Break the array into two halves.
      Mergesort the left half.
      Mergesort the right half.
      Merge the two subarrays into a sorted array.

> The main disadvantage of mergesort is that it uses a temporary array.

Mergesort uses a merge method to merge two sorted pieces of an array into a single sorted array. For example, suppose array a[0] ... a[n-1] is such that a[0] ... a[k] is sorted and a[k+1] ... a[n-1] is sorted, both parts in increasing order. Example:

a[0]	a[1]	a[2]	a[3]	a[4]	a[5]
2	5	8	9	1	6

In this case, a[0] ...a[3] and a[4] ...a[5] are the two sorted pieces. The method call merge(a,0,3,5) should produce the "merged" array:

a[0]	a[1]	a[2]	a[3]	a[4]	a[5]
1	2	5	6	8	9

The middle numerical parameter in merge (the 3 in this case) represents the index of the last element in the first "piece" of the array. The first and third numerical parameters are the lowest and highest index, respectively, of array a.

Here's what happens in mergesort:

1. Start with an unsorted list of n elements.
2. The recursive calls break the list into n sublists, each of length 1. Note that these n arrays, each containing just one element, are sorted!
3. Recursively merge adjacent pairs of lists. There are then approximately $n/2$ lists of length 2; then, approximately $n/4$ lists of approximate length 4, and so on, until there is just one list of length n.

An example of mergesort follows:

Break list into
n sublists of
length 1

Merge adjacent
pairs of lists

Analysis of Mergesort:

1. The major disadvantage of mergesort is that it needs a temporary array that is as large as the original array to be sorted. This could be a problem if space is a factor.
2. Mergesort is not affected by the initial ordering of the elements. Thus, best, worst, and average cases have similar run times.

Quicksort

Optional topic

For large *n*, quicksort is, on average, the fastest known sorting algorithm. Here is a recursive description of how quicksort works:

If there are at least two elements in the array
      Partition the array.
      Quicksort the left subarray.
      Quicksort the right subarray.

The `partition` method splits the array into two subarrays as follows: a *pivot* element is chosen at random from the array (often just the first element) and placed so that all items to the left of the pivot are less than or equal to the pivot, whereas those to the right are greater than or equal to it.

For example, if the array is 4, 1, 2, 7, 5, −1, 8, 0, 6, and a[0] = 4 is the pivot, the `partition` method produces

    −1   1   2   0   **4**   5   8   7   6

Here's how the partitioning works: Let a[0], 4 in this case, be the pivot. Markers up and down are initialized to index values 0 and *n* − 1, as shown. Move the up marker until a value less than the pivot is found, or down equals up. Move the down marker until a value greater than the pivot is found, or down equals up. Swap a[up] and a[down]. Continue the process until down equals up. This is the pivot position. Swap a[0] and a[pivotPosition].

Notice that the pivot element, 4, is in its final sorted position.

Analysis of Quicksort:

1. For the fastest run time, the array should be partitioned into two parts of roughly the same size.

The main disadvantage of quicksort is that its worst case behavior is very inefficient.

(continued)

2. If the pivot happens to be the smallest or largest element in the array, the split is not much of a split—one of the subarrays is empty! If this happens repeatedly, quicksort degenerates into a slow, recursive version of selection sort and is very inefficient.

3. The worst case for quicksort occurs when the partitioning algorithm repeatedly divides the array into pieces of size 1 and $n - 1$. An example is when the array is initially sorted in either order and the first or last element is chosen as the pivot. Some algorithms avoid this situation by initially shuffling up the given array (!) or selecting the pivot by examining several elements of the array (such as first, middle, and last) and then taking the median.

NOTE

For both quicksort and mergesort, when a subarray gets down to some small size m, it becomes faster to sort by straight insertion. The optimal value of m is machine-dependent, but it's approximately equal to 7.

SORTING ALGORITHMS IN JAVA

Unlike the container classes like `ArrayList`, whose elements must be objects, arrays can hold either objects or primitive types like `int` or `double`.

A common way of organizing code for sorting arrays is to create a sorter class with an array private instance variable. The class holds all the methods for a given type of sorting algorithm, and the constructor assigns the user's array to the private array variable.

Example

Selection sort for an array of `int`.

```
/* A class that sorts an array of ints from
 * largest to smallest using selection sort. */

public class SelectionSort
{
    private int[] a;

    //constructor
    public SelectionSort(int[] arr)
    { a = arr; }

    //Swap a[i] and a[j] in array a.
    private void swap(int i, int j)
    {
        int temp = a[i];
        a[i] = a[j];
        a[j] = temp;
    }
```

```
//Sort array a from largest to smallest using selection sort.
//Precondition: a is an array of ints.
public void selectionSort()
{
    int maxPos, max;

    for (int i = 0; i < a.length - 1; i++)
    {
        //find max element in a[i+1] to a[a.length-1]
        max = a[i];
        maxPos = i;
        for (int j = i + 1; j < a.length; j++)
            if (max < a[j])
            {
                max = a[j];
                maxPos = j;
            }
        swap(i, maxPos); //swap a[i] and a[maxPos]
    }
}
```

> Only `Comparable` objects can be sorted.

Note that in order to sort *objects*, the elements must be `Comparable` since you need to be able to compare them.

SEQUENTIAL SEARCH

Assume that you are searching for a key in a list of *n* elements. A sequential search starts at the first element and compares the key to each element in turn until the key is found or there are no more elements to examine in the list. If the list is sorted, in ascending order, say, stop searching as soon as the key is less than the current list element.

Analysis:

1. The best case has key in the first slot.
2. The worst case occurs if the key is in the last slot or not in the list. In the worst case, all *n* elements must be examined.
3. On average, there will be *n*/2 comparisons.

BINARY SEARCH

> Binary search works only if the array is sorted on the search key.

If the elements are in a *sorted* array, a divide-and-conquer approach provides a much more efficient searching algorithm. The following recursive pseudo-code algorithm shows how the *binary search* works.

Assume that a[low] ... a[high] is sorted in ascending order and that a method binSearch returns the index of key. If key is not in the array, it returns −1.

```
if (low > high)    //Base case. No elements left in array.
    return -1;
else
{
    mid = (low + high)/2;
    if (key is equal to a[mid])   //found the key
        return mid;
    else if (key is less than a[mid])  //key in left half of array
        < binSearch for key in a[low] to a[mid-1] >
    else     //key in right half of array
        < binSearch for key in a[mid+1] to a[high] >
}
```

NOTE

When `low` and `high` cross, there are no more elements to examine, and `key` is not in the array.

Example: suppose 5 is the key to be found in the following array:

```
a[0]  a[1]  a[2]  a[3]  a[4]  a[5]  a[6]  a[7]  a[8]
 1.    4     5.....7    9    12    15    20    .21
```

First pass: mid = (8+0)/2 = 4.   Check a[4].
Second pass: mid = (0+3)/2 = 1.   Check a[1].
Third pass: mid = (2+3)/2 = 2.   Check a[2]. Yes! Key is found.

Analysis of Binary Search:

1. In the best case, the key is found on the first try (i.e., `(low + high)/2` is the index of `key`.)
2. In the worst case, the key is not in the list or is at either end of a sublist. Here the n elements must be divided by 2 until there is just one element, and then that last element must be tested. An easy way to find the number of comparisons in the worst case is to round n up to the next power of 2 and take the exponent. For example, in the array above, $n = 9$. Suppose 21 were the key. Round 9 up to 16, which equals 2^4. Thus you would need four comparisons to find it. Try it!

Chapter Summary

You should not memorize any sorting code. You must, however, be familiar with the mechanism used in each of the sorting algorithms. For example, you should be able to explain how the merge method of mergesort works, or what the purpose of the pivot element in quicksort is. You should know the best and worst case situations for each of the sorting algorithms.

Be familiar with the sequential and binary search algorithms. You should know that a binary search is more efficient than a sequential search, and that a binary search can only be used for an array that is sorted on the search key.

MULTIPLE-CHOICE QUESTIONS ON SORTING AND SEARCHING

1. The decision to choose a particular sorting algorithm should be made based on

    I   Run-time efficiency of the sort
    II Size of the array
    III Space efficiency of the algorithm

    (A) I only
    (B) II only
    (C) III only
    (D) I and II only
    (E) I, II, and III

2. The following code fragment does a sequential search to determine whether a given integer, value, is stored in an array a[0] ... a[n-1].

    ```
    int i = 0;
    while (/* boolean expression */)
    {
        i++;
    }
    if (i == n)
        return -1;    //value not found
    else
        return i;     // value found at location i
    ```

    Which of the following should replace /* *boolean expression* */ so that the algorithm works as intended?
    (A) value != a[i]
    (B) i < n && value == a[i]
    (C) value != a[i] && i < n
    (D) i < n && value != a[i]
    (E) i < n || value != a[i]

3. A feature of data that is used for a binary search but not necessarily used for a sequential search is
    (A) length of list.
    (B) type of data.
    (C) order of data.
    (D) smallest value in the list.
    (E) median value of the data.

4. Array `unsortedArr` contains an unsorted list of integers. Array `sortedArr` contains a sorted list of integers. Which of the following operations is more efficient for `sortedArr` than `unsortedArr`? Assume the most efficient algorithms are used.

   I Inserting a new element
   II Searching for a given element
   III Computing the mean of the elements

   (A) I only
   (B) II only
   (C) III only
   (D) I and II only
   (E) I, II, and III

5. An algorithm for searching a large sorted array for a specific value x compares every third item in the array to x until it finds one that is greater than or equal to x. When a larger value is found, the algorithm compares x to the previous two items. If the array is sorted in increasing order, which of the following describes all cases when this algorithm uses fewer comparisons to find x than would a binary search?
   (A) It will never use fewer comparisons.
   (B) When x is in the middle position of the array
   (C) When x is very close to the beginning of the array
   (D) When x is very close to the end of the array
   (E) When x is not in the array

6. Assume that `a[0] ... a[N-1]` is an array of N positive integers and that the following assertion is true:

   $$a[0] > a[k] \text{ for all } k \text{ such that } 0 < k < N$$

   Which of the following *must* be true?
   (A) The array is sorted in ascending order.
   (B) The array is sorted in descending order.
   (C) All values in the array are different.
   (D) `a[0]` holds the smallest value in the array.
   (E) `a[0]` holds the largest value in the array.

7. The following code is designed to set `index` to the location of the first occurrence of `key` in array `a` and to set `index` to -1 if `key` is not in `a`.

   ```
   index = 0;
   while (a[index] != key)
       index++;
   if (a[index] != key)
       index = -1;
   ```

   In which case will this program *definitely* fail to perform the task described?
   (A) When `key` is the first element of the array
   (B) When `key` is the last element of the array
   (C) When `key` is not in the array
   (D) When `key` equals 0
   (E) When `key` equals `a[key]`

8. Refer to method search.

```
/* Precondition:  v[0]...v[v.length-1] are initialized.
 * Postcondition: Returns k such that -1 <= k <= v.length-1.
 *                If k >= 0 then v[k] == key. If k == -1,
 *                then key != any of the elements in v.  */
public static int search(int[] v, int key)
{
    int index = 0;
    while (index < v.length && v[index] < key)
        index++;
    if (v[index] == key)
        return index;
    else
        return -1;
}
```

Assuming that the method works as intended, which of the following should be added to the precondition of search?
(A) v is sorted smallest to largest.
(B) v is sorted largest to smallest.
(C) v is unsorted.
(D) There is at least one occurrence of key in v.
(E) key occurs no more than once in v.

Questions 9–13 are based on the binSearch method and the private instance variable a for some class:

```
private int[] a;

/* Does binary search for key in array a[0]...a[a.length-1],
 *     sorted in ascending order.
 * Postcondition: Returns index such that a[index]==key.
 *                If key not in a, returns -1.  */
public int binSearch(int key)
{
    int low = 0;
    int high = a.length - 1;
    while (low <= high)
    {
        int mid = (low + high) / 2;
        if (a[mid] == key)
            return mid;
        else if (a[mid] < key)
            low = mid + 1;
        else
            high = mid - 1;
    }
    return -1;
}
```

A binary search will be performed on the following list.

a[0]	a[1]	a[2]	a[3]	a[4]	a[5]	a[6]	a[7]
4	7	9	11	20	24	30	41

9. To find the key value 27, the search interval *after* the first pass through the `while` loop will be
    (A) `a[0] ... a[7]`
    (B) `a[5] ... a[6]`
    (C) `a[4] ... a[7]`
    (D) `a[2] ... a[6]`
    (E) `a[6] ... a[7]`

10. How many iterations will be required to determine that 27 is not in the list?
    (A) 1
    (B) 3
    (C) 8
    (D) 27
    (E) An infinite loop since 27 is not found

11. What will be stored in y after executing the following?

    ```
    int y = binSearch(4);
    ```

    (A) 20
    (B) 7
    (C) 4
    (D) 0
    (E) -1

12. If the test for the `while` loop is changed to

    ```
    while (low < high)
    ```

    the `binSearch` method does not work as intended. Which value in the given list will not be found?
    (A) 4
    (B) 7
    (C) 11
    (D) 24
    (E) 30

13. For `binSearch`, which of the following assertions will be true following every iteration of the `while` loop?
    (A) $key = a[mid]$ or key is not in a.
    (B) $a[low] \leq key \leq a[high]$
    (C) $low \leq mid \leq high$
    (D) $key = a[mid]$, or $a[low] \leq key \leq a[high]$
    (E) $key = a[mid]$, or $a[low] \leq key \leq a[high]$, or key is not in array a.

14. A large sorted array containing about 30,000 elements is to be searched for a value key using an iterative binary search algorithm. Assuming that key is in the array, which of the following is closest to the smallest number of iterations that will guarantee that key is found? Note: $10^3 \approx 2^{10}$.

   (A) 15
   (B) 30
   (C) 100
   (D) 300
   (E) 3000

For Questions 15–18 refer to the insertionSort method and the private instance variable a, both in a Sorter class.

```
private Comparable[] a;

/* Precondition:  a[0],a[1]...a[a.length-1] is an unsorted array
 *                of Comparable objects.
 * Postcondition: Array a is sorted in descending order.  */
public void insertionSort()
{
    for (int i = 1; i < a.length; i++)
    {
        Comparable temp = a[i];
        int j = i - 1;
        while (j >= 0 && temp.compareTo(a[j]) > 0)
        {
            a[j+1] = a[j];
            j--;
        }
        a[j+1] = temp;
    }
}
```

15. An array of Integer is to be sorted biggest to smallest using the insertionSort method. If the array originally contains

$$1 \quad 7 \quad 9 \quad 5 \quad 4 \quad 12$$

   what will it look like after the third pass of the for loop?
   (A) 9 7 1 5 4 12
   (B) 9 7 5 1 4 12
   (C) 12 9 7 1 5 4
   (D) 12 9 7 5 4 1
   (E) 9 7 12 5 4 1

16. When sorted biggest to smallest with insertionSort, which list will need the fewest changes of position for individual elements?
   (A) 5, 1, 2, 3, 4, 9
   (B) 9, 5, 1, 4, 3, 2
   (C) 9, 4, 2, 5, 1, 3
   (D) 9, 3, 5, 1, 4, 2
   (E) 3, 2, 1, 9, 5, 4

17. When sorted biggest to smallest with `insertionSort`, which list will need the greatest number of changes in position?
    (A) 5, 1, 2, 3, 4, 7, 6, 9
    (B) 9, 5, 1, 4, 3, 2, 1, 0
    (C) 9, 4, 6, 2, 1, 5, 1, 3
    (D) 9, 6, 9, 5, 6, 7, 2, 0
    (E) 3, 2, 1, 0, 9, 6, 5, 4

18. While typing the `insertionSort` method, a programmer by mistake enters

    ```
    while (temp.compareTo( a[j]) > 0)
    ```

    instead of

    ```
    while (j >= 0 && temp.compareTo( a[j]) > 0)
    ```

    Despite this mistake, the method works as intended the first time the programmer enters an array to be sorted in descending order. Which of the following could explain this?

    I   The first element in the array was the largest element in the array.
    II The array was already sorted in descending order.
    III The first element was less than or equal to all the other elements in the array.

    (A) I only
    (B) II only
    (C) III only
    (D) I and II only
    (E) II and III only

19. Consider the following class.

```
/* A class that sorts an array of objects from
 * largest to smallest using a selection sort. */
public class Sorter
{
    private Comparable[] a;

    public Sorter(Comparable[] arr)
    { a = arr; }

    /* Swap a[i] and a[j] in array a. */
    private void swap(int i, int j)
    { /* implementation not shown */ }

    /* Sort array a from largest to smallest using selection sort.
     * Precondition: a is an array of Comparable objects. */
    public void selectionSort()
    {
        for (int i = 0; i < a.length - 1; i++)
        {
            //find max element in a[i+1] to a[n-1]
            Comparable max = a[i];
            int maxPos = i;
            for (int j = i + 1; j < a.length; j++)
                if (max.compareTo(a[j]) < 0) //max less than a[j]
                {
                    max = a[j];
                    maxPos = j;
                }
            swap(i, maxPos);    //swap a[i] and a[maxPos]
        }
    }
}
```

If an array of Integer contains the following elements, what would the array look like after the third pass of selectionSort, sorting from high to low?

$$89 \quad 42 \quad -3 \quad 13 \quad 109 \quad 70 \quad 2$$

(A) 109   89   70   13   42   −3   2
(B) 109   89   70   42   13   2   −3
(C) 109   89   70   −3   2   13   42
(D)   89   42   13   −3   109   70   2
(E) 109   89   42   −3   13   70   2

20. The elements in a long list of integers are roughly sorted in decreasing order. No more than 5 percent of the elements are out of order. Which of the following is a valid reason for using an insertion sort rather than a selection sort to sort this list into decreasing order?

    I   There will be fewer comparisons of elements for insertion sort.
    II There will be fewer changes of position of elements for insertion sort.
    III There will be less space required for insertion sort.

    (A) I only
    (B) II only
    (C) III only
    (D) I and II only
    (E) I, II, and III

21. The code shown sorts array a[0] ...a[a.length-1] in descending order.

```
public static void sort(Comparable[] a)
{
    for (int i = 0; i < a.length - 1; i++)
        for (int j = 0; j < a.length - i - 1; j++)
            if (a[j].compareTo(a[j+1]) < 0)
                swap(a, j, j + 1);  //swap a[j] and a[j+1]
}
```

    This is an example of
    (A) selection sort.
    (B) insertion sort.
    (C) mergesort.
    (D) quicksort.
    (E) none of the above.

22. Which of the following is a valid reason why mergesort is a better sorting algorithm than insertion sort for sorting long lists?

    I   Mergesort requires less code than insertion sort.
    II Mergesort requires less storage space than insertion sort.
    III Mergesort runs faster than insertion sort.

    (A) I only
    (B) II only
    (C) III only
    (D) I and II only
    (E) II and III only

23. A large array of lowercase characters is to be searched for the pattern "pqrs." The first step in a very efficient searching algorithm is to look at characters with index
    (A) 0, 1, 2, ... until a "p" is encountered.
    (B) 0, 1, 2, ... until any letter in "p" ... "s" is encountered.
    (C) 3, 7, 11, ... until an "s" is encountered.
    (D) 3, 7, 11, ... until any letter in "p" ... "s" is encountered.
    (E) 3, 7, 11, ... until any letter other than "p" ... "s" is encountered.

24. The array `names[0]`, `names[1]`, ..., `names[9999]` is a list of 10,000 name strings. The list is to be searched to determine the location of some name `X` in the list. Which of the following preconditions is necessary for a binary search?
    (A) There are no duplicate names in the list.
    (B) The number of names N in the list is large.
    (C) The list is in alphabetical order.
    (D) Name `X` is definitely in the list.
    (E) Name `X` occurs near the middle of the list.

25. Consider the following method:

    ```
    //Precondition: a[0],a[1]...a[n-1] contain integers.
    public static int someMethod(int[] a, int n, int value)
    {
        if (n == 0)
            return -1;
        else
        {
            if (a[n-1] == value)
                return n - 1;
            else
                return someMethod(a, n - 1, value);
        }
    }
    ```

    The method shown is an example of
    (A) insertion sort.
    (B) mergesort.
    (C) selection sort.
    (D) binary search.
    (E) sequential search.

Optional topic

26. The `partition` method for quicksort partitions a list as follows:

    (i) A pivot element is selected from the array.
    (ii) The elements of the list are rearranged such that all elements to the left of the pivot are less than or equal to it; all elements to the right of the pivot are greater than or equal to it.

    Partitioning the array requires which of the following?
    (A) A recursive algorithm
    (B) A temporary array
    (C) An external file for the array
    (D) A swap algorithm for interchanging array elements
    (E) A merge method for merging two sorted lists

27. Assume that mergesort will be used to sort an array `arr` of n integers into increasing order. What is the purpose of the `merge` method in the mergesort algorithm?
    (A) Partition `arr` into two parts of roughly equal length, then merge these parts.
    (B) Use a recursive algorithm to sort `arr` into increasing order.
    (C) Divide `arr` into n subarrays, each with one element.
    (D) Merge two sorted parts of `arr` into a single sorted array.
    (E) Merge two sorted arrays into a temporary array that is sorted.

28. A binary search is to be performed on an array with 600 elements. In the *worst* case, which of the following best approximates the number of iterations of the algorithm?
    (A) 6
    (B) 10
    (C) 100
    (D) 300
    (E) 600

29. A worst case situation for insertion sort would be

       I A list in correct sorted order.
      II A list sorted in reverse order.
     III A list in random order.

    (A) I only
    (B) II only
    (C) III only
    (D) I and II only
    (E) II and III only

Optional topic

Questions 30 and 31 are based on the Sort interface and MergeSort and QuickSort classes shown below.

```
public interface Sort
{
    void sort();
}

public class MergeSort implements Sort
{
    private Comparable[] a;

    //constructor
    public MergeSort(Comparable[] arr)
    { a = arr; }

    //Merge a[lb] to a[mi] and a[mi+1] to a[ub].
    //Precondition: a[lb] to a[mi] and a[mi+1] to a[ub] both
    //              sorted in increasing order.
    private void merge(int lb, int mi, int ub)
    { /* Implementation not shown. */ }

    //Sort a[first]..a[last] in increasing order using mergesort.
    //Precondition: a is an array of Comparable objects.
    private void sort(int first, int last)
    {
        int mid;

        if (first != last)
        {
            mid = (first + last) / 2;
            sort(first, mid);
            sort(mid + 1, last);
            merge(first, mid, last);
        }
    }

    //Sort array a from smallest to largest using mergesort.
    //Precondition: a is an array of Comparable objects.
    public void sort()
    {
        sort(0, a.length - 1);
    }
}

public class QuickSort implements Sort
{
     private Comparable[] a;

    //constructor
    public QuickSort(Comparable[] arr)
    { a = arr; }

    //Swap a[i] and a[j] in array a.
    private void swap(int i, int j)
    { /* Implementation not shown. */ }
```

(continued)

```
//Returns the index pivPos such that a[first] to a[last]
//is partitioned.
//a[first..pivPos] <= a[pivPos] and a[pivPos..last] >= a[pivPos]
private int partition(int first, int last)
{ /* Implementation not shown. */ }


//Sort a[first]..a[last] in increasing order using quicksort.
//Precondition: a is an array of Comparable objects.
private void sort(int first, int last)
{
    if (first < last)
    {
        int pivPos = partition(first, last);
        sort(first, pivPos - 1);
        sort(pivPos + 1, last);
    }
}


//Sort array a in increasing order.
public void sort()
{
    sort(0, a.length - 1);
}
}
```

30. Notice that the `MergeSort` and `QuickSort` classes both have a private helper method that implements the recursive sort routine. For this example, which of the following is *not* a valid reason for having a helper method?

  I The helper method hides the implementation details of the sorting algorithm from the user.
  II A method with additional parameters is needed to implement the recursion.
  III Providing a helper method increases the run-time efficiency of the sorting algorithm.

  (A) I only
  (B) II only
  (C) III only
  (D) I and II only
  (E) I, II, and III

(continued)

31. A piece of code to test the `QuickSort` and `MergeSort` classes is as follows:

```
//Create an array of Comparable values
Comparable[] strArray = makeArray(strList);
writeList(strArray);
/* more code */
```

where `makeArray` creates an array of `Comparable` from a list `strList`. Which of the following replacements for /* *more code* */ is reasonable code to test `QuickSort` and `MergeSort`? You can assume `writeList` correctly writes out an array of `String`.

(A)
```
Sort q = new QuickSort(strArray);
Sort m = new MergeSort(strArray);
q.sort();
writeList(strArray);
m.sort();
writeList(strArray);
```

(B)
```
QuickSort q = new Sort(strArray);
MergeSort m = new Sort(strArray);
q.sort();
writeList(strArray);
m.sort();
writeList(strArray);
```

(C)
```
Sort q = new QuickSort(strArray);
Sort m = new MergeSort(strArray);
Comparable[] copyArray = makeArray(strList);
q.sort(0, strArray.length - 1);
writeList(strArray);
m.sort(0, copyArray.length - 1);
writeList(copyArray);
```

(D)
```
QuickSort q = new Sort(strArray);
Comparable[] copyArray = makeArray(strList);
MergeSort m = new Sort(strArray);
q.sort();
writeList(strArray);
m.sort();
writeList(copyArray);
```

(E)
```
Sort q = new QuickSort(strArray);
Comparable[] copyArray = makeArray(strList);
Sort m = new MergeSort(copyArray);
q.sort();
writeList(strArray);
m.sort();
writeList(copyArray);
```

32. Consider a binary search algorithm to search an ordered list of numbers. Which of the following choices is closest to the maximum number of times that such an algorithm will execute its main comparison loop when searching a list of 1 million numbers?
    (A) 6
    (B) 20
    (C) 100
    (D) 120
    (E) 1000

33. Consider these three tasks:

    I   A sequential search of an array of n names
    II A binary search of an array of n names in alphabetical order
    III An insertion sort into alphabetical order of an array of n names that are initially in random order

    For large n, which of the following lists these tasks in order (from least to greatest) of their average case run times?

    (A) II   I   III
    (B)   I   II   III
    (C) II III   I
    (D) III   I   II
    (E) III   II   I

Questions 34–36 refer to the Hi-Lo game described below.

Consider the problem of writing a Hi-Lo game in which a user thinks of an integer from 1 to 100 inclusive and the computer tries to guess that number. Each time the computer makes a guess, the user makes one of three responses:

- "lower" (i.e., the number is lower than the computer's guess)

- "higher" (i.e., the number is higher than the computer's guess)

- "you got it in *< however many >* tries!"

34. Suppose the game is programmed so that the computer uses a binary search strategy for making its guesses. What is the maximum number of guesses the computer could make before guessing the user's number?
    (A) 50
    (B) 25
    (C) 10
    (D) 7
    (E) 6

35. Suppose the computer used a *sequential search* strategy for guessing the user's number. What is the maximum number of guesses the computer could make before guessing the user's number?
    (A) 100
    (B) 99
    (C) 50
    (D) 25
    (E) 10

36. Using a sequential search strategy, how many guesses *on average* would the computer need to guess the number?
    (A) 100
    (B) 51
    (C) 50
    (D) 25
    (E) Fewer than 25

ANSWER KEY

1. E	13. E	25. E
2. D	14. A	26. D
3. C	15. B	27. D
4. B	16. B	28. B
5. C	17. A	29. B
6. E	18. D	30. C
7. C	19. A	31. E
8. A	20. A	32. B
9. C	21. E	33. A
10. B	22. C	34. D
11. D	23. D	35. A
12. A	24. C	36. C

ANSWERS EXPLAINED

1. **(E)** The time and space requirements of sorting algorithms are affected by all three of the given factors, so all must be considered when choosing a particular sorting algorithm.

2. **(D)** Choice B doesn't make sense: The loop will be exited as soon as a value is found that does *not* equal `a[i]`. Eliminate choice A because, if value is not in the array, `a[i]` will eventually go out of bounds. You need the `i < n` part of the boolean expression to avoid this. The test `i < n`, however, must precede `value != a[i]` so that if `i < n` fails, the expression will be evaluated as false, the test will be short-circuited, and an out-of-range error will be avoided. Choice C does not avoid this error. Choice E is wrong because both parts of the expression must be true in order to continue the search.

3. **(C)** The binary search algorithm depends on the array being sorted. Sequential search has no ordering requirement. Both depend on choice A, the length of the list, while the other choices are irrelevant to both algorithms.

4. **(B)** Inserting a new element is quick and easy in an unsorted array—just add it to the end of the list. Computing the mean involves finding the sum of the elements and dividing by n, the number of elements. The execution time is the same whether the list is sorted or not. Operation II, searching, is inefficient for an unsorted list, since a sequential search must be used. In `sortedArr`, the efficient binary search algorithm, which involves fewer comparisons, could be used. In fact, in a sorted list, even a sequential search would be more efficient than for an unsorted list: If the search item were not in the list, the search could stop as soon as the list elements were greater than the search item.

5. **(C)** Suppose the array has 1000 elements and x is somewhere in the first 8 slots. The algorithm described will find x using no more than five comparisons. A binary search, by contrast, will chop the array in half and do a comparison six

times before examining elements in the first 15 slots of the array (array size after each chop: 500, 250, 125, 62, 31, 15).

6. **(E)** The assertion states that the first element is greater than all the other elements in the array. This eliminates choices A and D. Choices B and C are incorrect because you have no information about the relative sizes of elements `a[1]...a[N-1]`.

7. **(C)** When `key` is not in the array, `index` will eventually be large enough that `a[index]` will cause an `ArrayIndexOutOfBoundsException`. In choices A and B, the algorithm will find `key` without error. Choice D won't fail if 0 is in the array. Choice E will work if `a[key]` is not out of range.

8. **(A)** The algorithm uses the fact that array `v` is sorted smallest to largest. The `while` loop terminates—which means that the search stops—as soon as `v[index] >= key`.

9. **(C)** The first pass uses the interval `a[0]...a[7]`. Since $mid = (0+7)/2 = 3$, `low` gets adjusted to $mid + 1 = 4$, and the second pass uses the interval `a[4]...a[7]`.

10. **(B)** First pass: compare 27 with `a[3]`, since `low = 0` `high = 7` $mid = (0+7)/2 = 3$. Second pass: compare 27 with `a[5]`, since `low = 4` `high = 7` $mid = (4+7)/2 = 5$. Third pass: compare 27 with `a[6]`, since `low = 6` `high = 7` $mid = (6+7)/2 = 6$. The fourth pass doesn't happen, since `low = 6`, `high = 5`, and therefore the test (`low <= high`) fails. Here's the general rule for finding the number of iterations when `key` is not in the list: If n is the number of elements, round n up to the nearest power of 2, which is 8 in this case. $8 = 2^3$, which implies 3 iterations of the "divide-and-compare" loop.

11. **(D)** The method returns the index of the `key` parameter, 4. Since `a[0]` contains 4, `binSearch(4)` will return 0.

12. **(A)** Try 4. Here are the values for `low`, `high`, and `mid` when searching for 4:

    First pass: `low = 0`,   `high = 7`,   `mid = 3`
    Second pass: `low = 0`,   `high = 2`,   `mid = 1`

After this pass, `high` gets adjusted to $mid - 1$, which is 0. Now `low` equals `high`, and the test for the `while` loop fails. The method returns -1, indicating that 4 wasn't found.

13. **(E)** When the loop is exited, either `key = a[mid]` (and `mid` has been returned) or `key` has not been found, in which case either `a[low]` $\le$ `key` $\le$ `a[high]` or `key` is not in the array. The correct assertion must account for all three possibilities.

14. **(A)** $30,000 = 1000 \times 30 \approx 2^{10} \times 2^5 = 2^{15}$. Since a successful binary search in the worst case requires $\log_2 n$ iterations, 15 iterations will guarantee that `key` is found. (Note that $30,000 < 2^{10} \times 2^5 = 32,768$.)

15. **(B)** Start with the second element in the array.

    After 1st pass: 7   1   9   5   4   12
    After 2nd pass: 9   7   1   5   4   12
    After 3rd pass: 9   7   5   1   4   12

16. **(B)** An insertion sort compares `a[1]` and `a[0]`. If they are not in the correct

order, a[0] is moved and a[1] is inserted in its correct position. a[2] is then inserted in its correct position, and a[0] and a[1] are moved if necessary, and so on. Since B has only one element out of order, it will require the fewest changes.

17. **(A)** This list is almost sorted in reverse order, which is the worst case for insertion sort, requiring the greatest number of comparisons and moves.

18. **(D)** j >= 0 is a stopping condition that prevents an element that is larger than all those to the left of it from going off the left end of the array. If no error occurred, it means that the largest element in the array was a[0], which was true in situations I and II. Omitting the j >= 0 test will cause a run-time (out-of-range) error whenever temp is bigger than all elements to the left of it (i.e., the insertion point is 0).

19. **(A)**

After 1st pass:	109	42	−3	13	89	70	2
After 2nd pass:	109	89	−3	13	42	70	2
After 3rd pass:	109	89	70	13	42	−3	2

20. **(A)** Look at a small array that is almost sorted:

$$10 \ 8 \ 9 \ 6 \ 2$$

For <u>insertion sort</u> you need four passes through this array.
The first pass compares 8 and 10—one comparison, no moves.
The second pass compares 9 and 8, then 9 and 10. The array becomes 10 9 8 6 2—two comparisons, two moves.
The third and fourth passes compare 6 and 8, and 2 and 6—no moves.
In summary, there are approximately one or two comparisons per pass and no more than two moves per pass.
For <u>selection sort</u>, there are four passes too.
The first pass finds the biggest element in the array and swaps it into the first position.
The array is still 10 8 9 6 2—four comparisons. There are two moves if your algorithm makes the swap in this case, otherwise no moves.
The second pass finds the biggest element from a[1] to a[4] and swaps it into the second position: 10 9 8 6 2—three comparisons, two moves.
For the third pass there are two comparisons, and one for the fourth. There are zero or two moves each time.
Summary: $4 + 3 + 2 + 1$ total comparisons and a possible two moves per pass.
Notice that reason I is valid. Selection sort makes the same number of comparisons irrespective of the state of the array. Insertion sort does far fewer comparisons if the array is almost sorted. Reason II is invalid. There are roughly the same number of data movements for insertion and selection. Insertion may even have more changes, depending on how far from their insertion points the unsorted elements are. Reason III is wrong because insertion and selection sorts have the same space requirements.

21. **(E)** In the first pass through the outer for loop, the smallest element makes its way to the end of the array. In the second pass, the next smallest element moves to the second last slot, and so on. This is different from the sorts in choices A through D; in fact, it is a bubble sort.

Optional topic

22. **(C)** Reject reason I. Mergesort requires both a merge and a mergeSort method—

more code than the relatively short and simple code for insertion sort. Reject reason II. The merge algorithm uses a temporary array, which means *more* storage space than insertion sort. Reason III is correct. For long lists, the "divide-and-conquer" approach of mergesort gives it a faster run time than insertion sort.

23. **(D)** Since the search is for a four-letter sequence, the idea in this algorithm is that if you examine every fourth slot, you'll find a letter in the required sequence very quickly. When you find one of these letters, you can then examine adjacent slots to check if you have the required sequence. This method will, on average, result in fewer comparisons than the strictly sequential search algorithm in choice A. Choice B is wrong. If you encounter a "q," "r," or "s" without a "p" first, you can't have found "pqrs." Choice C is wrong because you may miss the sequence completely. Choice E doesn't make sense.

24. **(C)** The main precondition for a binary search is that the list is ordered.

25. **(E)** This algorithm is just a recursive implementation of a sequential search. It starts by testing if the last element in the array, a[n-1], is equal to value. If so, it returns the index n - 1. Otherwise, it calls itself with n replaced by n - 1. The net effect is that it examines a[n-1], a[n-2], ... The base case, if (n == 0), occurs when there are no elements left to examine. In this case, the method returns −1, signifying that value was not in the array.

Optional topic

26. **(D)** The partition algorithm performs a series of swaps until the pivot element is swapped into its final sorted position (see p. 322). No temporary arrays or external files are used, nor is a recursive algorithm invoked. The merge method is used for mergesort, not quicksort.

27. **(D)** Recall the mergesort algorithm:

> Divide arr into two parts.
> Mergesort the left side.
> Mergesort the right side.
> Merge the two sides into a single sorted array.

The merge method is used for the last step of the algorithm. It does not do any sorting or partitioning of the array, which eliminates choices A, B, and C. Choice E is wrong because merge starts with a *single* array that has two sorted parts.

28. **(B)** Round 600 up to the next power of 2, which is $1024 = 2^{10}$. For the worst case, the array will be split in half $\log_2 1024 = 10$ times.

29. **(B)** If the list is sorted in reverse order, each pass through the array will involve the maximum possible number of comparisons and the maximum possible number of element movements if an insertion sort is used.

Optional topic

30. **(C)** Reason I is valid—it's always desirable to hide implementation details from users of a method. Reason II is valid too—since QuickSort and MergeSort implement the Sort interface, they must have a sort method with no parameters. But parameters are needed to make the recursion work. Therefore each sort requires a helper method with parameters. Reason III is invalid in this particular example of helper methods. There are many examples in which a helper method enhances efficiency (e.g., Example 2 on p. 291), but the sort example is not one of them.

31. **(E)** Since Sort is an interface, you can't create an instance of it. This eliminates choices B and D. The sort methods alter the contents of strArray. Thus invoking q.sort() followed by m.sort() means that m.sort will always operate on a

(continued)

sorted array, assuming quicksort works correctly! In order to test both quick-sort and mergesort on unsorted arrays, you need to make a copy of the original array or create a different array. Eliminate choice A (and B again!), which does neither of these. Choice C is wrong because it calls the *private* sort methods of the classes. The Sort interface has just a single *public* method, sort, with no arguments. The two classes shown must provide an implementation for this sort method, and it is this method that must be invoked in the client program.

32. **(B)** 1 million $= 10^6 = (10^3)^2 \approx (2^{10})^2 = 2^{20}$. Thus, there will be on the order of 20 comparisons.

33. **(A)** A binary search, on average, has a smaller run time than a sequential search. All of the sorting algorithms have greater run times than a sequential search. This is because a sequential search looks at each element once. A sorting algorithm, however, processes *other* elements in the array for each element it looks at.

34. **(D)** The computer should find the number in no more than seven tries. This is because the guessing interval is halved on each successive try:

$$
\begin{array}{lll}
(1) & 100 \div 2 = 50 & \text{numbers left to try} \\
(2) & 50 \div 2 = 25 & \text{numbers left to try} \\
(3) & 25 \div 2 = 13 & \text{numbers left to try} \\
(4) & 13 \div 2 = 7 & \text{numbers left to try} \\
(5) & 7 \div 2 = 4 & \text{numbers left to try} \\
(6) & 4 \div 2 = 2 & \text{numbers left to try} \\
(7) & 2 \div 2 = 1 & \text{number left to try}
\end{array}
$$

Seven iterations of the loop leaves just 1 number left to try!

35. **(A)** The maximum number of guesses is 100. A sequential search means that the computer starts at the first possible number, namely 1, and tries each successive number until it gets to 100. If the user's number is 100, the computer will take 100 guesses to reach it.

36. **(C)** On average the computer will make 50 guesses. The user is equally likely to pick any number between 1 and 100. Half the time it will be less than 50; half the time, greater than 50. So on the average, the distance of the number from 1 is 50.

The GridWorld Case Study

*Man is the only critter who feels the need
to label things as flowers and weeds.*
—*Anonymous*

Chapter Goals

- The classes in GridWorld: hierarchy and overview
- The Actor class
- The Location class
- The Rock and Flower classes
- The Bug and BoxBug classes
- The Critter class and ChameleonCritter classes
- The Grid interface
- The AbstractGrid class
- The BoundedGrid and UnboundedGrid classes

OVERVIEW

This chapter provides a complete summary of the code and narrative in the Grid-World Case Study. The full text can be found at the College Board website *http://www.collegeboard.com/student/testing/ap/compsci_a/case.html?compscia*.

The case study is a program that simulates actions and interactions of objects in a two-dimensional grid. The "actors" in the grid are displayed by a GUI (graphical user interface). The GUI can also add new actors to the grid and can invoke methods on all actors.

During a single step of the program, every occupant of the grid gets a chance to act. Each actor acts according to a clearly specified set of behaviors that can include moving, changing color, changing direction, removing other actors from the grid, depositing new actors in specified locations, and so on.

THE CLASSES

The following diagram displays the relationship between the testable classes in the case study.

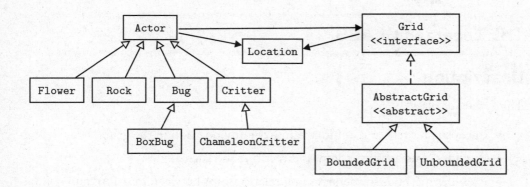

The diagram shows that each of these objects, `Flower`, `Rock`, `Bug`, and `Critter` *is-an* `Actor`. A `BoxBug` *is-a* `Bug`, and a `ChameleonCritter` *is-a* `Critter`. Also, `AbstractGrid` is an abstract class that implements the `Grid` interface. Each of `BoundedGrid` and `UnboundedGrid` *is-an* `AbstractGrid`. Every `Actor` *has-a* `Location` and `Grid`, and a `Grid` *has-a* `Location`.

NOTE

The `Location`, `Actor`, `Rock`, and `Flower` classes are "black box" classes whose code is not provided. You are, however, expected to know the specifications of their methods and constants. Code is provided for all of the other classes shown and is testable on the AP exam.

THE ACTORS

Here is a summary of what each actor does when it acts.

- A `Rock` does nothing.
- A `Flower` darkens its color.
- A `Bug` moves forward when it can. It can move into an empty spot or onto a flower. When it moves, it deposits a flower in its previous location. If it moves to a location occupied by a flower, that flower is removed from the grid. A bug cannot move if it is blocked in front by either another (nonflower) actor or the edge of the grid. When a bug is prevented from moving, it turns 45° to the right.
- A `BoxBug` moves like a `Bug`. Additionally, if it encounters no obstacles in its path, it traces out a square of flowers with a given side length. If a `BoxBug` is blocked from moving, it makes two right turns and starts again.
- A `Critter` gets a list of its adjacent neighboring actors and processes them by "eating" each actor that is not a rock or another critter. It then randomly selects one of the empty neighboring locations and moves there. If there are no available empty locations, a critter does not move.
- A `ChameleonCritter` gets a list of its adjacent neighbors, randomly picks one of them, and changes its color to that of the selected actor. The `ChameleonCritter` moves like a `Critter` but, additionally, it first changes its direction to face its new location before moving.

THE Location CLASS

Description

The Location class

- Encapsulates row and column values for any position in the grid.
- Provides constants for compass directions and turn angles.
- Provides methods for determining relationships between locations and compass directions.

The flower in the diagram is in row 1, column 2, or Location (1, 2).

There are eight constants that represent compass directions:

Constant	int Value
Location.NORTH	0
Location.EAST	90
Location.SOUTH	180
Location.WEST	270
Location.NORTHEAST	45
Location.SOUTHEAST	135
Location.SOUTHWEST	225
Location.NORTHWEST	315

The compass directions have integer values starting at 0 (north) and moving clockwise through 360 (degrees). The dashed arrow in the figure below represents a direction of 135 or Location.SOUTHEAST.

There are seven constants representing the most commonly used turn angles:

Constant	int **Value**
Location.LEFT	-90
Location.RIGHT	90
Location.HALF_LEFT	-45
Location.HALF_RIGHT	45
Location.FULL_CIRCLE	360
Location.HALF_CIRCLE	180
Location.AHEAD	0

To get an actor to turn through a given number of degrees, set its direction to the sum of its current direction and the turn angle. For example, to make an actor turn right (through 90°, clockwise)

$$\underbrace{\texttt{setDirection}}_{\text{change direction to}}(\underbrace{\texttt{getDirection()}}_{\text{current direction}} + \underbrace{\texttt{Location.RIGHT}}_{+90°});$$

In general, a class can be represented by a box diagram (shown below) in which private data and methods are completely enclosed within the shaded region, while public methods overlap the shaded region.[1]

The diagram below represents the Location class, and shows that there is one constructor, eight public methods, and two private instance variables.

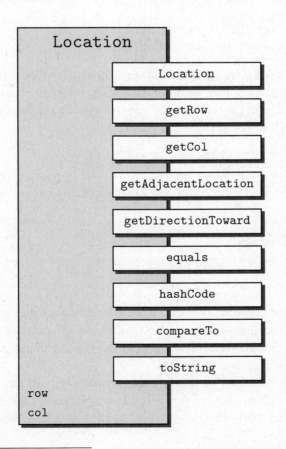

---

[1]The class diagrams are based on diagrams in *A Computer Science Tapestry* by Owen Astrachan and the Marine Biology Case Study narrative by Alyce Brady.

Methods

```
public Location(int r, int c)
```

Constructs a location with given row and column.

```
public int getRow()
public int getCol()
```

Accessor methods that return the row or column of the Location.

```
public Location getAdjacentLocation(int direction)
```

Returns the adjacent location in the compass direction closest to direction.

```
public int getDirectionToward(Location target)
```

Returns the direction, rounded to the nearest compass direction, from this location toward a target location.

```
public int hashCode()
```

Generates and returns a hash code for this Location (see p. 173).

```
public boolean equals(Object other)
public int compareTo(Object other)
```

These methods are used to compare Location objects. Two locations are equal if they have the same row and column values. Ascending order for locations is *row-major*, namely, start at (0, 0) and proceed row by row from left to right. For example, (0, 1) is less than (0, 2) and (1, 8) is less than (3, 0).

```
public String toString()
```

Returns a string representation of this Location in the form (row, col).

THE Actor CLASS

Description

The Actor class is the superclass for every creature or object that appears in the grid.

An Actor has a location, direction, and color, along with the capacity to change each of these instance variables. It has access to its grid. It can put itself in the grid, and also remove itself from it.

Here is the box diagram for the Actor class, showing only its public methods. (Since Actor is a black-box class, you are not privy to its private data and methods, nor the implementation of its methods.)

> Every creature in the grid is coded as a subclass of Actor.

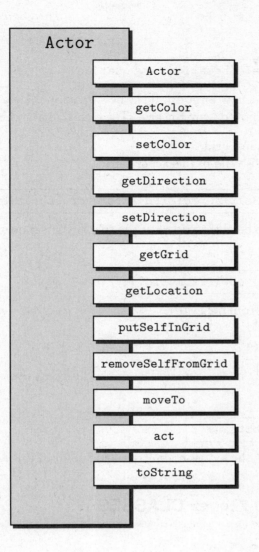

Methods

```
public Actor()
```

Default constructor. Constructs a blue actor facing north.

```
public Color getColor()
public int getDirection()
public Location getLocation()
```

Accessor methods. Return the color, direction, or location of this `Actor`. Note that the direction returned is an `int` from 0 through 359 (degrees).

```
public Grid<Actor> getGrid()
```

Accessor method. Returns the grid of this `Actor`, or `null` if the actor is not in the grid.

```
public void setColor(Color newColor)
public void setDirection(int newDirection)
```

Mutator methods. Change the color or direction of this `Actor` to the new value specified by the parameter.

```
public void moveTo(Location newLocation)
```

Moves this `Actor` to a new location. If the new location is already occupied, the actor in that location is removed from the grid. The `moveTo` method has two preconditions:

1. This `Actor` is in a grid.
2. `newLocation` is valid in this `Actor`'s grid.

```
public void putSelfInGrid(Grid<Actor> gr, Location loc)
```

Puts this `Actor` into the given grid gr at the specified location `loc`. A precondition is that `loc` is valid.

```
public void removeSelfFromGrid()
```

Removes this `Actor` from the grid.

```
public void act()
```

Reverses the direction of this actor. (The method is often overridden in sublcasses of `Actor`.)

```
public String toString()
```

Returns a string with the location, direction, and color of this `Actor`.

THE Rock AND Flower CLASSES

The Rock Class

A `Rock` acts by doing nothing. It has a default constructor that creates a black rock, and a second constructor that allows construction of a rock with a specified color. The act method is overridden—it has an empty body!

The Flower Class

A `Flower` acts by darkening its color. It has a default constructor that creates a pink flower, and a second constructor that allows construction of a flower with a specified color. The overridden act method darkens the flower by reducing the values of the red, green, and blue components of its color by a constant factor.

THE Bug CLASS

Description

A `Bug` is an `Actor` that moves forward in a straight line, turning only when it is blocked. A bug can be blocked by either the edge of the grid, or an actor that is not a flower.

As the bug moves, it steps on any flower in its path, causing the removal of that flower from the grid. After each step, the bug places a flower in its previous location.

Here is a box diagram for the Bug class. Methods inherited from Actor are not shown. Overridden methods are indicated with a double frame.

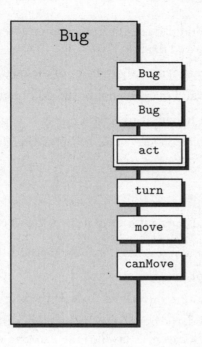

The diagram shows that a Bug has two constructors. The act method is overridden, and there are three additional public methods: turn, move, and canMove. Don't forget that Bug also inherits the following methods from Actor: getColor, setColor, getDirection, setDirection, getGrid, getLocation, putSelfInGrid, removeSelfFromGrid, moveTo, and toString.

Methods

```
public Bug()
```

Default constructor. Creates a red Bug.

```
public Bug(Color bugColor)
```

Constructor. Creates a Bug with the specified color.

Note that both of the constructors use the inherited setColor method.

```
public void act()
```

The Bug moves if it can; otherwise it turns.

Note that this is the only method of the Actor class that is overridden.

```
public void turn()
```

Turns this Bug 45° to the right without changing its location. It does it by adding Location.HALF_RIGHT to the bug's current direction.

```
public boolean canMove()
```

Returns true if this Bug can move, false otherwise. The bug is able to move if the location directly in front of it (a) is valid and (b) is empty or contains a flower. Here are the steps in the method:

- Get the bug's grid, and if it is null, return false. (Note that a bug's grid is null if another actor removed the bug.)
- Get the adjacent location directly in front of the bug.
- If this location is invalid (namely, out of the grid), return false.
- Get the actor in this neighboring location.
- If the actor is a flower or null (i.e., no actor there!), return true. Otherwise return false.

```
public void move()
```

Moves this Bug forward, placing a flower in its previous location. Here are the steps:

- Get the bug's grid, and if it is null, exit the method.
- Get the bug's current location.
- Get the adjacent location directly in front of the bug.
- If this location is valid, the bug moves there; otherwise it removes itself from the grid. (Note: If this location is invalid, the canMove method will return false, and move will not be called. So the test in this step is redundant, and is probably included as an extra precaution.)
- Create a flower that is the same color as the bug.
- Place the flower in the bug's previous location (which was saved in the second step.)

THE BoxBug CLASS

Description

A BoxBug is a Bug that moves in a square pattern if it is unimpeded. To create the square, a BoxBug has two private instance variables: sideLength, which is the number of steps in a side of its square, and steps, which keeps track of where the BoxBug is in creating a side. Whenever a side has been completed or the bug must start again because it encountered an obstacle, steps gets reset to zero.

Here is the box diagram for the BoxBug class.

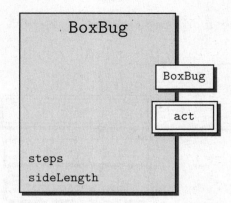

The diagram shows that BoxBug has two private instance variables, one constructor, and an overridden act method. In addition to inheriting all of the public methods of Actor, BoxBug inherits the methods turn, move, and canMove from Bug.

Methods

```
public BoxBug(int length)
```

Constructor. Sets sideLength to the specified length, and initializes steps to 0.

```
public void act()
```

This overridden method performs one step in the creation of the BoxBug's square. First, the method tests whether the bug is still in the process of making a side:

```
if (steps < sideLength...
```

If this is true, and the bug can move, the bug moves and steps is incremented. If the above piece of the test is false, it means that the bug has completed the current side, and must turn so that it can start a new side. It does this by calling turn twice, to create the 90° angle at the vertex of the square. (Recall that a single call to turn turns the bug through 45°.) After the bug has completed the 90° turn, steps is reset to zero in preparation for a new side. Notice that if steps < sideLength is true, but canMove() is false (BoxBug is blocked), the same preparation for a new side must occur (turn, turn, reset steps). If the BoxBug is unimpeded when creating its square, and the sideLength has value k, there will be $k + 1$ flowers on each side of the square.

THE Critter CLASS

Description

A Critter is an Actor with the following pattern of behavior.

- Get a list of neighboring actors.
- Process the actors.
- Get a list of possible locations to move to.
- Select a location from the list.
- Move there.

Here is the box diagram for the `Critter` class.

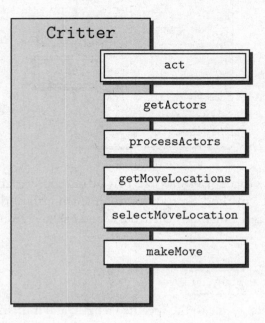

The diagram shows that the `Critter` class does not have an explicit constructor. This means that the default constructor of the `Actor` superclass will be invoked to create a blue `Critter` facing north. All other methods of `Actor` are inherited, and act is overridden. The other five methods are new methods for `Critter`.

Methods

```
public void act()
```

A `Critter` acts by getting a list of its neighbors, processing them, getting a list of possible locations to move to, selecting one of these, and then moving to the selected location.

```
public ArrayList<Actor> getActors()
```

Returns a list of adjacent neighboring actors.

```
public void processActors(ArrayList<Actor> actors)
```

Processes the actors. The `Critter` "eats" all actors that are not rocks or other critters. The actors are processed by iterating through the list of actors. Each actor is examined. If it is neither a rock nor a critter, the actor removes itself from the grid.

```
public ArrayList<Location> getMoveLocations()
```

Returns a list of valid, adjacent, empty, neighboring locations, which are the possible locations for the next move. The grid method `getEmptyAdjacentLocations` is used, with the critter's current location as its parameter.

```
public Location selectMoveLocation(ArrayList<Location> locs)
```

Selects the location for the next move from `locs`, a list of valid locations. Here are the steps.

- Assign n to be the length of the list.
- If n is zero, which means that there are no available locations, return the current location of the critter.
- Get a random `int` from 0 to $n - 1$ with the statement

    ```
    int r = (int) (Math.random() * n);
    ```

- Return the location at index r in the `locs` `ArrayList`.

```
public void makeMove(Location loc)
```

Moves this `Critter` to the specified location. A precondition is that `loc` is valid. The method is implemented with the statement

```
moveTo(loc);
```

Recall that `moveTo` is inherited from `Actor`.

THE `ChameleonCritter` CLASS

Description

A `ChameleonCritter` is a `Critter`. When it acts, a `ChameleonCritter` gets the same list of actors as a `Critter`, but instead of eating them, it randomly selects one actor and changes its color to that of the selected actor. A `ChameleonCritter` moves like a `Critter`, with one difference: Before it moves, it turns to face its new location.

Here is the box diagram for the `ChameleonCritter` class.

Notice that there is no constructor, which means that when a `ChameleonCritter` is created, the default constructor of `Actor` will be invoked, constructing a blue `ChameleonCritter` facing north.

Methods

```
public void processActors(ArrayList<Actor> actors)
```

Randomly selects an adjacent neighbor, and changes this `ChameleonCritter`'s color to that of the selected actor. Does nothing if there are no neighbors.

```
public void makeMove(Location loc)
```

Moves like a regular `Critter`, but before it moves, it turns to face its new location. To change direction, the `setDirection` method is used. The parameter used for the call to `setDirection` is the direction from the `ChameleonCritter`'s current location to `loc`:

```
getLocation().getDirectionToward(loc)
```

THE `Grid<E>` INTERFACE

Optional topic

The interface `Grid<E>` specifies methods that manipulate a grid of objects of type `E`. In the case study, `Grid<E>` is implemented by three classes, `AbstractGrid<E>`, `Bounded-Grid<E>`, and `UnboundedGrid<E>`. When the grid classes are used by clients, type `E` is replaced by `Actor`.

Methods

Listed below are the methods in the interface. These methods are commented and discussed in the classes that implement them.

```
public interface Grid<E>
{
    int getNumRows();
    int getNumCols();
    boolean isValid(Location loc);
    E put(Location loc, E obj);
    E remove(Location loc);
    E get(Location loc);
    ArrayList<Location> getOccupiedLocations();
    ArrayList<Location> getValidAdjacentLocations(Location loc);
    ArrayList<Location> getEmptyAdjacentLocations(Location loc);
    ArrayList<Location> getOccupiedAdjacentLocations(Location loc);
    ArrayList<E> getNeighbors(Location loc);
}
```

THE `AbstractGrid<E>` CLASS

Description

Optional topic

The `AbstractGrid<E>` class implements five methods of the `Grid<E>` interface that are common to both the `BoundedGrid<E>` and `UnboundedGrid<E>` classes. While no instance of an `AbstractGrid<E>` can be created, having this class avoids repeated code.

Here is the box diagram for the `AbstractGrid` class.

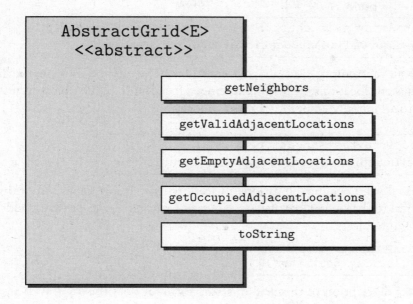

(continued)

Methods

Note that in every method below that has a loc parameter, there is a precondition that loc is valid in the grid.

```
public ArrayList<E> getNeighbors(Location loc)
```

Returns a list of all actors in locations adjacent to loc. It does this by traversing the locations in getOccupiedAdjacentLocations(loc), and adding the actors in those locations to an initially empty ArrayList<E>. Note that if neighbors is the ArrayList of actors to be returned, and neighborLoc is a Location in the traversal, the statement

```
neighbors.add(get(neighborLoc));
```

extracts the actor in neighborLoc and adds it to the neighbors list. Recall that add is an ArrayList method; but the get method used here is the Grid method that returns the object at its Location parameter.

```
public ArrayList<Location>
    getValidAdjacentLocations(Location loc)
```

Returns all valid locations adjacent to loc. Starting with north (at 0°), and going up in increments of 45, it gets the adjacent location in that direction, and, if that location is in the grid, adds it to an initially empty ArrayList of locations. If you do the math, you will see that the line

```
for (int i = 0; i < Location.FULL_CIRCLE / Location.HALF_RIGHT; i++)
```

is equivalent to

```
for (int i = 0; i < 8; i++)
```

The constants FULL_CIRCLE and HALF_RIGHT are used because 360/45 is much more descriptive than 8.

(continued)

```
public ArrayList<Location>
    getEmptyAdjacentLocations(Location loc)
```

Returns all valid empty locations adjacent to `loc`. The method traverses the list of `loc`'s valid adjacent locations. If it finds an empty location (i.e., the object in it is `null`), it adds it to an initially empty `ArrayList` of locations.

```
public ArrayList<Location>
    getOccupiedAdjacentLocations(Location loc)
```

Returns all valid occupied locations adjacent to `loc`. Implementation of this method is identical to that of `getEmptyAdjacentLocations` above, except that it adds locations that contain objects.

```
public String toString()
```

Returns a description of this grid in string form. It does this by traversing the occupied locations in the grid, and concatenating each location and occupying object to an initially empty string. The pieces of information for each location are separated by commas, which is the reason for this segment:

```
if (s.length() > 1)
    s += ", ";
```

What it means is: If there is at least one grid location described, add a comma to the string before starting the information for the next location. The test prevents the string from starting with a comma.

THE `BoundedGrid<E>` AND `UnboundedGrid<E>` CLASSES

Description

The grid classes provide an environment for the actors in GridWorld. A bounded grid is two-dimensional, with a finite number of rows and columns. Creatures in a bounded grid cannot escape its confines. An unbounded grid is also rectangular, but the number of rows and columns is unlimited.

Both `BoundedGrid<E>` and `UnboundedGrid<E>` extend `AbstractGrid<E>` which implements `Grid<E>`. This means that both of the grid classes inherit the five methods of `AbstractGrid<E>`, and *must* implement the remaining methods of `Grid<E>`.

Both the `BoundedGrid<E>` and `UnboundedGrid<E>` classes are represented in the following box diagram.

Both
BoundedGrid and
UnboundedGrid
extend
AbstractGrid
and implement
Grid.

(continued)

The diagram shows that each class has its own constructor, and each class implements the seven remaining Grid<E> methods that are not in AbstractGrid<E>. The inherited methods of AbstractGrid<E> are not shown: getValidAdjacentLocations, getEmptyAdjacentLocations, getOccupiedAdjacentLocations, getNeighbors, and toString.

The BoundedGrid<E> is implemented with a two-dimensional array of Object called occupantArray,

```
private Object[][] occupantArray;
```

The element type is Object, not E, because Java doesn't allow arrays of generic types. Still, all elements of occupantArray must be of type E, since the method that adds elements to this array, put, requires a parameter of type E for the object that is added.

The UnboundedGrid<E> is implemented with a map called occupantMap, in which a key of the map is a Location object and the corresponding value is an object of type E in that location:

```
private Map<Location, E> occupantMap;
```

Only those locations that contain an actor are keys of the map.

Methods

THE CONSTRUCTORS

For each class, the constructor creates an empty grid.

(continued)

BoundedGrid

```
public BoundedGrid(
    int rows, int cols)
```

Constructs an empty bounded grid with specified number of rows and columns. Throws an `IllegalArgumentException` if either parameter is negative.

```
public int getNumRows()
public int getNumCols()
```

BoundedGrid
Returns number of rows or columns in grid. Note that the number of rows is `occupantArray.length` and the number of columns is the length of the 0th row, `occupantArray[0].length`.

```
public boolean isValid(Location loc)
```

BoundedGrid
Returns true if `loc` is in bounds, false otherwise.

```
public ArrayList<Location> getOccupiedLocations()
```

Returns all occupied locations in this grid.

BoundedGrid

- A nested `for` loop traverses the rows and columns of the grid.
- Creates new `Location` from current row and column.
- Retrieves object at this location (using `get(loc)`).
- If object is not `null` (i.e., `loc` occupied), adds this location to `ArrayList`.

```
public E get(Location loc)
```

Returns the object at `loc`, or null if `loc` is unoccupied.

UnboundedGrid

```
public UnboundedGrid()
```

Creates an empty unbounded grid. Uses a `HashMap`.

UnboundedGrid
Always returns −1, since an `Unbounded-Grid` does not have a specific number of rows or columns.

UnboundedGrid
Always returns true.

UnboundedGrid

- Traverses key set of `occupantMap`, using a for-each loop.
- Adds each location in traversal to `ArrayList`. (All the keys are occupied locations.)

BoundedGrid

- An `IllegalArgumentException` is thrown if `loc` is invalid.
- Accesses object at `loc` by using the expression

  `occupantArray[loc.getRow()]`
  `    [loc.getCol()]`

- Before returning this object, cast to E.

UnboundedGrid

- A `NullPointerException` is thrown if `loc` is null.
- Accesses object at `loc` by using the expression

  `occupantMap.get(loc)`

  where get is a `Map` method.

`public E put(Location loc, E obj)`

Puts `obj` at location `loc` in this grid, and returns the previous occupant of that location. Returns `null` if `loc` was previously unoccupied.

BoundedGrid

- An `IllegalArgumentException` is thrown if `loc` is invalid.
- A `NullPointerException` is thrown if `obj` is null.
- Saves previous occupant at `loc`.
- Adds `obj` to `loc` using

  `occupantArray[loc.getRow()]`
  `  [loc.getCol()] = obj;`

- Returns previous occupant.

UnboundedGrid

- A `NullPointerException` is thrown if either `obj` or `loc` is null.
- Using the `Map` method put, returns result of

  `occupantMap.put(loc, obj)`

  (This creates a new mapping for `loc`, but returns the previous value that corresponded to `loc`.)

`public E remove(Location loc)`

Removes the object at `loc` and returns it. Returns `null` if `loc` is unoccupied.

BoundedGrid

- An `IllegalArgumentException` is thrown if `loc` is invalid.
- Retrieves object from `loc`:

  `E r = get(loc);`

  (Note: get is a `BoundedGrid` method.)
- Sets object in `loc` to null:

  `occupantArray[loc.getRow()]`
  `  [loc.getCol()] = null;`

- Returns r.

UnboundedGrid

- A `NullPointerException` is thrown if `loc` is null.
- Using `Map` method remove, removes mapping with `loc` as key, and returns previous object corresponding to `loc`:

  `return occupantMap.remove(loc);`

THE CASE STUDY AND THE AP EXAM

Approximately one-fourth of the AP exam will be devoted to questions on the case study. (This means five to ten multiple-choice questions and one free-response question.)

You must be familiar with the `Bug`, `BoxBug`, `Critter`, and `ChameleonCritter` classes, including their implementations. You should also be familiar with the documentation for the `Location`, `Actor`, `Rock`, and `Flower` classes, as well as the `Grid<E>` interface.

On the AP exam, all students will be provided with a Quick Reference that contains a list of methods for the preceding classes and interface. You will also receive source code for the `Bug`, `BoxBug`, `Critter`, and `ChameleonCritter` classes.

NOTE

1. The Javadoc comments `@param`, `@return`, and `@throws` are part of the AP Java subset. Here is an example.

```
/**
 * Puts obj at location loc in this grid, and returns
 * the object previously at this location.
 * Returns null if loc was previously unoccupied.
 * Precondition: obj is not null, and loc is valid in this grid.
 * @param loc the location where the object will be placed
 * @param obj the object to be placed
 * @return the object previously at the specified location
 * @throws IllegalArgumentException if the location is invalid
 * @throws NullPointerException if the object is null
 */
public E put(Location loc, E obj)
```

This will produce the following Javadoc output:

---

put

public E **put** (Location loc, E obj)

> Puts `obj` at location `loc` in this grid, and returns
> the object previously at this location.
> Returns `null` if `loc` was previously unoccupied.
> Precondition: `obj` is not `null`, and `loc` is valid in this grid.
>
> **Parameters:**
> > `loc` - the location where the object will be placed
> > `obj` - the object to be placed
>
> **Returns:**
> > the object previously at the specified location
>
> **Throws:**
> > `IllegalArgumentException` - if the location is invalid
> > `NullPointerException` - if the object is null

---

2. The GridWorld case study, including documentation, narrative, and code, can be found at *http://www.collegeboard.com/student/testing/ap/compsci_a/ case.html?compscia*.

Chapter Summary

Be thoroughly familiar with each of the actors in this world. Know how they move and act. In particular, you must know the inheritance relationships between the various actors. On the AP exam you are likely to be asked to write subclasses of Bug or Critter, or to write modified methods for some given superclass.

Find GridWorld in the Quick Reference guide, so you can become comfortable referring to this as you write your own code. By the time you get to the AP exam, it should be second nature to you to use the Quick Reference.

MULTIPLE-CHOICE QUESTIONS ON THE CASE STUDY

Before you begin, note that

- Some of the questions in this section provide code from the case study. On the AP exam, code will not be reproduced in the questions, since you will be provided with a copy of all code to be tested.

- The actors in GridWorld are represented in this book with the pictures shown below. Each actor is shown facing north. These pictures almost certainly will be different from those used on the AP exam!

    Actor   Bug   Flower   Rock   Critter   ChameleonCritter

1. Which of the following is a *false* statement about `Rock` and `Flower` behavior?
   (A) When a rock acts, it does nothing.
   (B) When a flower acts, it does nothing.
   (C) A flower never changes its location when it acts.
   (D) A rock never changes its location when it acts.
   (E) When a rock is placed in a location that contains a flower, the flower disappears from the grid.

2. Suppose a `Bug` starts out facing south. If the `turn` method is called for this bug, what will its resulting direction be?
   (A) North
   (B) Northeast
   (C) Northwest
   (D) Southeast
   (E) Southwest

3. Consider the BoxBug in the diagram.

If its sideLength is 3, which represents the result of executing act() once for this BoxBug?

(A)

(B)

(C)

(D)

(E)

4. What will be the effect of executing the following statement in a client class for Bug and BoxBug?

   ```
   Bug bb = new BoxBug();
   ```

   (A) A red BoxBug facing north will be created, with random sideLength.
   (B) A red BoxBug facing north will be created, with sideLength = 0.
   (C) A red BoxBug with random direction will be created, with sideLength = 0.
   (D) A BoxBug with random color and direction will be created, with sideLength = 0.
   (E) A compile-time error will occur.

5. Which is a good reason for using the Location class constants for the compass directions and commonly used turn angles?

   I   They enhance readability of code.

   II   There is no built-in Degree type in Java.

   III   They distinguish locations from directions.

   (A) I only
   (B) II only
   (C) III only
   (D) I and III only
   (E) I, II, and III

6. Which location will the bug occupy after it acts once?

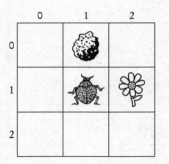

   (A) (1, 1)
   (B) (0, 1)
   (C) (1, 2)
   (D) (2, 1)
   (E) (1, 0)

7. Suppose you want to modify the behavior of a `Bug` as follows: Every time it moves to a new location, it drops a `Rock` rather than a `Flower` into its old location. Which of the following modifications to the `move` method of the `Bug` class will correctly achieve this?

    I Replace the last two "flower" lines with

```
Rock rock = new Rock();
rock.putSelfInGrid(gr, loc);
```

    II Replace the last two "flower" lines with

```
Rock rock = new Rock();
gr.put(loc, rock);
```

    III Replace the last two "flower" lines with

```
Rock rock = new Rock();
gr[loc.getRow()][loc.getCol()] = rock;
```

(A) I only
(B) II only
(C) III only
(D) I and II only
(E) I, II, and III

8. In which of the following situations will the `canMove` method of `Bug` return true?

I

II

III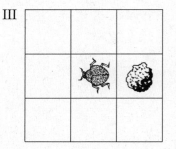

    (A) I only
    (B) II only
    (C) III only
    (D) I and II only
    (E) II and III only

9. What would be the effect of having a subclass of `Actor` called `SubActor` that does not override the `act` method?

    I A `SubActor` object would always be blue.

    II A `SubActor` object would always face north.

    III A `SubActor` object would remain in its original location when it acts.

    (A) I only
    (B) II only
    (C) III only
    (D) I and III only
    (E) I, II, and III

10. Consider a 4 × 4 bounded grid that contains a Bug at location (2, 3) facing east. What happens at this bug's turn to act?
    (A) It removes itself from the grid, leaving location (2, 3) empty.
    (B) It removes itself from the grid, leaving a flower in location (2, 3).
    (C) It moves to location (2, 4), leaving a flower in location (2, 3).
    (D) It remains in location (2, 3), and turns to face south.
    (E) It remains in location (2, 3), and turns to face southeast.

11. Consider a class PoisonousCritter that extends Critter. A PoisonousCritter marks its victims by changing the color of all its adjacent neighbors—except rocks—to green. Rocks remain unchanged. The PoisonousCritter then selects one of its victims at random, and "kills" it by moving into its location. Which groups of Critter methods will need to be overridden?

    I act and getActors

    II processActors and getMoveLocations

    III selectMoveLocation and makeMove

    (A) I only
    (B) II only
    (C) III only
    (D) II and III only
    (E) I, II, and III

12. A slight modification is made to the `BoxBug` class: One of the `turn` statements is removed. Here is the modified `act` method.

```
public void act()
{
    if (steps < sideLength && canMove())
    {
        move();
        steps++;
    }
    else
    {
        turn();
        steps = 0;
    }
}
```

Assuming that there are no impediments in the grid, which is a possible result of executing this code several times?

13. Suppose a subclass of `Critter`, `SmallCritter`, selects its next location by randomly selecting the location of an actor that occupies an adjacent neighboring grid location. The `getMoveLocations` of the `Critter` class will need to be overridden. Here is the specification for the overridden method.

```
/**
 * Gets the possible locations for the next move. Returns the
 * occupied neighboring locations.
 * Postcondition: The locations must be valid in the grid of this
 * SmallCritter.
 * @return a list of possible locations for the next move.
 */
public ArrayList<Location> getMoveLocations()
{ /* implementation code */ }
```

Which of the following is correct /* *implementation code* */ that will satisfy the postcondition?

(A) `return getGrid().getNeighbors(getLocation());`

(B) `return getGrid().getValidAdjacentLocations(getLocation());`

(C) `return getGrid().getOccupiedAdjacentLocations(getLocation());`

(D) `return getActors();`

(E) `return getActors().getLocations();`

14. Suppose a `ForwardCritter` extends `Critter`, and exists only in a bounded grid. A `ForwardCritter` has the following behavior when it acts.

   - It eats all actors in the grid (except for rocks and other critters) that are in a straight line in the direction that it is facing.
   - It then moves to a random empty location in the straight line in front of it.

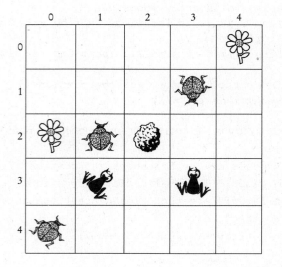

For example, the `ForwardCritter` at (3, 1) would eat the bug at (1, 3) and the flower at (0, 4), then it would randomly move to either (1, 3) or (0, 4). If it were the turn of the `ForwardCritter` at (3, 3) to act, it would eat the bug at (1, 3) and then randomly move to (2, 3), (1, 3), or (0, 3).

   In implementing the `ForwardCritter` class, which `Critter` methods would need to be overridden?

   I `getActors`

   II `processActors`

   III `getMoveLocations`

   (A) I only
   (B) II only
   (C) III only
   (D) I and III only
   (E) I, II, and III

15. Suppose the `Actor` class is modified to add a `Color` parameter to its constructor. If the `Critter` class is not changed, what will happen when the modified constructor is called to create a `Critter` in a client class?
   (A) A compile-time error will occur.
   (B) An exception will be thrown as soon as a color is selected.
   (C) A blue `Critter` will be created.
   (D) A `Critter` will be created with the same color as the `Actor`.
   (E) A dialog box will appear, allowing a `Critter` of any color to be created.

Refer to the grid shown for Questions 16 and 17.

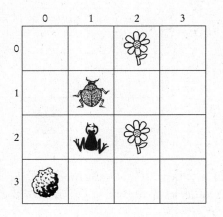

16. Suppose it is the turn of the `Critter` in location (2, 1) to act. What will be the value of `getActors().size()` for this `Critter`?
    (A) 1
    (B) 2
    (C) 3
    (D) 4
    (E) 5

17. Again, suppose it is the turn of the `Critter` in location (2, 1) to act. What will be the value of `getMoveLocations().size()` when `getMoveLocations` is called by this `Critter`'s act method?
    (A) 2
    (B) 3
    (C) 5
    (D) 7
    (E) 8

18. Consider the bounded grid shown.

The Flower in (0, 0) is yellow. The ChameleonCritter in (1, 1) is blue. The Bug in (2, 2) is purple. A valid setup after a call to act for the ChameleonCritter only is

(A)

ChameleonCritter is purple

(B)

ChameleonCritter is yellow

(C)

ChameleonCritter is yellow

(D)

ChameleonCritter is purple

(E)

ChameleonCritter is yellow

Refer to the grid shown for Questions 19 and 20.

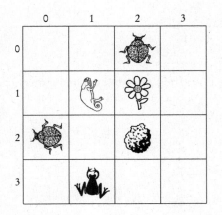

Location (0, 2) contains a green `Bug`.
Location (2, 0) contains a blue `Bug`.
Location (1, 1) contains a yellow `ChameleonCritter`.
Location (1, 2) contains a pink `Flower`.
Location (2, 2) contains a black `Rock`.
Location (3, 1) contains a red `Critter`.
The `ChameleonCritter` is about to act.

19. After the `ChameleonCritter` has acted, its color could *not* be
    (A) blue.
    (B) green.
    (C) pink.
    (D) black.
    (E) red.

20. After the `ChameleonCritter` has acted, its direction could *not* be
    (A) south.
    (B) southeast.
    (C) north.
    (D) northwest.
    (E) west.

For Questions 21 and 22, refer to the modified act method of the Critter class. The method has been changed by interchanging the lines

```
processActors(actors);
```

and

```
ArrayList<Location> moveLocs = getMoveLocations();
```

Here is the modified method:

```
public void act()
{
    if (getGrid() == null)
        return;
    ArrayList<Actor> actors = getActors();
    ArrayList<Location> moveLocs = getMoveLocations();
    processActors(actors);
    Location loc = selectMoveLocation(moveLocs);
    makeMove(loc);
}
```

21. Suppose that a Critter has at least one adjacent Bug. Which of the following *must* be true as a result of the modified act method for that Critter?
    (A) The Critter would eat a different group of actors.
    (B) The Critter would eat fewer actors.
    (C) There would be fewer locations available for the move.
    (D) The Critter would eat but not move.
    (E) There would be no change.

22. Suppose version 1 is the original version of act, and version 2 is the modified version of act. Let list1 represent the ArrayList<Location> as a result of calling getMoveLocations() in version 1, and let list2 represent the ArrayList<Location> returned by getMoveLocations() in version 2. Which of the following *could* be true, given that nothing is known about the surrounding actors for this Critter?

    I list1.size() == list2.size()

    II list1.size() > list2.size()

    III list1.size() < list2.size()

    (A) I only
    (B) II only
    (C) III only
    (D) I and II only
    (E) I and III only

23. For the 3 × 3 `BoundedGrid`, grid, shown, refer to the following code segment.

    ```
    Location loc = new Location(1, 2);
    ArrayList<Location> list = grid.getValidAdjacentLocations(loc);
    System.out.println(list);
    ```

    What will be output as a result of executing this code segment?
    (A) [(0, 2), (2, 2), (2, 1), (1, 1), (0, 1)]
    (B) [(2, 2), (2, 1), (1, 1), (0, 1), (0, 2)]
    (C) [(1, 1), (0, 1), (0, 2), (2, 2), (2, 1)]
    (D) [(0, 2), (0, 1), (1, 1), (2, 1), (2, 2)]
    (E) [(2, 2), (0, 2), (0, 1), (1, 1), (2, 1)]

24. A method is *deterministic* if, given the inputs to it, you can tell exactly what its result will be. A method is *probabilistic* if, given the inputs, there are various probabilities of different results. Which of the following is *false*?
    (A) Setting the original color of any `Actor` is deterministic.
    (B) The `getMoveLocations` method in the `Critter` class is probabilistic.
    (C) The `processActors` method in the `ChameleonCritter` class is probabilistic.
    (D) The `getActors` method in the `Critter` class is deterministic.
    (E) The process whereby a `BoxBug` receives its `sideLength` is deterministic.

25. Refer to the following statements concerning a 10 × 10 bounded grid.

    ```
    Location loc1 = new Location(1, 2);
    Location loc2 = loc1.getAdjacentLocation(110);
    ```

    What will `loc2` contain after executing these statements?
    (A) `Location.EAST`
    (B) `Location.SOUTHEAST`
    (C) (1, 3)
    (D) (2, 3)
    (E) (2, 2)

26. Consider the bounded grid shown.

Assume that the `act` method for each actor is invoked with the configuration as shown. Which of the following statements is *false*?

(A) The chameleon critters in locations (1, 2) and (2, 2) will change color but not location.

(B) The bugs in locations (0, 1) and (2, 0) will change direction but not location.

(C) The critter in location (1, 1) will change location.

(D) The flowers in locations (0, 0) and (2, 1) will change color.

(E) The rocks in locations (1, 0) and (0, 2) will change neither color nor location.

Refer to the `BoundedGrid` shown for Questions 27 and 28.

27. The `ChameleonCritter` in location (0, 1) is facing south. After it acts, its direction could *not* be
    (A) `Location.SOUTH`
    (B) `Location.WEST`
    (C) `Location.EAST`
    (D) `Location.SOUTHEAST`
    (E) `Location.SOUTHWEST`

28. Suppose that in the diagram the `ChameleonCritter` is blue, the `Flower` is red, and the `Rock` is black. What is *true* about the color of the `ChameleonCritter` after it acts?
    (A) It is a random color.
    (B) It is red or black, each of which is equally likely.
    (C) It must be red.
    (D) It must be blue.
    (E) It must be black.

29. Suppose a `Critter` has just one empty adjacent location just before its turn to act. What must be *true* after this `Critter` acts?

    I The `Critter` will be in that empty location.

    II The `Critter` will face the same direction that it faced before it acted.

    III After it moves, the only possible adjacent neighbors will be rocks and other critters.

    (A) I only
    (B) II only
    (C) III only
    (D) II and III only
    (E) I, II, and III

30. Which is a *false* statement about the grid classes?
    (A) In the `get` method of `BoundedGrid`, the object returned must be cast to `E` because `occupantArray` contains elements of type `Object`.
    (B) In the `UnboundedGrid` class, `getNumRows` and `getNumCols` must be implemented even though they are meaningless in this implementation.
    (C) The element returned by the `get` method of `UnboundedGrid` is not cast to `E` because values in the `Map` are declared to be of type `E`.
    (D) The `AbstractGrid` class must be abstract because it doesn't define all of the methods specified in the `Grid` interface.
    (E) The `occupantArray` of the `BoundedGrid` class contains references of type `Object` rather than type `E` to allow more flexibility in the types of elements that can be inserted into the grid.

31. Which is *true* about the `BoundedGrid` class?

    I It is a two-dimensional grid with a finite number of rows and columns.

    II An occupant of the grid can be an object of any type.

    III Empty locations in the grid have a value of `null`.

    (A) I only
    (B) II only
    (C) III only
    (D) I and III only
    (E) I, II, and III

32. In the `BoundedGrid` class, what would it mean if the following test were *true*?

    ```
    occupantArray[loc.getRow()][loc.getCol()] == null
    ```

    (A) The `occupantArray` has been constructed, but there is no actor in `occupantArray[loc.getRow()][loc.getCol()]`.
    (B) `loc` is an invalid location.
    (C) `loc` has not yet been constructed using `new`.
    (D) `occupantArray` has not yet been constructed using `new`.
    (E) An error has been made and an exception will be thrown.

33. The `isValid(loc)` method of `BoundedGrid` returns false if

    I `loc` is null.

    II `loc` is out of range.

    III The grid has not been constructed.

    (A) I only
    (B) II only
    (C) III only
    (D) I and II only
    (E) I, II, and III

(continued)

34. The current implementation of the grid classes allows for a given location to have eight adjacent neighbors: those on all four sides, and the four diagonally adjacent neighbors. Suppose the program will be changed so that any given location will have just four adjacent neighbors, those that are north, south, east, and west of the given location. Which of the following methods must be changed in order to achieve the modification described?

    I The constructors of the `BoundedGrid` and `UnboundedGrid` classes.

    II The `isValid` methods of the `BoundedGrid` and `UnboundedGrid` classes.

    III The `getValidAdjacentLocations` method of the `AbstractGrid` class.

(A) I only
(B) II only
(C) III only
(D) I and II only
(E) I, II, and III

ANSWER KEY

1. **B**	13. **C**	25. **C**
2. **E**	14. **D**	26. **B**
3. **A**	15. **A**	27. **D**
4. **E**	16. **C**	28. **C**
5. **A**	17. **D**	29. **B**
6. **A**	18. **E**	30. **E**
7. **A**	19. **E**	31. **D**
8. **E**	20. **B**	32. **A**
9. **C**	21. **C**	33. **B**
10. **E**	22. **D**	34. **C**
11. **B**	23. **A**	
12. **D**	24. **B**	

ANSWERS EXPLAINED

1. **(B)** When a flower acts, its color darkens.

2. **(E)** When a bug turns, its resulting direction is its current direction + 45°. In this case:

$$\text{final direction} = \texttt{getDirection()} + \texttt{Location.HALF\_RIGHT}$$
$$= 180 + 45$$
$$= 225$$
$$= \texttt{Location.SOUTHWEST}$$

3. **(A)** When `act()` is called for this `BoxBug`, the test

```
if (steps < sideLength && canMove())
```

will be false, since `canMove()` is false. Thus, the bug will execute two 45° turns, resulting in choice A. Choice B is wrong because it only makes *one* 45° turn. Choice C is the result when `act` is called *twice*. Choices D and E are wrong because a bug cannot move onto a rock.

4. **(E)** The error message will be

```
The constructor BoxBug() is undefined.
```

This is because the `BoxBug` constructor takes an `int` parameter representing the `sideLength` for the `BoxBug`. Here are the rules for subclasses and constructors.

- Constructors are not inherited.
- If no constructor is provided in a subclass, the default constructor in the superclass is invoked. If there is no default constructor in the superclass, there will be a compile-time error.

- If a constructor with parameters *is* provided in the subclass, but there is no default constructor, as is the case in the BoxBug class, you must use that constructor with parameters; otherwise you will get a compile-time error.

5. **(A)** The constants allow you to visualize directions at a glance. For example, setDirection(Location.WEST) is much clearer than setDirection(270). Reason II is bogus: A Degree type is unnecessary. (There's nothing wrong with representing a direction with an int—it's just more readable to use a constant.) Reason III is also spurious: A location is always easy to recognize because it has both a row and column component. This is easy to distinguish from an int that represents a direction.

6. **(A)** This bug will not change location because it is blocked by a rock. Its canMove method will return false, and the bug will turn instead of moving.

7. **(A)** Segment I is correct: A new rock places itself in the bug's old location and updates its location and direction. Segment II appears to work correctly. However, if the grid adds the rock, the rock does not know that its location and direction have been changed. In general, when adding or removing actors, do not use get and put from the Grid interface, since these methods don't update the location and direction values of the actor. Segment III is egregiously wrong: The variable gr is not a two-dimensional array, it is a Grid object.

8. **(E)** In diagram I the bug can't move because it is at the edge of the grid. In diagram II the bug moves onto the flower. In diagram III the location in front of the bug is empty, and the bug will move there.

9. **(C)** The act method of Actor does not change the location of the actor. A SubActor would inherit this method and exhibit the same behavior. Choice II is wrong because an Actor changes direction when it acts. Choices I and II both fail because an Actor has mutator methods setColor and setDirection, which would be inherited by SubActor.

10. **(E)** The situation before the bug acts is shown. Since the location in front of the bug is not valid, the canMove method for this bug will return false, and the bug will remain in its current location, but turn to face southeast (a half-turn to the right).

11. **(B)** Notice that to do its thing, the PoisonousCritter must get the adjacent actors, process them, get a list of possible move locations, randomly select one of these, and then move to it. This is what a regular Critter does, so act and getActors need not be changed. Both of the methods in group II must be changed: processActors turns the actors green, whereas the original method removes them. The getMoveLocations method must get a list of *occupied* locations, whereas the original method gets empty locations. Group III methods don't change at all: When a PoisonousCritter has a list of possible locations, it

randomly selects one and moves there. This is what a regular `Critter` does.

12. **(D)** Instead of turning right through 90°, the `BoxBug` now turns right through 45°. This produces the octagon in choice D. Choice A is wrong because the turn is through 90°. Choice B has a 135° turn then a 225° turn. In choice C, the `BoxBug` turns 45° left and then 45° right, while in choice E it turns 45° right and then 45° left. In the code, however, `turn` is a right turn.

13. **(C)** The method `getMoveLocations` returns an `ArrayList` of `Location` objects; so eliminate choices A and D, which return lists of `Actor` objects. Choice B is wrong because it will return empty as well as occupied locations, which was not required. Choice E is egregiously wrong: There is no `getLocations` method in the `ArrayList` class.

14. **(D)** Method I: `getActors` must be overridden because you are no longer getting the actors in neighboring locations. Method II: `processActors` should not be overridden, since once you have the list of actors, the action taken on them is no different from the action taken by regular critters (namely, they get eaten if they are not rocks or other critters). Method III: `getMoveLocations` must be overridden since you are no longer getting adjacent locations.

15. **(A)** A subclass does not inherit constructors from the superclass. If there is no constructor provided in the subclass, the compiler will provide a default constructor that calls the superclass default constructor. If the constructor in the superclass (`Actor` in this case) is not a default constructor, a compile-time error will occur when you try to construct a subclass object. Note that if a parameter is added to the `Actor` constructor, `Actor` no longer has a default constructor.

16. **(C)** The `getActors` method returns a list of adjacent actors. For the grid shown, the list will contain the flower at (2, 2), the rock at (3, 0), and the bug at (1, 1). Therefore the size of the list is 3.

17. **(D)** When the `Critter` acts it "eats" the nonrock and noncritter actors in the `getActors` list. Then, `getMoveLocations()` gets a list of adjacent, empty, neighboring locations. In this case the list contains (1, 0), (1, 1), (1, 2), (2, 2), (3, 2), (3, 1), and (2, 0)—seven elements. Notice that locations (1, 1) and (2, 2) are empty because the previous occupants have been eaten. The rock, however, is still there.

18. **(E)** The `ChameleonCritter` randomly chooses a neighboring actor and takes its color. Thus it will end up yellow or purple. It then randomly picks an empty adjacent location, moves into it, and ends up facing the direction in which it moved. Reject choices A and C: A `ChameleonCritter` does not eliminate its neighbors. Choice B is wrong because the `ChameleonCritter` *must* move if it can. Choice D is incorrect because the direction from location (1, 1) to location (2, 0) is southwest, and the `ChameleonCritter` didn't change its direction to southwest.

19. **(E)** The actors processed by any `Critter` must be in adjacent neighboring locations. Since location (3, 1) does not satisfy this condition, the red `Critter` in (3, 1) is not included in the `ChameleonCritter`'s `getActors` list.

20. **(B)** The `getMoveLocations()` method for the `ChameleonCritter` will contain the following locations: (2, 1), which is south of (1, 1); (0, 1), which is north of (1, 1); (0, 0), which is northwest of (1, 1); and (1, 0), which is west of (1, 1). Thus, the `ChameleonCritter` will end up facing south, north, northwest, or west. It cannot end up facing southeast because it cannot move to location (2, 2), which is southeast of (1, 1).

21. **(C)** The effect of the change is to get the list of empty adjacent neighboring locations *before* the "edible" neighboring actors have been removed. There would therefore be fewer empty locations available. Notice that choice D *may* be true (if all the neighboring locations were occupied before processing), but it is not necessarily true.

22. **(D)** See the explanation for the previous question on the effect of modifying the act method. Test I would be true if there were no adjacent actors to be eaten. Test II would be true if there were at least one adjacent actor to be eaten. Test III could never be true: The original version of the method creates the biggest possible list of available empty locations, since it removes some of the adjacent actors before the list is created.

23. **(A)** The algorithm in the getValidAdjacentLocations method starts with the adjacent location north of loc (0°) and, going up in increments of 45°, gets the adjacent location in that direction. If that location is in the grid, it adds it to the list.

24. **(B)** There is nothing random about how a Critter gets its list of possible move locations. It simply gets the list of empty neighboring locations. Choices A and E are true: The color and side length values are provided in the constructors. Choice C is true: A ChameleonCritter randomly selects an Actor whose color it will assume. Choice D is true: A Critter gets the list of actors that are in adjacent neighboring locations. There is no probability involved.

25. **(C)** The specification for getAdjacentLocation is to return the adjacent location that is in the compass direction nearest to its parameter. Since it does *not* return the nearest compass direction, reject choices A and B. The nearest compass direction to 110 is 90, or east. The adjacent location east of (1, 2) is location (1, 3).

26. **(B)** The bug in (2, 0) will move onto the flower in (2, 1). (The other bug, however, is blocked by the critter in (1, 1), and will turn right.) Each of the other choices is true. Choice A: The chameleon critters have no empty adjacent locations to move to. They will, however, randomly pick one of the neighboring actors and change color. Choice C: The critter will eat the bugs in (0, 1) and (2, 0) and the flowers in (0, 0) and (2, 1), making their locations available. The critter will randomly pick one of these and move. Choice D: Flowers get darker when they act. Choice E: Rocks do nothing when they act.

27. **(D)** The ChameleonCritter ends up facing the direction in which it moved. Since it cannot move onto the flower, it cannot end up facing southeast.

28. **(C)** The only actor in the ChameleonCritter's neighborhood is the red Flower. Therefore the ChameleonCritter ends up red.

29. **(B)** A Critter does not change direction when it acts. Statement I is wrong because a Critter can end up in the location of an actor that it ate. Statement

III is wrong because after a `Critter` moves to a different location, its adjacent neighbors are different from those that it had before the move.

30. **(E)** The type of elements in the array is `Object` because Java does not allow arrays of generic types. The following is illegal and will cause a compile-time error:

```
private E[][] occupantArray = new E[rows][cols];
```

31. **(D)** Statement II is false because the grid is declared as `BoundedGrid<E>`, which means that occupants of the grid must be objects of type `E`.

32. **(A)** In the constructor, the line

```
occupantArray = new Object[rows][cols];
```

creates a rows × cols two-dimensional array of `null` objects. Each slot represents an empty location. Notice in the `remove` method, the line

```
occupantArray[loc.getRow()][loc.getCol()] = null;
```

signifies that `loc` is now empty.

33. **(B)** The precondition for the method is that `loc` is not `null`. If `loc` is `null`, an exception is thrown. If the grid has not been constructed, the method call `grid.isValid(loc)` will throw a `NullPointerException` before any value can be returned.

34. **(C)** The only method that goes into the details of getting adjacent locations is the `getValidAdjacentLocations` method of the `AbstractGrid` class. Every other method that uses some subset of these locations starts by calling the method `getValidAdjacentLocations`. Note that each of the constructors of `BoundedGrid` and `UnboundedGrid` simply creates a grid containing no occupants.

Practice
Exams

Answer Sheet: Practice Exam Two

1. Ⓐ Ⓑ Ⓒ Ⓓ Ⓔ
2. Ⓐ Ⓑ Ⓒ Ⓓ Ⓔ
3. Ⓐ Ⓑ Ⓒ Ⓓ Ⓔ
4. Ⓐ Ⓑ Ⓒ Ⓓ Ⓔ
5. Ⓐ Ⓑ Ⓒ Ⓓ Ⓔ
6. Ⓐ Ⓑ Ⓒ Ⓓ Ⓔ
7. Ⓐ Ⓑ Ⓒ Ⓓ Ⓔ
8. Ⓐ Ⓑ Ⓒ Ⓓ Ⓔ
9. Ⓐ Ⓑ Ⓒ Ⓓ Ⓔ
10. Ⓐ Ⓑ Ⓒ Ⓓ Ⓔ
11. Ⓐ Ⓑ Ⓒ Ⓓ Ⓔ
12. Ⓐ Ⓑ Ⓒ Ⓓ Ⓔ
13. Ⓐ Ⓑ Ⓒ Ⓓ Ⓔ
14. Ⓐ Ⓑ Ⓒ Ⓓ Ⓔ

15. Ⓐ Ⓑ Ⓒ Ⓓ Ⓔ
16. Ⓐ Ⓑ Ⓒ Ⓓ Ⓔ
17. Ⓐ Ⓑ Ⓒ Ⓓ Ⓔ
18. Ⓐ Ⓑ Ⓒ Ⓓ Ⓔ
19. Ⓐ Ⓑ Ⓒ Ⓓ Ⓔ
20. Ⓐ Ⓑ Ⓒ Ⓓ Ⓔ
21. Ⓐ Ⓑ Ⓒ Ⓓ Ⓔ
22. Ⓐ Ⓑ Ⓒ Ⓓ Ⓔ
23. Ⓐ Ⓑ Ⓒ Ⓓ Ⓔ
24. Ⓐ Ⓑ Ⓒ Ⓓ Ⓔ
25. Ⓐ Ⓑ Ⓒ Ⓓ Ⓔ
26. Ⓐ Ⓑ Ⓒ Ⓓ Ⓔ
27. Ⓐ Ⓑ Ⓒ Ⓓ Ⓔ
28. Ⓐ Ⓑ Ⓒ Ⓓ Ⓔ

29. Ⓐ Ⓑ Ⓒ Ⓓ Ⓔ
30. Ⓐ Ⓑ Ⓒ Ⓓ Ⓔ
31. Ⓐ Ⓑ Ⓒ Ⓓ Ⓔ
32. Ⓐ Ⓑ Ⓒ Ⓓ Ⓔ
33. Ⓐ Ⓑ Ⓒ Ⓓ Ⓔ
34. Ⓐ Ⓑ Ⓒ Ⓓ Ⓔ
35. Ⓐ Ⓑ Ⓒ Ⓓ Ⓔ
36. Ⓐ Ⓑ Ⓒ Ⓓ Ⓔ
37. Ⓐ Ⓑ Ⓒ Ⓓ Ⓔ
38. Ⓐ Ⓑ Ⓒ Ⓓ Ⓔ
39. Ⓐ Ⓑ Ⓒ Ⓓ Ⓔ
40. Ⓐ Ⓑ Ⓒ Ⓓ Ⓔ

How to Calculate Your (Approximate) AP Computer Science Score

Multiple Choice

Number correct (out of 40)   =   _____   ⟸   Multiple-Choice Score

Free Response

Question 1   _____
                   (out of 9)

Question 2   _____
                   (out of 9)

Question 3   _____
                   (out of 9)

Question 4   _____
                   (out of 9)

Total   _____   ×   1.11   =   _____   ⟸   Free-Response Score
                                                                           (Do not round.)

Final Score

_____   +   _____   =   _____
Multiple-   Free-   Final Score
Choice   Response   (Round to nearest
Score   Score   whole number.)

Chart to Convert to AP Grade
Computer Science

Final Score Range	AP Grade[a]
60–80	5
45–59	4
33–44	3
25–32	2
0–24	1

[a]The score range corresponding to each grade varies from exam to exam and is approximate.

Practice Exam Two
COMPUTER SCIENCE
SECTION I

Time—1 hour and 15 minutes
Number of questions—40
Percent of total grade—50

Directions: Determine the answer to each of the following questions or incomplete statements, using the available space for any necessary scratchwork. Then decide which is the best of the choices given and fill in the corresponding oval on the answer sheet. Do not spend too much time on any one problem.

Notes:
- Assume that the classes in the Quick Reference have been imported where needed.
- Assume that variables and methods are declared within the context of an enclosing class.
- Assume that method calls that have no object or class name prefixed, and that are not shown within a complete class definition, appear within the context of an enclosing class.
- Assume that parameters in method calls are not `null` unless otherwise stated.

---

1. A large Java program was tested extensively and no errors were found. What can be concluded?
   (A) All of the preconditions in the program are correct.
   (B) All of the postconditions in the program are correct.
   (C) The program may have bugs.
   (D) The program has no bugs.
   (E) Every method in the program may safely be used in other programs.

GO ON TO THE NEXT PAGE.

Questions 2–4 refer to the `Worker` class below:

```
public class Worker
{
    private String myName;
    private double myHourlyWage;
    private boolean isUnionMember;

    //constructors

    public Worker()
    { /* implementation not shown */ }

    public Worker(String name, double hourlyWage, boolean union)
    { /* implementation not shown */ }

    //accessors getName, getHourlyWage, getUnionStatus not shown ...

    //modifiers

    //Permanently increase hourly wage by amt.
    public void incrementWage(double amt)
    { /* implementation of  incrementWage */ }

    //Switch value of isUnionMember from true to false and vice versa.
    public void changeUnionStatus()
    { /* implementation of  changeUnionStatus */ }
}
```

2. Refer to the `incrementWage` method. Which of the following is a correct
   / implementation of* `incrementWage` */?
   (A) `return myHourlyWage + amt;`
   (B) `return getHourlyWage() + amt;`
   (C) `myHourlyWage += amt;`
   (D) `getHourlyWage() += amt;`
   (E) `myHourlyWage = amt;`

GO ON TO THE NEXT PAGE.

3. Consider the method changeUnionStatus. Which is a correct
/* *implementation of* changeUnionStatus */?

```
    I if (isUnionMember)
          isUnionMember = false;
      else
          isUnionMember = true;

   II isUnionMember = !isUnionMember;

  III if (isUnionMember)
          isUnionMember = !isUnionMember;
```

(A) I only
(B) II only
(C) III only
(D) I and II only
(E) I, II, and III

4. A client method computePay will return a worker's pay based on the number of hours worked.

```
    //Precondition:  Worker w has worked the given number of hours.
    //Postcondition: Returns amount of pay for Worker w.
    public static double computePay(Worker w, double hours)
    { /* code */ }
```

Which replacement for /* *code* */ is correct?
(A) return myHourlyWage * hours;
(B) return getHourlyWage() * hours;
(C) return w.getHourlyWage() * hours;
(D) return w.myHourlyWage * hours;
(E) return w.getHourlyWage() * w.hours;

5. Consider this program segment. You may assume that wordList has been declared as ArrayList<String>.

```
    for (String s : wordList)
        if (s.length() < 4)
            System.out.println("SHORT WORD");
```

What is the maximum number of times that SHORT WORD can be printed?
(A) 3
(B) 4
(C) wordList.size()
(D) wordList.size() - 1
(E) s.length()

GO ON TO THE NEXT PAGE.

6. Refer to the following method.

```
public static int mystery(int n)
{
    if (n == 1)
        return 3;
    else
        return 3 * mystery(n - 1);
}
```

What value does mystery(4) return?
(A) 3
(B) 9
(C) 12
(D) 27
(E) 81

7. Refer to the following declarations:

```
String[] colors = {"red", "green", "black"};
List<String> colorList = new ArrayList<String>();
```

Which of the following correctly assigns the elements of the colors array to colorList? The final ordering of colors in colorList should be the same as in the colors array.

```
 I for (String col : colors)
        colorList.add(col);
```

```
 II for (String col : colorList)
        colors.add(col);
```

```
III for (int i = colors.length - 1; i >= 0; i--)
        colorList.add(i, colors[i]);
```

(A) I only
(B) II only
(C) III only
(D) II and III only
(E) I, II, and III

GO ON TO THE NEXT PAGE.

8. Often the most efficient computer algorithms use a divide-and-conquer approach, for example, one in which a list is repeatedly split into two pieces until a desired outcome is reached. Which of the following use a divide-and-conquer approach?

   I Mergesort
   II Insertion sort
   III Binary search

  (A) I only
  (B) II only
  (C) III only
  (D) I and III only
  (E) I, II, and III

9. An `Insect` class is to be written, containing the following data fields:
`age`, which will be initialized to 0 when an `Insect` is constructed.
`nextAvailableID`, which will be initialized to 0 outside the constructor and incremented each time an `Insect` is constructed.
`idNum`, which will be initialized to the current value of `nextAvailableID` when an `Insect` is constructed.
`position`, which will be initialized to the location in a garden where the `Insect` is placed when it is constructed.
`direction`, which will be initialized to the direction the `Insect` is facing when placed in the garden.
    Which variable in the `Insect` class should be static?
  (A) `age`
  (B) `nextAvailableID`
  (C) `idNum`
  (D) `position`
  (E) `direction`

Questions 10 and 11 refer to the classes `Address` and `Customer` given below.

```
public class Address
{
    private String myStreet;
    private String myCity;
    private String myState;
    private int myZipCode;

    //constructor
    public Address(String street, String city, String state, int zipCode)
    { /* implementation not shown */ }

    //accessors

    public String getStreet()
    { /* implementation not shown */ }

    public String getCity()
    { /* implementation not shown */ }

    public String getState()
    { /* implementation not shown */ }

    public int getZipCode()
    { /* implementation not shown */ }
}

public class Customer
{
    private String myName;
    private String myPhone;
    private Address myAddress;
    private int myID;

    //constructor
    public Customer(String name, String phone, Address addr, int ID)
    { /* implementation not shown */ }

    //accessors

    //Returns address of this customer.
    public Address getAddress()
    { /* implementation not shown */ }

    public String getName()
    { /* implementation not shown */ }

    public String getPhone()
    { /* implementation not shown */ }

    public int getID()
    { /* implementation not shown */ }
}
```

GO ON TO THE NEXT PAGE.

10. Which of the following correctly creates a `Customer` object `c`?

    I   `Address a = new Address("125 Bismark St", "Pleasantville",`
         `"NY", 14850);`
     `Customer c = new Customer("Jack Spratt", "747-1674", a, 7008);`

    II `Customer c = new Customer("Jack Spratt", "747-1674",`
        `"125 Bismark St, Pleasantville, NY 14850", 7008);`

    III `Customer c = new Customer("Jack Spratt", "747-1674",`
        `new Address("125 Bismark St", "Pleasantville", "NY", 14850),`
        `7008);`

(A) I only
(B) II only
(C) III only
(D) I and II only
(E) I and III only

11. Consider an `AllCustomers` class that has private instance variable

```
private Customer[] custList;
```

Given the ID number of a particular customer, a method of the class, `locate`, must find the correct `Customer` record and return the name of that customer. Here is the method `locate`:

```
/* Precondition:  custList contains a complete list of Customer
 *                objects. idNum matches the ID number data member
 *                of one of the Customer objects.
 * Postcondition: The name of the customer whose ID number
 *                matches idNum is returned.  */
public String locate(int idNum)
{
    for (Customer c : custList)
        if (c.getID() == idNum)
            return c.getName();
    return null;      //idNum not found
}
```

A more efficient algorithm for finding the matching `Customer` object could be used if
(A) `Customer` objects were in alphabetical order by name.
(B) `Customer` objects were sorted by phone number.
(C) `Customer` objects were sorted by ID number.
(D) the `custList` array had fewer elements.
(E) the `Customer` class did not have an `Address` data member.

GO ON TO THE NEXT PAGE.

12. Refer to method `removeWord`.

```
//Precondition:  wordList is an ArrayList of String objects.
//Postcondition: All occurrences of word have been removed from
                 wordList.
public static void removeWord(ArrayList<String> wordList,
                                                String word)
{
    for (int i = 0; i < wordList.size(); i++)
        if ((wordList.get(i)).equals(word))
            wordList.remove(i);
}
```

The method does not always work as intended. Consider the method call

```
removeWord(wordList, "cat");
```

For which of the following lists will this method call fail?
(A) The cat sat on the mat
(B) The cat cat sat on the mat mat
(C) The cat sat on the cat
(D) cat
(E) The cow sat on the mat

GO ON TO THE NEXT PAGE.

13. Consider the following method that will access a square matrix mat:

```
//Precondition: mat is initialized and is a square matrix
public static void printSomething(int [][] mat)
{
    for (int r=0; r<mat.length; r++)
    {
        for (int c=0; c<=r; c++)
            System.out.print(mat[r][c] + " ");
        System.out.println();
    }
}
```

Suppose mat is originally

```
0 1 2 3
4 5 6 7
3 2 1 0
7 6 5 4
```

After the method call printSomething(mat) the output will be

(A) 0 1 2 3
     4 5 6 7
     3 2 1 0
     7 6 5 4

(B) 0
     4 5
     3 2 1
     7 6 5 4

(C) 0 1 2 3
     4 5 6
     3 2
     7

(D) 0
     4
     3
     7

(E) There will be no output. An ArrayIndexOutOfBoundsException will be thrown.

14. Consider two different ways of storing a set of nonnegative integers in which there are no duplicates.

Method One: Store the integers explicitly in an array in which the number of elements is known. For example, in this method, the set {6, 2, 1, 8, 9, 0} can be represented as follows:

0	1	2	3	4	5
6	2	1	8	9	0

6 elements

Method Two: Suppose that the range of the integers is 0 to MAX. Use a boolean array indexed from 0 to MAX. The index values represent the possible values in the set. In other words, each possible integer from 0 to MAX is represented by a different position in the array. A value of true in the array means that the corresponding integer is in the set, a value of false means that the integer is not in the set. For example, using this method for the same set above, {6, 2, 1, 8, 9, 0}, the representation would be as follows (T = true, F = false):

0	1	2	3	4	5	6	7	8	9	10	...	MAX
T	T	T	F	F	F	T	F	T	T	F	...	F

The following operations are to be performed on the set of integers:

   I Search for a target value in the set.
  II Print all the elements of the set.
 III Return the number of elements in the set.

Which statement is *true*?
(A) Operation I is more efficient if the set is stored using Method One.
(B) Operation II is more efficient if the set is stored using Method Two.
(C) Operation III is more efficient if the set is stored using Method One.
(D) Operation I is equally efficient for Methods One and Two.
(E) Operation III is equally efficient for Methods One and Two.

15. An algorithm for finding the average of N numbers is

$$\text{average} = \frac{\text{sum}}{N}$$

where N and sum are both integers. In a program using this algorithm, a programmer forgot to include a test that would check for N equal to zero. If N is zero, when will the error be detected?
(A) At compile time
(B) At edit time
(C) As soon as the value of N is entered
(D) During run time
(E) When an incorrect result is output

GO ON TO THE NEXT PAGE.

16. What is wrong with this interface?

```
public interface Bad
{
    void someMethod(String password)
    {
        System.out.println("Psst! The password is " + password);
    }
}
```

(A) A method in an interface should be declared `public`.
(B) A method in an interface should be declared `abstract`.
(C) There should not be a method implementation.
(D) There should be a class implementation provided.
(E) There should not be any method parameters.

17. Consider a program that deals with various components of different vehicles. Which of the following is a reasonable representation of the relationships among some classes that may comprise the program? Note that an open up-arrow denotes an inheritance relationship and a down-arrow denotes a composition relationship.

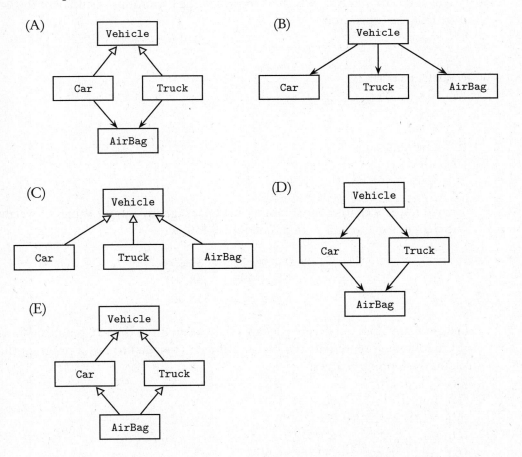

18. Consider the following program segment:

```
//Precondition: a[0]...a[n-1] is an initialized array of
//               integers, 0 < n <= a.length.
    int c = 0;
    for (int i = 0; i < n; i++)
        if (a[i] >= 0)
        {
            a[c] = a[i];
            c++;
        }
    n = c;
```

Which is the best postcondition for the segment?
(A) a[0]...a[n-1] has been stripped of all positive integers.
(B) a[0]...a[n-1] has been stripped of all negative integers.
(C) a[0]...a[n-1] has been stripped of all nonnegative integers.
(D) a[0]...a[n-1] has been stripped of all occurrences of zero.
(E) The updated value of n is less than or equal to the value of n before execution of the segment.

19. If a, b, and c are integers, which of the following conditions is sufficient to *guarantee* that the expression

```
a < c || a < b && !(a == c)
```

evaluates to true?
(A) a < c
(B) a < b
(C) a > b
(D) a == b
(E) a == c

20. Airmail Express charges for shipping small packages by integer values of weight. The charges for a weight w in pounds are as follows:

$$0 < w \leq 2 \quad \$4.00$$
$$2 < w \leq 5 \quad \$8.00$$
$$5 < w \leq 20 \quad \$15.00$$

The company does not accept packages that weigh more than 20 pounds. Which of the following represents the best set of data (weights) to test a program that calculates shipping charges?
(A) 0, 2, 5, 20
(B) 1, 4, 16
(C) −1, 1, 2, 3, 5, 16, 20
(D) −1, 0, 1, 2, 3, 5, 16, 20, 22
(E) All integers from −1 through 22

GO ON TO THE NEXT PAGE.

Questions 21–22 are based on the following class declaration:

```
public class AutoPart
{
    private String myDescription;
    private int myPartNum;
    private double myPrice;

    //constructor
    public AutoPart(String description, int partNum, double price)
    { /* implementation not shown */ }

    //accessors

    public String getDescription()
    { return myDescription; }

    public int getPartNum()
    { return myPartNum; }

    public double getPrice()
    { return myPrice; }
}
```

GO ON TO THE NEXT PAGE.

21. This question refers to the findCheapest method below, which occurs in a class that has an array of AutoPart as one of its private data fields:

```
private AutoPart[] allParts;
```

The findCheapest method examines an array of AutoPart and returns the part number of the AutoPart with the lowest price whose description matches the partDescription parameter. For example, several of the AutoPart elements may have "headlight" as their description field. Different headlights will differ in both price and part number. If the partDescription parameter is "headlight", then findCheapest will return the part number of the cheapest headlight.

```
/* Precondition:  allParts contains at least one element whose
 *                description matches partDescription.
 * Postcondition: Returns the part number of the cheapest AutoPart
 *                whose description matches partDescription.  */
public int findCheapest(String partDescription)
{
    AutoPart part = null;        //AutoPart with lowest price so far
    double min = LARGEVALUE;     //larger than any valid price
    for (AutoPart p : allParts)
    {
        /* more code */
    }
    return part.getPartNum();
}
```

Which of the following replacements for /* *more code* */ will achieve the intended postcondition of the method?

```
I if (p.getPrice() < min)
  {
      min = p.getPrice();
      part = p;
  }
```

```
II if (p.getDescription().equals(partDescription))
       if (p.getPrice() < min)
       {
           min = p.getPrice();
           part = p;
       }
```

```
III if (p.getDescription().equals(partDescription))
        if (p.getPrice() < min)
            return p.getPartNum();
```

(A) I only
(B) II only
(C) III only
(D) I and II only
(E) I and III only

22. Consider the following method:

```
//Precondition: ob1 and ob2 are distinct Comparable objects.
//Return smaller of ob1 and ob2.
public static Comparable min(Comparable ob1, Comparable ob2)
{
    if (ob1.compareTo(ob2) < 0)
        return ob1;
    else
        return ob2;
}
```

A method in the same class has these declarations:

```
AutoPart p1 = new AutoPart(<suitable values>);
AutoPart p2 = new AutoPart(<suitable values>);
```

Which of the following statements will cause an error?

```
I  System.out.println(min(p1.getDescription(),
   p2.getDescription()));
```

```
II  System.out.println(min(((String) p1).getDescription(),
      ((String) p2).getDescription()));
```

```
III  System.out.println(min(p1, p2));
```

(A) None
(B) I only
(C) II only
(D) III only
(E) II and III only

23. This question is based on the following declarations:

```
String strA = "CARROT", strB = "Carrot", strC = "car";
```

Given that all uppercase letters precede all lowercase letters when considering alphabetical order, which is true?

(A) strA.compareTo(strB) < 0 && strB.compareTo(strC) > 0
(B) strC.compareTo(strB) < 0 && strB.compareTo(strA) < 0
(C) strB.compareTo(strC) < 0 && strB.compareTo(strA) > 0
(D) !(strA.compareTo(strB) == 0) && strB.compareTo(strA) < 0
(E) !(strA.compareTo(strB) == 0) && strC.compareTo(strB) < 0

Questions 24–26 refer to the `ThreeDigitInteger` and `ThreeDigitCode` classes below.

```java
public class ThreeDigitInteger
{
    private int myHundredsDigit;
    private int myTensDigit;
    private int myOnesDigit;
    private int myValue;

    //constructor
    //value is a 3-digit int.
    public ThreeDigitInteger(int value)
    { /* implementation not shown */ }

    //Return sum of digits for this ThreeDigitInteger.
    public int digitSum()
    { /* implementation not shown */ }

    //Return sum of hundreds digit and tens digit.
    public int twoDigitSum()
    { /* implementation not shown */ }

    //other methods not shown
        ...
}

public class ThreeDigitCode extends ThreeDigitInteger
{
    private boolean myIsValid;

    //constructor
    //value is a 3-digit int.
    public ThreeDigitCode(int value)
    { /* implementation code */ }

    /* Returns true if ThreeDigitCode is valid, false otherwise.
     * ThreeDigitCode is valid if and only if the remainder when the
     * sum of the hundreds and tens digits is divided by 7 equals the
     * ones digit. Thus 362 is valid while 364 is not.  */
    public boolean isValid()
    { /* implementation not shown */ }
}
```

GO ON TO THE NEXT PAGE.

24. Which is a *true* statement about the classes shown?
    (A) The `ThreeDigitInteger` class inherits the `isValid` method from the class `ThreeDigitCode`.
    (B) The `ThreeDigitCode` class inherits all of the private instance variables and public accessor methods from the `ThreeDigitInteger` class.
    (C) The `ThreeDigitCode` class inherits the constructor from the class `ThreeDigitInteger`.
    (D) The `ThreeDigitCode` class can directly access all the private variables of the `ThreeDigitInteger` class.
    (E) The `ThreeDigitInteger` class can access the `myIsValid` instance variable of the `ThreeDigitCode` class.

25. Which is correct /* *implementation code* */ for the `ThreeDigitCode` constructor?

    I `super(value);`
       `myIsValid = isValid();`

    II `super(value, valid);`

    III `super(value);`
       `myIsValid = twoDigitSum() % 7 == myOnesDigit;`

    (A) I only
    (B) II only
    (C) III only
    (D) I and III only
    (E) I, II, and III

26. Refer to these declarations in a client program:

    ```
    ThreeDigitInteger code = new ThreeDigitCode(127);
    ThreeDigitInteger num = new ThreeDigitInteger(456);
    ```

    Which of the following subsequent tests will *not* cause an error?

    I `if (code.isValid())`
       `...`

    II `if (num.isValid())`
       `...`

    III `if (((ThreeDigitCode) code).isValid())`
       `...`

    (A) I only
    (B) II only
    (C) III only
    (D) I and II only
    (E) I and III only

GO ON TO THE NEXT PAGE.

27. Consider the following hierarchy of classes:

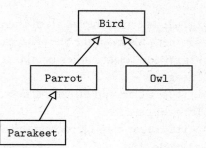

Assuming that each class has a valid default constructor, which of the following declarations in a client program are correct?

```
  I Bird b1 = new Parrot();
    Bird b2 = new Parakeet();
    Bird b3 = new Owl();

 II Parakeet p = new Parrot();
    Owl o = new Bird();

III Parakeet p = new Bird();
```

(A) I only
(B) II only
(C) III only
(D) II and III only
(E) I, II, and III

28. Consider an array `arr` and a list `list` that is an `ArrayList<String>`. Both `arr` and `list` are initialized with string values. Which of the following code segments correctly appends all the strings in `arr` to the end of `list`?

```
  I for (String s : arr)
        list.add(s);

 II for (String s : arr)
        list.add(list.size(), s);

III for (int i = 0; i < arr.length; i++)
        list.add(arr[i]);
```

(A) I only
(B) II only
(C) III only
(D) I and III only
(E) I, II, and III

GO ON TO THE NEXT PAGE.

29. Refer to the `nextIntInRange` method below:

```
/* Postcondition: Returns a random integer in the range
 *                low to high, inclusive. */
public int nextIntInRange(int low, int high)
{
    return /* expression */
}
```

Which /* *expression* */ will always return a value that satisfies the postcondition?

(A) `(int) (Math.random() * high) + low;`

(B) `(int) (Math.random() * (high - low)) + low;`

(C) `(int) (Math.random() * (high - low + 1)) + low;`

(D) `(int) (Math.random() * (high + low)) + low;`

(E) `(int) (Math.random() * (high + low - 1)) + low;`

30. Consider the following `mergeSort` method and the private instance variable `a` both in the same `Sorter` class:

```
private Comparable[] a;

/* Sorts a[first] to a[last] in increasing order using mergesort. */
public void mergeSort(int first, int last)
{
    if (first != last)
    {
        int mid = (first + last) / 2;
        mergeSort(first, mid);
        mergeSort(mid + 1, last);
        merge(first, mid, last);
    }
}
```

Method `mergeSort` calls method `merge`, which has this header:

```
/* Merge a[lb] to a[mi] and a[mi+1] to a[ub].
 * Precondition: a[lb] to a[mi] and a[mi+1] to a[ub] both
 *               sorted in increasing order.  */
private void merge(int lb, int mi, int ub)
```

If the first call to `mergeSort` is `mergeSort(0,3)`, how many *further* calls will there be to `mergeSort` before an array `b[0]...b[3]` is sorted?

(A) 2

(B) 3

(C) 4

(D) 5

(E) 6

GO ON TO THE NEXT PAGE.

31. A large hospital maintains a list of patients' records in no particular order. To find the record of a given patient, which represents the most efficient method that will work?

   (A) Do a sequential search on the name field of the records.
   (B) Do a binary search on the name field of the records.
   (C) Use insertion sort to sort the records alphabetically by name; then do a sequential search on the name field of the records.
   (D) Use mergesort to sort the records alphabetically by name; then do a sequential search on the name field of the records.
   (E) Use mergesort to sort the records alphabetically by name; then do a binary search on the name field of the records.

Use the following information for Questions 32 and 33.

Here is a diagram that shows the relationship between some of the classes that will be used in a program to draw a banner with block letters.

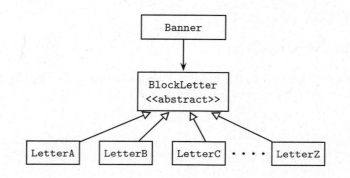

The diagram shows that the `Banner` class uses `BlockLetter` objects, and that the `BlockLetter` class has 26 subclasses, representing block letters from A to Z.

   The `BlockLetter` class has an abstract `draw` method

```
public abstract void draw();
```

Each of the subclasses shown implements the `draw` method in a unique way to draw its particular letter. The `Banner` class gets an array of `BlockLetter` and has a method to draw all the letters in this array.

   Here is a partial implementation of the `Banner` class:

```
public class Banner
{
    private BlockLetter[] letters;
    private int numLetters;

    //constructor. Gets the letters for the Banner.
    public Banner()
    {
        numLetters = <some integer read from user input>
        letters = getLetters();
    }
```

GO ON TO THE NEXT PAGE.

```
//Return an array of block letters.
public BlockLetter[] getLetters()
{
    String letter;
    letters = new BlockLetter[numLetters];
    for (int i = 0; i < numLetters; i++)
    {
        < read in capital letter >

        if (letter.equals("A"))
            letters[i] = new LetterA();
        else if (letter.equals("B"))
            letters[i] = new LetterB();
            ...                  //similar code for C through Y
        else
            letters[i] = new LetterZ();
    }
    return letters;
}

//Draw all the letters in the Banner.
public void drawLetters()
{
    for (BlockLetter letter : letters)
        letter.draw();
}

//Other methods not shown.
    ...
}
```

32. You are given the information that `BlockLetter` is an abstract class that is used in the program. Which of the following can you conclude about the class?

    I   All of its methods *must* be abstract.

    II It *must* have at least one subclass.

    III No instances of `BlockLetter` can be created.

    (A) I only
    (B) II only
    (C) III only
    (D) II and III only
    (E) I, II, and III

33. Which is a *true* statement about method `drawLetters`?
    (A) It is an overloaded method in the `Banner` class.
    (B) It is an overridden method in the `Banner` class.
    (C) It uses polymorphism to draw the correct letters.
    (D) It will cause a compile-time error because `draw` is not implemented in the `BlockLetter` class.
    (E) It will cause a run-time error because `draw` is not implemented in the `BlockLetter` class.

GO ON TO THE NEXT PAGE.

34. A programmer has a file of names. She is designing a program that sends junk mail letters to everyone on the list. To make the letters sound personal and friendly, she will extract each person's first name from the name string. She plans to create a parallel file of first names only. For example,

fullName	firstName
Ms. Anjali DeSouza	Anjali
Dr. John Roufaiel	John
Mrs. Mathilda Concia	Mathilda

Here is a method intended to extract the first name from a full name string.

```
/* Precondition:  fullName starts with a title followed by a period.
 *                A single space separates the title, first name,
 *                and last name.
 * Postcondition: Returns the first name only.  */
public static String getFirstName(String fullName)
{
    final String BLANK = " ";
    String temp, firstName;

    /* code to extract first name */

    return firstName;
}
```

Which represents correct /* *code to extract first name* */?

```
 I  int k = fullName.indexOf(BLANK);
    temp = fullName.substring(k + 1);
    k = temp.indexOf(BLANK);
    firstName = temp.substring(0, k);

 II int k = fullName.indexOf(BLANK);
    firstName = fullName.substring(k + 1);
    k = firstName.indexOf(BLANK);
    firstName = firstName.substring(0, k);

III int firstBlank = fullName.indexOf(BLANK);
    int secondBlank = fullName.indexOf(BLANK);
    firstName = fullName.substring(firstBlank + 1, secondBlank + 1);
```

(A) I only
(B) II only
(C) III only
(D) I and II only
(E) I, II, and III

Questions 35–40 involve reasoning about the code from the GridWorld Case Study. A Quick Reference to the case study is provided as part of this exam. The actors in GridWorld are represented in this book with the pictures shown below. Each actor is shown facing north. These pictures almost certainly will be different from those used on the AP exam!

35. Suppose a Bug is at the edge of a grid, facing south, as shown.

Which of the following correctly represents the state of this part of the grid after the act method has been called twice, assuming no other actors enter it?

(A)

(B)

(C)

(D)

(E)

GO ON TO THE NEXT PAGE.

36. Which of the following always makes an actor reverse direction?

    I `setDirection(180);`

    II `setDirection(getDirection() + Location.HALF_CIRCLE);`

    III `setDirection(getDirection() - 180);`

    (A) I only
    (B) II only
    (C) III only
    (D) II and III only
    (E) I, II, and III

37. Here is the implementation of the act method in the `Rock` class.

    ```
    public void act()
    { }
    ```

    What would be the effect of omitting this piece of code from the `Rock` class?

    I A `Rock` would change location at its turn to act.

    II A `Rock` would change direction at its turn to act.

    III A `Rock` would change color at its turn to act.

    (A) I only
    (B) II only
    (C) III only
    (D) I and II only
    (E) II and III only

38. Which is (are) *true* about the behavior of a `BoxBug` that moves in a grid with many obstacles?

    I It will make smaller and smaller squares.

    II It will remove itself from the grid when it can no longer move forward.

    III It will step on obstacles until it reaches its `sideLength`.

    (A) None
    (B) I only
    (C) II only
    (D) I and II only
    (E) I and III only

GO ON TO THE NEXT PAGE.

39. Consider a subclass of `Critter` called `CannibalCritter`. A `CannibalCritter` eats only flowers and other critters. Its behavior is otherwise identical to that of a `Critter`. The only method that needs to be overridden in the `CannibalCritter` class is `processActors`. Here is the method.

```
/**
 * Processes the actors.
 * Implemented to "eat" (i.e., remove) all actors that
 * are critters or flowers.
 * @param actors the actors to be processed
 */
public void processActors(ArrayList<Actor> actors)
{
    for (Actor a : actors)
    {
        if ( /* test */ )
            a.removeSelfFromGrid();
    }
}
```

Which replacement for /* *test* */ produces the desired behavior for a `CannibalCritter`?

(A) `a instanceof Critter && a instanceof Flower`

(B) `!(a instanceof Critter) && !(a instanceof Flower)`

(C) `a instanceof Critter || a instanceof Flower`

(D) `!(a instanceof Critter) || !(a instanceof Flower)`

(E) `!(a instanceof Critter || a instanceof Flower)`

40. Refer to the bounded grid shown.

Location (0, 0) contains a `ChameleonCritter` facing southwest.

Location (1, 1) contains a `Bug` facing north.

Location (2, 1) contains a `Critter` facing north.

Which is *true* about the actors in the grid?

(A) If it were the `ChameleonCritter`'s turn to act, it could end up in location (0, 1).

(B) If it were the `Rock`'s turn to act, it could end up in location (1, 1).

(C) If it were the `Bug`'s turn to act, it would end up in location (0, 1).

(D) If it were the `Critter`'s turn to act, it could end up in location (1, 2).

(E) If it were the `Flower`'s turn to act, it would end up in location (0, 2).

END OF SECTION I

COMPUTER SCIENCE
SECTION II

Time—1 hour and 45 minutes
Number of questions—4
Percent of total grade—50

Directions: SHOW ALL YOUR WORK. REMEMBER THAT
PROGRAM SEGMENTS ARE TO BE WRITTEN IN Java.

Write your answers in <u>pencil only</u> in the booklet provided.

Notes:

- Assume that the classes in the Quick Reference have been imported where needed.

- Unless otherwise stated, assume that parameters in method calls are not null and that methods are called only when their preconditions are satisfied.

- In writing solutions for each question, you may use any of the accessible methods that are listed in classes defined in that question. Writing significant amounts of code that can be replaced by a call to one of these methods may not receive full credit.

---

1. Consider a program that keeps track of transactions in a large department store. Both sales and returns are recorded. Three classes—Transaction, Sale, and Return—are used in the program, related as in the following inheritance hierarchy:

The diagram shows that both the Sale and Return classes are subclasses of the Transaction class.

The Transaction class is defined below:

```
public class Transaction
{
    private String myDescription;
    private int myNumItems;
    private double myItemCost;
    public static final double TAX_RATE = 0.07;

    //constructor
    public Transaction(String description, int numItems,
                          double itemCost)
    {
        myDescription = description;
        myNumItems = numItems;
        myItemCost = itemCost;
    }

    //accessors
    public String getDescription()
    { return myDescription; }

    public int getNumItems()
    { return myNumItems; }

    public double getItemCost()
    { return myItemCost; }

    public double getTotal()
    {
        double cost = myNumItems * myItemCost;
        double tax = cost * TAX_RATE;
        return cost + tax;
    }
}
```

(a) Write the code for the `Sale` class. Each `Sale` includes

- A description of the item being sold.
- The number of this item being sold.
- The cost of this item.
- Whether the sale is cash or credit, stored as a boolean variable.
- A 10 percent discount for cash, with 10 percent stored as a final variable.

When a new `Sale` is created, it must be assigned an item description, the number being sold, the cost of this item, and whether the sale is cash or credit. Operations on a `Sale` include the following:

- Retrieve the description of the item being sold.
- Retrieve the quantity of the item being sold.
- Retrieve the cost of the item being sold.
- Retrieve whether the sale is cash or credit.
- Calculate the total for the sale. In calculating this total, a 10 percent discount for paying cash should be applied to the cost before the tax is calculated. Hint: Discount is discount rate × cost.

Write the code for the `Sale` class below.

GO ON TO THE NEXT PAGE.

(b) A class called `DailyTransactions` has the following private instance variable:

```
/** The list of all transactions in a single day, including
 *   sales and returns */
private Transaction[] allTransactions;
```

Write `findTransactionAverage`, a method for the `DailyTransactions` class, which computes the average of all transactions in a given day. The transactions are contained in the array `allTransactions`, where each object is a `Sale` or `Return`. The method `findTransactionAverage` should

- Compute the total for all transactions.
- Divide by the number of transactions. (You may assume that there's at least one transaction.)
- Return the average.

Note that when an item is returned to the store, the amount paid is returned to the customer. For this reason, the `getTotal` method in the `Return` class returns a *negative* quantity.

Complete `findTransactionAverage` below:

```
/** @return the transaction average for one day
 *   Precondition:  allTransactions contains the day's transactions,
 *                  each of which may be a Sale or a Return.
 */
public double findTransactionAverage()
```

2. Consider a system for processing names and addresses from a mailing list. A `Recipients` class will be used as part of this system. The lines in the mailing list are stored in an `ArrayList<String>`, a private instance variable in the `Recipients` class. The blank line that separates recipients in the mailing list is stored as the empty string in this list, and the final element in the list is an empty string.
A portion of the mailing list is shown below, with the corresponding part of the `ArrayList`.

```
Mr. J. Adams
6 Rose St.
Ithaca, NY 14850

Jack S. Smith
12 Posy Way
Suite 201
Glendale, CA 91203

Ms. M.K. Delgado
2 River Dr.
New York, NY 10013

        ...
```

0	1	2	3	4
"Mr. J. Adams"	"6 Rose St."	"Ithaca, NY 14850"	""	"Jack S. Smith"

5	6	7	8	9
"12 Posy Way"	"Suite #201"	"Glendale, CA 91023"	""	"Ms. M.K. Delgado"

10	11	12
"2 River Dr."	"New York, NY 10013"	""

...

The Recipients class that processes this data is shown below.

```
public class Recipients
{
    /** The list of lines in the mailing list */
    private List<String> lines;

    /**
     * Constructor. Fill lines with mailing list data.
     * Postcondition: Each element in lines is one line of the mailing list.
     *                Lines appear in the list in the same order
     *                that they appear in the mailing list.
     *                Blank line separators in the mailing list are stored
     *                as empty strings.
     */
    public Recipients()
    { /* implementation not shown */ }

    /**
     * Postcondition: Returns the city contained in the cityZip string
     *                of an address.
     * @param  cityZip contains the city, state, and
     *         zipcode line of an address
     * @return the city substring contained in cityZip
     */
    public String extractCity(String cityZip)
    { /* to be implemented in part (a) */ }

    /**
     * Precondition:  The recipient name is the first line of each
     *                label on the mailing list.
     * Postcondition: Prints a list of recipient names to console,
     *                one per line.
     */
    public void printNames()
    { /* to be implemented in part (b) */ }
```

GO ON TO THE NEXT PAGE.

```
        /**
         * Postcondition: Returns the address of the recipient with
         *                the specified name.
         * @param name a name in the lines ArrayList
         * @return the address of the recipient with the given name
         */
        public String getAddress(String name)
        {/* to be implemented in part (c) */}

        // other methods not shown
    }
```

(a) Write the `extractCity` method of the `Recipients` class. In the `cityZip` parameter the city is followed by a comma, then one blank space, then two capital letters for a state abbreviation, then a space and 5-digit zip code. For example, if `cityZip` is "Ithaca, NY 14850", the method call `extractCity(cityZip)` should return "Ithaca".

> Information repeated from the beginning of the question
>
> `public class Recipients`
>
> `private List<String> lines`
> `public Recipients()`
> `public String extractCity(String cityZip)`
> `public void printNames()`
> `public String getAddress(String name)`

Complete method `extractCity` below.

```
/**
 * Postcondition: Returns the city contained in the cityZip string
 *                of an address.
 * @param  cityZip contains the city, state, and
 *         zipcode line of an address
 * @return the city substring contained in cityZip
 */
public String extractCity(String cityZip)
```

(b) Write the `printNames` method of the `Recipients` class. Method `printNames` prints the names of all recipients to the console, one per line. For the sample part of the mailing list shown at the beginning of the question, the output for `printNames` would be:

```
Mr. J. Adams
Jack S. Smith
Ms. M.K. Delgado
```

GO ON TO THE NEXT PAGE.

Complete method `printNames` below.

```
/**
 * Precondition:   The recipient name is the first line of each
 *                 label on the mailing list.
 * Postcondition: Prints a list of recipient names to console,
 *                 one per line.
 */
public void printNames()
```

(c) Write the `getAddress` method of the `Recipients` class. This method should return a string that contains only the address of the corresponding name parameter. For example, if name is `"Jack S. Smith"`, a string containing the three subsequent lines of his address should be returned. This string should contain line breaks in appropriate places, including after the last line of the address. This ensures that the address will have the proper address format when printed by a client class.

Complete method `getAddress` below.

```
/**
 * Postcondition: Returns the address of the recipient with
 *                 the specified name.
 * @param name a name in the lines ArrayList
 * @return the address of the recipient with the given name
 */
public String getAddress(String name)
```

3. In this question you will write the code for three methods in a `MagicSquare` class.

An $n \times n$ *magic square* is a square array of n^2 distinct integers arranged such that the n numbers along any row, column, major diagonal, or minor diagonal have the same sum. Shown below are two magic squares.

8	1	6
3	5	7
4	9	2

16	2	3	13
5	11	10	8
9	7	6	12
4	14	15	1

The `MagicSquare` class has two private instance variables, a two-dimensional array `myMat`, and a final variable `SIZE`. In the matrices shown above, the one on the left has `SIZE` 3, while the one on the right has `SIZE` 4.

The `MagicSquare` class is given below.

```
public class MagicSquare
{
    private int[][] myMat;
    private final int SIZE;

    /**
     * Creates a SIZE × SIZE matrix of integers by setting
     * it equal to the specified matrix.
     * @param matrix a SIZE × SIZE matrix of integers
     * Postcondition: myMat may or may not be a magic square.
     */
    public MagicSquare(int[][] matrix)
    {
        myMat = matrix;
        if (myMat == null)
            SIZE=0;
        else
            SIZE = myMat.length;
    }

    /**
     * Displays matrix on screen.
     */
    public void writeMatrix()
    { /* implementation not shown */ }

    /**
     * Precondition: 0 <= row < SIZE.
     * @param row a row in the matrix
     * @return the sum of elements in row
     */
    public int sumRow(int row)
    { /* to be implemented in part (a) */ }

    /**
     * Precondition: 0 <= col < SIZE.
     * @param col a column in the matrix
     * @return the sum of elements in col
     */
    public int sumCol(int col)
    { /* implementation not shown */ }

    /**
     * @return the sum of elements in the major diagonal
     */
    public int sumMajorDiag()
    { /* implementation not shown */ }

    /**
     * @return the sum of elements in the minor diagonal
     */
    public int sumMinorDiag()
    { /* to be implemented in part (b) */ }
```

GO ON TO THE NEXT PAGE.

```
    /**
     * Precondition: myMat is a square matrix of integers,
     *               which may or may not be a magic square.
     * @return true if myMat is a magic square, false otherwise
     */
    public boolean isMagic()
    { /* to be implemented in part (c) */ }
}
```

(a) Write the `MagicSquare` method `sumRow`. This method should return the sum of the elements in `row`, its parameter. Your code should work for any square matrix, irrespective of whether it's a magic square or not.

Complete method `sumRow` started below.

```
    /**
     * Precondition: 0 <= row < SIZE.
     * @param row a row in the matrix
     * @return the sum of elements in row
     */
    public int sumRow(int row)
```

(b) Write the `MagicSquare` method `sumMinorDiag`. This method should return the sum of the elements in the minor diagonal. The minor diagonal extends from the top right corner of the matrix to the lower left corner, as shown in the two matrices below.

8	1	6
3	5	7
4	9	2

16	2	3	13
5	11	10	8
9	7	6	12
4	14	15	1

Your code should work for any square matrix, irrespective of whether it's a magic square or not.

Complete method `sumMinorDiag` started below.

```
    /**
     * @return the sum of elements in the minor diagonal
     */
    public int sumMinorDiag()
```

GO ON TO THE NEXT PAGE.

(c) Write the MagicSquare method isMagic. This method should return true if myMat is a magic square, false otherwise. In writing isMagic you may use any methods in the MagicSquare class, and assume they work as specified.

Information repeated from the beginning of the question

```
public class MagicSquare

private int[][] myMat
private final int SIZE
public MagicSquare(int[][] matrix)
public void writeMatrix()
public int sumRow(int row)
public int sumCol(int col)
public int sumMajorDiag()
public int sumMinorDiag()
public boolean isMagic()
```

Complete method isMagic started below.

```
/**
 * Precondition: myMat is a square matrix of integers,
 *               which may or may not be a magic square.
 * @return true if myMat is a magic square, false otherwise
 */
public boolean isMagic()
```

4. This question involves reasoning about the code from the GridWorld Case Study. A Quick Reference to the case study is provided as part of this exam.

Consider a new type of Bug, a JiveBug that dances when it acts. First, it turns. Then, it either stays where it is, or moves forward if it can. Each of these actions is equally likely. Some of the times that it moves forward, it tosses a flower in front of it to the right, according to a specified probability and if the "toss" location is valid.

A partial definition of JiveBug is shown below. Notice that the move method of Bug is overridden: Even though a JiveBug moves like a regular Bug, it no longer drops a flower in its path. Instead, it sometimes tosses a flower. The act and turn methods are also overridden.

```
public class JiveBug extends Bug
{
    private double probOfFlowerToss;
    private int[] myTurns = { /* selection of turns from Location.LEFT,
        Location.RIGHT, Location.HALF_LEFT,
        Location.HALF_RIGHT, Location.FULL_CIRCLE,
        Location.HALF_CIRCLE */ }
```

```
/**
 * Constructs a JiveBug that dances when it acts,
 * and sometimes throws a flower according to the specified
 * probability.
 * @param probToss the probability of tossing a flower
 */
public JiveBug(double probToss)
{
    probOfFlowerToss = probToss;
}
/**
 * Gets a randomly selected turn from myTurns.
 * @return a randomly selected turn constant
 */
public int getDanceTurn()
{ /* to be implemented in part (a) */ }
/**
 * Gets a dance turn, and then turns.
 */
public void turn()
{ /* to be implemented in part (b) */ }

/**
 * Moves forward, like a Bug.
 * Attempts to toss a flower that is the same color as itself.
 */
public void move()
{
    Grid<Actor> gr = getGrid();
    if (gr == null)
        return;
    Location loc = getLocation();
    Location next = loc.getAdjacentLocation(getDirection());
    if (gr.isValid(next))
        moveTo(next);
    else
        removeSelfFromGrid();
    tossFlower();
}
/**
 * Tosses a flower some fraction of the time, given by
 * probOfFlowerToss. A JiveBug tosses a flower in front
 * of itself to the right, if that location is valid.
 * The flower is the same color as the JiveBug.
 */
public void tossFlower()
{ /* to be implemented in part (c) */ }
/**
 * A JiveBug starts by turning when it acts.
 * Then, it is equally likely that it will stay where it is
 * or attempt to move.
 */
public void act()
{ /* to be implemented in part (d) */ }
}
```

GO ON TO THE NEXT PAGE.

(a) Write the `getDanceTurn` method of `JiveBug`. This method randomly returns a turn from the `myTurns` array.
Complete method `getDanceTurn` below.

```
/**
 * Gets a randomly selected turn from myTurns.
 * @return a randomly selected turn constant
 */
public int getDanceTurn()
```

(b) Override the `turn` method from the `Bug` class. The overridden method should get a turn value from its `myTurns` array, and make that turn.
Complete the `turn` method below.

```
/**
 * Gets a dance turn, and then turns.
 */
public void turn()
```

(c) Write the `tossFlower` method for `JiveBug`. Method `tossFlower` causes a flower that is the same color as the `JiveBug` to be tossed some fraction of the time, given by `probOfFlowerToss`, if the toss location is valid. When it tosses a flower, a `JiveBug` tosses it into the location that is in front of it and to its right.
Here are some toss locations for a `JiveBug` that has just moved:

Complete method `tossFlower` below.

```
/**
 * Tosses a flower some fraction of the time, given by
 * probOfFlowerToss. A JiveBug tosses a flower in front
 * of itself to the right, if that location is valid.
 * The flower is the same color as the JiveBug.
 */
public void tossFlower()
```

(d) Override the `act` method of the `Bug` class. A `JiveBug` acts by turning. Then it either stays where it is, or, with equal probability, moves forward if it can.
Complete the `act` method below.

```
/**
 * A JiveBug starts by turning when it acts.
 * Then, it is equally likely that it will stay where it is
 * or attempt to move.
 */
public void act()
```

END OF EXAMINATION

ANSWER KEY (Section I)

1. C	15. D	29. C
2. C	16. C	30. E
3. D	17. A	31. A
4. C	18. B	32. D
5. C	19. A	33. C
6. E	20. D	34. D
7. A	21. B	35. C
8. D	22. E	36. D
9. B	23. C	37. B
10. E	24. B	38. A
11. C	25. A	39. C
12. B	26. C	40. C
13. B	27. A	
14. C	28. E	

ANSWERS EXPLAINED

Section I

1. **(C)** Testing a program thoroughly does not prove that a program is correct. For a large program, it is generally impossible to test every possible set of input data.

2. **(C)** The private instance variable myHourlyWage must be incremented by amt. Eliminate choice E, which doesn't *increment* myHourlyWage; it simply *replaces* it by amt. Choice D is wrong because you can't use a method call as the left-hand side of an assignment. Choices A and B are wrong because the incrementWage method is void and should not return a value.

3. **(D)** The value of the boolean instance variable isUnionMember must be changed to the opposite of what it currently is. Segments I and II both achieve this. Note that !true has a value of false and !false a value of true. Segment III fails to do what's required if the current value of isUnionMember is false.

4. **(C)** computePay is a client method and, therefore, cannot access the private variables of the class. This eliminates choices A and D. The method getHourlyWage() must be accessed with the dot member construct; thus, choice B is wrong, and choice C is correct. Choice E is way off base—hours is not part of the Worker class, so w.hours is meaningless.

5. **(C)** If s.length() < 4 for all strings in wordList, then SHORT WORD will be printed on each pass through the for loop. Since there are wordList.size() passes through the loop, the maximum number of times that SHORT WORD can be printed is wordList.size().

6. **(E)**

$$\begin{aligned} \text{mystery}(4) &= 3 * \text{mystery}(3) \\ &= 3 * 3 * \text{mystery}(2) \\ &= 3 * 3 * 3 * \text{mystery}(1) \\ &= 3 * 3 * 3 * 3 \\ &= 81 \end{aligned}$$

7. **(A)** The declaration of the `colors` array makes the following assignments: `colors[0] = "red"`, `colors[1] = "green"`, and `colors[2] = "black"`. The loop in segment I adds these values to `colorList` in the correct order. Segment II fails because `colors` is an array and therefore can't use the `get` method. The code also confuses the lists. Segment III, in its first pass through the loop, attempts to add `colors[2]` to index position 2 of `colorList`. This will cause an `IndexOutOfBoundsException` to be thrown, since index positions 0 and 1 do not yet exist!

8. **(D)** Mergesort repeatedly splits an array of n elements in half until there are n arrays containing one element each. Now adjacent arrays are successively merged until there is a single merged, sorted array. A binary search repeatedly splits an array into two, narrowing the region that may contain the key. Insertion sort, however, does no array splitting. It takes elements one at a time and finds their insertion point in the sorted piece of the array. Elements are shifted to allow correct insertion of each element. Even though this algorithm maintains the array in two parts—a sorted part and yet-to-be-sorted part—this is not a divide-and-conquer approach.

9. **(B)** A static variable is shared by all instances of the class. "Static" means that there will be just one memory slot allocated, no matter how many `Insects` are constructed. All instances of `Insect` access the same information stored in that slot. When an `Insect` is created, it will get tagged with the current value of `nextAvailableID` for that memory slot, which will then be incremented for the next `Insect` created. All of the other variables—`age`, `idNum`, `position`, `direction`—are specific to one instance of `Insect` and should therefore be private instance variables in the class.

10. **(E)** A new `Address` object must be created, to be used as the `Address` parameter in the `Customer` constructor. To do this correctly requires the keyword `new` preceding the `Address` constructor. Segment II omits `new` and does not use the `Address` constructor correctly. (In fact, it inserts a new `String` object in the `Address` slot of the `Customer` constructor.)

11. **(C)** The algorithm used in method `locate` is a sequential search, which may have to examine all the objects to find the matching one. A binary search, which repeatedly discards a chunk of the array that does not contain the key, is more efficient. However, it can only be used if the values being examined—in this case customer ID numbers—are sorted. Note that it doesn't help to have the array sorted by name or phone number since the algorithm doesn't look at these values.

12. **(B)** The `remove` method of `ArrayList` removes the indicated element, shifts the remaining elements down one slot (i.e., it does not leave gaps in the list), and adjusts the size of the list. Consider the list in choice B. The index values are shown:

```
The cat cat sat on the mat mat
 0   1   2   3   4   5   6   7
```

After the first occurrence of cat has been removed:

```
The cat sat on the mat mat
 0   1   2   3   4   5   6
```

The value of i, which was 1 when cat was removed, has now been incremented to 2 in the for loop. This means that the word to be considered next is sat. The second occurrence of cat has been missed. Thus, the given code will fail whenever occurrences of the word to be removed are consecutive. You fix it by not allowing the index to increment when a removal occurs:

```
int i = 0;
while (i < wordList.size())
{
    if ((wordList.get(i)).equals(word))
        wordList.remove(i);
    else
        i++;
}
```

13. **(B)** When r is 0, c goes from 0 to 0, and just one element, mat[0][0], will be printed. When r is 1, c goes from 0 to 1, and two elements, mat[1][0] and mat[1][1], will be printed, and so on. When r is 3, all four elements of row 3 will be printed.

14. **(C)** To return the number of elements in the set for Method One requires no more than returning the number of elements in the array. For Method Two, however, the number of cells that contain true must be counted, which requires a test for each of the MAX values. Note that searching for a target value in the set is more efficient for Method Two. For example, to test whether 2 is in the set, simply check if a[2] == true. In Method One, a sequential search must be done, which is less efficient. To print all the elements in Method One, simply loop over the known number of elements and print. Method Two is less efficient because the whole array must be examined: Each cell must be tested for true before printing.

15. **(D)** An ArithmeticException will be thrown at run time. Note that if N were of type double, no exception would be thrown. The variable sum would be assigned the value Infinity, and the error would only be detected in the output.

16. **(C)** An interface should provide method declarations only. No code! Note that the methods are automatically public and abstract, so there is no need to specify this explicitly.

17. **(A)** The correct diagram uses two up arrows to show that a Car *is-a* Vehicle and a Truck *is-a* Vehicle (inheritance relationship). The two down arrows indicate that a Car *has-a* AirBag and a Truck *has-a* AirBag (composition relationship). In each of the incorrect choices, at least one of the relationships does not make sense. For example, in choice B a Vehicle *has-a* Truck, and in choice E an AirBag *is-a* Car.

18. **(B)** The postcondition should be a true assertion about the major action of the segment. The segment overwrites the elements of array a with the nonnegative elements of a. Then n is adjusted so that now the array a[0]...a[n-1] contains

just nonnegative integers. Note that even though choice E is a correct assertion about the program segment, it is not a good postcondition because it doesn't describe the main modification to array a (namely all negative integers have been removed).

19. **(A)** Note the order of precedence for the expressions involved: (1) parentheses, (2) !, (3) <, (4) ==, (5) &&, (6) ||. This means that a < c, a < b, and !(a == b) will all be evaluated before || and && are considered. The given expression then boils down to value1 || (value2 && value3), since && has higher precedence than ||. Notice that if value1 is true, the whole expression is true since (true || any) evaluates to true. Thus, a < c will guarantee that the expression evaluates to true. None of the other conditions will guarantee an outcome of true. For example, suppose a < b (choice B). If a == c, then the whole expression will be false because you get F || F.

20. **(D)** Test data should always include a value from each range in addition to all boundary values. The given program should also handle the cases in which weights over 20 pounds or any negative weights are entered. Note that choice E contains redundant data. There is no new information to be gained in testing two weights from the same range—both 3 and 4 pounds, for example.

21. **(B)** Segment II correctly checks that the part descriptions match and keeps track of the current part with minimum price. If this is not done, the part whose number must be returned will be lost. Segment I is incorrect because it doesn't check that partDescription matches the description of the current part being examined in the array. Thus, it simply finds the AutoPart with the lowest price, which is not what was required. Segment III incorrectly returns the part number of the first part it finds with a matching description.

22. **(E)** Statement I is fine: The parameters are String objects. Statement II will throw a ClassCastException because an AutoPart cannot be cast to a String. Statement III will fail because p1 and p2 are not Comparable objects.

23. **(C)** Ordering of strings involves a character-by-character comparison starting with the leftmost character of each string. Thus, strA precedes strB (since "A" precedes "a") or strA.compareTo(strB) < 0. This eliminates choices B and D. Eliminate choices A and E since strB precedes strC (because "C" precedes "c") and therefore strB.compareTo(strC) < 0. Note that string1.compareTo(string2) == 0 if and only if string1 and string2 are equal strings.

24. **(B)** ThreeDigitCode is a subclass of ThreeDigitInteger and therefore inherits all the instance variables and methods of ThreeDigitInteger except constructors. All of the statements other than B are false. For choice A, ThreeDigitInteger is the superclass and therefore cannot inherit from its subclass. For choice C, constructors are never inherited (see p. 132). For choice D, a subclass can access private variables of the superclass through accessor methods only (see p. 132). For choice E, a superclass cannot access any additional instance variables of its subclass.

25. **(A)** Implementation II is wrong because the constructor has no boolean validity parameter. Implementation III is wrong because a subclass cannot access a private instance variable of its superclass.

26. **(C)** A compile-time error will occur for both tests I and II because at com-

pile time the types of code and num are both ThreeDigitInteger, and the class ThreeDigitInteger does not have an isValid method. To avoid this error, the code object must be cast to ThreeDigitCode, its actual type. Note that if you try to cast num to ThreeDigitCode, you'll get a run-time error (ClassCastException) because num is not an instance of ThreeDigitCode.

27. **(A)** The *is-a* relationship must work from right-to-left: a Parrot *is-a* Bird, a Parakeet *is-a* Bird, and an Owl *is-a* Bird. All are correct. This relationship fails in declarations II and III: a Parrot is not necessarily a Parakeet, a Bird is not necessarily an Owl, and a Bird is not necessarily a Parakeet.

28. **(E)** All three segments traverse the array, accessing one element at a time, and appending it to the end of the ArrayList. In segment II, the first parameter of the add method is the position in list where the next string s will be added. Since list.size() increases by one after each insertion, this index is correctly updated in each pass through the for-each loop.

29. **(C)** Suppose you want random integers from 2 to 8, that is, low = 2 and high = 8. This is 7 possible integers, so you need

        (int) (Math.random() * 7)

    which produces 0, 1, 2, ..., or 6. Therefore the quantity

        (int) (Math.random() * 7) + 2

    produces 2, 3, 4, ..., or 8. The only expression that yields the right answer with these values is

        (int) (Math.random() * (high - low + 1)) + low;

30. **(E)** Here is a "box diagram" for mergeSort(0,3). The boldface numbers 1–6 show the order in which the mergeSort calls are made.

The mergeSort calls in which first == last are base case calls, which means that there will be no further method calls.

31. **(A)** Since the records are not sorted, the quickest way to find a given name is to start at the beginning of the list and sequentially search for that name. Choices C, D, and E will all work, but it's inefficient to sort and then search because all sorting algorithms take longer than simply inspecting each element. Choice B won't work: A binary search can only be used for a sorted list.

32. **(D)** Statement I is false: An abstract class may have *no* abstract methods. The point about an abstract class is that it represents an abstract concept, and no instance of it will ever be created. The only instances that will be created are instances of its subclasses. Statement II *must* be true, since you are told the abstract class is actually used in the program. Statement III is true because an abstract class cannot be instantiated.

33. **(C)** The draw method is polymorphic, which means that it is a superclass method that is overridden in at least one of its subclasses. During run time, there is dynamic binding between the calling object and the method, that is, the actual instance is bound to its particular overridden method. In the drawLetters method, the correct version of draw is called during each iteration of the for loop, and a banner with the appropriate letters is drawn.

34. **(D)** Suppose fullName is Dr. John Roufaiel. In segment I the expression fullName.indexOf(BLANK) returns 3. Then temp gets assigned the value of fullName.substring(4), which is John Roufaiel. Next k gets assigned the value temp.indexOf(BLANK), namely 4, and firstName gets assigned temp.substring(0, 4), which is all the characters from 0 to 3 inclusive, namely John. Note that segment II works the same way, except firstName gets assigned John Roufaiel and then reassigned John. This is not good style, since a variable name should document its contents as precisely as possible. Still, the code works. Segment III fails because indexOf returns the *first* occurrence of its String parameter. Thus, firstBlank and secondBlank will both contain the same value, 3.

35. **(C)** The first time it acts, the bug can't move forward, so it turns 45° right. (Choice B is the situation after it acts once.) The second call to act has the bug move forward, leaving a flower in its original location (choice C, the correct answer). Choice A is wrong because if the bug doesn't move, it turns. Choice D fails because a bug cannot move onto a rock. Choice E is wrong because it doesn't reflect the fact that the bug turned to face southwest when it couldn't move the first time. After its second turn it would still be facing southwest.

36. **(D)** Adding 180 to or subtracting 180 from the actor's current direction will reverse that actor's direction. Note that Location.HALF_CIRCLE has a value of 180. Statement I is wrong because the method call setDirection(180) causes the actor to face south, which does not necessarily reverse its direction.

37. **(B)** With no override of act, a Rock will do what an Actor does, namely change direction.

38. **(A)** Statement I is wrong because the sideLength does not get changed when obstacles are encountered. The BoxBug tends to make rectangles, rather than squares, since it turns when it cannot move forward. Statement II is false: When a Bug cannot move forward, it turns. Statement III is false: A Bug steps on flowers, but not on other actors. Its behavior is to turn when it encounters obstacles, not to step on them.

39. **(C)** Here is the logic of choice C: If a is a Critter or a Flower, remove it. This is

what was required. Choice A says: If a is both a `Critter` *and* a `Flower` ... —not possible! Choice B: If a is neither a `Critter` nor a `Flower`, remove it. Wrong action! Choice E is equivalent to choice B. Choice D: If a is not a `Critter` or a is not a `Flower`, remove it. This test will evaluate to `true` no matter what a is!

40. **(C)** The `Bug` would move onto the `Flower`. Every other choice is false: Choice A: `ChameleonCritters` do not displace other actors. Choice B: `Rocks` do not move. Choice D: `Critters` do not eat rocks. Choice E: `Flowers` do not move.

Section II

1. (a)
```
public class Sale extends Transaction
{
    private boolean myIsCash;
    private final double CASH_DISCOUNT = 0.1;

    //constructor
    public Sale(String description, int numItems,
        double itemCost, boolean isCash)
    {
        super(description, numItems, itemCost);
        myIsCash = isCash;
    }

    //Return true if Sale is cash, false otherwise.
    public boolean getIsCash()
    { return myIsCash; }

    public double getTotal()
    {
        double cost = getNumItems() * getItemCost();
        if (myIsCash)
        {
            double discount = cost * CASH_DISCOUNT;
            cost = cost - discount;
        }
        double tax = cost * TAX_RATE;
        return cost + tax;
    }
}
```

(b)
```
public double findTransactionAverage()
{
    double sum = 0;
    for (Transaction t : allTransactions)
        sum += t.getTotal();
    return sum / allTransactions.length;
}
```

NOTE

- In part (a), the solution shows some comments. In general, you don't need to provide comments for your code on the exam. However, short comments to clarify what you're doing are fine.
- The Sale class inherits all of the accessors from the Transaction superclass. The getDescription, getNumItems, and getItemCost methods should not be redefined. Their implementation doesn't change. The getTotal method, however, is different in the Sale class and therefore must be overridden.
- In part (b), the fact that getTotal is negative for a Return object means that the correct amount will automatically be added to the sum if the Transaction is a Return. The method is polymorphic and will call the appropriate getTotal method, depending on whether the Transaction t is a Sale or a Return.

2. (a)
```
public String extractCity(String cityZip)
{
    int commaPos = cityZip.indexOf(",");
    return cityZip.substring(0, commaPos);
}
```

(b)
```
public void printNames()
{
    System.out.println(lines.get(0));
    int index = 1;
    while(index < lines.size() - 1)
    {
        if (lines.get(index).equals(""))
            System.out.println(lines.get(index + 1));
        index++;
    }
}
```

(c)
```
public String getAddress(String name)
{
    int index = 0;
    while(index < lines.size() && !name.equals(lines.get(index)))
        index++;
    index++;
    String s = "";
    while (!(lines.get(index).equals("")))
    {
        s += lines.get(index) + "\n";
        index++;
    }
    return s;
}
```

NOTE

- In part (b), the empty string signals that the next element in the list will be a name. This is why you should be careful that you don't miss the first name in the list, which is at index 0. Notice, too, that you can avoid the empty string at the end of the list by having

  ```
  index < lines.size() - 1
  ```

  as the test in the `while` loop. If you don't do this, the final

  ```
  lines.get(index + 1)
  ```

  will cause an `IndexOutOfBoundsException`.
- Part (c) first finds the name that matches the parameter, and then builds a string out of the next two or three lines that comprise the address. Again, the empty string signals that the end of the address has been reached.
- The escape character string, `"\n"`, inserts a line break into the string.

3. (a)
```
public int sumRow(int row)
{
    int sum = 0;
    for (int col = 0; col < SIZE; col++)
        sum += myMat[row][col];
    return sum;
}
```

(b)
```
public int sumMinorDiag()
{
    int sum = 0;
    for (int i = 0; i < SIZE; i++)
        sum += myMat[i][SIZE-i-1];
    return sum;
}
```

(c)
```
public boolean isMagic()
{
    int sum = sumRow(0);
    for (int i = 0; i < SIZE; i++)
    {
        if (sumRow(i) != sum || sumCol(i)!= sum)
        {
            return false;
        }
    }
    return sumMajorDiag() == sum && sumMinorDiag() == sum;
}
```

NOTE

- In part (a), notice that instead of the test `col < SIZE`, you could use `col < myMat[row].length`, where `myMat[row].length` is the length of row.
- In part (c), the line

  ```
  int sum = sumRow(0);
  ```

  could just as easily be

  ```
  int sum = sumCol(0);
  ```

  You need to store one of the sums so that you can compare it to the other row and column sums.
- In part (c), if you are still in the method after exiting the `for` loop, it means that the sum of every row equals the sum of every column. All that still needs to be checked is whether the sums of the diagonals equal that same sum.
- In part (c), the last line of code is equivalent to

  ```
  if(sumMajorDiag() == sum && sumMinorDiag() == sum)
      return true;
  else
      return false;
  ```

4. (a)
```
public int getDanceTurn()
{
    int n = myTurns.length;
    int r = (int) (Math.random() * n);
    return myTurns[r];
}
```

(b)
```
public void turn()
{ setDirection(getDirection() + getDanceTurn()); }
```

(c)
```
public void tossFlower()
{
    if (Math.random() < probOfFlowerToss)
    {
        Grid<Actor> gr = getGrid();
        int tossDirection = getDirection() + Location.HALF_RIGHT;
        Location currentLoc = getLocation();
        Location tossLoc =
                currentLoc.getAdjacentLocation(tossDirection);
        if (gr.isValid(tossLoc))
        {
            Flower flower = new Flower(getColor());
            flower.putSelfInGrid(gr, tossLoc);
        }
    }
}
```

(d)
```
public void act()
{
    turn();
    if (Math.random() < 0.5)
        if (canMove())
            move();
}
```

NOTE

- In part (a), you cannot make assumptions about the number of turns in the myTurns array. You must therefore use myTurns.length.
- In part (b), you must use the method getDanceTurn defined in part (a). You will not get full credit if you reimplement code.

Answer Sheet: Practice Exam Three

1. Ⓐ Ⓑ Ⓒ Ⓓ Ⓔ

2. Ⓐ Ⓑ Ⓒ Ⓓ Ⓔ

3. Ⓐ Ⓑ Ⓒ Ⓓ Ⓔ

4. Ⓐ Ⓑ Ⓒ Ⓓ Ⓔ

5. Ⓐ Ⓑ Ⓒ Ⓓ Ⓔ

6. Ⓐ Ⓑ Ⓒ Ⓓ Ⓔ

7. Ⓐ Ⓑ Ⓒ Ⓓ Ⓔ

8. Ⓐ Ⓑ Ⓒ Ⓓ Ⓔ

9. Ⓐ Ⓑ Ⓒ Ⓓ Ⓔ

10. Ⓐ Ⓑ Ⓒ Ⓓ Ⓔ

11. Ⓐ Ⓑ Ⓒ Ⓓ Ⓔ

12. Ⓐ Ⓑ Ⓒ Ⓓ Ⓔ

13. Ⓐ Ⓑ Ⓒ Ⓓ Ⓔ

14. Ⓐ Ⓑ Ⓒ Ⓓ Ⓔ

15. Ⓐ Ⓑ Ⓒ Ⓓ Ⓔ

16. Ⓐ Ⓑ Ⓒ Ⓓ Ⓔ

17. Ⓐ Ⓑ Ⓒ Ⓓ Ⓔ

18. Ⓐ Ⓑ Ⓒ Ⓓ Ⓔ

19. Ⓐ Ⓑ Ⓒ Ⓓ Ⓔ

20. Ⓐ Ⓑ Ⓒ Ⓓ Ⓔ

21. Ⓐ Ⓑ Ⓒ Ⓓ Ⓔ

22. Ⓐ Ⓑ Ⓒ Ⓓ Ⓔ

23. Ⓐ Ⓑ Ⓒ Ⓓ Ⓔ

24. Ⓐ Ⓑ Ⓒ Ⓓ Ⓔ

25. Ⓐ Ⓑ Ⓒ Ⓓ Ⓔ

26. Ⓐ Ⓑ Ⓒ Ⓓ Ⓔ

27. Ⓐ Ⓑ Ⓒ Ⓓ Ⓔ

28. Ⓐ Ⓑ Ⓒ Ⓓ Ⓔ

29. Ⓐ Ⓑ Ⓒ Ⓓ Ⓔ

30. Ⓐ Ⓑ Ⓒ Ⓓ Ⓔ

31. Ⓐ Ⓑ Ⓒ Ⓓ Ⓔ

32. Ⓐ Ⓑ Ⓒ Ⓓ Ⓔ

33. Ⓐ Ⓑ Ⓒ Ⓓ Ⓔ

34. Ⓐ Ⓑ Ⓒ Ⓓ Ⓔ

35. Ⓐ Ⓑ Ⓒ Ⓓ Ⓔ

36. Ⓐ Ⓑ Ⓒ Ⓓ Ⓔ

37. Ⓐ Ⓑ Ⓒ Ⓓ Ⓔ

38. Ⓐ Ⓑ Ⓒ Ⓓ Ⓔ

39. Ⓐ Ⓑ Ⓒ Ⓓ Ⓔ

40. Ⓐ Ⓑ Ⓒ Ⓓ Ⓔ

How to Calculate Your (Approximate) AP Computer Science Score

Multiple Choice

Number correct (out of 40)   =   _____   ⟸ Multiple-Choice Score

Free Response

Question 1   _____
              (out of 9)

Question 2   _____
              (out of 9)

Question 3   _____
              (out of 9)

Question 4   _____
              (out of 9)

Total   _____   ×   1.11   =   _____   ⟸ Free-Response Score
                                                    (Do not round.)

Final Score

_____   +   _____   =   _____
Multiple-   Free-   Final Score
Choice   Response   (Round to nearest
Score   Score   whole number.)

Chart to Convert to AP Grade
Computer Science

Final Score Range	AP Grade[a]
60–80	5
45–59	4
33–44	3
25–32	2
0–24	1

[a]The score range corresponding to each grade varies from exam to exam and is approximate.

Practice Exam Three
COMPUTER SCIENCE
SECTION I

Time—1 hour and 15 minutes
Number of questions—40
Percent of total grade—50

Directions: Determine the answer to each of the following questions or incomplete statements, using the available space for any necessary scratchwork. Then decide which is the best of the choices given and fill in the corresponding oval on the answer sheet. Do not spend too much time on any one problem.

Notes:
- Assume that the classes in the Quick Reference have been imported where needed.
- Assume that variables and methods are declared within the context of an enclosing class.
- Assume that method calls that have no object or class name prefixed, and that are not shown within a complete class definition, appear within the context of an enclosing class.
- Assume that parameters in method calls are not `null` unless otherwise stated.

---

1. What output is produced by the following line of code?

   ```
   System.out.println("\"This is\n very strange\"");
   ```

   (A) \This is\n very strange\

   (B) "This is very strange"

   (C) This is
       very strange

   (D) \"This is
       very strange\"

   (E) "This is
       very strange"

2. A certain class, `SomeClass`, contains a method with the following header:

   ```
   public int getValue(int n)
   ```

   Suppose that methods with the following headers are now added to `SomeClass`:

   I `public int getValue()`

   II `public double getValue(int n)`

   III `public int getValue(double n)`

   Which of the above headers will cause an error?
   (A) None
   (B) I only
   (C) II only
   (D) III only
   (E) I and III only

3. Consider the following statement:

   ```
   int num = /* expression */;
   ```

   Which of the following replacements for `/* expression */` creates in `num` a random integer from 2 to 50, including 2 and 50?
   (A) `(int)(Math.random() * 50) - 2`
   (B) `(int)(Math.random() * 49) - 2`
   (C) `(int)(Math.random() * 49) + 2`
   (D) `(int)(Math.random() * 50) + 2`
   (E) `(int)(Math.random() * 48) + 2`

4. Consider the following code segment.

   ```
   int num = 0, score = 10;
   if (num != 0 && score / num > SOME_CONSTANT)
       statement1;
   else
       statement2;
   ```

   What is the result of executing this statement?
   (A) An `ArithmeticException` will be thrown.
   (B) A syntax error will occur.
   (C) *statement1*, but not *statement2*, will be executed.
   (D) *statement2*, but not *statement1*, will be executed.
   (E) Neither *statement1* nor *statement2* will be executed; control will pass to the first statement following the `if` statement.

5. Refer to the following class header.

   ```
   public class SomeClass implements Comparable
   {   ...
   ```

   Of the following, which is the best specification for writing the `compareTo` method in this class?
   (A) `public int compareTo(Object obj)`
   (B) `public void compareTo(Object obj)`
   (C) `public int compareTo(Object obj1, Object obj2)`
   (D) `public void compareTo(Object obj1, Object obj2)`
   (E) `public boolean compareTo(Object obj)`

6. Consider the following inheritance hierarchy.

   Which of the following declarations will *not* cause an error? You may assume that each of the classes above has a default constructor.

   I `WheatCereal w = new Cereal();`

   II `Cereal c1 = new Cereal();`

   III `Cereal c2 = new RiceCereal();`

   (A) I only
   (B) II only
   (C) III only
   (D) I and III only
   (E) I, II, and III

Questions 7 and 8 refer to the following class definitions.

```
public interface Class1
{ void method1(); }

public class Class2 implements Class1
{
    public void method1()
    { /* implementation not shown */ }

    //private instance variables and other methods not shown
    ...
}

public class Class3 extends Class2
{
    public void method2(Class3 other)
    { /* implementation not shown */ }

    //private instance variables and other methods not shown
    ...
}
```

7. Assuming that both Class2 and Class3 have default constructors, which is (are) valid in a client class?

   I   `Class1 c1 = new Class2();`

   II `Class2 c2 = new Class3();`

   III `Class1 c3 = new Class3();`

   (A) I only
   (B) II only
   (C) III only
   (D) I and II only
   (E) I, II, and III

8. Consider the following declarations in a client class.

   ```
   Class3 ob3 = new Class3();
   Class2 ob2 = new Class2();
   ```

   Which method calls would be legal?

   I   `ob3.method1();`

   II `ob2.method2(ob3);`

   III `ob3.method2(ob2);`

   (A) I only
   (B) II only
   (C) III only
   (D) II and III only
   (E) I, II, and III

GO ON TO THE NEXT PAGE.

9. Refer to the following program segment.

```
for (int n = 50; n > 0; n = n / 2)
    System.out.println(n);
```

How many lines of output will this segment produce?
(A) 50
(B) 49
(C) 7
(D) 6
(E) 5

10. Let `list` be an `ArrayList<String>` containing only these elements:

```
"John", "Mary", "Harry", "Luis"
```

Which of the following statements will cause an error to occur?

 I `list.set(2, "6");`

 II `list.add(4, "Pat");`

III `String s = list.get(4);`

(A) I only
(B) II only
(C) III only
(D) II and III only
(E) I, II, and III

11. Consider the following static method.

```
public static int compute(int n)
{
    for (int i = 1; i < 4; i++)
        n *= n;
    return n;
}
```

Which of the following could replace the body of `compute`, so that the new version returns the identical result as the original for all n?
(A) `return 4 * n;`
(B) `return 8 * n;`
(C) `return 64 * n;`
(D) `return (int) Math.pow(n, 4);`
(E) `return (int) Math.pow(n, 8);`

GO ON TO THE NEXT PAGE.

12. Consider the following method.

```
public int mystery (int n)
{
    if (n == 0)
        return 0;
    else if (n % 2 == 1)
        return n;
    else
        return n + mystery(n - 1);
}
```

What will be returned by a call to mystery(6)?
(A) 6
(B) 11
(C) 12
(D) 27
(E) 30

13. Consider the following code segment.

```
int num1 = value1, num2 = value2, num3 = value3;
while (num1 > num2 || num1 > num3)
{
    /* body of loop */
}
```

You may assume that value1, value2, and value3 are int values. Which of the following is sufficient to guarantee that /* *body of loop* */ will never be executed?
(A) There is no statement in /* *body of loop* */ that leads to termination
(B) num1 < num2
(C) num1 < num3
(D) num1 > num2 && num1 > num3
(E) num1 < num2 && num1 < num3

14. Which is true of the following boolean expression, given that x is a variable of type double?

```
3.0 == x * (3.0 / x)
```

(A) It will always evaluate to false.
(B) It may evaluate to false for some values of x.
(C) It will evaluate to false only when x is zero.
(D) It will evaluate to false only when x is very large or very close to zero.
(E) It will always evaluate to true.

GO ON TO THE NEXT PAGE.

Use the program description below for Questions 15–17.

A car dealer needs a program that will maintain an inventory of cars on his lot. There are three types of cars: sedans, station wagons, and SUVs. The model, year, color, and price need to be recorded for each car, plus any additional features for the different types of cars. The program must allow the dealer to

- Add a new car to the lot.
- Remove a car from the lot.
- Correct any data that's been entered.
- Display information for any car.

15. The programmer decides to have these classes: `Car`, `Inventory`, `Sedan`, `SUV`, and `StationWagon`. Which statement is *true* about the relationships between these classes and their attributes?

    I There are no inheritance relationships between these classes.
    II The `Inventory` class *has-a* list of `Car` objects.
    III The `Sedan`, `StationWagon`, and `SUV` classes are independent of each other.

(A) I only
(B) II only
(C) III only
(D) I and II only
(E) II and III only

16. Suppose that the programmer decides to have a `Car` class and an `Inventory` class. The `Inventory` class will maintain a list of all the cars on the lot. Here are some of the methods in the program:

```
addCar          //adds a car to the lot
removeCar       //removes a car from the lot
displayCar      //displays all the features of a given car
setColor        //sets the color of a car to a given color
                //May be used to correct data
getPrice        //returns the price of a car
displayAllCars  //displays features for every car on the lot
```

In each of the following, a class and a method are given. Which is the *least* suitable choice of class to be responsible for the given method?
(A) Car, setColor
(B) Car, removeCar
(C) Car, getPrice
(D) Car, displayCar
(E) Inventory, displayAllCars

17. Suppose `Car` is a superclass and `Sedan`, `StationWagon`, and `SUV` are subclasses of `Car`. Which of the following is the most likely method of the `Car` class to be overridden by at least one of the subclasses (`Sedan`, `StationWagon`, or `SUV`)?

    (A) `setColor(newColor)`   //sets color of Car to newColor
    (B) `getModel()`   //returns model of Car
    (C) `displayCar()`   //displays all features of Car
    (D) `setPrice(newPrice)`   //sets price of Car to newPrice
    (E) `getYear()`   //returns year of Car

18. Consider the following segment of code.

    ```
    String word = "conflagration";
    int x = word.indexOf("flag");
    String s = word.substring(0, x);
    ```

    What will be the result of executing the above segment?
    (A) A syntax error will occur.
    (B) String s will be the empty string.
    (C) String s will contain "flag".
    (D) String s will contain "conf".
    (E) String s will contain "con".

19. Consider the following class declaration:

    ```
    public abstract class AClass
    {
        private int v1;
        private double v2;

        //methods of the class
            ...
    }
    ```

    Which is *true* about `AClass`?
    (A) Any program using this class will have an error: An abstract class cannot contain private instance variables.
    (B) `AClass` *must* have a constructor with two parameters in order to initialize v1 and v2.
    (C) At least one method of `AClass` must be abstract.
    (D) A client program that uses `AClass` must have another class that is a subclass of `AClass`.
    (E) In a client program, more than one instance of `AClass` can be created.

GO ON TO THE NEXT PAGE.

20. A class of 30 students rated their computer science teacher on a scale of 1 to 10 (1 means awful and 10 means outstanding). The `responses` array is a 30-element integer array of the student responses. An 11-element array `freq` will count the number of occurrences of each response. For example, `freq[6]` will count the number of students who responded 6. The quantity `freq[0]` will not be used.

Here is a program that counts the students' responses and outputs the results.

```
public class StudentEvaluations
{
    public static void main(String args[])
    {
        int[] responses = {6,6,7,8,10,1,5,4,6,7,
                           5,4,3,4,4,9,8,6,7,10,
                           6,7,8,8,9,6,7,8,9,2};
        int[] freq = new int[11];
        for (int i = 0; i < responses.length; i++)
            freq[responses[i]]++;
        //output results
        System.out.print("rating" + "   " + "frequency\n");
        for (int rating = 1; rating < freq.length; rating++)
            System.out.print(rating + "   " +
                freq[rating] + "\n");
    }
}
```

Suppose the last entry in the initializer list for the `responses` array was incorrectly typed as 12 instead of 2. What would be the result of running the program?
(A) A rating of 12 would be listed with a frequency of 1 in the output table.
(B) A rating of 1 would be listed with a frequency of 12 in the output table.
(C) An `ArrayIndexOutOfBoundsException` would be thrown.
(D) A `StringIndexOutOfBoundsException` would be thrown.
(E) A `NullPointerException` would be thrown.

GO ON TO THE NEXT PAGE.

Questions 21–23 are based on the three classes below:

```java
public class Employee
{
    private String myName;
    private int myEmployeeNum;
    private double mySalary, myTaxWithheld;

    public Employee(String name, int empNum, double salary,
        double taxWithheld)
    { /* implementation not shown */ }

    //Returns pre-tax salary
    public double getSalary()
    { return mySalary; }

    public String getName()
    { return myName; }

    public int getEmployeeNum()
    { return myEmployeeNum; }

    public double getTax()
    { return myTaxWithheld; }

    public double computePay()
    { return mySalary - myTaxWithheld; }
}

public class PartTimeEmployee extends Employee
{
    private double myPayFraction;

    public PartTimeEmployee(String name, int empNum, double salary,
        double taxWithheld, double payFraction)
    { /* implementation not shown */ }

    public double getPayFraction()
    { return myPayFraction; }

    public double computePay()
    { return getSalary() * myPayFraction - getTax();}
}

public class Consultant extends Employee
{
    private static final double BONUS = 5000;

    public Consultant(String name, int empNum, double salary,
        double taxWithheld)
    { /* implementation not shown */ }

    public double computePay()
    { /* implementation code */ }
}
```

GO ON TO THE NEXT PAGE.

21. The `computePay` method in the `Consultant` class redefines the `computePay` method of the `Employee` class to add a bonus to the salary after subtracting the tax withheld. Which represents correct /* *implementation code* */ of `computePay` for `Consultant`?

    I `return super.computePay() + BONUS;`

    II `super.computePay();`
       `return getSalary() + BONUS;`

    III `return getSalary() - getTax() + BONUS;`

    (A) I only
    (B) II only
    (C) III only
    (D) I and III only
    (E) I and II only

22. Consider these valid declarations in a client program:

    ```
    Employee e = new Employee("Noreen Rizvi", 304, 65000, 10000);
    Employee p = new PartTimeEmployee("Rafael Frongillo", 287, 40000,
        7000, 0.8);
    Employee c = new Consultant("Dan Lepage", 694, 55000, 8500);
    ```

    Which of the following method calls will cause an error?
    (A) `double x = e.computePay();`
    (B) `double y = p.computePay();`
    (C) `String n = c.getName();`
    (D) `int num = p.getEmployeeNum();`
    (E) `double g = p.getPayFraction();`

23. Consider the `writePayInfo` method:

```
//Writes Employee name and pay on one line.
public static void writePayInfo(Employee e)
{ System.out.println(e.getName() + " " + e.computePay()); }
```

The following piece of code invokes this method:

```
Employee[] empList = new Employee[3];
empList[0] = new Employee("Lila Fontes", 1, 10000, 850);
empList[1] = new Consultant("Momo Liu", 2, 50000, 8000);
empList[2] = new PartTimeEmployee("Moses Wilks", 3, 25000, 3750,
    0.6);
for (Employee e : empList)
    writePayInfo(e);
```

What will happen when this code is executed?
(A) A list of employees' names and corresponding pay will be written to the screen.
(B) A `NullPointerException` will be thrown.
(C) A `ClassCastException` will be thrown.
(D) A compile-time error will occur, with the message that the `getName` method is not in the `Consultant` class.
(E) A compile-time error will occur, with the message that an instance of an `Employee` object cannot be created.

24. Consider an array `arr` that is initialized with `int` values. The following code fragment stores in `count` the number of positive values in `arr`.

```
int count = 0, index = 0;
while (index < arr.length)
{
    if (arr[index] > 0)
        count++;
    index++;
}
```

Which of the following code fragments is equivalent to the above segment?

```
I   int count = 0;
    for (int num : arr)
    {
        if (arr[num] > 0)
            count++;
    }
```

```
II  int count = 0;
    for (int num : arr)
    {
        if (num > 0)
            count++;
    }
```

```
III int count = 0;
    for (int i = 0; i < arr.length; i++)
    {
        if (arr[i] > 0)
            count++;
    }
```

(A) I only
(B) II only
(C) III only
(D) II and III only
(E) I and III only

GO ON TO THE NEXT PAGE.

25. A square matrix is declared as

    ```
    int[][] mat = new int[SIZE][SIZE];
    ```

    where SIZE is an appropriate integer constant. Consider the following method:

    ```
    public static void mystery(int[][] mat, int value, int top, int left,
        int bottom, int right)
    {
        for (int i = left; i <= right; i++)
        {
            mat[top][i] = value;
            mat[bottom][i] = value;
        }
        for (int i = top + 1; i <= bottom - 1; i++)
        {
            mat[i][left] = value;
            mat[i][right] = value;
        }
    }
    ```

    Assuming that there are no out-of-range errors, which best describes what method mystery does?
    (A) Places value in corners of the rectangle with corners (top, left) and (bottom, right).
    (B) Places value in the diagonals of the square with corners (top, left) and (bottom, right).
    (C) Places value in each element of the rectangle with corners (top, left) and (bottom, right).
    (D) Places value in each element of the border of the rectangle with corners (top, left) and (bottom, right).
    (E) Places value in the topmost and bottommost rows of the rectangle with corners (top, left) and (bottom, right).

26. Which of the following statements about a class SomeClass that implements an interface is (are) true?

    I It is illegal to create an instance of SomeClass.

    II Any superclass of SomeClass must also implement that interface.

    III SomeClass must implement every method of the interface.

    (A) None
    (B) I only
    (C) II only
    (D) III only
    (E) II and III only

27. Assume that a `Book` class implements `Comparable`. The following method is intended to return the index of the "smallest" book, namely the book that would appear first in a sorted list of `Book` objects.

```
//Precondition: books is initialized with Book objects.
//               books.length > 0.
public static int findMin(Book[] books)
{
    int minPos = 0;
    for (int index = 1; index < books.length; index++)
    {
        if ( /* condition */ )
        {
            minPos = index;
        }
    }
    return minPos;
}
```

Which of the following should be used to replace /* *condition* */ so that `findMin` works as intended?

(A) `books[minPos] > books[index]`

(B) `books[index] > books[minPos]`

(C) `books[index].compareTo(books[minPos]) > 0`

(D) `books[index].compareTo(books[minPos]) >= 0`

(E) `books[index].compareTo(books[minPos]) < 0`

28. Refer to the static method `removeNegs` shown below.

```
//Precondition:  list is an ArrayList<Integer>.
//Postcondition: All negative values have been removed from list.
public static void removeNegs(List<Integer> list)
{
    int index = 0;
    while (index < list.size())
    {
        if (list.get(index).intValue() < 0)
        {
            list.remove(index);
        }
        index++;
    }
}
```

For which of the following lists will the method *not* work as intended?

(A) 6 -1 -2 5

(B) -1 2 -3 4

(C) 2 4 6 8

(D) -3

(E) 1 2 3 -8

29. A sorted list of 120 integers is to be searched to determine whether the value 100 is in the list. Assuming that the most efficient searching algorithm is used, what is the maximum number of elements that must be examined?
    (A) 7
    (B) 8
    (C) 20
    (D) 100
    (E) 120

30. Consider a sorted array arr of n elements, where n is large and n is even. Under which conditions will a sequential search of arr be faster than a binary search?

    I The target is not in the list.

    II The target is in the first position of the list.

    III The target is in arr[1 + n/2].

    (A) I only
    (B) II only
    (C) III only
    (D) I and III only
    (E) II and III only

GO ON TO THE NEXT PAGE.

31. Refer to the following data field and method.

```
private int[] arr;

//Precondition: arr.length > 0, and index < arr.length.
public void remove(int index)
{
    int[] b = new int[arr.length - 1];
    int count = 0;
    for (int i = 0; i < arr.length; i++)
    {
        if (i != index)
        {
            b[count] = arr[i];
            count++;
        }
    }
    //assertion
    arr = b;
}
```

Which of the following assertions is true when the //assertion line is reached during execution of remove?
(A) b[k] == arr[k] for 0 <= k < arr.length.
(B) b[k] == arr[k + 1] for 0 <= k < arr.length.
(C) b[k] == arr[k] for 0 <= k <= index, and
    b[k] == arr[k + 1] for index < k < arr.length - 1.
(D) b[k] == arr[k] for 0 <= k < index, and
    b[k] == arr[k + 1] for index <= k < arr.length - 1.
(E) b[k] == arr[k] for 0 <= k < index, and
    b[k] == arr[k + 1] for index <= k < arr.length.

32. When an integer is represented in base 16 (hexadecimal), the digits 0, 1, 2, 3, 4, 5, 6, 7, 8, 9, A, B, C, D, E, F are used, where A–F represent the numbers 10–15. If base 16 is represented with the subscript $_{hex}$ and base 10 is represented with the subscript $_{dec}$, then the decimal number 196 could be represented in hexadecimal as shown below:

$$196_{dec} = C4_{hex}$$

Which of the following is equal to $2AF_{hex}$?
(A) 27_{dec}
(B) 300_{dec}
(C) 687_{dec}
(D) 4002_{dec}
(E) 6896_{dec}

GO ON TO THE NEXT PAGE.

Questions 33–35 refer to the `TennisPlayer`, `GoodPlayer`, and `WeakPlayer` classes below. These classes are to be used in a program to simulate a game of tennis.

```
public abstract class TennisPlayer
{
    private String myName;

    //constructor
    public TennisPlayer(String name)
    { myName = name; }

    public String getName()
    { return myName; }

    public abstract boolean serve();
    public abstract boolean serviceReturn();
}

public class GoodPlayer extends TennisPlayer
{
    //constructor
    public GoodPlayer(String name)
    { /* implementation not shown */ }

    //Postcondition: Return true if serve is in (80% probability),
    //               false if serve is out (20% probability).
    public boolean serve()
    { /* implementation not shown */ }

    //Postcondition: Return true if service return is in
    //               (70% probability), false if service return
    //               is out (30% probability).
    public boolean serviceReturn()
    { /* implementation not shown */ }
}

public class WeakPlayer extends TennisPlayer
{
    //constructor
    public WeakPlayer(String name)
    { /* implementation not shown */ }

    //Postcondition: Return true if serve is in (45% probability),
    //               false if serve is out (55% probability).
    public boolean serve()
    { /* implementation not shown */ }

    //Postcondition: Return true if service return is in
    //               (30% probability), false if service return
    //               is out (70% probability).
    public boolean serviceReturn()
    { /* implementation not shown */ }
}
```

GO ON TO THE NEXT PAGE.

33. Which of the following declarations will cause an error? You may assume all the constructors are correctly implemented.
    (A) `TennisPlayer t = new TennisPlayer("Smith");`
    (B) `TennisPlayer g = new GoodPlayer("Jones");`
    (C) `TennisPlayer w = new WeakPlayer("Henry");`
    (D) `TennisPlayer p = null;`
    (E) `WeakPlayer q = new WeakPlayer("Grady");`

34. Refer to the serve method in the `WeakPlayer` class:

    ```
    //Postcondition: Return true if serve is in (45% probability),
    //               false if serve is out (55% probability).
    public boolean serve()
    { /* implementation */ }
    ```

    Which of the following replacements for /* *implementation* */ satisfy the post-condition of the serve method?

    ```
     I double value = Math.random();
       return value >= 0 || value < 0.45;

    II double value = Math.random();
       return value < 0.45;

   III int val = (int) (Math.random() * 100);
       return val < 45;
    ```

    (A) I only
    (B) II only
    (C) III only
    (D) II and III only
    (E) I, II, and III

35. Consider the following class definition:

```
public class Beginner extends WeakPlayer
{
    private double myCostOfLessons;

    //methods of Beginner class
        ...
}
```

Refer to the following declarations and method in a client program:

```
TennisPlayer g = new GoodPlayer("Sam");
TennisPlayer w = new WeakPlayer("Harry");
TennisPlayer b = new Beginner("Dick");

public void giveEncouragement(WeakPlayer t)
{ /* implementation not shown */ }
```

Which of the following method calls will *not* cause an error?
(A) `giveEncouragement((WeakPlayer) g);`
(B) `giveEncouragement((WeakPlayer) b);`
(C) `giveEncouragement((Beginner) w);`
(D) `giveEncouragement(w);`
(E) `giveEncouragement(b);`

Questions 36–39 involve reasoning about the code from the GridWorld Case Study. A Quick Reference to the case study is provided as part of this exam.

The following images will be used to represent creatures in GridWorld (each is shown facing north):

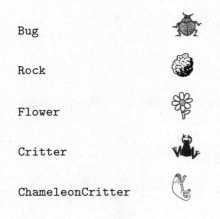

Bug

Rock

Flower

Critter

ChameleonCritter

GO ON TO THE NEXT PAGE.

36. Consider the grid shown.

The Critter in location (1, 2) is about to act. Which of the following is a possible result of executing act for this Critter?

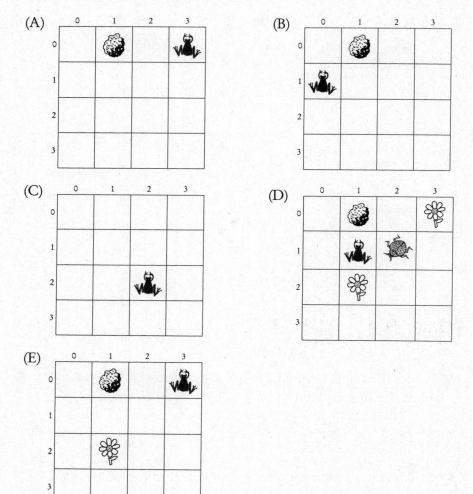

37. Refer to the following statements.

```
Location loc1 = new Location(1, 3);
Location loc2 = new Location(2, 1);
Location loc3 = new Location(3, 2);
Location loc4 = loc1.getAdjacentLocation(40);
Location loc5 = loc2.getAdjacentLocation(200);
```

Which is (are) *true*?

I `loc2.getDirectionToward(loc3)` returns 135.

II `loc1.compareTo(loc5) == 0`

III `loc4.getAdjacentLocation(230).equals(loc1)`

(A) I only
(B) II only
(C) III only
(D) I and III only
(E) I, II, and III

38. Refer to the turn method of the Bug class:

```
public void turn()
{
    setDirection(getDirection() + Location.HALF_RIGHT);
}
```

Suppose the body of the method were changed to

```
setDirection(getDirection() + Location.RIGHT);
```

Which would have to be true as a result of this change?

I A Bug would never move in a diagonal path.

II The getDirection() method for a Bug would return either north, south, east, or west, and no other values.

III Two calls to act() would cause a Bug to turn 180 degrees to the right, namely, to reverse its direction.

(A) None
(B) I only
(C) II only
(D) III only
(E) I, II, and III

GO ON TO THE NEXT PAGE.

39. Consider writing a subclass of Bug called TriangleBug. A TriangleBug moves in a right triangular pattern, as shown.

In order to create this pattern, the TriangleBug has no actors blocking its path, and always starts near the right edge of the grid, facing west. Its final location is the same as its starting location. A private instance variable, side, keeps track of which side of the triangle the bug is currently traversing (either 1, 2, or 3). When the pattern is complete, the bug stops. Here is the implementation of the TriangleBug class.

```
public class TriangleBug extends Bug
{
    private int steps;
    private int sideLength;
    private int side;

    /**
     * Constructs a triangle bug that traces a right triangle of a
     * given side length.
     * @param length the side length
     */
    public TriangleBug(int length)
    {
        steps = 0;
        sideLength = length;
        side = 1;
        setDirection(Location.WEST);
    }
```

GO ON TO THE NEXT PAGE.

```
        public void act()
        {
            if (side < 4)
            {
                if (steps < sideLength && canMove())
                {
                    move();
                    steps++;
                    if (steps == sideLength)
                        side++;
                }
                else
                {
                    steps = 0;
                /* more code */
                }
            }
        }
    }
```

Which replacement for /* *more code* */ leads to the correct triangular pattern?

(A) `turn();`
    `turn();`

(B) `turn();`
    `turn();`
    `turn();`

(C) `turn();`
    `turn();`
    `if (side == 3)`
        `turn();`

(D) `turn();`
    `if (side == 3)`
        `turn();`

(E) `turn();`
    `if (side == 3)`
    `{`
        `turn();`
        `turn();`
    `}`

40. When a client class constructs a ChameleonCritter why is it blue, facing north?
    (A) It inherits the constructor from the Critter class.
    (B) It inherits the constructor from the Actor class.
    (C) It inherits the methods getColor() and getDirection() from the Actor class.
    (D) The compiler adds the following code to the ChameleonCritter class:

    ```
    public ChameleonCritter()
    { super(); }
    ```
    which calls the default constructor from the Actor class.
    (E) The compiler adds the following code to the ChameleonCritter class:

    ```
    public ChameleonCritter()
    {
        setColor(Color.BLUE);
        setDirection(Location.NORTH);
    }
    ```

END OF SECTION I

COMPUTER SCIENCE
SECTION II

Time—1 hour and 45 minutes
Number of questions—4
Percent of total grade—50

Directions: SHOW ALL YOUR WORK. REMEMBER THAT
PROGRAM SEGMENTS ARE TO BE WRITTEN IN Java.

Write your answers in pencil only in the booklet provided.

Notes:

- Assume that the classes in the Quick Reference have been imported where needed.

- Unless otherwise stated, assume that parameters in method calls are not null and that methods are called only when their preconditions are satisfied.

- In writing solutions for each question, you may use any of the accessible methods that are listed in classes defined in that question. Writing significant amounts of code that can be replaced by a call to one of these methods may not receive full credit.

---

1. Pig Latin is a made-up language sometimes used by children. Here are the rules for converting an English word to Pig Latin. If the word begins with a consonant, move the consonant to the end of the word and add "ay" after it. If the word begins with a vowel, add "yay" to the end of the word.
Examples:

English	Pig Latin
dog	ogday
Apple	Appleyay
easy	easyyay
Cattle	attleCay

Consider the following incomplete declarations of a `PigLatinConverter` class that allows a line of text to be converted to Pig Latin. The line of text is stored internally as a `String`.

```
public class PigLatinConverter
{
    private String myLine;

    /**
     * @param ch a single-character string
     * @return true if ch is a vowel, false otherwise
     */
    private boolean isVowel(String ch)
    { /* implementation not shown */}

    /**
     * Precondition: word is not null and may begin with a
     *               vowel or consonant.
     * @param word the word to be converted to Pig Latin
     * @return the Pig Latin form of word
     */
    public String toPig(String word)
    { /* to be implemented in part (a) */}

    /**
     * Precondition:  myLine contains at least one word.
     *                Words are separated by exactly one space.
     *                There is no punctuation in myLine.
     * Postcondition: myLine is unchanged.
     * @return a list of words in myLine
     */
    private List<String> getLineWords()
    { /* to be implemented in part (b) */}

    /**
     * Precondition:  myLine contains at least one word.
     *                Words are separated by exactly one space.
     *                There is no punctuation in myLine.
     * Postcondition: myLine has been converted to Pig Latin.
     *                The Pig Latin words are separated by one
     *                space.
     */
    public void pigLatin()
    { /* to be implemented in part (c) */}

    //Constructors and other methods not shown.
}
```

(a) Write the `PigLatinConverter` method `toPig` as described earlier. For example, the method call `toPig("hello")` will return the String `"ellohay"`, and the method call `toPig("elephant")` will return the String `"elephantyay"`.

GO ON TO THE NEXT PAGE.

Complete method `toPig` below.

```
/**
 * Precondition: word is not null and may begin with a
 *               vowel or consonant.
 * @param word the word to be converted to Pig Latin
 * @return the Pig Latin form of word
 */
public String toPig(String word)
```

(b) Write the `PigLatinConverter` method `getLineWords`. The method returns an `ArrayList` of words contained in `myLine`. You may assume that `myLine` contains at least one word, that there is no punctuation, and that the words in `myLine` are separated by one space.

For example, if `myLine` is the `String`

`"What a lovely day"`

a call to `getLineWords()` will return the `ArrayList`

`["What", "a", "lovely", "day"]`

```
Information repeated from the beginning of the question

public class PigLatinConverter

private String myLine
private boolean isVowel(String ch)
public String toPig(String word)
private List<String> getLineWords()
public void pigLatin()
```

Complete method `getLineWords` below.

```
/**
 * Precondition:  myLine contains at least one word.
 *                Words are separated by exactly one space.
 *                There is no punctuation in myLine.
 * Postcondition: myLine is unchanged.
 * @return a list of words in myLine
 */
private List<String> getLineWords()
```

(c) Write the `PigLatinConverter` method `pigLatin`. This method converts all the words in `myLine` to Pig Latin.

For example, if `myLine` is the `String`

`"What a lovely day"`

a call to `pigLatin()` will change `myLine` to the `String`

`"hatWay ayay ovelylay ayday"`

In writing `pigLatin`, you may call methods `toPig` and `getLineWords` from parts (a) and (b), as well as the `isVowel` method. Assume that all these methods work as specified, regardless of what you wrote in parts (a) and (b).

> Information repeated from the beginning of the question
>
> ```
> public class PigLatinConverter
> ```
>
> ```
> private String myLine
> private boolean isVowel(String ch)
> public String toPig(String word)
> private List<String> getLineWords()
> public void pigLatin()
> ```

Complete method `pigLatin` below.

```
/**
 * Precondition:  myLine contains at least one word.
 *                Words are separated by exactly one space.
 *                There is no punctuation in myLine.
 * Postcondition: myLine has been converted to Pig Latin.
 *                The Pig Latin words are separated by one
 *                space.
 */
public void pigLatin()
```

2. The following class, `DigitalClock` is designed to display and manipulate a digital clock. The incomplete class declaration is shown below.

```
public class DigitalClock
{
    /**
     * Constructs a DigitalClock set at the specified hour and minute.
     * @param hour the specified hour
     * @param minute the specified minute
     */
    public DigitalClock(int hour, int minute)
    { /* implementation not shown */ }

    /**
     * Advances the time on the DigitalClock by one minute.
     */
    public void advanceTime()
    { /* implementation not shown */ }

    /**
     * @return true if this DigitalClock is defective, false otherwise
     */
    public boolean isDefective()
    { /* implementation not shown */ }

    //There may be instance variables, constructors, and methods that
    //are not shown.
}
```

GO ON TO THE NEXT PAGE.

Consider the following class, `AllClocks`, which stores and manipulates a list of `DigitalClock` objects.

```
public class AllClocks
{
    /** The list of digital clocks */
    private List<DigitalClock> clocks;

    /** Advance the time by one minute on all the clocks.  */
    public void advanceTimeOnAll()
    { /* to be implemented in part (a) */ }

    /** Remove all defective clocks from the list.  */
    public void removeDefective()
    { /* to be implemented in part (b) */ }

    /**
     * Replace all defective clocks with a new clock set at 12:30,
     * that is, hours 12 and minutes 30.
     */
    public void replaceDefective()
    { /* to be implemented in part (c) */ }

    //There may be constructors and methods that are not shown.
}
```

(a) Write the `AllClocks` method `advanceTimeOnAll`, which advances the time by one minute on all the clocks in the `ArrayList` clocks.

Complete method `advanceTimeOnAll` below.

```
/** Advance the time by one minute on all the clocks.  */
public void advanceTimeOnAll()
```

(b) Write the `AllClocks` method `removeDefective`, which removes all defective clocks from the `ArrayList` clocks.

Complete method `removeDefective` below.

```
/** Remove all defective clocks from the list.  */
public void removeDefective()
```

(c) Write the `AllClocks` method `replaceDefective`, which replaces each defective clock with a new clock set at 12:30.

Complete method `replaceDefective` below.

```
/**
 * Replace all defective clocks with a new clock set at 12:30,
 * that is, hours 12 and minutes 30.
 */
public void replaceDefective()
```

GO ON TO THE NEXT PAGE.

3. Consider the problem of keeping track of the available seats in a theater. Theater seats can be represented with a two-dimensional array of integers, where a value of 0 shows a seat is available, while a value of 1 indicates that the seat is occupied. For example, the array below shows the current seat availability for a show in a small theater.

	[0]	[1]	[2]	[3]	[4]	[5]
[0]	0	0	1	1	0	1
[1]	0	1	0	1	0	1
[2]	1	0	0	0	0	0

The seat at slot [1][3] is taken, but seat [0][4] is still available. A show can be represented by the Show class shown below.

```java
public class Show
{
    /** The seats for this show */
    private int[][] mySeats;

    private final int SEATS_PER_ROW = <some integer value>;
    private final int NUM_ROWS = <some integer value>;

    /** Returns true if the seat with the specified row and seat
     *  number is an aisle seat, false otherwise.
     *  @param row the row number
     *  @param seatNumber the seat number
     *  @return true if an aisle seat, false otherwise
     */
    public boolean isAisleSeat (int row, int seatNumber)
    { /* to be implemented in part (a) */ }

    /** Reserve two adjacent seats and return true if this was
     *  successfully done.
     *  If two adjacent seats could not be found, leave the state
     *  of the show unchanged, and return false.
     *  @return true if two adjacent seats were found, false
     *  otherwise
     */
    public boolean twoTogether()
    { /* to be implemented in part (b) */ }

    /** Return the lowest seat number in the specified row for a
     *  block of empty adjacent seats. If no such block exists,
     *  return -1.
     *  @param row the row number
     *  @param seatsNeeded the number of adjacent empty seats needed
     *  @return lowest seat number for a block of needed adjacent
     *  seats or -1 if no such block exists
     */
    public int findAdjacent(int row, int seatsNeeded)
    { /* to be implemented in part (c) */ }

    //There may be instance variables, constructors, and methods
    //that are not shown.
}
```

GO ON TO THE NEXT PAGE.

(a) Write the `Show` method `isAisleSeat`, which should return `true` if the seat with the specified row and seat number is an aisle seat, `false` otherwise. Aisle seats are the first and the last columns of the two-dimensional array representing the theater. For example, in the diagram shown above, if `show` is a `Show` variable, here are some results of calling the `isAisleSeat` method.

Method call	Return value
show.isAisleSeat(2,5)	true
show.isAisleSeat(0,4)	false
show.isAisleSeat(1,0)	true

Complete method `isAisleSeat` below.

```
/** Returns true if the seat with the specified row and seat
 *  number is an aisle seat, false otherwise.
 *  @param row the row number
 *  @param seatNumber the seat number
 *  @return true if an aisle seat, false otherwise
 */
public boolean isAisleSeat (int row, int seatNumber)
```

(b) Write the `Show` method `twoTogether`, which reserves two adjacent seats and returns `true` if this was successfully done. If it is not possible to find two adjacent seats that are unoccupied, the method should leave the show unchanged and return `false`. For example, suppose this is the state of a show.

	[0]	[1]	[2]	[3]	[4]	[5]
[0]	0	0	1	1	0	1
[1]	0	1	0	1	0	1
[2]	1	0	0	0	1	1

A call to `twoTogether` should return `true`, and the final state of the show could be any one of the following three configurations.

	[0]	[1]	[2]	[3]	[4]	[5]
[0]	1	1	1	1	0	1
[1]	0	1	0	1	0	1
[2]	1	0	0	0	1	1

OR

	[0]	[1]	[2]	[3]	[4]	[5]
[0]	0	0	1	1	0	1
[1]	0	1	0	1	0	1
[2]	1	1	1	0	1	1

OR

	[0]	[1]	[2]	[3]	[4]	[5]
[0]	0	0	1	1	0	1
[1]	0	1	0	1	0	1
[2]	1	0	1	1	1	1

GO ON TO THE NEXT PAGE.

For the following state of a show, a call to twoTogether should return `false` and leave the two-dimensional array as shown.

	[0]	[1]	[2]	[3]	[4]	[5]
[0]	0	1	0	1	1	0
[1]	1	1	0	1	0	1
[2]	0	1	1	1	1	1

Information repeated from the beginning of the question

```
public class Show

private int[][] mySeats
private final int SEATS_PER_ROW
private final int NUM_ROWS
public boolean isAisleSeat (int row, int seatNumber)
public boolean twoTogether()
public int findAdjacent(int row, int seatsNeeded)
```

Complete method twoTogether below.

```
/** Reserve two adjacent seats and return true if this was
 *  successfully done.
 *  If two adjacent seats could not be found, leave the state
 *  of the show unchanged, and return false.
 *  @return true if two adjacent seats were found, false
 *  otherwise
 */
public boolean twoTogether()
```

(c) Write the Show method findAdjacent, which finds the lowest seat number in the specified row for a block of empty adjacent seats. If no such block exists, the findAdjacent method should return -1. No changes should be made to the state of the show, irrespective of the value returned.
For example, suppose the diagram of seats is as shown.

	[0]	[1]	[2]	[3]	[4]	[5]
[0]	0	1	1	0	0	0
[1]	0	0	0	0	1	1
[2]	1	0	0	1	0	0

The following table shows some examples of calling findAdjacent for show.

Method call	Return value
show.findAdjacent(0,3)	3
show.findAdjacent(1,3)	0 or 1
show.findAdjacent(2,2)	1 or 4
show.findAdjacent(1,5)	-1

GO ON TO THE NEXT PAGE.

Complete method `findAdjacent` below.

```
/** Return the lowest seat number in the specified row for a
 * block of empty adjacent seats. If no such block exists,
 * return -1.
 * @param row the row number
 * @param seatsNeeded the number of adjacent empty seats needed
 * @return lowest seat number for a block of needed adjacent
 * seats or -1 if no such block exists
 */
public int findAdjacent(int row, int seatsNeeded)
```

4. This question involves reasoning about the code from the GridWorld Case Study. A Quick Reference to the case study is provided as part of this exam.

Consider modifying the `Critter` class so that a `Critter` has the capability of breeding. Every time it acts, it removes the neighboring critters, as before. Then, if this `Critter` meets the probability requirements for breeding, it breeds into each empty neighboring location by placing a new `Critter` there. If the `Critter` does not breed, it moves, as before, into one of the empty neighboring locations. A partial definition of the modified `Critter` class is shown below.

```
public class Critter extends Actor
{
    private double myProbBreeding;
    private boolean myBreed;

    /**
     * Constructor. Creates a Critter with the given probability of
     * breeding. myBreed is set to false.
     * @param probBreeding the probability of breeding
     */
    public Critter(double probBreeding)
    { /* to be implemented in part (a) */ }

    /**
     * A critter breeds by getting a list of its empty neighboring
     * locations, and placing a new Critter in each.
     */
    private void breed()
    { /* to be implemented in part (b) */ }

    /**
     * A critter acts by getting a list of its neighbors, and
     * processing them. If it passes the probability test for
     * breeding, then it breeds into each of the empty neighboring
     * locations. If not, it gets the possible locations to move
     * to, selects one of them, and moves to the selected location.
     */
    public void act()
    { /* to be implemented in part (c) */ }

    //methods getActors, processActors, getMoveLocations,
    // selectMoveLocation, and makeMove remain unchanged, and are
    // not shown ...
}
```

GO ON TO THE NEXT PAGE.

(a) Write the constructor for the modified `Critter` class. The constructor creates a blue `Critter` facing north, whose probability of breeding is as specified in its parameter. The private instance variable `myBreed` is set to false.

Complete the `Critter` constructor below.

```
/**
 * Constructor. Creates a Critter with the given probability of
 * breeding. myBreed is set to false.
 * @param probBreeding the probability of breeding
 */
public Critter(double probBreeding)
```

(b) Write the private helper method `breed`. This method places a new blue `Critter` facing north into each of the empty neighboring adjacent locations. Each new `Critter` has the same probability of breeding as its parent critter.

Complete method `breed` below.

```
/**
 * A critter breeds by getting a list of its empty neighboring
 * locations, and placing a new Critter in each.
 */
private void breed()
```

(c) Write the modified act method in the `Critter` class. The act method processes actors as before, "eating" each neighboring adjacent `Actor` that is neither a `Rock` nor another `Critter`. Then it uses a random number to determine whether this `Critter` will breed or not. If the random number is within the probability range for breeding, the `Critter` will breed; otherwise it will move as in the original act method.

Complete method act below.

```
/**
 * A critter acts by getting a list of its neighbors, and
 * processing them. If it passes the probability test for
 * breeding, then it breeds into each of the empty neighboring
 * locations. If not, it gets the possible locations to move
 * to, selects one of them, and moves to the selected location.
 */
public void act()
```

END OF EXAMINATION

ANSWER KEY (Section I)

1. E	15. E	29. A
2. C	16. B	30. B
3. C	17. C	31. D
4. D	18. E	32. C
5. A	19. D	33. A
6. C	20. C	34. D
7. E	21. D	35. B
8. A	22. E	36. A
9. D	23. A	37. D
10. C	24. D	38. A
11. E	25. D	39. C
12. B	26. A	40. D
13. E	27. E	
14. B	28. A	

ANSWERS EXPLAINED

Section I

1. **(E)** The string parameter in the line of code uses two escape characters:
   \", which means print a double quote.
   \n, which means print a newline character (i.e., go to the next line).

2. **(C)** The intent of the programmer is to have overloaded getValue methods in SomeClass. Overloaded methods have different signatures, where the signature of a method includes the name and parameter types only. Thus, the signature of the original method is getValue(int). The signature in header I is getValue(). The signature in header II is getValue(int). The signature in header III is getValue(double). Since the signature in header II is the same as that of the given method, the compiler will flag it and say that the method already exists in SomeClass. Note: The return type of a method is not included in its signature.

3. **(C)** The expression (int)(Math.random() * 49) produces a random integer from 0 through 48. (Note that 49 is the number of possibilities for num.) To shift this range from 2 to 50, add 2 to the expression.

4. **(D)** Short-circuit evaluation of the boolean expression will occur. The expression (num != 0) will evaluate to false, which makes the entire boolean expression false. Therefore the expression (score/num > SOME_CONSTANT) will not be evaluated. Hence no division by zero will occur, and there will be no ArithmeticException thrown. When the boolean expression has a value of false, only the else part of the statement, *statement2*, will be executed.

5. **(A)** The header for `compareTo` in the `Comparable` interface is

    ```
    public int compareTo(Object other);
    ```

    Thus, when implementing `Comparable`, this form of the header must be used.

6. **(C)** Declarations I and II fail because you can't create an instance of an abstract class. Additionally, declaration I fails this test: `Cereal` *is-a* `WheatCereal`? No. Notice that declaration III passes this test: `RiceCereal` *is-a* `Cereal`? Yes.

7. **(E)** All satisfy the *is-a* test! `Class2` *is-a* `Class1`. `Class3` *is-a* `Class2`. `Class3` *is-a* `Class1`. Note: Since `Class3` is a subclass of `Class2`, it automatically implements any interfaces implemented by `Class2`, its superclass.

8. **(A)** Method call I works because `Class3` inherits all the methods of `Class2`. Method call II fails because `Class2`, the superclass, does not inherit the methods of `Class3`, its subclass. Method call III uses a parameter that fails the *is-a* test: `ob2` is *not* a `Class3`, which the parameter requires.

9. **(D)** After each execution of the loop body, n is divided by 2. Thus, the loop will produce output when n is 50, 25, 12, 6, 3, and 1. The final value of n will be 1 / 2, which is 0, and the test will fail.

10. **(C)** Statement III will cause an `IndexOutOfBoundsException` because there is no slot 4. The final element, `"Luis"`, is in slot 3. Statement I is correct: It replaces the string `"Harry"` with the string `"6"`. It may look peculiar in the list, but the syntax is correct. Statement II looks like it may be out of range because there is no slot 4. It is correct, however, because you must be allowed to add an element to the end of the list.

11. **(E)** The effect of the given algorithm is to raise n to the 8th power.
    When $i = 1$, the result is $n * n = n^2$.
    When $i = 2$, the result is $n^2 * n^2 = n^4$.
    When $i = 3$, the result is $n^4 * n^4 = n^8$.

12. **(B)** Since n == 6 fails the two base case tests, method call `mystery(6)` returns `6 + mystery(5)`. Since 5 satisfies the second base case test, `mystery(5)` returns 5 and there are no more recursive calls. Thus, `mystery(6)` = 6 + 5 = 11.

13. **(E)** In order for /* *body of loop* */ not to be executed, the test must be false the first time it is evaluated. A compound OR test will be false if and only if both pieces of the test are false. Thus, choices B and C are insufficient. Choice D fails because it guarantees that both pieces of the test will be *true*. Choice A is wrong because /* *body of loop* */ may be executed many times, until the computer runs out of memory (an infinite loop!).

14. **(B)** Although the expression is always algebraically true for nonzero x, the expression may evaluate to false. This could occur because of round-off error in performing the division and multiplication operations. Whether the right-hand side of the expression evaluates to exactly 3.0 depends on the value of x. Note that if x is zero, the expression will be evaluated to `false` because the right-hand side will be assigned a value of `Infinity`.

15. **(E)** Statement I is false: The `Sedan`, `StationWagon`, and `SUV` classes should all be subclasses of `Car`. Each one satisfies the *is-a* `Car` relationship. Statement II is true: The main task of the `Inventory` class should be to keep an updated list of `Car` objects. Statement III is true: A class is independent of another class if it does not require that class to implement its methods.

16. **(B)** The `Inventory` class is responsible for maintaining the list of all cars on the lot. Therefore methods like `addCar`, `removeCar`, and `displayAllCars` must be the responsibility of this class. The `Car` class should contain the `setColor`, `getPrice`, and `displayCar` methods, since all these pertain to the attributes of a given `Car`.

17. **(C)** Each subclass may contain additional attributes for the particular type of car that are not in the `Car` superclass. Since `displayCar` displays all features of a given car, this method should be overridden to display the original plus additional features.

18. **(E)** The expression `word.indexOf("flag")` returns the index of the first occurrence of `"flag"` in the calling string, `word`. Thus, x has value 3. (Recall that the first character in `word` is at index 0.) The method call `word.substring(0, x)` is equivalent to `word.substring(0, 3)`, which returns the substring in `word` from 0 to 2, namely `"con"`. The character at index 3 is not included.

19. **(D)** A program that uses an abstract class must have at least one subclass that is *not* abstract, since instances of abstract classes cannot be created. Thus, choice E is false. Choice A is false: An abstract class can contain any number of private instance variables, each of which is inherited by a subclass of `AClass`. Choice B is wrong—for example `v1` and `v2` could be initialized in a default constructor (constructor with no parameters). Choice C is incorrect: The point of an abstract class is that no instances of it will be created. The class does not need to contain any abstract methods.

20. **(C)** If the `responses` array contained an invalid value like 12, the program would attempt to add 1 to `freq[12]`. This is out of bounds for the `freq` array.

21. **(D)** Implementation I calls `super.computePay()`, which is equivalent to the `computePay` method in the `Employee` superclass. The method returns the quantity `mySalary - myTaxWithheld`. The `BONUS` is then correctly added to this expression, as required. Implementation III correctly uses the public accessor methods `getSalary` and `getTax` that the `Consultant` class has inherited. Note that the `Consultant` class does not have access to the private instance variables `mySalary` and `myTaxWithheld` even though it inherits them from the `Employee` class. Implementation II incorrectly returns the salary plus `BONUS`—there is no tax withheld. The expression `super.computePay()` returns a value equal to salary minus tax. But this is neither stored nor included in the `return` statement.

22. **(E)** Note that p is declared to be of type `Employee`, and the `Employee` class does not have a `getPayFraction` method. To avoid the error, p must be cast to `PartTimeEmployee` as follows:

```
double g = ((PartTimeEmployee) p).getPayFraction();
```

23. **(A)** The code does exactly what it looks like it should. The `writePayInfo` parameter is of type `Employee` and each element of the `empList` array *is-a* `Employee` and therefore does not need to be downcast to its actual instance type. There is no `ClassCastException` (choice C) since nowhere is there an attempt made to cast an object to a class of which it is not an instance. None of the array elements is null; therefore, there is no `NullPointerException` (choice B). Choice D won't happen because the `getName` method is inherited by both the `Consultant` and `PartTimeEmployee` classes. Choice E would occur if the `Employee` superclass were abstract, but it's not.

24. **(D)** Segment I is incorrect because num is not an index in the loop: It is a value in the array. Thus, the correct test is if (num > 0), which is correctly used in segment II. Segment III is a regular for loop, exactly equivalent to the given while loop.

25. **(D)** The first for loop places value in the top and bottom rows of the defined rectangle. The second for loop fills in the remaining border elements on the sides. Note that the top + 1 and bottom - 1 initializer and terminating conditions avoid filling in the corner elements twice.

26. **(A)** Statement I is false: An *interface* may not be instantiated, but a class that implements the interface can be instantiated, provided it is not an abstract class. Statement II is false: Any subclass of SomeClass will automatically implement the interface, but not necessarily the superclass. For example, suppose a super-class Animal has a subclass Bird. And suppose Bird implements CanFly, which is an interface with a single method, fly. Clearly, Animal shouldn't implement CanFly—not all animals fly. Statement III appears to be true: This is what it means for a class to implement an interface—it's a promise that the class will contain all methods of that interface. This is not true, however, if SomeClass is an abstract class. Any method of the interface that is not implemented in SomeClass then automatically becomes an abstract method of SomeClass and must be implemented by any nonabstract subclass of SomeClass.

27. **(E)** Eliminate choices A and B: When comparing Book objects, you cannot use simple inequality operators; you *must* use compareTo. For the calling object to be *less than* the parameter object, use the *less than* 0 test (a good way to remember this!).

28. **(A)** Method removeNegs will not work whenever there are consecutive negative values in the list. This is because removal of an element from an ArrayList causes the elements to the right of it to be shifted left to fill the "hole." The index in the given algorithm, however, always moves one slot to the right. Therefore in choice A, when -1 is removed, -2 will be passed over, and the final list will be 6 -2 5.

29. **(A)** If the list is sorted, a binary search is the most efficient algorithm to use. Binary search chops the current part of the array being examined in half, until you have found the element you are searching for, or there are no elements left to look at. In the worst case, you will need to divide by 2 seven times:

$$120/2 \rightarrow 60$$
$$60/2 \rightarrow 30$$
$$30/2 \rightarrow 15$$
$$15/2 \rightarrow 7$$
$$7/2 \rightarrow 3$$
$$3/2 \rightarrow 1$$
$$1/2 \rightarrow 0$$

30. **(B)** When the target is in the first position of the list, a sequential search will find it in the first comparison. The binary search, which examines a middle element first, will not. Condition I is a worst case situation for both the sequential search ($O(n)$) and binary search ($O(\log n)$). Condition III is approximately the middle of the list, but it won't be found on the first try of the binary search. (The first

8383 try examines arr[n/2].) Still, the target *will* be located within fewer than $\log n$ tries, whereas the sequential search will need more than $n/2$ tries.

31. **(D)** The `remove` method removes from `arr` the element `arr[index]`. It does this by copying all elements from `arr[0]` up to but not including `arr[index]` into array `b`. Thus, `b[k] == arr[k]` for `0 <= k < index` is true. Then it copies all elements from `arr[index + 1]` up to and including `arr[arr.length - 1]` into `b`. Since no gaps are left in `b`, `b[k] == arr[k + 1]` for `index <= k < arr.length - 1`. The best way to see this is with a small example. If `arr` is 2, 6, 4, 8, 1, 7, and the element at `index 2` (namely the 4) is to be removed, here is the picture:

```
b[0] == arr[0]
b[1] == arr[1]
b[2] == arr[3]
b[3] == arr[4]
b[4] == arr[5]
```

Notice that `arr.length` is 6, but `k` ends at 4.

32. **(C)**
$$2\text{AF}_{\text{hex}} = (F)(16^0) + (A)(16^1) + (2)(16^2)$$
$$= (15)(1) + (10)(16) + (2)(256)$$
$$= 15 + 160 + 512$$
$$= 687_{\text{dec}}$$

33. **(A)** Choice A is illegal because you cannot create an instance of an abstract class.

34. **(D)** The statement

```
double value = Math.random();
```

generates a random `double` in the range $0 \leq \text{value} < 1$. Since random doubles are uniformly distributed in this interval, 45 percent of the time you can expect `value` to be in the range $0 \leq \text{value} < 0.45$. Therefore, a test for `value` in this range can be a test for whether the serve of a `WeakPlayer` went in. Since `Math.random()` never returns a negative number, the test in implementation II, `value < 0.45`, is sufficient. The test in implementation I would be correct if `||` were changed to `&&` ("or" changed to "and"—both parts must be true). Implementation III also works. The expression

```
(int) (Math.random() * 100)
```

returns a random integer from 0 to 99, each equally likely. Thus, 45 percent of the time, the integer `val` will be in the range $0 \leq \text{val} \leq 44$. Therefore, a test for `val` in this range can be used to test whether the serve was in.

35. **(B)** Choice B is fine: `b`, the `Beginner`, *is-a* `WeakPlayer`. Choices A and C will each cause a `ClassCastException` to be thrown: You can't cast a `GoodPlayer` to a `WeakPlayer` and you can't cast a `WeakPlayer` to a `Beginner`. Choices D and E

will each cause a compile-time error: The parameter must be of type `WeakPlayer`, but `w` and `b` are declared to be of type `TennisPlayer`. Each of these choices can be corrected by casting the parameter to `WeakPlayer`.

36. **(A)** A `Critter` gets all adjacent actors and eats those that are not rocks or other critters. Then it moves to one of the adjacent empty locations. Eliminate choices D and E, since the flower and the bug are still in the picture. Also, eliminate choice C, since the rock is gone. Choice B is wrong because the `Critter` moved to a nonadjacent location.

37. **(D)** Locations 1 – 5 are labeled l_1, l_2, l_3, l_4, and l_5.

Notice that `loc4` is adjacent to `loc1` in the direction 45 (the nearest compass direction to 40). Similarly, `loc5` is adjacent to `loc2` in the direction 180 (the nearest compass direction to 200). Statement III gets the adjacent location to `loc4` in the direction 225, the nearest compass direction to 230. This location is (1, 3) or `loc1`. Statement II is false since `Location (1, 3)` is not equal to `Location (3, 1)`.

38. **(A)** Statement I is false because a `Bug` could have its direction set to 45 (northeast), or 135 (southeast), or 225 (southwest), or 315 (northwest). With no obstructions on the grid, this bug would then move forward in a diagonal path. Statement II would only be true if the default constructor were used to create the `Bug`, making it face north. Otherwise, a `Bug` can be created to have any direction d, where $0 \leq d < 360$. Statement III would be true only if the bug were blocked, and therefore unable to move both times. A `Bug` turns only if it can't move.

39. **(C)** There are two situations where a `TriangleBug` needs to turn:

When `side` becomes 2:   When `side` becomes 3:

Notice that when `side` switches to 2, two half turns of 45° must be made, and when `side` switches to 3, three half turns must be made, in order for the bug to be facing the correct direction. Choice C is the only sequence of statements that does this correctly.

40. **(D)** If the `Actor` class did not have a default constructor, there would be a compile-time error. Choices A and B are wrong because constructors are never

inherited. Choice C is a true statement, but it has nothing to do with the construction of a subclass object! Choice E is fanciful: The compiler simply does not make this kind of decision for the programmer.

Section II

1. (a)
```
public String toPig(String word)
{
    if (isVowel (word.substring(0, 1)))
        return word + "yay";
    else
        return word.substring(1) + word.substring(0, 1) + "ay";
}
```

(b)
```
private List<String> getLineWords()
{
    String line = myLine;
    List<String> list = new ArrayList<String>();
    int blankIndex = line.indexOf(" ");
    while (blankIndex != -1)
    {
        list.add(line.substring(0, blankIndex));
        line = line.substring(blankIndex + 1);
        blankIndex = line.indexOf(" ");
    }
    list.add(line);
    return list;
}
```

(c)
```
public void pigLatin()
{
    List<String> words = getLineWords();
    myLine = "";
    for (String word : words)
        myLine += " " + toPig(word);
}
```

NOTE

- In part (b), the postcondition of `getLineWords` specifies that `myLine` should be unchanged. This is the reason for the local variable `line`.
- The idea in part (b) is that while there are still blanks in the line, you will chop off the first word and add it to `list`. When you are done, don't forget to add the remaining word (the part of the line that has no more blanks) to `list`.

2. (a)
```
public void advanceTimeOnAll()
{
    for (DigitalClock c : clocks)
        c.advanceTime();
}
```

(b)
```
public void removeDefective()
{
    int index = 0;
    while (index < clocks.size())
    {
        if (clocks.get(index).isDefective())
            clocks.remove(index);
        else
            index++;
    }
}
```

Alternatively, you can use an iterator.

```
public void removeDefective()
{
    Iterator<DigitalClock> itr = clocks.iterator();
    while (itr.hasNext())
    {
        if (itr.next().isDefective())
            itr.remove();
    }
}
```

(c)
```
public void replaceDefective()
{
    int index = 0;
    while (index < clocks.size())
    {
        if (clocks.get(index).isDefective())
            clocks.set(index, new DigitalClock(12, 30));
        index++;
    }
}
```

Alternatively, you can use a list iterator.

```
public void replaceDefective()
{
    ListIterator<DigitalClock> itr = clocks.listIterator();
    while (itr.hasNext())
    {
        if (itr.next().isDefective())
            itr.set(new DigitalClock(12, 30));
    }
}
```

NOTE

- A for-each loop can be used to access and modify each element in a list. Thus, it is OK to use it in `advanceTimeOnAll`.
- A for-each loop cannot be used for removing or replacing elements in a list. Thus, `removeDefective` and `replaceDefective` both need index traversals and use of the `ArrayList` methods `get`, `set`, and `remove`. Alternatively, if you have learned about iterators, you can use the `remove` method of `Iterator` to "remove all occurrences of ...," and the `set` method of `ListIterator` to "replace all occurrences of ...."
- You need to be especially careful in part (b) if you don't use an iterator. The `remove` method of `ArrayList` shifts elements to the left to close the "hole" when an item is removed. This means that you must only increment the index when you don't remove an element! If you increment the index when you have just performed `remove`, the next `DigitalClock` object will be shifted left without being tested, and you may inadvertently leave a defective clock in the list.

3. (a)
```
public boolean isAisleSeat (int row, int seatNumber)
{
    return seatNumber == 0 || seatNumber == SEATS_PER_ROW - 1;
}
```

(b)
```
public boolean twoTogether()
{
    for (int r = 0; r < NUM_ROWS; r++)
        for (int c = 0; c < SEATS_PER_ROW-1; c++)
            if (mySeats[r][c] == 0 && mySeats[r][c+1] == 0)
            {
                mySeats[r][c] = 1;
                mySeats[r][c+1] = 1;
                return true;
            }
    return false;
}
```

(c)
```
public int findAdjacent(int row, int seatsNeeded)
{
    int index = 0, count = 0, lowIndex = 0;
    while (index < SEATS_PER_ROW)
    {
        while (index < SEATS_PER_ROW && mySeats[row][index] == 0)
        {
            count++;
            index++;
            if (count == seatsNeeded)
                return lowIndex;
        }
        count = 0;
        index++;
        lowIndex = index;
    }
    return -1;
}
```

NOTE

- In part (a), the seat numbers go from 0 to SEATS_PER_ROW - 1.
- In part (b), you need the test c < SEATS_PER_ROW-1, because when you refer to mySeats[r][c+1], you must worry about going off the end of the row and causing an ArrayIndexOutOfBounds exception.
- In part (c), every time you increment index, you need to test that it is in range. This is why you need this test twice: index < SEATS_PER_ROW.
- In part (c), every time you reset the count, you need to reset the lowIndex, because this is the value you're asked to return.
- In parts (b) and (c), the final return statements are executed only if all rows in the show have been examined unsuccessfully.

4. (a)
```
public Critter(double probBreeding)
{
    super();
    myProbBreeding = probBreeding;
    myBreed = false;
}
```

(b)
```
    private void breed()
    {
        ArrayList<Location> breedLocs =
            getGrid().getEmptyAdjacentLocations(getLocation());
        for (Location loc : breedLocs)
        {
            Critter c = new Critter(myProbBreeding);
            c.putSelfInGrid(getGrid(), loc);
        }
    }
```

(c)
```
    public void act()
    {
        if (getGrid() == null)
            return;
        ArrayList<Actor> actors = getActors();
        processActors(actors);
        myBreed = Math.random() < myProbBreeding;
        if(myBreed)
        {
            breed();
        }
        else
        {
            ArrayList<Location> moveLocs = getMoveLocations();
            Location loc = selectMoveLocation(moveLocs);
            makeMove(loc);
        }
    }
```

NOTE

- In part (a), the line super() is optional. The compiler automatically calls the constructor of the superclass to initialize the inherited private instance variables (like color, direction, and so on). Since the Actor class has a default constructor, omitting the line will not cause an error. If you *do* include the line, it must be the first line of code in the implementation of the constructor.
- In part (c), the first three statements are executed whether the Critter breeds or not. In other words, first the Critter eats, then it either breeds or moves.

Appendix: Glossary of Useful Computer Terms

I hate definitions.
—*Benjamin Disraeli*, Vivian Grey *(1826)*

API library: Applications Program Interface library. A library of classes for use in other programs. The library provides standard interfaces that hide the details of the implementations.

Applet: A graphical Java program that runs in a web browser or applet viewer.

Application: A stand-alone Java program stored in and executed on the user's local computer.

Bit: From "binary digit." Smallest unit of computer memory, taking on only two values, 0 or 1.

Buffer: A temporary storage location of limited size. Holds values waiting to be used.

Byte: Eight bits. Similarly, megabyte (MB, 10^6 bytes) and gigabyte (GB, 10^9 bytes).

Bytecode: Portable (machine-independent) code, intermediate between source code and machine language. It is produced by the Java compiler and interpreted (executed) by the Java Virtual Machine.

Cache: A small amount of "fast" memory for the storage of data. Typically, the most recently accessed data from disk storage or "slow" memory is saved in the main memory cache to save time if it's retrieved again.

Compiler: A program that translates source code into object code (machine language).

CPU: The central processing unit (computer's brain). It controls the interpretation and execution of instructions. It consists of the arithmetic/logic unit, the control unit, and some memory, usually called "on-board memory" or cache memory. Physically, the CPU consists of millions of microscopic transistors on a chip.

Debugger: A program that helps find errors by tracing the values of variables in a program.

GUI: Graphical user interface.

Hardware: The physical components of computers. These are the ones you can touch, for example, the keyboard, monitor, printer, CPU chip.

Hertz (Hz): One cycle per second. It refers to the speed of the computer's internal clock and gives a measure of the CPU speed. Similarly, megahertz (MHz, 10^6 Hz) and gigahertz (GHz, 10^9 Hz).

Hexadecimal number system: Base 16.

High-level language: A human-readable programming language that enables instructions that require many machine steps to be coded concisely, for example, Java, C++, Pascal, BASIC, FORTRAN.

HTML: Hypertext Markup Language. The instructions read by web browsers to format web pages, link to other websites, and so on.

IDE: Integrated Development Environment. Provides tools such as an editor, compiler, and debugger that work together, usually with a graphical interface. Used for creating software in a high-level language.

Interpreter: A program that reads instructions that are not in machine language and executes them one at a time.

Javadoc: A program that extracts comments from Java source files and produces documentation files in HTML. These files can then be viewed with a web browser.

JVM (Java Virtual Machine): An interpreter that reads and executes Java bytecode on any local machine.

Linker: A program that links together the different modules of a program into a single executable program after they have been compiled into object code.

Low-level language: Assembly language. This is a human-readable version of machine language, where each machine instruction is coded as one statement. It is translated into machine language by a program called an assembler. Each different kind of CPU has its own assembly language.

Mainframe computer: A large computer, typically used by large institutions, such as government agencies and big businesses.

Microcomputer: Personal computer.

Minicomputer: Small mainframe.

Modem: A device that connects a computer to a phone line or TV cable.

Network: Several computers linked together so that they can communicate with each other and share resources.

Object code: Machine language. Produced by compiling source code.

Operating system: A program that controls access to and manipulation of the various files and programs on the computer. It also provides the interface for user interaction with the computer. Some examples: Windows, MacOS, and Linux.

Primary memory: RAM. This gets erased when you turn off your computer.

RAM: Random Access Memory. This stores the current program and the software to run it.

ROM: Read Only Memory. This is permanent and nonerasable. It contains, for example, programs that boot up the operating system and check various components of the hardware. In particular, ROM contains the BIOS (Basic Input Output System)—a program that handles low-level communication with the keyboard, disk drives, and so on.

SDK: Sun's Java Software Development Kit. A set of tools for developing Java software.

Secondary memory: Hard drive, disk, magnetic tapes, CD-ROM, and so on.

Server: The hub of a network of computers. Stores application programs, data, mail messages, and so on, and makes them available to all computers on the network.

Software: Computer programs written in some computer language and executed on the hardware after conversion to machine language. If you can install it on your hard drive, it's software (e.g., programs, spreadsheets, word processors).

Source code: A program in a high-level language like Java, C++, Pascal, or FORTRAN.

Swing: A Java toolkit for implementing graphical user interfaces.

Transistor: Microscopic semiconductor device that can serve as an on-off switch.

URL: Uniform Resource Locator. An address of a web page.

Workstation: Desktop computer that is faster and more powerful than a microcomputer.

Index

How to Use the CD-ROM

The software is not installed on your computer; it runs directly from the CD-ROM. Barron's CD-ROM includes an "autorun" feature that automatically launches the application when the CD is inserted into the CD-ROM drive. In the unlikely event that the autorun feature is disabled, follow the manual launching instructions below.

Windows®

1. Click on the Start button and choose "My Computer."
2. Double-click on the CD-ROM drive, which is named **AP_Computer Science**.
3. Double-click **AP_Computer Science** to launch the program.

MAC®

1. Double-click the CD-ROM icon.
2. Double-click the **AP_Computer Science** icon to start the program.

SYSTEM REQUIREMENTS

Microsoft® Windows®
Processor: Intel® Pentium® II 450MHz,
AMD Athlon® 600MHz or faster processor
(or equivalent).
Memory: 128MB of RAM.
Graphics Memory: 128MB.
Color Display: 1024 x 768
Platforms:
Windows 7, Windows Vista,
Windows XP.

MAC® OS X
Processor: Intel Core™ Duo
1.33GHz or faster processor.
Memory: 256MB of RAM.
Graphics Memory: 128MB.
Color Display: 1024 x 768
Platforms:
Mac OS X 10.4 (Intel) and higher.